EVERYMAN, I will go with thee,

and be thy guide,

In thy most need to go by thy side

CHRISTOPHER MARLOWE

Son of a shoemaker, born at Canterbury in 1564. Educated at King's School, Canterbury, and Corpus Christi College, Cambridge. Killed in a brawl at Deptford in 1593.

MARLOWE

Plays and Poems

EDITED AND INTRODUCED BY
M. R. RIDLEY

DENT : LONDON
EVERYMAN'S LIBRARY
DUTTON : NEW YORK

Made in Great Britain
at the
Aldine Press · Letchworth · Herts
for
J. M. DENT & SONS LTD
Aldine House · Albemarle Street · London
This edition was first published in Everyman's Library in 1909
Revised edition 1955
Reprinted 1973

Published in the U.S.A. by arrangement with
J. M. Dent & Sons Ltd

No. 383 Hardback ISBN 0 460 00383 6
No. 1383 Paperback ISBN 0 460 01383 1

INTRODUCTION

CHRISTOPHER MARLOWE was born in Canterbury, the son of a shoemaker of that city, in 1564. He was thus an exact contemporary of Shakespeare, some years younger than Lyly, Kyd, Greene, and Peele, and three years older than Nashe. He died in 1593, stabbed in the course of a quarrel in an inn at Deptford. Of the events of his life we know very little. He was educated at King's School, Canterbury, and then at Corpus Christi College, Cambridge, where he took his B.A. in 1583. He may have served as a soldier in the Low Countries, and there is some reason to think that he was one of Walsingham's secret service agents. In 1589 he was arrested on suspicion of complicity in a murder, but released after a fortnight's imprisonment. Less than a fortnight before his death, as a result of allegations made against him of atheism and treason, he was 'apprehended,' but not imprisoned, by order of the Privy Council. The precise circumstances of his death are the subject of the first, and probably the most brilliant and convincing, of those pieces of literary detection with which Dr Leslie Hotson has during the last thirty years enlivened and illuminated Elizabethan studies; but a discussion of them is hardly to the present purpose.

All, then, that we can be said to know about Marlowe, apart from a few dates, is that he wrote a number of works. He translated, probably while still at Cambridge, the first book of Lucan's *Pharsalia*, and Ovid's *Amores*. Of short poems only one can with any certainty be ascribed to him. Towards the end of his life he began what was to be a considerable narrative poem on the story of Hero and Leander, but he had written no more than 800 lines when he died. He also wrote seven plays (one of them possibly with some collaboration from Nashe): *The Tragedy of Dido, Queen of Carthage*; *Tamburlaine the Great*, in two parts, described as 'tragical discourses'; *The Tragical History of Dr Faustus*; *The Famous Tragedy of the Rich Jew of Malta*; *The Troublesome Reign and Lamentable Death of Edward the Second, King of England*; and *The Massacre at Paris*. A brief examination of the intrinsic quality of these works, and of the contribution which, through them, Marlowe made to the progress of English poetry and drama, forms the rest of this introduction.

I have included in this edition the translation of the first book of the *Pharsalia*, and, as a specimen, that of thirteen (about a sixth of the whole) of Ovid's *Amores*. All Marlowe's translation is very obviously prentice work. But when the apprentice is going later to be a great poet even his immature work is usually worth examination, and here one can watch Marlowe tentatively, and often clumsily, experimenting with the two metres which he later so richly developed, blank verse and the decasyllabic couplet. The translation is often clumsy and sometimes incorrect, so that even as a 'clandestine refuge for schoolboys' it would be found a perilous asylum by its users. The line-for-line method of translation almost inevitably entailed clumsiness, and some of the incorrectness is due to Marlowe's use of an incorrect text, but some of the blunders are plain howlers, like the often quoted misreading (or rather, oddly enough for Marlowe, mis-hearing) of *cānebat* as *cănebat*. It appears that Marlowe, though—as his later work very clearly shows—widely read in the Latin classics, was far from being an accurate scholar. But the defects are offset by occasional beauties of both diction and rhythm. In the *Amores* Marlowe shows some real perception of both the capacities and limitations of his metrical form, and every now and then there is a foretaste of the richer and sweeter melodies of *Hero and Leander*, while the Lucan shows that he has already moved some distance from the jog-trot of *Gorboduc* and Surrey's *Aeneid*, and is on the road which will lead, however far they yet lie ahead, to the magnificences of *Tamburlaine* and *Dr Faustus*.

The date of the composition of *Dido, Queen of Carthage* is uncertain. It was first published in 1594, with a title-page which stated that it had been played by the children of Her Majesty's chapel, and written by Marlowe and Nashe. The internal evidence for Nashe's collaboration is very slight; the style is not like that of Nashe's only extant dramatic work, but there are a few words used in a sense in which Nashe elsewhere used them and Marlowe did not. It is probable that Nashe revised the play for publication, and prefixed to it an elegy on the death of Marlowe; but this does not preclude the possibility that he had collaborated more extensively in earlier days when the play was first written and before his own style was formed. As it stands the play reads like unmistakable early Marlowe. It has the attractively naïve immaturity of Peele, as it appears in *The Arraignment of Paris* and *David and Bathsabe*; it has much of Marlowe's own sweetness, though very little of his later power; and, with its extensive adaptations of and translations from Virgil, it suggests a very youthful, perhaps undergraduate, performance, of the same period as the Ovid and Lucan translations. But it has one or two touches of something a good deal more powerful, though undisciplined and crude, like the description of the death of Priam, which is almost certainly the passage which Shakespeare parodied in *Hamlet*.

I included the writing of *Tamburlaine* among the few facts which we know about Marlowe. But we do not, strictly speaking, 'know' that he wrote it. No author is mentioned either on the title-pages of the early editions or in contemporary records of the play's performance. Nor does Heywood's stage prologue to *The Jew of Malta* help matters, since (unless we are resolute to retain an extremely awkward piece of punctuation, which is almost certainly a compositor's vagary) he is not claiming that Marlowe wrote *Tamburlaine*, but that Tamburlaine and the Jew were among Alleyn's famous roles.

But of indirect evidence there is some (such as allusions in other writers) and of internal evidence a great deal. What one may call the negative evidence is the strongest of all. Both the conception and the style of *Tamburlaine* are highly individual, and there is no writer of the time who could conceivably have written it except the man who wrote *The Jew of Malta* and *Dr Faustus*, and whose authorship of those plays is acknowledged. Hence, though even so notable a scholar as Malone, and Robinson, who in 1826 was the first to edit Marlowe's works, both rejected his authorship, for the last hundred years Marlowe's authorship of *Tamburlaine* has been universally accepted.

And with this play Marlowe stormed the Elizabethan stage, swept the Elizabethan audiences off their feet, and started English tragedy on its triumphal progress, not only kindling his immediate successors with the fires of his imagination, but also developing, from very crude material, for their use and that of poets long after them, a superb vehicle of expression. Up to the time of *Tamburlaine*, which we can fix with some certainty at 1587–8, there had been some robust comedy, of considerable vigour but little finish (like *Ralph Roister Doister* and *Gammer Gurton's Needle*), and some pleasant but light pieces by Lyly and Peele, like *Campaspe* and *The Arraignment of Paris*. There had been a few so-called tragedies, constructed on foreign models, of some finish but no vigour at all. Of these the best known is *Gorboduc*, first played in 1561, and apparently popular enough to justify its printing a few years later. This popularity is, to us, most surprising, since, quite apart from the tedious jog-trot of the verse, the play is a lifeless performance, with no character of enough vitality to stand out from the ruck of the rest of the pasteboards. There was, it seemed, in the literal sense of the colloquial phrase, 'no future' in English tragedy, and indeed any observer in the early days of 1587 might reasonably have forecast that the next ten years were going to be an age of the novel rather than of the drama. With the first performance of *Tamburlaine* the whole picture changed, almost overnight. The Elizabethan audience had been given what it wanted, recognized the fact, and clamoured for more. For *Tamburlaine*, for all its manifest defects, is clearly a 'big' piece of work. Marlowe had the instinct to create a single great and dominant figure, and set him striding and ranting gloriously across the boards. The first part of the play is not a tragedy at all, not even a 'tragical discourse'. It is a triumphal pageant, culminating in the great conqueror's felicitous marriage to Zenocrate. It is full of poetry, of a kind hitherto unheard, falling sometimes to empty bombast, but rising often to exultant and fiery magnificence, and once or twice to an exquisite beauty more lyrical than dramatic, as in the famous passage in v. ii, which begins 'What is beauty . . .' It is a matter of dispute whether Marlowe had the second part in mind while writing the first; my guess is that he had, but in any case we get, I think, a clearer insight into Marlowe if we examine the two parts not in isolation but as two closely related parts of one whole. In the second part there are specifically tragic elements. Not only are there the deaths of Zenocrate and Tamburlaine, but there is some sort of dramatic progress, not merely a succession of conquests. Tamburlaine is no longer just the invincible conqueror; he becomes the megalomaniac, first seeing himself as the destined instrument of the gods, then provoking Nemesis by his insolent defiance of the very gods whose instrument he professes to be, and finally facing the last adversary against whom even he is powerless. And even as early as this there are touches which ought to save us from the facile judgment that 'Marlowe is a poet, not a dramatist.' No doubt his powers are primarily poetic, but he had also a dramatic sense. The entry of Zenocrate discovering the bloody corpses of Bajazeth and Zabina is dramatic, or crudely melodramatic, and it was devised by a man with an eye for *stage* effect, not the effect on a reader. And in the second part there is not only some notion of a sub-plot, however lightly sketched, in the episode of Olympia, but there is also a surprising bit of character delineation in the brief vignette of the unwarlike Caliphas refusing to go out to battle. Of the poetry I shall say more later.

The Jew of Malta, probably Marlowe's next play, was first performed in 1591, but the earliest text of it which we have is that of 1633, after it had been handled, and, one suspects, mishandled, in at least one revision and probably in two. And an unequal and disconcerting piece of work it is. For the first two Acts the Jew is a commanding figure, of the same calibre as Tamburlaine, and inspired by the same motive, though the power which he lusts for is to come by gold and not by conquest. And his characterization is considerably better rounded than Tamburlaine's. Then suddenly the play goes to pieces and degenerates into what has been not unjustly described as a 'savage farce'. It is, as the prologue announces, a 'Machiavellian' tragedy, but the label neither explains nor excuses the weak treatment of its second half, and one must suppose either that Marlowe's energy unaccountably flagged, or that, though there is no reason to suppose that he was not himself responsible for the melodramatic outline of the plot, some other writer unhappily changed his treatment of the latter part of it.

Edward II, first printed in 1594, and probably first performed in 1592, is a wholly different work from any of its predecessors. It is a chronicle play, it has no great central figure, it shows much increased subtlety of characterization, and much more sense of dramatic interaction between characters; but the poetry has lost almost all the earlier fire, and moves almost throughout at a competently pedestrian level. And the choice of subject is a surprising one. One would have expected Marlowe, if he had determined on a chronicle play, to choose one which would have offered him a figure like, for example, Henry V, into whose mouth he could have appropriately put great passages of the rhodomontade of which he knew he was so complete a master. But far from it; he chooses a neurotic weakling, who offers a chance of interesting psychological study, and can, properly handled, be made pathetic, but is as far removed as may be from any kind of grandeur. Add to this the treatment of Mortimer and Isabella, which, even though sometimes abrupt and clumsy, is yet a *dramatist*'s treatment, and one sees how far Marlowe has moved along the road towards a fully developed drama of character.

The problem of the date of *Dr Faustus* is unhappily a vexed one. It used to be generally accepted that the play immediately followed *Tamburlaine*, say in 1588 or 1589. This produced a satisfying picture of Marlowe's dramatic development. He wrote first three plays in each of which there was one supereminent central character, and no other character who more than momentarily enlisted attention; all three central characters were driven on by soaring and relentless ambition, and all three uttered magnificent poetry. He then wrote *Edward II*. But some thirty years ago Dr F. S. Boas marshalled evidence leading to the conclusion that the play cannot be dated before 1592. I fancy that Dr Boas himself was not too happy about the conclusion, but it seems to me very hard to refute the evidence, and not much easier to get round it. A detailed examination of the evidence would be out of place here, but in the briefest summary it is as follows: It is clear that in writing *Dr Faustus* Marlowe made very considerable use of a particular English translation of a German *Faustbuch*; the earliest extant edition of this translation was published in 1592; the saving supposition of an earlier edition which has disappeared is based on fact, but it appears that this earlier edition anteceded the one we have by only a few months, not by the necessary four years. The way round the evidence is to assume that Marlowe had not only seen, but over a period of working days been allowed to use, the manuscript of the translation some years before it was published. This would at the time have been far from impossible, but the assumption that it occurred is not one that we should readily make unless in more desperate straits than those in which we here find ourselves. For the picture which the new dating presents is not at all an incredible one. Marlowe writes *Tamburlaine* and *The Jew*. Then, perhaps not quite satisfied with the second, he breaks new ground with *Edward II*, and perhaps also *The Massacre at Paris*. Finally, feeling that neither of these has quite 'set his genius', he casts back to the type of the earlier two plays and far surpasses both of them in dramatic tension and in splendour of poetry. In one way indeed the new picture is more, not less, easy of acceptance than the old. The sudden jump in technique from *Tamburlaine* to *Dr Faustus* is, when one really examines it, more startling than the complete change of method involved in the transition from *Tamburlaine* or *The Jew* to *Edward II*. It is not just that there is more beautiful poetry in *Dr Faustus* than in *Tamburlaine*; it is that the verse is infinitely more flexible, the work of a far maturer and more assured craftsman.

In any case, whatever its date, *Dr Faustus* must surely be held to mark the summit of Marlowe's achievement. The subject no doubt appealed to him urgently. In no other of his plays are we so vividly aware of his restless aspiring spirit, beating against the bars of earthly confines. In no other does the poetry rise with such exultant ease to such peaks of dawn-flushed splendour. In no other, and indeed hardly in the whole range of English drama, is there a scene comparable for sheer passionate and tragic intensity with Faustus' last hour on earth.

The Massacre at Paris must have been written later than August 1589, when Henri III of France died, and was probably written some time in 1592, since Henslowe's diary notes it as a new play in January 1592–3. The only early edition is undated. In type it is similar to *Edward II* and may well have immediately preceded or succeeded it. It has been unduly neglected by the critics, probably in part because of the very unsatisfactory (? pirated) text which is all we have. It is not a distinguished play, but a quite workmanlike one, in which Marlowe handles his source competently, accepting it where it will serve and adapting it with some skill where it will not. Its main interest for the student of Marlowe lies in its reminiscences of other plays. Guise sometimes reminds one of Tamburlaine, sometimes of the Jew; and there is a good deal of Edward II in Henri III. And much of the characterization is like that in *Edward II*, showing some insight, but sketchy in execution. Hence it is a reasonable guess that the play succeeded rather than preceded *Edward II*, that Marlowe, finding that he had made something of a hit with a chronicle play of the past, followed it up with another, based on almost contemporary history with its obvious topical appeal.

Hero and Leander is almost certainly Marlowe's last work, left unfinished at his death. It is an exquisitely lovely piece of work, full of the ardour and tenderness of youth, and, technically, a superlative achievement, moving smoothly without monotony, and rich without cloying. A measure of its quality is offered by a comparison with *Venus and Adonis* and Keats' *Endymion.* I have followed, somewhat reluctantly, the usual practice, and appended to Marlowe's eight hundred lines the completion of the poem by Chapman. But I find it hard to understand why anyone should wish to overlay the fire and air of Marlowe with the laboured scholarship, the ponderous conceits, personifications, and philosophizing of Chapman. The proper place for the completion is, I think, in the works of Chapman, and only there, since it is good Chapman but very bad Marlowe.

Lastly a few words about Marlowe's verse. An examination of it is, I think, of importance quite apart from the study of Marlowe, because an understanding of what he did affects one's appreciation of much English poetry from his own time to our own, and because this understanding of the vital revolution which he achieved is hampered by a frequently repeated misstatement. It is accepted that Marlowe was the real creator of the most famous, the noblest, and the most versatile of our English measures, the unrhymed decasyllabic line which we know as blank verse. Experiments had been made in this metre twenty and more years before Marlowe, notably by Sackville and Norton in *Gorboduc* and by Surrey in his translation from the *Aeneid.* The results which they produced were of an intolerably tedious monotony. And they failed because, so far as one can judge, they were working on the wrong principle. They were trying, very rightly, to produce an English equivalent to that metre which, because of its nearness to, and yet sufficient difference from, the rhythms of ordinary speech, had been accepted by the Athenian dramatists as the suitable metre for their purpose. This was the 'Iambic trimeter,' a twelve-syllable line with an iambic (⏑ –) base in which spondee (– –) or, occasionally, dactyl (– ᴗ ᴗ) or tribrach (ᴗ ᴗ ᴗ), might be substituted for iamb in certain feet. The experimenters were perceptive enough to see that in the more slowly moving English language five feet would be preferable to the six feet of the Greek. But they wholly failed to reckon with the difference between a language which relied for its metrical effects on 'quantity' and one which relied on accent. Hence, taking a 'foot' in which a stressed syllable followed an unstressed as being the nearest English equivalent to the Greek quantitative iamb, they heard their English decasyllable as a series of five iambic feet. The result was, inevitably, such passages as this—a typical passage from *Gorboduc*:

> Your lasting age shall be their longer stay,
> For cares of kings, that rule as you have ruled,
> For public wealth and not for private joy,
> Do waste man's life, and hasten crooked age,
> With furrowed face and with enfeebled limbs,
> To draw on creeping death a swifter pace.
> They two yet young shall bear the parted reign
> With greater ease, than one, now old, alone,
> Can wield the whole, for whom much harder is
> With lessened strength the double weight to bear.

It will be noticed that (*a*) there are almost uniformly five stresses to the line, each marking a foot, (*b*) these stresses are roughly uniform in weight, (*c*) the substitution of spondee (– –, or, in English, two consecutive stresses) for iamb is uncommon, and 'reversed stress,' i.e. the substitution of trochee (– ᴗ) for iamb, almost unknown, and (*d*) most of the lines are end-stopped. The general effect is a tiresomely repetitive and gently oscillatory motion. It is clear that unless Marlowe, or someone with as sensitive an ear as Marlowe's, had effected a revolution, blank verse would never have been the great measure which it is.

What then was it that Marlowe did? Here we encounter the misstatement which I mentioned. A tacit line of argument seems to be as follows: *Gorboduc* is very monotonous; *Gorboduc* is heavily end-stopped; *Tamburlaine* is much less monotonous than *Gorboduc*. All three premises may be readily granted; but we are then presented with the quite fallacious conclusion, stated or implied, that *Tamburlaine* is therefore less heavily end-stopped than *Gorboduc*, and that Marlowe's chief contribution to blank verse is that, even as early as *Tamburlaine*, he reduced the amount of end-stopping. Marlowe in fact did nothing of the kind. If anyone will take the slight trouble to take three passages of say twenty lines apiece at random from each play he is likely to find that (though the monotonous regularity of *Gorboduc* sometimes seduces one into making a pause where no pause should be) the passages from *Tamburlaine* are more, not less, heavily end-stopped than those from *Gorboduc*. Marlowe's revolution was much more fundamental and vital. It concerned, not end-stopping, but the internal structure of the single line. Marlowe had an ear acute enough to perceive that though the base, the 'norm,' of English blank verse was to be the five-stress 'iambic' line, and though the hearer's awareness of that norm must not be lost, yet few lines should strictly conform to the norm, and that five is, so far from being the desirable, almost the forbidden, number. The effective stresses should often be fewer than five; the line should fall naturally into four, or three, or sometimes even only two, groups of sounds; and the substitution of other feet for the iamb should be freely admitted. By the use of these devices, singly or in combination, blank verse is transformed from a stiff and monotonous into a most flexible and varied metre; and when, as with the later Shakespeare and with Milton, the proportion of run-on lines is greatly increased, the range of the metre becomes almost unlimited.

Marlowe did not at first wholly master all his own devices, nor always use them wisely. But here are some examples of what he could do, which will demonstrate his advance on *Gorboduc*:

> Dreadless of blows, of bloody wounds, and death; (p. 86)

Here there are five stresses but only three groups of sound, and the first foot has a trochee for an iamb; otherwise the line is regular iambic and the groups each end with the end of a foot. Here are four well-known lines (p. 20):

> Is it not brave to be a king, Techelles!—
> Usumcasane and Theridamas,
> Is it not passing brave to be a king,
> And ride in triumph through Persepolis?

In the first line, three groups and only three stresses, since no natural conduct of the voice can throw a stress on to either 'it' or 'be'; and a feminine ending. In the second line, two groups, divided in the middle of a foot, and four stresses. In the third, three stresses, and two groups divided at the end of the third foot. In the fourth, there are three groups, the second ending in mid-foot, and three stresses of which the first two are hammer strokes, accentuated by the repetition of the long *i*. This is a trick of which Marlowe is particularly fond and of which he is a master, the lightening of some stresses to vanishing point and enforcing the impact on those that remain. It would be hard to find a line like this last in the whole of *Gorboduc*. But it will be noticed that in those four lines, though there are several feet of the ˘ ˘ form, with no stress, there is no example of the reversed stress, nor even of the spondee. In *Dr Faustus* Marlowe is using much greater freedom, and the whole twenty lines of the famous invocation to Helen (p. 154) are worth study. I have space to draw attention to one or two points only. The first three lines are a kind of epitome of blank verse development.

> Was this the face that launch'd a thousand ships?
> And burnt the topless towers of Ilium?—
> Sweet Helen, make me immortal with a kiss.—

The first line is completely regular, five iambic feet, five stresses. The second is equally regular in stress, but falls into three groups, each ending with the foot. But the third is wholly different. It falls into three groups, with the divisions in mid-foot; it has only four stresses, two of which are in the first foot (*Sweet He-*); it thus opens with a spondee and also has an anapaest (˘ ˘ –, *me immor-*) in the middle. In the passage as a whole seven of the twenty lines open with a stress. There are at one point two consecutive lines which illustrate the delicate skill with which Marlowe can play variations:

> Clad in the beauty of a thousand stars;
> Brighter art thou than flaming Jupiter.

Each line begins with a trochee, and each has four stresses, the incidence of the first two of which is identical; but because of the slight pause after 'thou' while there is no pause after the first syllable of 'beauty,' and of the differing distribution of the third and fourth stresses, the effect of the two lines is subtly but manifestly different. Finally, in Faustus's last terrific speech there is a line which shows how far Marlowe now knew he could push freedom without its becoming unmetrical licence:

> See, see, where Christ's blood streams in the firmament.

Five heavy stresses crowded into the first six syllables; and yet that is unmistakably an English blank verse line, and a wonderful one. It is Marlowe's greatest gift to the poets, his fellow countrymen, who came after him, that he learned to write lines like those himself and so made possible the writing of others like

> To the Propontis and the Hellespont

or

> After life's fitful fever he sleeps well

or

> That beats upon the high shore of this world

or

> To the last syllable of recorded time

or

> O dark, dark, dark, amid the blaze of noon,
> Irrecoverably dark, total eclipse

M. R. RIDLEY.

1955.

SELECT BIBLIOGRAPHY

The probable dates of composition, and of first performance, of the individual plays are given in the brief accounts of each play. Of modern editions there are those by Robinson, 1826; Dyce, 1850; Cunningham, 1870; Bullen, 1885; Tucker Brooke, 1910 (text only).

Individual plays have been edited as follows: *Tamburlaine*, A. Wagner, 1885; U. Ellis-Fermor, 1930. *Dido*, C. F. Tucker Brooke, 1930. *The Jew of Malta*, A. Wagner, 1889; H. S. Bennett, 1931. *Edward II*, H. B. Charlton and A. D. Waller, 1933. *Dr Faustus*, H. Breymann, 1889; F. S. Boas, 1932. *The Massacre at Paris*, H. S. Bennett, 1931.

The poems were edited by R. Bell in 1856, by the same Editor for the Bohn edition in 1876, and by L. C. Martin in 1931. Out of a considerable number of works of biography and criticism the following may be mentioned: J. H. Ingram, *Christopher Marlowe and his Associates*, 1904; J. Leslie Hotson, *The Death of Christopher Marlowe*, 1925; U. Ellis-Fermor, *Christopher Marlowe*, 1927; S. Tannenbaum, *The Assassination of Christopher Marlowe*, 1928; C. F. Tucker Brooke, *Life of Marlowe*, 1930; M. Eccles, *Marlowe in London*, 1934; M. K. Mincoff, *Christopher Marlowe, a Study of his Development*, Sofia, 1937; John Bakeless, *Christopher Marlowe*, 1938; F. S. Boas, *Christopher Marlowe*, 1940; P. H. Kocher, *Christopher Marlowe*, 1946; C. Norman, *The Muses' Darling*, 1948; F. P. Wilson, *Marlowe and the Early Shakespeare*, 1953; J. B. Steane, *Marlowe: A Critical Study*, 1964.

CONTENTS

THE FIRST PART OF

TAMBURLAINE THE GREAT

DRAMATIS PERSONÆ

MYCETES, *King of Persia.*
COSROE, *his brother.*
MEANDER, THERIDAMAS, ORTYGIUS, CENEUS, MENAPHON, } *Persian lords.*
TAMBURLAINE, *a Scythian shepherd.*
TECHELLES, USUMCASANE, } *his followers.*
BAJAZETH, *Emperor of the Turks.*
KING OF FEZ.
KING OF MOROCCO.
KING OF ARGIER.
KING OF ARABIA.
SOLDAN OF EGYPT.
GOVERNOR OF DAMASCUS.
AGYDAS, MAGNETES, } *Median lords.*
CAPOLIN, *an Egyptian.*
PHILEMUS, BASSOES, LORDS, CITIZENS, MOORS, SOLDIERS, *and* ATTENDANTS.

ZENOCRATE, *daughter to the Soldan of Egypt.*
ANIPPE, *her maid.*
ZABINA, *wife to* BAJAZETH.
EBEA, *her maid.*
VIRGINS OF DAMASCUS.

THE PROLOGUE

FROM jigging veins of rhyming mother-wits,
And such conceits as clownage keeps in pay,
We'll lead you to the stately tent of war,
Where you shall hear the Scythian Tamburlaine
Threatening the world with high astounding terms,
And scourging kingdoms with his conquering sword.
View but his picture in this tragic glass,
And then applaud his fortunes as you please.

ACT I

SCENE I

Enter MYCETES, COSROE, MEANDER, THERIDAMAS, ORTYGIUS, CENEUS, MENAPHON, *with others.*

Myc. Brother Cosroe, I find myself agriev'd;
Yet insufficient to express the same,
For it requires a great and thundering speech:
Good brother, tell the cause unto my lords;
I know you have a better wit than I.

Cos. Unhappy Persia,—that in former age
Hast been the seat of mighty conquerors,
That, in their prowess and their policies,
Have triumph'd over Afric, and the bounds
Of Europe where the sun dares scarce appear
For freezing meteors and congealed cold,—
Now to be rul'd and govern'd by a man
At whose birthday Cynthia with Saturn join'd,
And Jove, the Sun, and Mercury denied
To shed their influence in his fickle brain!
Now Turks and Tartars shake their swords at thee,
Meaning to mangle all thy provinces.

Myc. Brother, I see your meaning well enough,
And through your planets I perceive you think
I am not wise enough to be a king:
But I refer me to my noblemen,
That know my wit, and can be witnesses.
I might command you to be slain for this,—
Meander, might I not?

Mean. Not for so small a fault, my sovereign lord.

Myc. I mean it not, but yet I know I might—
Yet live; yea, live; Mycetes wills it so.—
Meander, thou, my faithful counsellor,
Declare the cause of my conceived grief,
Which is, God knows, about that Tamburlaine,
That, like a fox in midst of harvest-time,
Doth prey upon my flocks of passengers;
And, as I hear, doth mean to pull my plumes:
Therefore 'tis good and meet for to be wise.

Mean. Oft have I heard your majesty complain
Of Tamburlaine, that sturdy Scythian thief,

That robs your merchants of Persepolis
Trading by land unto the Western Isles,
And in your confines with his lawless train
Daily commits incivil outrages,
Hoping (misled by dreaming prophecies)
To reign in Asia, and with barbarous arms
To make himself the monarch of the East:
But, ere he march in Asia, or display
His vagrant ensign in the Persian fields,
Your grace hath taken order by Theridamas,
Charg'd with a thousand horse, to apprehend
And bring him captive to your highness' throne.

Myc. Full true thou speak'st, and like thyself, my lord,
Whom I may term a Damon for thy love:
Therefore 'tis best, if so it like you all,
To send my thousand horse incontinent
To apprehend that paltry Scythian.
How like you this, my honourable lords?
Is it not a kingly resolution?

Cos. It cannot choose, because it comes from you.

Myc. Then hear thy charge, valiant Theridamas,
The chiefest captain of Mycetes' host,
The hope of Persia, and the very legs
Whereon our state doth lean as on a staff,
That holds us up and foils our neighbour foes:
Thou shalt be leader of this thousand horse,
Whose foaming gall with rage and high disdain
Have sworn the death of wicked Tamburlaine.
Go frowning forth; but come thou smiling home,
As did Sir Paris with the Grecian dame:
Return with speed; time passeth swift away;
Our life is frail, and we may die to-day.

Ther. Before the moon renew her borrow'd light,
Doubt not, my lord and gracious sovereign,
But Tamburlaine and that Tartarian rout
Shall either perish by our warlike hands,
Or plead for mercy at your highness' feet.

Myc. Go, stout Theridamas; thy words are swords,
And with thy looks thou conquerest all thy foes.
I long to see thee back return from thence,
That I may view these milk-white steeds of mine
All loaden with the heads of killed men,
And, from their knees even to their hoofs below,

Besmear'd with blood that makes a dainty show.
Ther. Then now, my lord, I humbly take my leave.
Myc. Theridamas, farewell ten thousand times.
[*Exit Theridamas.*
Ah, Menaphon, why stay'st thou thus behind,
When other men press forward for renown?
Go, Menaphon, go into Scythia,
And foot by foot follow Theridamas.
Cos. Nay, pray you, let him stay; a greater [task]
Fits Menaphon than warring with a thief:
Create him pro-rex of all Africa,
That he may win the Babylonians' hearts,
Which will revolt from Persian government,
Unless they have a wiser king than you.
Myc. Unless they have a wiser king than you!
These are his words; Meander, set them down.
Cos. And add this to them,—that all Asia
Lament to see the folly of their king.
Myc. Well, here I swear by this my royal seat—
Cos. You may do well to kiss it, then.
Myc. Emboss'd with silk as best beseems my state,
To be reveng'd for these contemptuous words!
O where is duty and allegiance now?
Fled to the Caspian or the Ocean main?
What, shall I call thee brother? no, a foe;
Monster of nature, shame unto thy stock,
That dar'st presume thy sovereign for to mock!—
Meander, come: I am abus'd, Meander.
[*Exeunt all except Cosroe and Menaphon.*
Men. How now, my lord! what, mated and amaz'd
To hear the king thus threaten like himself!
Cos. Ah, Menaphon, I pass not for his threats!
The plot is laid by Persian noblemen
And captains of the Median garrisons
To crown me emperor of Asia:
But this it is that doth excruciate
The very substance of my vexed soul,
To see our neighbours, that were wont to quake
And tremble at the Persian monarch's name,
Now sit and laugh our regiment to scorn;
And that which might resolve me into tears,
Men from the farthest equinoctial line
Have swarm'd in troops into the Eastern India,

Lading their ships with gold and precious stones,
And made their spoils from all our provinces.
Men. This should entreat your highness to rejoice,
Since Fortune gives you opportunity
To gain the title of a conqueror
By curing of this maimed empery.
Afric and Europe bordering on your land,
And continent to your dominions,
How easily may you, with a mighty host,
Pass into Græcia, as did Cyrus once,
And cause them to withdraw their forces home,
Lest you subdue the pride of Christendom!
[*Trumpet within.*
Cos. But, Menaphon, what means this trumpet's sound?
Men. Behold, my lord, Ortygius and the rest
Bringing the crown to make you emperor!

Re-enter ORTYGIUS *and* CENEUS, *with others, bearing a crown.*

Orty. Magnificent and mighty prince Cosroe,
We, in the name of other Persian states
And commons of this mighty monarchy,
Present thee with th' imperial diadem.
Cen. The warlike soldiers and the gentlemen,
That heretofore have fill'd Persepolis
With Afric captains taken in the field,
Whose ransom made them march in coats of gold,
With costly jewels hanging at their ears,
And shining stones upon their lofty crests,
Now living idle in the walled towns,
Wanting both pay and martial discipline,
Begin in troops to threaten civil war,
And openly exclaim against the king:
Therefore, to stay all sudden mutinies,
We will invest your highness emperor;
Whereat the soldiers will conceive more joy
Than did the Macedonians at the spoil
Of great Darius and his wealthy host.
Cos. Well, since I see the state of Persia droop
And languish in my brother's government,
I willingly receive th' imperial crown,
And vow to wear it for my country's good,
In spite of them shall malice my estate.
Orty. And, in assurance of desir'd success,

We here do crown thee monarch of the East,
Emperor of Asia and Persia;
Great lord of Media and Armenia;
Duke of Africa and Albania,
Mesopotamia and of Parthia,
East India and the late-discover'd isles;
Chief lord of all the wide vast Euxine Sea;
And of the ever-raging Caspian Lake.

All. Long live Cosroe, mighty emperor!

Cos. And Jove may never let me longer live
Than I may seek to gratify your love,
And cause the soldiers that thus honour me
To triumph over many provinces!
By whose desires of discipline in arms
I doubt not shortly but to reign sole king.
And with the army of Theridamas
(Whither we presently will fly, my lords,)
To rest secure against my brother's force.

Orty. We knew, my lord, before we brought the crown,
Intending your investion so near
The residence of your despised brother,
The lords would not be too exasperate
To injury or suppress your worthy title;
Or, if they would, there are in readiness
Ten thousand horse to carry you from hence,
In spite of all suspected enemies.

Cos. I know it well, my lord, and thank you all.

Orty. Sound up the trumpets, then.

[*Trumpets sounded.*

All. God save the king! [*Exeunt.*

SCENE II

Enter TAMBURLAINE *leading* ZENOCRATE, TECHELLES, USUMCASANE, AGYDAS, MAGNETES, Lords, *and* Soldiers *loaden with treasure.*

Tamb. Come, lady, let not this appal your thoughts;
The jewels and the treasure we have ta'en
Shall be reserv'd, and you in better state
Than if you were arriv'd in Syria,
Even in the circle of your father's arms,
The mighty Soldan of Ægyptia.

Zeno. Ah, shepherd, pity my distressed plight!

(If, as thou seem'st, thou art so mean a man,)
And seek not to enrich thy followers
By lawless rapine from a silly maid,
Who, travelling with these Median lords
To Memphis, from my uncle's country of Media,
Where, all my youth, I have been governed,
Have pass'd the army of the mighty Turk,
Bearing his privy-signet and his hand
To safe conduct us thorough Africa.
Mag. And, since we have arrived in Scythia,
Besides rich presents from the puissant Cham,
We have his highness' letters to command
Aid and assistance, if we stand in need.
Tamb. But now you see these letters and commands
Are countermanded by a greater man;
And through my provinces you must expect
Letters of conduct from my mightiness,
If you intend to keep your treasure safe,
But, since I love to live at liberty
As easily may you get the Soldan's crown
As any prizes out of my precinct;
For they are friends that help to wean my state
Till men and kingdoms help to strengthen it
And must maintain my life exempt from servitude—
But, tell me, madam, is your grace betroth'd?
Zeno. I am, my lord,—for so you do import.
Tamb. I am a lord, for so my deeds shall prove;
And yet a shepherd by my parentage.
But, lady, this fair face and heavenly hue
Must grace his bed that conquers Asia,
And means to be a terror to the world,
Measuring the limits of his empery
By east and west, as Phœbus doth his course—
Lie here, ye weeds, that I disdain to wear!
This complete armour and this curtle-axe
Are adjuncts more beseeming Tamburlaine.—
And, madam, whatsoever you esteem
Of this success, and loss unvalued,
Both may invest you empress of the East;
And these that seem but silly country swains
May have the leading of so great an host
As with their weight shall make the mountains quake,
Even as when windy exhalations,

Fighting for passage, tilt within the earth.
Tech. As princely lions, when they rouse themselves,
Stretching their paws, and threatening herds of beasts,
So in his armour looketh Tamburlaine.
Methinks I see kings kneeling at his feet,
And he with frowning brows and fiery looks
Spurning their crowns from off their captive heads.
Usum. And making thee and me, Techelles, kings,
That even to death will follow Tamburlaine.
Tamb. Nobly resolv'd, sweet friends and followers!
These lords perhaps do scorn our estimates,
And think we prattle with distemper'd spirits:
But, since they measure our deserts so mean,
That in conceit bear empires on our spears,
Affecting thoughts coequal with the clouds,
They shall be kept our forced followers
Till with their eyes they view us emperors.
Zeno. The gods, defenders of the innocent,
Will never prosper your intended drifts,
That thus oppress poor friendless passengers.
Therefore at least admit us liberty,
Even as thou hop'st to be eternised
By living Asia's mighty emperor.
Agyd. I hope our lady's treasure and our own
May serve for ransom to our liberties:
Return our mules and empty camels back,
That we may travel into Syria,
Where her betrothed lord, Alcidamus,
Expects the arrival of her highness' person.
Mag. And wheresoever we repose ourselves,
We will report but well of Tamburlaine.
Tamb. Disdains Zenocrate to live with me?
Or you, my lord, to be my followers?
Think you I weigh this treasure more than you?
Not all the gold in India's wealthy arms
Shall buy the meanest soldier in my train.
Zenocrate, lovelier than the love of Jove,
Brighter than is the silver Rhodope,
Fairer than whitest snow on Scythian hills,
Thy person is more worth to Tamburlaine
Than the possession of the Persian crown,
Which gracious stars have promis'd at my birth.
A hundred Tartars shall attend on thee,

Mounted on steeds swifter than Pegasus;
Thy garments shall be made of Median silk,
Enchas'd with precious jewels of mine own,
More rich and valurous than Zenocrate's;
With milk-white harts upon an ivory sled
Thou shalt be drawn amidst the frozen pools,
And scale the icy mountains' lofty tops,
Which with thy beauty will be soon resolv'd:
My martial prizes, with five hundred men,
Won on the fifty-headed Volga's waves,
Shall we all offer to Zenocrate,
And then myself to fair Zenocrate.
Tech. What now! in love?
Tamb. Techelles, women must be flattered:
But this is she with whom I am in love.

Enter a Soldier.

Sold. News, news!
Tamb. How now! what's the matter?
Sold. A thousand Persian horsemen are at hand,
Sent from the king to overcome us all.
Tamb. How now, my lords of Egypt and Zenocrate!
Now must your jewels be restor'd again,
And I, that triumph'd so, be overcome?
How say you, lordlings? is not this your hope?
Agyd. We hope yourself will willingly restore them.
Tamb. Such hope, such fortune, have the thousand horse.
Soft ye, my lords, and sweet Zenocrate!
You must be forced from me ere you go—
A thousand horsemen! we five hundred foot!
An odds too great for us to stand against.
But are they rich? and is their armour good?
Sold. Their plumed helms are wrought with beaten gold,
Their swords enamell'd, and about their necks
Hang massy chains of gold down to the waist;
In every part exceeding brave and rich.
Tamb. Then shall we fight courageously with them?
Or look you I should play the orator?
Tech. No; cowards and faint-hearted runaways
Look for orations when the foe is near:
Our swords shall play the orators for us.
Usum. Come, let us meet them at the mountain-foot.
And with a sudden and an hot alarum

Drive all their horses headlong down the hill.
Tech. Come, let us march.
Tamb. Stay, Techelles; ask a parley first.

The Soldiers *enter.*

Open the mails, yet guard the treasure sure:
Lay out our golden wedges to the view,
That their reflections may amaze the Persians;
And look we friendly on them when they come:
But, if they offer word or violence,
We'll fight, five hundred men-at-arms to one,
Before we part with our possession;
And 'gainst the general we will lift our swords,
And either lance his greedy thirsting throat,
Or take him prisoner, and his chain shall serve
For manacles till he be ransom'd home.
Tech. I hear them come: shall we encounter them?
Tamb. Keep all your standings, and not stir a foot:
Myself will bide the danger of the brunt.

Enter THERIDAMAS, *with others.*

Ther. Where is this Scythian Tamburlaine?
Tamb. Whom seek'st thou, Persian? I am Tamburlaine.
Ther. Tamburlaine!
A Scythian shepherd so embellished
With nature's pride and richest furniture!
His looks do menace heaven and dare the gods;
His fiery eyes are fix'd upon the earth,
As if he now devis'd some stratagem,
Or meant to pierce Avernus' darksome vaults
To pull the triple-headed dog from hell.
Tamb. Noble and mild this Persian seems to be,
If outward habit judge the inward man.
Tech. His deep affections make him passionate.
Tamb. With what a majesty he rears his looks!—
In thee, thou valiant man of Persia,
I see the folly of thy emperor.
Art thou but captain of a thousand horse,
That by characters graven in thy brows,
And by thy martial face and stout aspect,
Deserv'st to have the leading of an host?
Forsake thy king, and do but join with me,
And we will triumph over all the world:

I hold the Fates bound fast in iron chains,
And with my hand turn Fortune's wheel about;
And sooner shall the sun fall from his sphere
Than Tamburlaine be slain or overcome.
Draw forth thy sword thou mighty man-at-arms,
Intending but to raze my charmed skin,
And Jove himself will stretch his hand from heaven
To ward the blow, and shield me safe from harm.
See, how he rains down heaps of gold in showers,
As if he meant to give my soldiers pay!
And, as a sure and grounded argument
That I shall be the monarch of the East,
He sends this Soldan's daughter rich and brave,
To be my queen and portly emperess.
If thou wilt stay with me, renowmed man,
And lead thy thousand horse with my conduct,
Besides thy share of this Egyptian prize,
Those thousand horse shall sweat with martial spoil
Of conquer'd kingdoms and of cities sack'd:
Both we will walk upon the lofty cliffs;
And Christian merchants, that with Russian stems
Plough up huge furrows in the Caspian Sea,
Shall vail to us as lords of all the lake;
Both we will reign as consuls of the earth,
And mighty kings shall be our senators.
Jove sometime masked in a shepherd's weed;
And by those steps that he hath scal'd the heavens
May we become immortal like the gods.
Join with me now in this my mean estate,
(I call it mean, because, being yet obscure,
The nations far-remov'd admire me not,)
And when my name and honour shall be spread
As far as Boreas claps his brazen wings,
Or fair Bootes sends his cheerful light,
Then shalt thou be competitor with me,
And sit with Tamburlaine in all his majesty.

Ther. Not Hermes, prolocutor to the gods,
Could use persuasions more pathetical.

Tamb. Nor are Apollo's oracles more true
Than thou shalt find my vaunts substantial.

Tech. We are his friends; and if the Persian king
Should offer present dukedoms to our state,
We think it loss to make exchange for that

We are assur'd of by our friend's success.
Usum. And kingdoms at the least we all expect,
Besides the honour in assured conquests,
Where kings shall crouch unto our conquering swords,
And hosts of soldiers stand amaz'd at us,
When with their fearful tongues they shall confess,
These are the men that all the world admires.
Ther. What strong enchantments tice my yielding soul?
Ah, these resolved, noble Scythians!
But shall I prove a traitor to my king?
Tamb. No; but the trusty friend of Tamburlaine.
Ther. Won with thy words, and conquer'd with thy looks,
I yield myself, my men, and horse to thee,
To be partaker of thy good or ill,
As long as life maintains Theridamas.
Tamb. Theridamas, my friend, take here my hand,
Which is as much as if I swore by heaven,
And call'd the gods to witness of my vow.
Thus shalt my heart be still combin'd with thine
Until our bodies turn to elements,
And both our souls aspire celestial thrones.—
Techelles and Casane, welcome him.
Tech. Welcome, renowmed Persian, to us all!
Usum. Long may Theridamas remain with us!
Tamb. These are my friends, in whom I more rejoice
Than doth the king of Persia in his crown;
And, by the love of Pylades and Orestes,
Whose statues we adore in Scythia,
Thyself and them shall never part from me
Before I crown you kings in Asia.
Make much of them, gentle Theridamas,
And they will never leave thee till the death.
Ther. Nor thee nor them, thrice-noble Tamburlaine
Shall want my heart to be with gladness pierc'd,
To do you honour and security.
Tamb. A thousand thanks, worthy Theridamas.—
And now, fair madam, and my noble lords,
If you will willingly remain with me,
You shall have honours as your merits be;
Or else you shall be forc'd with slavery.
Agyd. We yield unto thee, happy Tamburlaine.
Tamb. For you, then, madam, I am out of doubt.
Zeno. I must be pleas'd perforce,—wretched Zenocrate!

[*Exeunt.*

ACT II

SCENE I

Enter Cosroe, Menaphon, Ortygius, *and* Ceneus, *with* Soldiers.

Cos. Thus far are we towards Theridamas,
And valiant Tamburlaine, the man of fame,
The man that in the forehead of his fortune
Bears figures of renown and miracle.
But tell me, that hast seen him, Menaphon,
What stature wields he, and what personage?
Men. Of stature tall, and straightly fashioned
Like his desire, lift upwards and divine;
So large of limbs, his joints so strongly knit,
Such breadth of shoulders as might mainly bear
Old Atlas' burden; 'twixt his manly pitch,
A pearl more worth than all the world is plac'd,
Wherein by curious sovereignty of art
Are fix'd his piercing instruments of sight,
Whose fiery circles bear encompassed
A heaven of heavenly bodies in their spheres,
That guides his steps and actions to the throne
Where honour sits invested royally;
Pale of complexion, wrought in him with passion,
Thirsting with sovereignty and love of arms;
His lofty brows in folds do figure death,
And in their smoothness amity and life;
About them hangs a knot of amber hair,
Wrapped in curls, as fierce Achilles' was,
On which the breath of heaven delights to play
Making it dance with wanton majesty;
His arms and fingers long and sinewy,
Betokening valour and excess of strength;—
In every part proportion'd like the man
Should make the world subdu'd to Tamburlaine.
Cos. Well hast thou pourtray'd in thy terms of life
The face and personage of a wondrous man:
Nature doth strive with Fortune and his stars
To make him famous in accomplish'd worth;
And well his merits shew him to be made
His fortune's master and the king of men,

That could persuade, at such a sudden pinch,
With reasons of his valour and his life,
A thousand sworn and overmatching foes.
Then, when our powers in points of swords are join'd,
And clos'd in compass of the killing bullet,
Though strait the passage and the port be made
That leads to palace of my brother's life,
Proud is his fortune if we pierce it not;
And, when the princely Persian diadem
Shall overweigh his weary witless head,
And fall, like mellow'd fruit, with shakes of death
In fair Persia noble Tamburlaine
Shall be my regent, and remain as king.

Orty. In happy hour we have set the crown
Upon your kingly head, that seeks our honour
In joining with the man ordain'd by heaven
To further every action to the best.

Cen. He that with shepherds and a little spoil
Durst, in disdain of wrong and tyranny,
Defend his freedom 'gainst a monarchy,
What will he do supported by a king,
Leading a troop of gentlemen and lords,
And stuff'd with treasure for his highest thoughts!

Cos. And such shall wait on worthy Tamburlaine.
Our army will be forty thousand strong,
When Tamburlaine and brave Theridamas
Have met us by the river Araris;
And all conjoin'd to meet the witless king,
That now is marching near to Parthia,
And, with unwilling soldiers faintly arm'd,
To seek revenge on me and Tamburlaine;
To whom, sweet Menaphon, direct me straight.

Men. I will, my lord. [*Exeunt.*

SCENE II

Enter MYCETES, MEANDER, *with other* Lords; *and* Soldiers.

Myc. Come, my Meander, let us to this gear.
I tell you true, my heart is swoln with wrath
On this same thievish villain Tamburlaine,
And of that false Cosroe, my traitorous brother.
Would it not grieve a king to be so abus'd,

And have a thousand horsemen ta'en away?
And, which is worst, to have his diadem
Sought for by such scald knaves as love him not?
I think it would: well, then, by heavens I swear,
Aurora shall not peep out of her doors,
But I will have Cosroe by the head,
And kill proud Tamburlaine with point of sword.
Tell you the rest, Meander: I have said.

Mean. Then, having pass'd Armenian deserts now,
And pitch'd our tents under the Georgian hills,
Whose tops are cover'd with Tartarian thieves,
That lie in ambush, waiting for a prey,
What should we do but bid them battle straight,
And rid the world of those detested troops?
Lest, if we let them linger here a while,
They gather strength by power of fresh supplies.
This country swarms with vile outragious men
That live by rapine and by lawless spoil,
Fit soldiers for the wicked Tamburlaine;
And he that could with gifts and promises
Inveigle him that led a thousand horse,
And make him false his faith unto his king,
Will quickly win such as are like himself.
Therefore cheer up your minds; prepare to fight:
He that can take or slaughter Tamburlaine,
Shall rule the province of Albania;
Who brings that traitor's head, Theridamas,
Shall have a government in Media,
Beside the spoil of him and all his train:
But, if Cosroe (as our spials say,
And as we know) remains with Tamburlaine,
His highness' pleasure is that he should live,
And be reclaim'd with princely lenity.

Enter a Spy.

Spy. An hundred horsemen of my company,
Scouting abroad upon these champion plains,
Have view'd the army of the Scythians;
Which make report it far exceeds the king's.

Mean. Suppose they be in number infinite,
Yet being void of martial discipline,
All running headlong after greedy spoils,
And more regarding gain than victory,

Like to the cruel brothers of the earth,
Sprung of the teeth of dragons venomous,
Their careless swords shall lance their fellows' throats
And make us triumph in their overthrow.
Myc. Was there such brethren, sweet Meander, say,
That sprung of teeth of dragons venomous?
Mean. So poets say, my lord.
Myc. And 'tis a pretty toy to be a poet.
Well, well, Meander, thou art deeply read;
And having thee, I have a jewel sure.
Go on, my lord, and give your charge, I say;
Thy wit will make us conquerors to-day.
Mean. Then, noble soldiers, to entrap these thieves
That live confounded in disorder'd troops,
If wealth or riches may prevail with them,
We have our camels laden all with gold,
Which you that be but common soldiers
Shall fling in every corner of the field;
And, while the base-born Tartars take it up,
You, fighting more for honour than for gold,
Shall massacre those greedy-minded slaves;
And, when their scatter'd army is subdu'd,
And you march on their slaughter'd carcasses,
Share equally the gold that bought their lives,
And live like gentlemen in Persia.
Strike up the drum, and march courageously:
Fortune herself doth sit upon our crests.
Myc. He tells you true, my masters; so he does.—
Drums, why sound ye not when Meander speaks?
[*Exeunt, drums sounding.*

SCENE III

Enter COSROE, TAMBURLAINE, THERIDAMAS, TECHELLES, USUMCASANE, *and* ORTYGIUS, *with others.*

Cos. Now, worthy Tamburlaine, have I repos'd
In thy approved fortunes all my hope.
What think'st thou, man, shall come of our attempts?
For, even as from assured oracle,
I take thy doom for satisfaction.
Tamb. And so mistake you not a whit, my lord;
For fates and oracles [of] heaven have sworn
To royalise the deeds of Tamburlaine,

And make them blest that share in his attempts
And doubt you not but, if you favour me,
And let my fortunes and my valour sway
To some direction in your martial deeds,
The world will strive with hosts of men-at-arms
To swarm unto the ensign I support.
The hosts of Xerxes, which by fame is said
To drink the mighty Parthian Araris,
Was but a handful to that we will have:
Our quivering lances, shaking in the air,
And bullets, like Jove's dreadful thunderbolts,
Enroll'd in flames and fiery smouldering mists,
Shall threat the gods more than Cyclopian wars;
And with our sun-bright armour, as we march,
We'll chase the stars from heaven, and dim their eyes
That stand and muse at our admired arms.

Ther. You see, my lord, what working words he hath;
But, when you see his actions top his speech,
Your speech will stay, or so extol his worth
As I shall be commended and excus'd
For turning my poor charge to his direction:
And these his two renowmed friends, my lord,
Would make one thrust and strive to be retain'd
In such a great degree of amity.

Tech. With duty and with amity we yield
Our utmost service to the fair Cosroe.

Cos. Which I esteem as portion of my crown.
Usumcasane and Techelles both,
When she that rules in Rhamnus' golden gates,
And makes a passage for all prosperous arms,
Shall make me solely emperor of Asia,
Then shall your meeds and valours be advanc'd
To rooms of honour and nobility.

Tamb. Then haste, Cosroe, to be king alone,
That I with these my friends and all my men
May triumph in our long-expected fate.
The king, your brother, is now hard at hand:
Meet with the fool, and rid your royal shoulders
Of such a burden as outweighs the sands
And all the craggy rocks of Caspia.

Enter a Messenger.

Mes. My lord,
We have discovered the enemy

Ready to charge you with a mighty army.
Cos. Come, Tamburlaine; now whet thy winged sword,
And lift thy lofty arm into the clouds,
That it may reach the king of Persia's crown,
And set it safe on my victorious head.
Tamb. See where it is, the keenest curtle-axe
That e'er made passage thorough Persian arms!
These are the wings shall make it fly as swift
As doth the lightning or the breath of heaven,
And kill as sure as it swiftly flies.
Cos. Thy words assure me of kind success:
Go, valiant soldier, go before, and charge
The fainting army of that foolish king.
Tamb. Usumcasane and Techelles, come:
We are enow to scare the enemy,
And more than needs to make an emperor.
[*Exeunt to the battle.*

SCENE IV

Enter MYCETES, *with his crown in his hand.*

Myc. Accurs'd be he that first invented war!
They knew not, ah, they knew not, simple men,
How those were hit by pelting cannon-shot
Stand staggering like a quivering aspen-leaf
Fearing the force of Boreas' boisterous blasts!
In what a lamentable case were I,
If nature had not given me wisdom's lore!
For kings are clouts that every man shoots at,
Our crown the pin that thousands seek to cleave:
Therefore in policy I think it good
To hide it close; a goodly stratagem,
And far from any man that is a fool:
So shall not I be known; or if I be,
They cannot take away my crown from me.
Here will I hide it in this simple hole.

Enter TAMBURLAINE.

Tamb. What, fearful coward, straggling from the camp,
When kings themselves are present in the field!
Myc. Thou liest.
Tamb. Base villain, darest thou give me the lie?
Myc. Away! I am the king; go; touch me not.

Thou break'st the law of arms, unless thou kneel,
And cry me " mercy, noble king! "
Tamb. Are you the witty king of Persia?
Myc. Ay, marry, am I: have you any suit to me?
Tamb. I would entreat you to speak but three wise words.
Myc. So I can when I see my time.
Tamb. Is this your crown?
Myc. Ay: didst thou ever see a fairer?
Tamb. You will not sell it, will you?
Myc. Such another word, and I will have thee executed. Come, give it me.
Tamb. No; I took it prisoner.
Myc. You lie; I gave it you.
Tamb. Then 'tis mine.
Myc. No; I mean I let you keep it.
Tamb. Well, I mean you shall have it again.
Here, take it for a while: I lend it thee,
Till I may see thee hemm'd with armed men;
Then shalt thou see me pull it from thy head:
Thou art no match for mighty Tamburlaine. [*Exit.*
Myc. O gods, is this Tamburlaine the thief?
I marvel much he stole it not away.
[*Trumpets within sound to the battle: he runs out.*

SCENE V

Enter COSROE, TAMBURLAINE, MENAPHON, MEANDER, ORTYGIUS, THERIDAMAS. TECHELLES, USUMCASANE, *with others.*

Tamb. Hold thee, Cosroe; wear two imperial crowns;
Think thee invested now as royally,
Even by the mighty hand of Tamburlaine,
As if as many kings as could encompass thee
With greatest pomp had crown'd thee emperor.
Cos. So do I, thrice-renowmed man-at-arms;
And none shall keep the crown but Tamburlaine:
Thee do I make my regent of Persia,
And general lieutenant of my armies.—
Meander, you, that were our brother's guide,
And chiefest counsellor in all his acts,
Since he is yielded to the stroke of war,
On your submission we with thanks excuse,
And give you equal place in our affairs.

Mean. Most happy emperor, in humblest terms
I vow my service to your majesty,
With utmost virtue of my faith and duty.
Cos. Thanks, good Meander.—Then, Cosroe, reign,
And govern Persia in her former pomp.
Now send embassage to thy neighbour kings,
And let them know the Persian king is chang'd,
From one that knew not what a king should do,
To one that can command what 'longs thereto.
And now we will to fair Persepolis
With twenty thousand expert soldiers.
The lords and captains of my brother's camp
With little slaughter take Meander's course,
And gladly yield them to my gracious rule.—
Ortygius and Menaphon, my trusty friends,
Now will I gratify your former good,
And grace your calling with a greater sway.
Orty. And as we ever aim'd at your behoof,
And sought your state all honour it deserv'd,
So will we with our powers and our lives
Endeavour to preserve and prosper it.
Cos. I will not thank thee, sweet Ortygius;
Better replies shall prove my purposes.—
And now, Lord Tamburlaine, my brother's camp
I leave to thee and to Theridamas,
To follow me to fair Persepolis;
Then will we march to all those Indian mines
My witless brother to the Christians lost,
And ransom them with fame and usury:
And, till thou overtake me, Tamburlaine,
(Staying to order all the scatter'd troops,)
Farewell, lord regent and his happy friends.
I long to sit upon my brother's throne.
Mean. Your majesty shall shortly have your wish,
And ride in triumph through Persepolis.
[*Exeunt all except Tamb., Ther., Tech., and Usum.*
Tamb. And ride in triumph through Persepolis!—
Is it not brave to be a king, Techelles!—
Usumcasane and Theridamas,
Is it not passing brave to be a king,
And ride in triumph through Persepolis?
Tech. O, my lord, it is sweet and full of pomp!
Usum. To be a king, is half to be a god.

Ther. A god is not so glorious as a king:
I think the pleasure they enjoy in heaven,
Cannot compare with kingly joys in earth;—
To wear a crown enchas'd with pearl and gold,
Whose virtues carry with it life and death;
To ask and have, command and be obey'd;
When looks breed love, with looks to gain the prize,
Such power attractive shines in princes' eyes.
Tamb. Why, say, Theridamas, wilt thou be a king?
Ther. Nay, though I praise it, I can live without it.
Tamb. What say my other friends? will you be kings?
Tech. Ay, if I could, with all my heart, my lord.
Tamb. Why, that's well said, Techelles: so would I:—
And so would you my masters, would you not?
Usum. What then, my lord?
Tamb. Why, then, Casane, shall we wish for aught
The world affords in greatest novelty,
And rest attemptless, faint, and destitute?
Methinks we should not. I am strongly mov'd,
That if I should desire the Persian crown,
I could attain it with a wondrous ease:
And would not all our soldiers soon consent,
If we should aim at such a dignity?
Ther. I know they would with our persuasions.
Tamb. Why, then, Theridamas, I'll first assay
To get the Persian kingdom to myself;
Then thou for Parthia; they for Scythia and Media;
And, if I prosper, all shall be as sure
As if the Turk, the Pope, Afric, and Greece,
Came creeping to us with their crowns a-piece.
Tech. Then shall we send to this triumphing king,
And bid him battle for his novel crown?
Usum. Nay, quickly, then, before his room be hot.
Tamb. 'Twill prove a pretty jest, in faith, my friends.
Ther. A jest to charge on twenty thousand men!
I judge the purchase more important far.
Tamb. Judge by thyself, Theridamas, not me;
For presently Techelles here shall haste
To bid him battle ere he pass too far,
And lose more labour than the gain will quite:
Then shalt thou see this Scythian Tamburlaine
Make but a jest to win the Persian crown.—
Techelles, take a thousand horse with thee,

And bid him turn him back to war with us,
That only made him king to make us sport:
We will not steal upon him cowardly,
But give him warning and more warriors:
Haste thee, Techelles; we will follow thee.
[*Exit Techelles.*
What saith Theridamas?
Ther. Go on, for me. [*Exeunt.*

SCENE VI

Enter COSROE, MEANDER, ORTYGIUS, *and* MENAPHON, *with* Soldiers.

Cos. What means this devilish shepherd, to aspire
With such a giantly presumption,
To cast up hills against the face of heaven,
And dare the force of angry Jupiter?
But, as he thrust them underneath the hills,
And press'd out fire from their burning jaws,
So will I send this monstrous slave to hell,
Where flames shall ever feed upon his soul.
Mean. Some powers divine, or else infernal, mix'd
Their angry seeds at his conception;
For he was never sprung of human race,
Since with the spirit of his fearful pride,
He dares so doubtlessly resolve of rule,
And by profession be ambitious.
Orty. What god, or fiend, or spirit of the earth,
Or monster turned to a manly shape,
Or of what mould or mettle he be made,
What star or fate soever govern him,
Let us put on our meet encountering minds;
And, in detesting such a devilish thief,
In love of honour and defence of right,
Be arm'd against the hate of such a foe,
Whether from earth, or hell, or heaven he grow.
Cos. Nobly resolv'd, my good Ortygius;
And since we all have suck'd one wholesome air,
And with the same proportion of elements
Resolve, I hope we are resembled,
Vowing our loves to equal death and life.
Let's cheer our soldiers to encounter him,
That grievous image of ingratitude,

That fiery thirster after sovereignty,
And burn him in the fury of that flame
That none can quench but blood and empery.
Resolve, my lords and loving soldiers, now
To save your king and country from decay.
Then strike up, drum; and all the stars that make
The loathsome circle of my dated life,
Direct my weapon to his barbarous heart,
That thus opposeth him against the gods,
And scorns the powers that govern Persia!

[*Exeunt, drums sounding.*

SCENE VII

Alarms of battle within. Then enter COSROE *wounded,* TAMBURLAINE, THERIDAMAS, TECHELLES, USUMCASANE, *with others.*

Cos. Barbarous and bloody Tamburlaine,
Thus to deprive me of my crown and life!—
Treacherous and false Theridamas,
Even at the morning of my happy state,
Scarce being seated in my royal throne,
To work my downfall and untimely end!
An uncouth pain torments my grieved soul
And death arrests the organ of my voice,
Who, entering at the breach thy sword hath made,
Sacks every vein and artier of my heart.—
Bloody and insatiate Tamburlaine!

Tamb. The thirst of reign and sweetness of a crown,
That caus'd the eldest son of heavenly Ops
To thrust his doting father from his chair,
And place himself in the imperial heaven,
Mov'd me to manage arms against thy state.
What better precedent than mighty Jove?
Nature, that fram'd us of four elements
Warring within our breasts for regiment,
Doth teach us all to have aspiring minds:
Our souls, whose faculties can comprehend
The wondrous architecture of the world,
And measure every wandering planet's course,
Still climbing after knowledge infinite,
And always moving as the restless spheres,
Will us to wear ourselves, and never rest,

Until we reach the ripest fruit of all,
That perfect bliss and sole felicity,
The sweet fruition of an earthly crown.

Ther. And that made me to join with Tamburlaine;
For he is gross and like the massy earth
That moves not upwards, nor by princely deeds
Doth mean to soar above the highest sort.

Tech. And that made us the friends of Tamburlaine,
To lift our swords against the Persian king.

Usum. For as, when Jove did thrust old Saturn down,
Neptune and Dis gain'd each of them a crown,
So do we hope to reign in Asia,
If Tamburlaine be plac'd in Persia.

Cos. The strangest men that ever nature made!
I know not how to take their tyrannies.
My bloodless body waxeth chill and cold.
And with my blood my life slides through my wound;
My soul begins to take her flight to hell,
And summons all my senses to depart:
The heat and moisture, which did feed each other,
For want of nourishment to feed them both,
Are dry and cold; and now doth ghastly Death
With greedy talons gripe my bleeding heart,
And like a harpy tires on my life.—
Theridamas and Tamburlaine, I die:
And fearful vengeance light upon you both!

[*Dies.—Tamburlaine takes Cosroe's crown, and puts it on his own head.*

Tamb. Not all the curses which the Furies breathe
Shall make me leave so rich a prize as this.
Theridamas, Techelles, and the rest,
Who think you now is king of Persia?

All. Tamburlaine! Tamburlaine!

Tamb. Though Mars himself, the angry god of arms,
And all the earthly potentates conspire
To dispossess me of this diadem,
Yet will I wear it in despite of them,
As great commander of this eastern world,
If you but say that Tamburlaine shall reign.

All. Long live Tamburlaine, and reign in Asia!

Tamb. So; now it is more surer on my head
Than if the gods had held a parliament,
And all pronounc'd me king of Persia. [*Exeunt.*

ACT III

SCENE I

Enter BAJAZETH, *the* KINGS OF FEZ, MOROCCO, *and* ARGIER, *with others, in great pomp.*

Baj. Great kings of Barbary, and my portly bassoes,
We hear the Tartars and the eastern thieves,
Under the conduct of one Tamburlaine,
Presume a bickering with your emperor,
And think to rouse us from our dreadful siege
Of the famous Grecian Constantinople.
You know our army is invincible;
As many circumcised Turks we have,
And warlike bands of Christians renied,
As hath the ocean or the Terrene sea
Small drops of water when the moon begins
To join in one her semicircled horns:
Yet would we not be brav'd with foreign power,
Nor raise our siege before the Grecians yield,
Or breathless lie before the city-walls

K. of Fez. Renowmed emperor and mighty general,
What, if you sent the bassoes of your guard
To charge him to remain in Asia,
Or else to threaten death and deadly arms
As from the mouth of mighty Bajazeth?

Baj. Hie thee, my basso, fast to Persia;
Tell him thy lord, the Turkish emperor,
Dread lord of Afric, Europe, and Asia,
Great king and conqueror of Græcia,
The ocean, Terrene, and the Coal-black sea,
The high and highest monarch of the world,
Wills and commands, (for say not I entreat,)
Not once to set his foot in Africa,
Or spread his colours in Græcia,
Lest he incur the fury of my wrath:
Tell him I am content to take a truce,
Because I hear he bears a valiant mind:
But if, presuming on his silly power,
He be so mad to manage arms with me,
Then stay thou with him,—say, I bid thee so;
And if, before the sun have measur'd heaven

With triple circuit, thou regreet us not,
We mean to take his morning's next arise
For messenger he will not be reclaim'd,
And mean to fetch thee in despite of him.

Baj. Most great and puissant monarch of the earth,
Your basso will accomplish your behest,
And shew your pleasure to the Persian,
As fits the legate of the stately Turk. [*Exit.*

K. of Arg. They say he is the king of Persia;
But, if he dare attempt to stir your siege,
'Twere requisite he should be ten times more,
For all flesh quakes at your magnificence.

Baj. True, Argier; and trembles at my looks.

K. of Mor. The spring is hinder'd by your smothering host;
For neither rain can fall upon the earth,
Nor sun reflex his virtuous beams thereon,
The ground is mantled with such multitudes.

Baj. All this is true as holy Mahomet;
And all the trees are blasted with our breaths.

K. of Fez. What thinks your greatness best to be achiev'd
In pursuit of the city's overthrow?

Baj. I will the captive pioners of Argier
Cut off the water that by leaden pipes
Runs to the city from the mountain Carnon;
Two thousand horse shall forage up and down,
That no relief or succour come by land;
And all the sea my galleys countermand:
Then shall our footmen lie within the trench,
And with their cannons, mouth'd like Orcus' gulf,
Batter the walls, and we will enter in;
And thus the Grecians shall be conquered. [*Exeunt.*

SCENE II

Enter ZENOCRATE, AGYDAS, ANIPPE, *with others.*

Agyd. Madam Zenocrate, may I presume
To know the cause of these unquiet fits
That work such trouble to your wonted rest?
'Tis more than pity such a heavenly face
Should by heart's sorrow wax so wan and pale,
When your offensive rape by Tamburlaine
(Which of your whole displeasures should be most)

Hath seem'd to be digested long ago.
Zeno. Although it be digested long ago,
As his exceeding favours have deserv'd,
And might content the Queen of Heaven, as well
As it hath chang'd my first-conceiv'd disdain;
Yet since a farther passion feeds my thoughts
With ceaseless and disconsolate conceits.
Which dye my looks so lifeless as they are,
And might, if my extremes had full events,
Make me the ghastly counterfeit of death.
Agyd. Eternal heaven sooner be dissolv'd,
And all that pierceth Phœbus' silver eye,
Before such hap fall to Zenocrate!
Zeno. Ah, life and soul, still hover in his breast,
And leave my body senseless as the earth,
Or else unite you to his life and soul,
That I may live and die with Tamburlaine!

Enter, behind, TAMBURLAINE, *with* TECHELLES, *and others.*

Agyd. With Tamburlaine! Ah, fair Zenocrate,
Let not a man so vile and barbarous,
That holds you from your father in despite,
And keeps you from the honours of a queen,
(Being suppos'd his worthless concubine,)
Be honour'd with your love but for necessity!
So, now the mighty Soldan hears of you,
Your highness needs not doubt but in short time
He will, with Tamburlaine's destruction,
Redeem you from this deadly servitude.
Zeno. Leave to wound me with these words,
And speak of Tamburlaine as he deserves:
The entertainment we have had of him
Is far from villany or servitude,
And might in noble minds be counted princely.
Agyd. How can you fancy one that looks so fierce,
Only dispos'd to martial stratagems?
Who, when he shall embrace you in his arms,
Will tell how many thousand men he slew;
And, when you look for amorous discourse,
Will rattle forth his facts of war and blood,
Too harsh a subject for your dainty ears.
Zeno. As looks the sun through Nilus' flowing stream,

Or when the Morning holds him in her arms,
So looks my lordly love, fair Tamburlaine;
His talk much sweeter than the Muses' song
They sung for honour 'gainst Pierides,
Or when Minerva did with Neptune strive:
And higher would I rear my estimate
Than Juno, sister to the highest god,
If I were match'd with mighty Tamburlaine.

Agyd. Yet be not so inconstant in your love,
But let the young Arabian live in hope,
After your rescue to enjoy his choice.
You see, though first the king of Persia,
Being a shepherd, seem'd to love you much,
Now, in his majesty, he leaves those looks,
Those words of favour, and those comfortings,
And gives no more than common courtesies.

Zeno. Thence rise the tears that so disdain my cheeks,
Fearing his love through my unworthiness.

[*Tamburlaine goes to her, and takes her away lovingly by the hand, looking wrathfully on Agydas, and says nothing. Exeunt all except Agydas.*

Agyd. Betray'd by fortune and suspicious love,
Threaten'd with frowning wrath and jealousy,
Surpris'd with fear of hideous revenge,
I stand aghast; but most astonied
To see his choler shut in secret thoughts,
And wrapt in silence of his angry soul:
Upon his brows was pourtray'd ugly death;
And in his eyes the fury of his heart,
That shone as comets, menacing revenge,
And cast a pale complexion on his cheeks.
As when the seaman sees the Hyades
Gather an army of Cimmerian clouds,
(Auster and Aquilon with winged steeds,
All sweating, tilt about the watery heavens,
With shivering spears enforcing thunder-claps,
And from their shields strike flames of lightening,)
All-fearful folds his sails, and sounds the main,
Lifting his prayers to the heavens for aid
Against the terror of the winds and waves;
So fares Agydas for the late-felt frowns,
That sent a tempest to my daunted thoughts,
And make my soul divine her overthrow.

Re-enter TECHELLES *with a naked dagger, and* USUMCASANE.

Tech. See you, Agydas, how the king salutes you!
He bids you prophesy what it imports.
Agyd. I prophesied before, and now I prove
The killing frowns of jealousy and love.
He needed not with words confirm my fear,
For words are vain where working tools present
The naked action of my threaten'd end:
It says, Agydas, thou shalt surely die,
And of extremities elect the least;
More honour and less pain it may procure,
To die by this resolved hand of thine
Than stay the torments he and heaven have sworn.
Then haste, Agydas, and prevent the plagues
Which thy prolonged fates may draw on thee:
Go wander free from fear of tyrant's rage,
Removed from the torments and the hell
Wherewith he may excruciate thy soul;
And let Agydas by Agydas die,
And with this stab slumber eternally. [*Stabs himself.*
Tech. Usumcasane, see, how right the man
Hath hit the meaning of my lord and king!
Usum. Faith, and, Techelles, it was manly done;
And, since he was so wise and honourable,
Let us afford him now the bearing hence,
And crave his triple-worthy burial.
Tech. Agreed, Casane; we will honour him.
[*Exeunt, bearing out the body.*

SCENE III

Enter TAMBURLAINE, TECHELLES, USUMCASANE, THERIDAMAS, *a* Basso, ZENOCRATE, ANIPPE, *with others.*

Tamb. Basso, by this thy lord and master knows
I mean to meet him in Bithynia:
See, how he comes! tush, Turks are full of brags,
And menace more than they can well perform.
He meet me in the field, and fetch thee hence!
Alas, poor Turk! his fortune is too weak
T' encounter with the strength of Tamburlaine:
View well my camp, and speak indifferently;
Do not my captains and my soldiers look

As if they meant to conquer Africa?
Bas. Your men are valiant, but their number few,
And cannot terrify his mighty host:
My lord, the great commander of the world,
Besides fifteen contributory kings,
Hath now in arms ten thousand janizaries,
Mounted on lusty Mauritanian steeds,
Brought to the war by men of Tripoly;
Two hundred thousand footmen that have serv'd
In two set battles fought in Græcia;
And for the expediton of this war,
If he think good, can from his garrisons
Withdraw as many more to follow him.
Tech. The more he brings, the greater is the spoil;
For, when they perish by our warlike hands,
We mean to set our footmen on their steeds,
And rifle all those stately janizars.
Tamb. But will those kings accompany your lord?
Bas. Such as his highness please: but some must stay
To rule the provinces he late subdu'd.
Tamb. [*To his Officers*]. Then fight courageously: their crowns are yours,
This hand shall set them on your conquering heads
That made me emperor of Asia.
Usum. Let him bring millions infinite of men,
Unpeopling Western Africa and Greece,
Yet we assure us of the victory.
Ther. Even he, that in a trice vanquish'd two kings
More mighty than the Turkish emperor,
Shall rouse him out of Europe, and pursue
His scatter'd army till they yield or die.
Tamb. Well said, Theridamas! speak in that mood;
For *will* and *shall* best fitteth Tamburlaine,
Whose smiling stars give him assured hope
Of martial triumph ere he meets his foes.
I that am term'd the Scourge and Wrath of God,
The only fear and terror of the world,
Will first subdue the Turk, and then enlarge
Those Christian captives which you keep as slaves,
Burdening their bodies with your heavy chains,
And feeding them with thin and slender fare;
That naked row about the Terrene sea,
And, when they chance to rest or breathe a space,

Are punish'd with bastones so grievously
That they lie panting on the galleys' side,
And strive for life at every stroke they give.
These are the cruel pirates of Argier,
That damned train, the scum of Africa,
Inhabited with straggling runagates,
That make quick havoc of the Christian blood:
But, as I live, that town shall curse the time
That Tamburlaine set foot in Africa.

Enter BAJAZETH, Bassoes, *the* KINGS OF FEZ, MOROCCO, *and* ARGIER; ZABINA *and* EBEA.

Baj. Bassoes and janizaries of my guard,
Attend upon the person of your lord,
The greatest potentate of Africa.
Tamb. Techelles and the rest, prepare your swords;
I mean t' encounter with that Bajazeth.
Baj. Kings of Fez, Morocco, and Argier,
He calls me Bajazeth, whom you call lord!
Note the presumption of this Scythian slave!—
I tell thee, villain, those that lead my horse
Have to their names titles of dignity;
And dar'st thou bluntly call me Bajazeth?
Tamb. And know thou, Turk, that those which lead my horse
Shall lead thee captive thorough Africa;
And dar'st thou bluntly call me Tamburlaine?
Baj. By Mahomet my kinsman's sepulchre,
And by the holy Alcoran I swear,
He shall be made a chaste and lustless eunuch,
And in my sarell tend my concubines;
And all his captains, that thus stoutly stand,
Shall draw the chariot of my emperess,
Whom I have brought to see their overthrow!
Tamb. By this my sword that conquer'd Persia.
Thy fall shall make me famous through the world!
I will not tell thee how I'll handle thee,
But every common soldier of my camp
Shall smile to see thy miserable state.
K. of Fez. What means the mighty Turkish emperor,
To talk with one so base as Tamburlaine?
K. of Morocco. Ye Moors and valiant men of Barbary,
How can ye suffer these indignities?
K. of Arg. Leave words, and let them feel your lances' points,

Which glided through the bowels of the Greeks.
Baj. Well said, my stout contributory kings!
Your threefold army and my hugy host
Shall swallow up these base-born Persians.
Tech. Puissant, renowm'd, and mighty Tamburlaine,
Why stay we thus prolonging of their lives?
Ther. I long to see those crowns won by our swords,
That we may rule as kings of Africa.
Usum. What coward would not fight for such a prize?
Tamb. Fight all courageously, and be you kings:
I speak it, and my words are oracles.
Baj. Zabina, mother of three braver boys
Than Hercules, that in his infancy
Did pash the jaws of serpents venomous;
Whose hands are made to gripe a warlike lance,
Their shoulders broad for complete armour fit,
Their limbs more large and of a bigger size
Than all the brats y-sprung from Typhon's loins;
Who, when they come unto their father's age,
Will batter turrets with their manly fists;—
Sit here upon this royal chair of state,
And on thy head wear my imperial crown,
Until I bring this sturdy Tamburlaine
And all his captains bound in captive chains.
Zab. Such good success happen to Bajazeth!
Tamb. Zenocrate, the loveliest maid alive,
Fairer than rocks of pearl and precious stone,
The only paragon of Tamburlaine;
Whose eyes are brighter than the lamps of heaven,
And speech more pleasant than sweet harmony;
That with thy looks canst clear the darken'd sky,
And calm the rage of thundering Jupiter;
Sit down by her, adorned with my crown,
As if thou wert the empress of the world
Stir not, Zenocrate, until thou see
Me march victoriously with all my men,
Triumphing over him and these his kings,
Which I will bring as vassals to thy feet;
Till then, take thou my crown, vaunt of my worth,
And manage words with her, as we will arms.
Zeno. And may my love, the king of Persia,
Return with victory and free from wound!
Baj. Now shalt thou feel the force of Turkish arms,

Which lately made all Europe quake for fear.
I have of Turks, Arabians, Moors, and Jews,
Enough to cover all Bithynia:
Let thousands die: their slaughter'd carcasses
Shall serve for walls and bulwarks to the rest;
And as the heads of Hydra, so my power,
Subdu'd, shall stand as mighty as before:
If they should yield their necks unto the sword,
Thy soldiers' arms could not endure to strike
So many blows as I have heads for them.
Thou know'st not, foolish-hardy Tamburlaine,
What 'tis to meet me in the open field,
That leave no ground for thee to march upon.

Tamb. Our conquering swords shall marshal us the way
We use to march upon the slaughter'd foe,
Trampling their bowels with our horses' hoofs,
Brave horses bred on the white Tartarian hills.
My camp is like to Julius Cæsar's host,
That never fought but had the victory;
Nor in Pharsalia was there such hot war
As these, my followers, willingly would have.
Legions of spirits, fleeting in the air,
Direct our bullets and our weapons' points,
And make your strokes to wound the senseless light;
And when she sees our bloody colours spread,
Then Victory begins to take her flight,
Resting herself upon my milk-white tent.—
But come, my lords, to weapons let us fall;
The field is ours, the Turk, his wife, and all.
[*Exit with his followers.*

Baj. Come, kings and bassoes, let us glut our swords,
That thirst to drink the feeble Persians' blood.
[*Exit with his followers.*

Zab. Base concubine, must thou be plac'd by me
That am the empress of the mighty Turk?

Zeno. Disdainful Turkess, and unreverend boss,
Call'st thou me concubine, that am betroth'd
Unto the great and mighty Tamburlaine?

Zab. To Tamburlaine, the great Tartarian thief!

Zeno. Thou wilt repent these lavish words of thine
When thy great basso-master and thyself
Must plead for mercy at his kingly feet,
And sue to me to be your advocate.

Zab. And sue to thee! I tell thee, shameless girl,
Thou shalt be laundress to my waiting-maid.—
How lik'st thou her, Ebea? will she serve?
Ebea. Madam, she thinks perhaps she is too fine;
But I shall turn her into other weeds,
And make her dainty fingers fall to work.
Zeno. Hear'st thou, Anippe, how thy drudge doth talk?
And how my slave, her mistress, menaceth?
Both for their sauciness shall be employ'd
To dress the common soldiers' meat and drink;
For we will scorn they should come near ourselves.
Anip. Yet sometimes let your highness send for them
To do the work my chambermaid disdains.
[*They sound to the battle within.*
Zeno. Ye gods and powers that govern Persia,
And made my lordly love her worthy king,
Now strengthen him against the Turkish Bajazeth,
And let his foes, like flocks of fearful roes
Pursu'd by hunters, fly his angry looks,
That I may see him issue conqueror!
Zab. Now, Mahomet, solicit God himself,
And make him rain down murdering shot from heaven,
To dash the Scythians' brains, and strike them dead,
That dare to manage arms with him
That offer'd jewels to thy sacred shrine
When first he warr'd against the Christians!
[*They sound again to the battle within.*
Zeno. By this the Turks lie weltering in their blood,
And Tamburlaine is lord of Africa.
Zab. Thou art deceiv'd. I heard the trumpets sound
As when my emperor overthrew the Greeks,
And led them captive into Africa.
Straight will I use thee as thy pride deserves;
Prepare thyself to live and die my slave.
Zeno. If Mahomet should come from heaven and swear
My royal lord is slain or conquered,
Yet should he not persuade me otherwise
But that he lives and will be conqueror.

Re-enter BAJAZETH, *pursued by* TAMBURLAINE.

Tamb. Now, king of bassoes, who is conqueror?
Baj. Thou, by the fortune of this damned foil.
Tamb. Where are your stout contributory kings?

Re-enter TECHELLES, THERIDAMAS, *and* USUMCASANE.

Tech. We have their crowns; their bodies strow the field.
Tamb. Each man a crown! why, kingly fought, i'faith.
Deliver them into my treasury.
Zeno. Now let me offer to my gracious lord
His royal crown again so highly won.
Tamb. Nay, take the Turkish crown from her, Zenocrate,
And crown me emperor of Africa.
Zab. No, Tamburlaine; though now thou gat the best,
Thou shalt not yet be lord of Africa.
Ther. Give her the crown, Turkess, you were best.
[*Takes it from her.*
Zab. Injurious villains, thieves, runagates,
How dare you thus abuse my majesty?
Ther. Here, madam, you are empress; she is none.
[*Gives it to Zenocrate.*
Tamb. Not now, Theridamas; her time is past:
The pillars, that have bolster'd up those terms,
Are faln in clusters at my conquering feet.
Zab. Though he be prisoner, he may be ransom'd.
Tamb. Not all the world shall ransom Bajazeth.
Baj. Ah, fair Zabina! we have lost the field;
And never had the Turkish emperor
So great a foil by any foreign foe.
Now will the Christian miscreants be glad,
Ringing with joy their superstitious bells,
And making bonfires for my overthrow:
But, ere I die, those foul idolaters
Shall make me bonfires with their filthy bones;
For, though the glory of this day be lost,
Afric and Greece have garrisons enough
To make me sovereign of the earth again.
Tamb. Those walled garrisons will I subdue,
And write myself great lord of Africa:
So from the East unto the furthest West
Shall Tamburlaine extend his puissant arm.
The galleys and those pilling brigandines,
That yearly sail to the Venetian gulf,
And hover in the Straits for Christians' wreck,
Shall lie at anchor in the Isle Asant,
Until the Persian fleet and men-of-war,
Sailing along the oriental sea,

Have fetch'd about the Indian continent,
Even from Persepolis to Mexico,
And thence unto the Straits of Jubalter;
Where they shall meet and join their force in one,
Keeping in awe the Bay of Portingale,
And all the ocean by the British shore;
And by this means I'll win the world at last.

Baj. Yet set a ransom on me, Tamburlaine.

Tamb. What, think'st thou Tamburlaine esteems thy gold?
I'll make the kings of India, ere I die,
Offer their mines, to sue for peace, to me.
And dig for treasure to appease my wrath.—
Come, bind them both, and one lead in the Turk;
The Turkess let my love's maid lead away.
[*They bind them.*

Baj. Ah, villains, dare you touch my sacred arms?
O Mahomet! O sleepy Mahomet!

Zab. O cursed Mahomet, that mak'st us thus
The slaves to Scythians rude and barbarous!

Tamb. Come, bring them in; and for this happy conquest
Triumph, and solemnise a martial feast. [*Exeunt.*

ACT IV

SCENE I

Enter the Soldan of Egypt, Capolin, Lords, *and a* Messenger.

Sold. Awake, ye men of Memphis! hear the clang
Of Scythian trumpets; hear the basilisks,
That, roaring, shake Damascus' turrets down!
The rogue of Volga holds Zenocrate,
The Soldan's daughter, for his concubine,
And, with a troop of thieves and vagabonds,
Hath spread his colours to our high disgrace,
While you, faint-hearted base Egyptians,
Lie slumbering on the flowery banks of Nile,
As crocodiles that unaffrighted rest
While thundering cannons rattle on their skins.

Mess. Nay, mighty Soldan, did your greatness see
The frowning looks of fiery Tamburlaine,
That with his terror and imperious eyes

Commands the hearts of his associates,
It might amaze your royal majesty.
Sold. Villain, I tell thee, were that Tamburlaine
As monstrous as Gorgon prince of hell,
The Soldan would not start a foot from him.
But speak, what power hath he?
Mess. Mighty lord,
Three hundred thousand men in armour clad,
Upon their prancing steeds, disdainfully
With wanton paces trampling on the ground;
Five hundred thousand footmen threatening shot,
Shaking their swords, their spears, and iron bills,
Environing their standard round, that stood
As bristle-pointed as a thorny wood;
Their warlike engines and munition
Exceed the forces of their martial men.
Sold. Nay, could their numbers countervail the stars,
Or ever-drizzling drops of April showers,
Or wither'd leaves that autumn shaketh down,
Yet would the Soldan by his conquering power
So scatter and consume them in his rage,
That not a man should live to rue their fall.
Capo. So might your highness, had you time to sort
Your fighting men, and raise your royal host;
But Tamburlaine by expedition
Advantage takes of your unreadiness.
Sold. Let him take all th' advantages he can:
Were all the world conspir'd to fight for him,
Nay, were he devil, as he is no man,
Yet in revenge of fair Zenocrate,
Whom he detaineth in despite of us,
This arm should send him down to Erebus,
To shroud his shame in darkness of the night.
Mess. Pleaseth your mightiness to understand,
His resolution far exceedeth all.
The first day when he pitcheth down his tents,
White is their hue, and on his silver crest,
A snowy feather spangled-white he bears,
To signify the mildness of his mind,
That, satiate with spoil, refuseth blood:
But, when Aurora mounts the second time,
As red as scarlet is his furniture;
Then must his kindled wrath be quench'd with blood,

Not sparing any that can manage arms:
But, if these threats move not submission,
Black are his colours, black pavilion;
His spear, his shield, his horse, his armour, plumes,
And jetty feathers, menace death and hell;
Without respect of sex, degree, or age,
He razeth all his foes with fire and sword.

Sold. Merciless villain, peasant, ignorant
Of lawful arms or martial discipline!
Pillage and murder are his usual trades:
The slave usurps the glorious name of war.
See, Capolin, the fair Arabian king,
That hath been disappointed by this slave
Of my fair daughter and his princely love,
May have fresh warning to go war with us,
And be reveng'd for her disparagement. [*Exeunt.*

SCENE II

Enter TAMBURLAINE, TECHELLES, THERIDAMAS, USUMCASANE, ZENOCRATE, ANIPPE, *two* Moors *drawing* BAJAZETH *in a cage, and* ZABINA *following him.*

Tamb. Bring out my footstool.
[*They take Bajazeth out of the cage.*

Baj. Ye holy priests of heavenly Mahomet,
That, sacrificing, slice and cut your flesh,
Staining his altars with your purple blood,
Make heaven to frown, and every fixed star
To suck up poison from the moorish fens,
And pour it in this glorious tyrant's throat!

Tamb. The chiefest god, first mover of that sphere
Enchas'd with thousands ever-shining lamps,
Will sooner burn the glorious frame of heaven
Than it should so conspire my overthrow.
But, villain, thou that wishest this to me,
Fall prostrate on the low disdainful earth,
And be the footstool of great Tamburlaine,
That I may rise into my royal throne.

Baj. First shalt thou rip my bowels with thy sword,
And sacrifice my heart to death and hell,
Before I yield to such a slavery.

Tamb. Base villain, vassal, slave to Tamburlaine,
Unworthy to embrace or touch the ground

That bears the honour of my royal weight;
Stoop, villain, stoop! stoop; for so he bids
That may command thee piecemeal to be torn,
Or scatter'd like the lofty cedar-trees
Struck with the voice of thundering Jupiter.

Baj. Then, as I look down to the damned fiends,
Fiends, look on me! and thou, dread god of hell,
With ebon sceptre strike this hateful earth,
And make it swallow both of us at once!

[*Tamburlaine gets up on him into his chair.*

Tamb. Now clear the triple region of the air,
And let the Majesty of Heaven behold
Their scourge and terror tread on emperors.
Smile, stars that reign'd at my nativity,
And dim the brightness of your neighbour lamps;
Disdain to borrow light of Cynthia!
For I, the chiefest lamp of all the earth,
First rising in the east with mild aspect,
But fixed now in the meridian line,
Will send up fire to your turning spheres,
And cause the sun to borrow light of you,
My sword struck fire from his coat of steel.
Even in Bithynia, when I took this Turk;
As when a fiery exhalation,
Wrapt in the bowels of a freezing cloud,
Fighting for passage, make[s] the welkin crack,
And casts a flash of lightning to the earth:
But, ere I march to wealthy Persia,
Or leave Damascus and th' Egyptian fields,
As was the fame of Clymene's brain-sick son
That almost brent the axle-tree of heaven,
So shall our swords, our lances, and our shot
Fill all the air with fiery meteors;
Then, when the sky shall wax as red as blood,
It shall be said I made it red myself,
To make me think of naught but blood and war.

Zab. Unworthy king, that by thy cruelty
Unlawfully usurp'st the Persian seat,
Dar'st thou, that never saw an emperor
Before thou met my husband in the field,
Being thy captive, thus abuse his state,
Keeping his kingly body in a cage,
That roofs of gold and sun-bright palaces

Should have prepar'd to entertain his grace?
And treading him beneath thy loathsome feet,
Whose feet the kings of Africa have kiss'd?

Tech. You must devise some torment worse, my lord,
To make these captives rein their lavish tongues.

Tamb. Zenocrate, look better to your slave.

Zeno. She is my handmaid's slave, and she shall look
That these abuses flow not from her tongue.—
Chide her, Anippe.

Anip. Let these be warnings, then, for you, my slave,
How you abuse the person of the king;
Or else I swear to have you whipt stark nak'd.

Baj. Great Tamburlaine, great in my overthrow,
Ambitious pride shall make thee fall as low,
For treading on the back of Bajazeth,
That should be horsed on four mighty kings.

Tamb. Thy names, and titles, and thy dignities
Are fled from Bajazeth, and remain with me,
That will maintain it 'gainst a world of kings.—
Put him in again. [*They put him into the cage.*

Baj. Is this a place for mighty Bajazeth?
Confusion light on him that helps thee thus.

Tamb. There, while he lives, shall Bajazeth be kept;
And, where I go, be thus in triumph drawn;
And thou, his wife, shall feed him with the scraps
My servitors shall bring thee from my board;
For he that gives him other food than this,
Shall sit by him, and starve to death himself:
This is my mind, and I will have it so.
Not all the kings and emperors of the earth,
If they would lay their crowns before my feet,
Shall ransom him, or take him from his cage:
The ages that shall talk of Tamburlaine,
Even from this day to Plato's wondrous year,
Shall talk how I have handled Bajazeth:
These Moors, that drew him from Bithynia
To fair Damascus, where we now remain,
Shall lead him with us wheresoe'er we go.—
Techelles, and my loving followers,
Now may we see Damascus' lofty towers,
Like to the shadows of Pyramides
That with their beauties grace the Memphian fields.
The golden stature of their feather'd bird,

That spreads her wings upon the city walls,
Shall not defend it from our battering shot:
The townsmen mask in silk and cloth of gold,
And every house is as a treasury;
The men, the treasure, and the town are ours.
Ther. Your tents of white now pitch'd before the gates,
And gentle flags of amity display'd,
I doubt not but the governor will yield,
Offering Damascus to your majesty.
Tamb. So shall he have his life, and all the rest:
But, if he stay until the bloody flag
Be once advanc'd on my vermilion tent,
He dies, and those that kept us out so long;
And, when they see me march in black array,
With mournful streamers hanging down their heads
Were in that city all the world contain'd,
Not one should scape, but perish by our swords.
Zeno. Yet would you have some pity for my sake,
Because it is my country and my father's.
Tamb. Not for the world, Zenocrate, if I have sworn.—
Come; bring in the Turk. [*Exeunt*

SCENE III

Enter SOLDAN, KING OF ARABIA, CAPOLIN, *and* Soldiers, *with streaming colours.*

Sold. Methinks we march as Meleager did,
Environed with brave Argolian knights,
To chase the savage Calydonian boar,
Or Cephalus, with lusty Theban youths,
Against the wolf that angry Themis sent
To waste and spoil the sweet Aonian fields.
A monster of five hundred thousand heads,
Compact of rapine, piracy, and spoil,
The scum of men, the hate and scourge of God,
Raves in Egyptia, and annoyeth us:
My lord, it is the bloody Tamburlaine,
A sturdy felon, and a base-bred thief,
By murder raised to the Persian crown,
That dares control us in our territories.
To tame the pride of this presumptuous beast,
Join your Arabians with the Soldan's power;
Let us unite our royal bands in one,

And hasten to remove Damascus' siege.
It is a blemish to the majesty
And high estate of mighty emperors,
That such a base usurping vagabond
Should brave a king, or wear a princely crown.
K. of Ar. Renowmed Soldan, have you lately heard
The overthrow of mighty Bajazeth
About the confines of Bithynia?
The slavery wherewith he persecutes
The noble Turk and his great emperess?
Sold. I have, and sorrow for his bad success;
But, noble lord of great Arabia,
Be so persuaded that the Soldan is
No more dismay'd with tidings of his fall,
Than in the haven when the pilot stands,
And views a stranger's ship rent in the winds,
And shivered against a craggy rock:
Yet in compassion to his wretched state,
A sacred vow to heaven and him I make,
Confirming it with Ibis' holy name,
That Tamburlaine shall rue the day, the hour,
Wherein he wrought such ignominious wrong
Unto the hallow'd person of a prince,
Or kept the fair Zenocrate so long,
As concubine, I fear, to feed his lust.
K. of Ar. Let grief and fury hasten on revenge;
Let Tamburlaine for his offences feel
Such plagues as heaven and we can pour on him:
I long to break my spear upon his crest,
And prove the weight of his victorious arm;
For fame, I fear, hath been too prodigal
In sounding through the world his partial praise.
Sold. Capolin, hast thou survey'd our powers?
Capol. Great emperors of Egypt and Arabia,
The number of your hosts united is,
A hundred and fifty thousand horse,
Two hundred thousand foot, brave men-at-arms,
Courageous and full of hardiness,
As frolic as the hunters in the chase
Of savage beasts amid the desert woods.
K. of Ar. My mind presageth fortunate success;
And, Tamburlaine, my spirit doth foresee
The utter ruin of thy men and thee.

Sold. Then rear your standards; let your sounding drums
Direct our soldiers to Damascus' walls.—
Now, Tamburlaine, the mighty Soldan comes,
And leads with him the great Arabian king,
To dim thy baseness and obscurity,
Famous for nothing but for theft and spoil;
To raze and scatter thy inglorious crew
Of Scythians and slavish Persians. [*Exeunt*.

SCENE IV

A banquet set out; and to it come TAMBURLAINE *all in scarlet*, ZENOCRATE, THERIDAMAS, TECHELLES, USUMCASANE, BAJAZETH *drawn in his cage*, ZABINA, *and others*.

Tamb. Now hang our bloody colours by Damascus,
Reflexing hues of blood upon their heads,
While they walk quivering on their city-walls,
Half-dead for fear before they feel my wrath.
Then let us freely banquet, and carouse
Full bowls of wine unto the god of war,
That means to fill your helmets full of gold,
And make Damascus' spoils as rich to you
As was to Jason Colchos' golden fleece.—
And now, Bajazeth, hast thou any stomach?

Baj. Ay, such a stomach, cruel Tamburlaine, as I could willingly feed upon thy blood-raw heart.

Tamb. Nay, thine own is easier to come by: pluck out that; and 'twill serve thee and thy wife.— Well, Zenocrate, Techelles, and the rest, fall to your victuals.

Baj. Fall to, and never may your meat digest!—
Ye Furies, that can mask invisible,
Dive to the bottom of Avernus' pool,
And in your hands bring hellish poison up,
And squeeze it in the cup of Tamburlaine!
Or, winged snakes of Lerna, cast your stings,
And leave your venoms in this tyrant's dish!

Zab. And may this banquet prove as ominous
As Progne's to th' adulterous Thracian king
That fed upon the substance of his child!

Zeno. My lord, how can you suffer these
Outrageous curses by these slaves of yours?

Tamb. To let them see, divine Zenocrate,
I glory in the curses of my foes,

Having the power from the empyreal heaven
To turn them all upon their proper heads.

Tech. I pray you, give them leave, madam; this speech is a goodly refreshing for them.

Ther. But, if his highness would let them be fed, it would do them more good.

Tamb. Sirrah, why fall you not to? are you so daintily brought up, you cannot eat your own flesh?

Baj. First, legions of devils shall tear thee in pieces.

Usum. Villain, knowest thou to whom thou speakest?

Tamb. O, let him alone.—Here; eat, sir; take it from my sword's point, or I'll thrust it to thy heart.

[*Bajazeth takes the food, and stamps upon it.*

Ther. He stamps it under his feet, my lord.

Tamb. Take it up, villain, and eat it; or I will make thee slice the brawns of thy arms into carbonadoes and eat them.

Usum. Nay, 'twere better he killed his wife, and then she shall be sure not to be starved, and he be provided for a month's victual beforehand.

Tamb. Here is my dagger: despatch her while she is fat; for, if she live but a while longer, she will fall into a consumption with fretting, and then she will not be worth the eating.

Ther. Dost thou think that Mahomet will suffer this?

Tech. 'Tis like he will, when he cannot let it.

Tamb. Go to; fall to your meat. What, not a bit!—Belike he hath not been watered to-day: give him some drink.

[*They give Bajazeth water to drink, and he flings it on the ground.*

Fast, and welcome, sir, while hunger make you eat.
—How now, Zenocrate! doth not the Turk and his wife make a goodly show at a banquet?

Zeno. Yes, my lord.

Ther. Methinks 'tis a great deal better than a consort of music.

Tamb. Yet music would do well to cheer up Zenocrate. Pray thee, tell why art thou so sad? if thou wilt have a song, the Turk shall strain his voice: but why is it?

Zeno. My lord, to see my father's town besieg'd,
The country wasted, where myself was born,
How can it but afflict my very soul?

If any love remain in you, my lord,
Or if my love unto your majesty
May merit favour at your highness' hands,
Then raise your siege from fair Damascus' walls,
And with my father take a friendly truce.

Tamb. Zenocrate, were Egypt Jove's own land,
Yet would I with my sword make Jove to stoop.
I will confute those blind geographers
That make a triple region in the world,
Excluding regions which I mean to trace,
And with this pen reduce them to a map,
Calling the provinces, cities, and towns,
After my name and thine, Zenocrate:
Here at Damascus will I make the point
That shall begin the perpendicular:
And wouldst thou have me buy thy father's love
With such a loss? tell me, Zenocrate.

Zeno. Honour still wait on happy Tamburlaine!
Yet give me leave to plead for him, my lord.

Tamb. Content thyself: his person shall be safe,
And all the friends of fair Zenocrate,
If with their lives they will be pleas'd to yield,
Or may be forced to make me emperor;
For Egypt and Arabia must be mine.—
Feed, you slave; thou mayst think thyself happy to be fed from my trencher.

Baj. My empty stomach, full of idle heat,
Draws bloody humours from my feeble parts,
Preserving life by hastening cruel death.
My veins are pale; my sinews hard and dry;
My joints benumb'd; unless I eat, I die.

Zab. Eat, Bajazeth; let us live in spite of them, looking some happy power will pity and enlarge us.

Tamb. Here, Turk; wilt thou have a clean trencher?

Baj. Ay, tyrant, and more meat.

Tamb. Soft, sir! you must be dieted; too much eating will make you surfeit.

Ther. So it would, my lord, 'specially having so small a walk and so little exercise.

[*A second course is brought in of crowns.*

Tamb. Theridamas, Techelles, and Casane, here are the cates you desire to finger, are they not?

Ther. Ay, my lord: but none save kings must feed with these.

Tech. 'Tis enough for us to see them, and for Tamburlaine only to enjoy them.

Tamb. Well; here is now to the Soldan of Egypt, the King of Arabia, and the Governor of Damascus. Now, take these three crowns, and pledge me, my contributory kings. I crown you here, Theridamas, king of Argier; Techelles, king of Fez; and Usumcasane, king of Morocco.—How say you to this, Turk? these are not your contributory kings.

Baj. Nor shall they long be thine, I warrant them.

Tamb. Kings of Argier, Morocco, and of Fez,
You that have marched with happy Tamburlaine
As far as from the frozen place of heaven
Unto the watery Morning's ruddy bower,
And thence by land unto the torrid zone,
Deserve these titles I endow you with
By valour and by magnanimity.
Your births shall be no blemish to your fame;
For virtue is the fount whence honour springs,
And they are worthy she investeth kings.

Ther. And, since your highness hath so well vouchsaf'd,
If we deserve them not with higher meeds
Than erst our states and actions have retained,
Take them away again, and make us slaves.

Tamb. Well said, Theridamas: when holy Fates
Shall stablish me in strong Ægyptia,
We mean to travel to th' antarctic pole,
Conquering the people underneath our feet,
And be renowm'd as never emperors were.—
Zenocrate, I will not crown thee yet,
Until with greater honours I be grac'd. [*Exeunt.*

ACT V

SCENE I

Enter the Governor of Damascus *with three or four* Citizens, *and four* Virgins *with branches of laurel in their hands.*

Gov. Still doth this man, or rather god of war,
Batter our walls and beat our turrets down;
And to resist with longer stubbornness,
Or hope of rescue from the Soldan's power,
Were but to bring our wilful overthrow,

And make us desperate of our threatened lives.
We see his tents have now been altered
With terrors to the last and cruel'st hue;
His coal-black colours, everywhere advanc'd,
Threaten our city with a general spoil;
And, if we should with common rites of arms
Offer our safeties to his clemency,
I fear the custom proper to his sword,
Which he observes as parcel of his fame,
Intending so to terrify the world,
By any innovation or remorse
Will never be dispens'd with till our deaths.
Therefore, for these our harmless virgins' sakes,
Whose honours and whose lives rely on him,
Let us have hope that their unspotted prayers,
Their blubber'd cheeks, and hearty humble moans
Will melt his fury into some remorse,
And use us like a loving conqueror.

First Virg. If humble suits or imprecations
(Utter'd with tears of wretchedness and blood
Shed from the heads and hearts of all our sex,
Some made your wives, and some your children,)
Might have entreated your obdurate breasts
To entertain some care of our securities
Whilst only danger beat upon our walls,
These more than dangerous warrants of our death
Had never been erected as they be,
Nor you depend on such weak helps as we.

Gov. Well, lovely virgins, think our country's care,
Our love of honour, loath to be enthrall'd
To foreign powers and rough imperious yokes,
Would not with too much cowardice or fear,
Before all hope of rescue were denied,
Submit yourselves and us to servitude.
Therefore, in that your safeties and our own,
Your honours, liberties, and lives were weigh'd
In equal care and balance with our own,
Endure as we the malice of our stars,
The wrath of Tamburlaine and power of wars;
Or be the means the overweighing heavens
Have kept to qualify these hot extremes,
And bring us pardon in your cheerful looks.

Sec. Virg. Then here, before the Majesty of Heaven

And holy patrons of Ægyptia,
With knees and hearts submissive we entreat
Grace to our words and pity to our looks,
That this device may prove propitious,
And through the eyes and ears of Tamburlaine
Convey events of mercy to his heart;
Grant that these signs of victory we yield
May bind the temples of his conquering head,
To hide the folded furrows of his brows,
And shadow his displeased countenance
With happy looks of ruth and lenity.
Leave us, my lord, and loving countrymen:
What simple virgins may persuade, we will.

Gov. Farewell, sweet virgins, on whose safe return
Depends our city, liberty, and lives.
[*Exeunt all except the Virgins.*

Enter TAMBURLAINE, *all in black and very melancholy,* TECHELLES, THERIDAMAS, USUMCASANE, *with others.*

Tamb. What, are the turtles fray'd out of their nests?
Alas, poor fools, must you be first shall feel
The sword destruction of Damascus?
They knew my custom; could they not as well
Have sent ye out when first my milk-white flags,
Through which sweet Mercy threw her gentle beams,
Reflexed them on their disdainful eyes,
As now when fury and incensed hate
Flings slaughtering terror from my coal-black tents,
And tells for truth submission comes too late?

First Vir. Most happy king and emperor of the earth,
Image of honour and nobility,
For whom the powers divine have made the world,
And on whose throne the holy Graces sit;
In whose sweet person is compris'd the sum
Of Nature's skill and heavenly majesty;
Pity our plights! O, pity poor Damascus!
Pity old age, within whose silver hairs
Honour and reverence evermore have reign'd!
Pity the marriage-bed, where many a lord,
In prime and glory of his loving joy,
Embraceth now with tears of ruth and blood
The jealous body of his fearful wife,
Whose cheeks and hearts, so punish'd with conceit,

To think thy puissant never-stayed arm
Will part their bodies, and prevent their souls
From heavens of comfort yet their age might bear,
Now wax all pale and wither'd to the death,
As well for grief our ruthless governor
Hath thus refus'd the mercy of thy hand,
(Whose sceptre angels kiss and Furies dread,)
As for their liberties, their loves, or lives!
O, then, for these, and such as we ourselves,
For us, for infants, and for all our bloods,
That never nourish'd thought against thy rule,
Pity, O pity, sacred emperor,
The prostrate service of this wretched town;
And take in sign thereof this gilded wreath,
Whereto each man of rule hath given his hand,
And wish'd, as worthy subjects, happy means
To be investers of thy royal brows
Even with the true Egyptian diadem!

Tamb. Virgins, in vain you labour to prevent
That which mine honour swears shall be perform'd.
Behold my sword; what see you at the point?

First Vir. Nothing but fear and fatal steel, my lord.

Tamb. Your fearful minds are thick and misty, then,
For there sits death; there sits imperious Death,
Keeping his circuit by the slicing edge.
But I am pleas'd you shall not see him there;
He now is seated on my horsemen's spears,
And on their points his fleshless body feeds.—
Techelles, straight go charge a few of them
To charge these dames, and shew my servant Death,
Sitting in scarlet on their armed spears.

Virgins. O, pity us!

Tamb. Away with them, I say, and shew them Death!

[*The Virgins are taken out by Techelles and others.*

I will not spare these proud Egyptians,
Nor change my martial observations
For all the wealth of Gihon's golden waves,
Or for the love of Venus, would she leave
The angry god of arms and lie with me.
They have refus'd the offer of their lives,
And know my customs are as peremptory
As wrathful planets, death, or destiny.

Re-enter TECHELLES.

What, have your horsemen shown the virgins Death?
Tech. They have, my lord, and on Damascus' walls
Have hoisted up their slaughtered carcasses.
Tamb. A sight as baneful to their souls, I think,
As are Thessalian drugs or mithridate:
But go, my lords, put the rest to the sword.
[*Exeunt all except Tamburlaine.*
Ah, fair Zenocrate!—divine Zenocrate!
Fair is too foul an epithet for thee,—
That in thy passion for thy country's love,
And fear to see thy kingly father's harm,
With hair dishevell'd wip'st thy watery cheeks;
And, like to Flora in her morning's pride,
Shaking her silver tresses in the air,
Rain'st on the earth resolved pearl in showers,
And sprinklest sapphires on thy shining face,
Where Beauty, mother to the Muses, sits,
And comments volumes with her ivory pen,
Taking instructions from thy flowing eyes;
Eyes, when that Ebena steps to heaven,
In silence of thy solemn evening's walk,
Making the mantle of the richest night,
The moon, the planets, and the meteors, light;
There angels in their crystal armours fight
A doubtful battle with my tempted thoughts
For Egypt's freedom and the Soldan's life,
His life that so consumes Zenocrate;
Whose sorrows lay more siege unto my soul
Than all my army to Damascus' walls;
And neither Persia's sovereign nor the Turk
Troubled my senses with conceit of foil
So much by much as doth Zenocrate.
What is beauty, saith my sufferings, then?
If all the pens that ever poets held
Had fed the feeling of their masters' thoughts,
And every sweetness that inspir'd their hearts,
Their minds, and muses on admired themes;
If all the heavenly quintessence they still
From their immortal flowers of poesy,
Wherein, as in a mirror, we perceive
The highest reaches of a human wit;

If these had made one poem's period,
And all combin'd in beauty's worthiness,
Yet should there hover in their restless heads
One thought, one grace, one wonder, at the least,
Which into words no virtue can digest.
But how unseemly is it for my sex,
My discipline of arms and chivalry,
My nature, and the terror of my name,
To harbour thoughts effeminate and faint!
Save only that in beauty's just applause,
With whose instinct the soul of man is touched;
And every warrior that is rapt with love
Of fame, of valour, and of victory,
Must needs have beauty beat on his conceits:
I thus conceiving, and subduing both,
That which hath stoop'd the chiefest of the gods,
Even from the fiery-spangled veil of heaven,
To feel the lovely warmth of shepherds' flames,
And march in cottages of strowed reeds,
Shall give the world to note, for all my birth,
That virtue solely is the sum of glory,
And fashions men with true nobility.—
Who's within there?

Enter Attendants.

Hath Bajazeth been fed to-day?

Attend. Ay, my lord.

Tamb. Bring him forth; and let us know if the town be ransacked. [*Exeunt Attendants.*

Enter TECHELLES, THERIDAMAS, USUMCASANE, *and others.*

Tech. The town is ours, my lord, and fresh supply
Of conquest and of spoil is offer'd us.

Tamb. That's well, Techelles. What's the news?

Tech. The Soldan and the Arabian king together
March on us with such eager violence
As if there were no way but one with us.

Tamb. No more there is not, I warrant thee, Techelles.

Attendants *bring in* BAJAZETH *in his cage, followed by* ZABINA.
Exeunt Attendants.

Ther. We know the victory is ours, my lord;
But let us save the reverend Soldan's life
For fair Zenocrate that so laments his state.

Tamb. That will we chiefly see unto, Theridamas,

For sweet Zenocrate, whose worthiness
Deserves a conquest over every heart.—
And now, my footstool, if I lose the field,
You hope of liberty and restitution?—
Here let him stay, my masters, from the tents,
Till we have made us ready for the field.—
Pray for us, Bajazeth; we are going.
[*Exeunt all except Bajazeth and Zabina.*

Baj. Go, never to return with victory!
Millions of men encompass thee about,
And gore thy body with as many wounds!
Sharp forked arrows light upon thy horse!
Furies from the black Cocytus' lake,
Break up the earth, and with their fire-brands
Enforce thee run upon the baneful pikes!
Vollies of shot pierce through thy charmed skin,
And every bullet dipt in poison'd drugs!
Or roaring cannons sever all thy joints,
Making thee mount as high as eagles soar!

Zab. Let all the swords and lances in the field
Stick in his breast as in their proper rooms!
At every pore let blood come dropping forth,
That lingering pains may massacre his heart,
And madness send his damned soul to hell!

Baj. Ah, fair Zabina! we may curse his power,
The heavens may frown, the earth for anger quake;
But such a star hath influence in his sword
As rules the skies and countermands the gods
More than Cimmerian Styx or Destiny:
And then shall we in this detested guise,
With shame, with hunger, and with horror stay,
Griping our bowels with retorqued thoughts,
And have no hope to end our ecstasies.

Zab. Then is there left no Mahomet, no God,
No fiend, no fortune, nor no hope of end
To our infamous, monstrous slaveries.
Gape, earth, and let the fiends infernal view
A hell as hopeless and as full of fear
As are the blasted banks of Erebus,
Where shaking ghosts with ever-howling groans
Hover about the ugly ferryman,
To get a passage to Elysium!
Why should we live?—O. wretches, beggars, slaves!—

Why live we, Bajazeth, and build up nests
So high within the region of the air,
By living long in this oppression,
That all the world will see and laugh to scorn
The former triumphs of our mightiness
In this obscure infernal servitude?

Baj. O life, more loathsome to my vexed thoughts
Than noisome parbreak of the Stygian snakes,
Which fills the nooks of hell with standing air,
Infecting all the ghosts with cureless griefs!
O dreary engines of my loathed sight,
That see my crown, my honour, and my name
Thrust under yoke and thraldom of a thief,
Why feed ye still on day's accursed beams,
And sink not quite into my tortur'd soul?
You see my wife, my queen, and emperess,
Brought up and propped by the hand of Fame,
Queen of fifteen contributory queens,
Now thrown to rooms of black abjection,
Smeared with blots of basest drudgery,
And villainess to shame, disdain, and misery.
Accursed Bajazeth, whose words of ruth,
That would with pity cheer Zabina's heart,
And make our souls resolve in ceaseless tears,
Sharp hunger bites upon and gripes the root
From whence the issue of my thoughts do break!
O poor Zabina! O my queen, my queen!
Fetch me some water for my burning breast,
To cool and comfort me with longer date,
That, in the shorten'd sequel of my life,
I may pour forth my soul into thine arms
With words of love, whose moaning intercourse
Hath hitherto been stay'd with wrath and hate
Of our expressless bann'd inflictions.

Zab. Sweet Bajazeth, I will prolong thy life
As long as any blood or spark of breath
Can quench or cool the torments of my grief. [*Exit.*

Baj. Now, Bajazeth, abridge thy baneful days,
And beat thy brains out of thy conquer'd head,
Since other means are all forbidden me,
That may be ministers of my decay.
O highest lamp of ever-living Jove,
Accursed day, infected with my griefs,

Hide now thy stained face in endless night,
And shut the windows of the lightsome heavens!
Let ugly Darkness with her rusty coach,
Engirt with tempests, wrapt in pitchy clouds,
Smother the earth with never-fading mists,
And let her horses from their nostrils breathe
Rebellious winds and dreadful thunder-claps,
That in this terror Tamburlaine may live,
And my pin'd soul, resolv'd in liquid air,
May still excruciate his tormented thoughts!
Then let the stony dart of senseless cold
Pierce through the centre of my wither'd heart,
And make a passage for my loathed life!
[*He brains himself against the cage.*

Re-enter ZABINA.

Zab. What do mine eyes behold? my husband dead!
His skull all riven in twain! his brains dash'd out,
The brains of Bajazeth, my lord and sovereign!
O Bajazeth, my husband and my lord!
O Bajazeth! O Turk! O emperor!

Give him his liquor? not I. Bring milk and fire, and my blood I bring him again.—Tear me in pieces—give me the sword with a ball of wild-fire upon it.—Down with him! down with him!—Go to my child; away, away, away! ah, save that infant! save him, save him!—I, even I, speak to her.—The sun was down—streamers white, red, black.—Here, here, here!—Fling the meat in his face—Tamburlaine, Tamburlaine!—Let the soldiers be buried.—Hell, death, Tamburlaine, hell!—Make ready my coach, my chair, my jewels.—I come, I come, I come!
[*She runs against the cage, and brains herself.*

Enter ZENOCRATE *with* ANIPPE.

Zeno. Wretched Zenocrate! that liv'st to see
Damascus' walls dy'd with Egyptian blood,
Thy father's subjects and thy countrymen;
The streets strow'd with dissever'd joints of men,
And wounded bodies gasping yet for life;
But most accurs'd, to see the sun-bright troop
Of heavenly virgins and unspotted maids
(Whose looks might make the angry god of arms
To break his sword and mildly treat of love)

On horsemen's lances to be hoisted up,
And guiltlessly endure a cruel death;
For every fell and stout Tartarian steed,
That stamp'd on others with their thundering hoofs,
When all their riders charg'd their quivering spears,
Began to check the ground and rein themselves,
Gazing upon the beauty of their looks.
Ah, Tamburlaine, wert thou the cause of this,
That term'st Zenocrate thy dearest love?
Whose lives were dearer to Zenocrate
Than her own life, or aught save thine own love.
But see, another bloody spectacle!
Ah, wretched eyes, the enemies of my heart,
How are ye glutted with these grievous objects,
And tell my soul more tales of bleeding ruth!—
See, see, Anippe, if they breathe or no.

Anip. No breath, nor sense, nor motion, in them both:
Ah, madam, this their slavery hath enforc'd,
And ruthless cruelty of Tamburlaine!

Zeno. Earth, cast up fountains from thy entrails,
And wet thy cheeks for their untimely deaths;
Shake with their weight in sign of fear and grief!
Blush, heaven, that gave them honour at their birth,
And let them die a death so barbarous!
Those that are proud of fickle empery
And place their chiefest good in earthly pomp,
Behold the Turk and his great emperess!
Ah, Tamburlaine my love, sweet Tamburlaine,
That fights for sceptres and for slippery crowns,
Behold the Turk and his great emperess!
Thou that, in conduct of thy happy stars,
Sleep'st every night with conquest on thy brows,
And yet wouldst shun the wavering turns of war,
In fear and feeling of the like distress,
Behold the Turk and his great emperess!
Ah, mighty Jove and holy Mahomet,
Pardon my love! O, pardon his contempt
Of earthly fortune and respect of pity;
And let not conquest, ruthlessly pursu'd,
Be equally against his life incens'd
In this great Turk and hapless emperess!
And pardon me that was not mov'd with ruth
To see them live so long in misery!—

Ah, what may chance to thee, Zenocrate?

Anip. Madam, content yourself, and be resolv'd,
Your love hath Fortune so at his command,
That she shall stay, and turn her wheel no more,
As long as life maintains his mighty arm
That fights for honour to adorn your head.

Enter PHILEMUS.

Zeno. What other heavy news now brings Philemus?

Phil. Madam, your father, and the Arabian king,
The first affecter of your excellence,
Come now, as Turnus 'gainst Æneas did,
Armed with lance into the Ægyptian fields,
Ready for battle 'gainst my lord the king.

Zeno. Now shame and duty, love and fear present
A thousand sorrows to my martyr'd soul,
Whom should I wish the fatal victory,
When my poor pleasures are divided thus,
And rack'd by duty from my cursed heart?
My father and my first-betrothed love
Must fight against my life and present love;
Wherein the change I use condemns my faith,
And makes my deeds infamous through the world:
But, as the gods, to end the Trojans' toil,
Prevented Turnus of Lavinia,
And fatally enrich'd Æneas' love,
So, for a final issue to my griefs,
To pacify my country and my love,
Must Tamburlaine by their resistless powers,
With virtue of a gentle victory,
Conclude a league of honour to my hope;
Then, as the powers divine have pre-ordain'd,
With happy safety of my father's life
Send like defence of fair Arabia.

[*They sound to the battle within; and Tamburlaine enjoys the victory: after which, the King of Arabia enters wounded.*

K. of Ar. What cursed power guides the murdering hands
Of this infamous tyrant's soldiers,
That no escape may save their enemies,
Nor fortune keep themselves from victory?
Lie down, Arabia, wounded to the death,
And let Zenocrate's fair eyes behold,

That, as for her thou bear'st these wretched arms,
Even so for her thou diest in these arms,
Leaving thy blood for witness of thy love.

Zeno. Too dear a witness for such love, my lord!
Behold Zenocrate, the cursed object
Whose fortunes never mastered her griefs;
Behold her wounded in conceit for thee,
As much as thy fair body is for me!

K. of Ar. Then shall I die with full contented heart,
Having beheld divine Zenocrate,
Whose sight with joy would take away my life
As now it bringeth sweetness to my wound,
If I had not been wounded as I am.
Ah, that the deadly pangs I suffer now
Would lend an hour's licence to my tongue,
To make discourse of some sweet accidents
Have chanc'd thy merits in this worthless bondage,
And that I might be privy to the state
Of thy deserv'd contentment and thy love!
But, making now a virtue of thy sight,
To drive all sorrow from my fainting soul,
Since death denies me further cause of joy,
Depriv'd of care, my heart with comfort dies,
Since thy desired hand shall close mine eyes. [*Dies.*

Re-enter TAMBURLAINE, *leading the* SOLDAN; TECHELLES, THERIDAMAS, USUMCASANE, *with others.*

Tamb. Come, happy father of Zenocrate,
A title higher than thy Soldan's name.
Though my right hand have thus enthralled thee,
Thy princely daughter here shall set thee free;
She that hath calm'd the fury of my sword,
Which had ere this been bath'd in streams of blood
As vast and deep as Euphrates or Nile.

Zeno. O sight thrice-welcome to my joyful soul,
To see the king, my father, issue safe
From dangerous battle of my conquering love!

Sold. Well met, my only dear Zenocrate,
Though with the loss of Egypt and my crown!

Tamb. 'Twas I, my lord, that gat the victory;
And therefore grieve not at your overthrow,
Since I shall render all into your hands,
And add more strength to your dominions

Than ever yet confirm'd th' Egyptian crown.
The god of war resigns his room to me,
Meaning to make me general of the world:
Jove, viewing me in arms, looks pale and wan,
Fearing my power should pull him from his throne:
Where'er I come the Fatal Sisters sweat,
And grisly Death, by running to and fro,
To do their ceaseless homage to my sword:
And here in Afric, where it seldom rains,
Since I arriv'd with my triumphant host,
Have swelling clouds, drawn from wide-gaping wounds,
Been oft resolv'd in bloody purple showers,
A meteor that might terrify the earth,
And make it quake at every drop it drinks:
Millions of souls sit on the banks of Styx,
Waiting the back-return of Charon's boat;
Hell and Elysium swarm with ghosts of men
That I have sent from sundry foughten fields
To spread my fame through hell and up to heaven:
And see, my lord, a sight of strange import,—
Emperors and kings lie breathless at my feet;
The Turk and his great empress, as it seems,
Left to themselves while we were at the fight,
Have desperately despatch'd their slavish lives:
With them Arabia, too, hath left his life:
All sights of power to grace my victory;
And such are objects fit for Tamburlaine,
Wherein, as in a mirror, may be seen
His honour, that consists in shedding blood
When men presume to manage arms with him.

Sold. Mighty hath God and Mahomet made thy hand,
Renowmed Tamburlaine, to whom all kings
Of force must yield their crowns and emperies;.
And I am pleas'd with this my overthrow,
If, as beseems a person of thy state,
Thou hast with honour us'd Zenocrate.

Tamb. Her state and person want no pomp, you see;
And for all blot of foul inchastity,
I record heaven, her heavenly self is clear:
Then let me find no further time to grace
Her princely temples with the Persian crown;
But here these kings that on my fortunes wait,
And have been crowned for proved worthiness

Even by this hand that shall establish them,
Shall now, adjoining all their hands with mine,
Invest her here the Queen of Persia.
What saith the noble Soldan, and Zenocrate?
Sold. I yield with thanks and protestations
Of endless honour to thee for her love.
Tamb. Then doubt I not but fair Zenocrate
Will soon consent to satisfy us both.
Zeno. Else should I much forget myself, my lord.
Ther. Then let us set the crown upon her head,
That long hath linger'd for so high a seat.
Tech. My hand is ready to perform the deed;
For now her marriage-time shall work us rest.
Usum. And here's the crown, my lord; help set it on.
Tamb. Then sit thou down, divine Zenocrate;
And here we crown thee Queen of Persia,
And all the kingdoms and dominions
That late the power of Tamburlaine subdu'd.
As Juno, when the giants were suppress'd,
That darted mountains at her brother Jove,
So looks my love, shadowing in her brows
Triumphs and trophies for my victories;
Or as Latona's daughter, bent to arms,
Adding more courage to my conquering mind.
To gratify the sweet Zenocrate,
Egyptians, Moors, and men of Asia,
From Barbary unto the Western India,
Shall pay a yearly tribute to thy sire;
And from the bounds of Afric to the banks
Of Ganges shall his mighty arm extend.—
And now, my lords and loving followers,
That purchas'd kingdoms by your martial deeds,
Cast off your armour, put on scarlet robes,
Mount up your royal places of estate,
Environed with troops of noblemen,
And there make laws to rule your provinces:
Hang up your weapons on Alcides' post[s];
For Tamburlaine takes truce with all the world.—
Thy first-betrothed love, Arabia,
Shall we with honour, as beseems, entomb
With this great Turk and his fair emperess.
Then, after all these solemn exequies,
We will our rites of marriage solemnise. [*Exeunt.*

THE SECOND PART OF

TAMBURLAINE THE GREAT

DRAMATIS PERSONÆ

TAMBURLAINE, *King of Persia.*
CALYPHAS, AMYRAS, CELEBINUS, } his sons.
THERIDAMAS, *King of Argier.*
TECHELLES, *King of Fez.*
USUMCASANE, *King of Morocco.*
ORCANES, *King of Natolia.*
KING OF TREBIZON.
KING OF SORIA.
KING OF JERUSALEM.
KING OF AMASIA.
GAZELLUS, *Viceroy of Byron.*
URIBASSA.
SIGISMUND, *King of Hungary.*
FREDERICK, BALDWIN, } *lords of Buda and Bohemia.*
CALLAPINE, *son to* BAJAZETH, *and prisoner to* TAMBURLAINE.
ALMEDA, *his keeper.*
GOVERNOR OF BABYLON.
CAPTAIN OF BALSERA.
HIS SON.
ANOTHER CAPTAIN.
MAXIMUS, PERDICAS, PHYSICIANS, LORDS, CITIZENS, MESSENGERS, SOLDIERS, *and* ATTENDANTS.
ZENOCRATE, *wife to* TAMBURLAINE.
OLYMPIA, *wife to the* CAPTAIN OF BALSERA.
TURKISH CONCUBINES.

THE PROLOGUE

THE general welcomes Tamburlaine receiv'd.
When he arrived last upon the stage,
Have made our poet pen his Second Part,
Where death cuts off the progress of his pomp,
And murderous Fates throw all his triumphs down.
But what became of fair Zenocrate,
And with how many cities' sacrifice
He celebrated her sad funeral,
Himself in presence shall unfold at large.

ACT I

SCENE I

Enter ORCANES *king of Natolia,* GAZELLUS *viceroy of Byron,* URIBASSA, *and their train, with drums and trumpets.*

Orc. Egregious viceroys of these eastern parts,
Plac'd by the issue of great Bajazeth,

And sacred lord, the mighty Callapine,
Who lives in Egypt prisoner to that slave
Which kept his father in an iron cage,—
Now have we march'd from fair Natolia
Two hundred leagues, and on Danubius' banks
Our warlike host, in complete armour, rest,
Where Sigismund, the king of Hungary,
Should meet our person to conclude a truce:
What! shall we parley with the Christian?
Or cross the stream, and meet him in the field?

Gaz. King of Natolia, let us treat of peace:
We all are glutted with the Christians' blood,
And have a greater foe to fight against,—
Proud Tamburlaine, that now in Asia,
Near Guyron's head, doth set his conquering feet,
And means to fire Turkey as he goes:
'Gainst him, my lord, you must address your power.

Uri. Besides, King Sigismund hath brought from Christendom
More than his camp of stout Hungarians,—
Sclavonians, Almains, Rutters, Muffs, and Danes,
That with the halberd, lance, and murdering axe,
Will hazard that we might with surety hold.

Orc. Though from the shortest northern parallel,
Vast Grantland, compass'd with the Frozen Sea,
(Inhabited with tall and sturdy men,
Giants as big as hugy Polypheme,)
Millions of soldiers cut the arctic line,
Bringing the strength of Europe to these arms,
Our Turkey blades shall glide through all their throats,
And make this champion mead a bloody fen:
Danubius' stream, that runs to Trebizon,
Shall carry, wrapt within his scarlet waves,
As martial presents to our friends at home,
The slaughter'd bodies of these Christians:
The Terrene main, wherein Danubius' falls,
Shall by this battle be the bloody sea:
The wandering sailors of proud Italy
Shall meet those Christians, fleeting with the tide,
Beating in heaps against their argosies,
And make fair Europe, mounted on her bull,
Trapp'd with the wealth and riches of the world,
Alight, and wear a woful mourning weed.

Gaz. Yet, stout Orcanes, pro-rex of the world,
Since Tamburlaine hath muster'd all his men,
Marching from Cairo northward, with his camp,
To Alexandria and the frontier towns,
Meaning to make a conquest of our land,
'Tis requisite to parle for a peace
With Sigismund, the king of Hungary,
And save our forces for the hot assaults
Proud Tamburlaine intends Natolia.

Orc. Viceroy of Byron, wisely hast thou said.
My realm, the centre of our empery,
Once lost, all Turkey would be overthrown;
And for that cause the Christians shall have peace.
Sclavonians, Almains, Rutters, Muffs, and Danes,
Fear not Orcanes, but great Tamburlaine;
Nor he, but Fortune that hath made him great.
We have revolted Grecians, Albanese,
Sicilians, Jews, Arabians, Turks, and Moors,
Natolians, Sorians, black Egyptians,
Illyrians, Thracians, and Bithynians,
Enough to swallow forceless Sigismund,
Yet scarce enough t' encounter Tamburlaine.
He brings a world of people to the field,
From Scythia to the oriental plage
Of India, where raging Lantchidol
Beats on the regions with his boisterous blows,
That never seaman yet discovered.
All Asia is in arms with Tamburlaine,
Even from the midst of fiery Cancer's tropic
To Amazonia under Capricorn;
And thence, as far as Archipelago,
All Afric is in arms with Tamburlaine:
Therefore, viceroy, the Christians must have peace.

Enter SIGISMUND, FREDERICK, BALDWIN, *and their train, with drums and trumpets.*

Sig. Orcanes, (as our legates promis'd thee,)
We, with our peers, have cross'd Danubius' stream,
To treat of friendly peace or deadly war.
Take which thou wilt; for, as the Romans us'd,
I here present thee with a naked sword:
Wilt thou have war, then shake this blade at me;

If peace, restore it to my hands again,
And I will sheathe it, to confirm the same.

Orc. Stay, Sigismund: forgett'st thou I am he
That with the cannon shook Vienna-walls,
And made it dance upon the continent,
As when the massy substance of the earth
Quiver[s] about the axle-tree of heaven?
Forgett'st thou that I sent a shower of darts,
Mingled with powder'd shot and feather'd steel,
So thick upon the blink-ey'd burghers' heads,
That thou thyself, then County Palatine,
The King of Boheme, and the Austric Duke,
Sent heralds out, which basely on their knees,
In all your names, desir'd a truce of me?
Forgett'st thou that, to have me raise my siege,
Waggons of gold were set before my tent,
Stampt with the princely fowl that in her wings
Carries the fearful thunderbolts of Jove?
How canst thou think of this, and offer war?

Sig. Vienna was besieg'd, and I was there,
Then County Palatine, but now a king,
And what we did was in extremity.
But now, Orcanes, view my royal host,
That hides these plains, and seems as vast and wide
As doth the desert of Arabia
To those that stand on Bagdet's lofty tower,
Or as the ocean to the traveller
That rests upon the snowy Appenines;
And tell me whether I should stoop so low,
Or treat of peace with the Natolian king.

Gaz. Kings of Natolia and of Hungary,
We came from Turkey to confirm a league,
And not to dare each other to the field.
A friendly parle might become you both.

Fred. And we from Europe, to the same intent;
Which if your general refuse or scorn,
Our tents are pitch'd, our men stand in array,
Ready to charge you ere you stir your feet.

Orc. So prest are we: but yet, if Sigismund
Speak as a friend, and stand not upon terms,
Here is his sword; let peace be ratified
On these conditions specified before,
Drawn with advice of our ambassadors.

Sig. Then here I sheathe it, and give thee my hand,
Never to draw it out, or manage arms
Against thyself or thy confederates,
But, whilst I live, will be at truce with thee.
Orc. But, Sigismund, confirm it with an oath,
And swear in sight of heaven and by thy Christ.
Sig. By Him that made the world and sav'd my soul,
The Son of God and issue of a maid,
Sweet Jesus Christ, I solemnly protest
And vow to keep this peace inviolable!
Orc. By sacred Mahomet, the friend of God,
Whose holy Alcoran remains with us,
Whose glorious body, when he left the world,
Clos'd in a coffin mounted up the air,
And hung on stately Mecca's temple-roof,
I swear to keep this truce inviolable!
Of whose conditions and our solemn oaths,
Sign'd with our hands, each shall retain a scroll,
As memorable witness of our league.
Now, Sigismund, if any Christian king
Encroach upon the confines of thy realm,
Send word, Orcanes of Natolia
Confirm'd this league beyond Danubius' stream,
And they will, trembling, sound a quick retreat;
So am I fear'd among all nations.
Sig. If any heathen potentate or king
Invade Natolia, Sigismund will send
A hundred thousand horse train'd to the war,
And back'd by stout lanciers of Germany,
The strength and sinews of the imperial seat.
Orc. I thank thee, Sigismund; but, when I war,
All Asia Minor, Africa, and Greece,
Follow my standard and my thundering drums.
Come, let us go and banquet in our tents:
I will despatch chief of my army hence
To fair Natolia and to Trebizon,
To stay my coming 'gainst proud Tamburlaine:
Friend Sigismund, and peers of Hungary,
Come, banquet and carouse with us a while,
And then depart we to our territories. [*Exeunt.*

SCENE II

Enter CALLAPINE, *and* ALMEDA *his keeper.*

Call. Sweet Almeda, pity the ruthful plight
Of Callapine, the son of Bajazeth,
Born to be monarch of the western world,
Yet here detain'd by cruel Tamburlaine.
Alm. My lord, I pity it, and with my heart
Wish your release; but he whose wrath is death,
My sovereign lord, renowmed Tamburlaine,
Forbids you further liberty than this.
Call. Ah, were I now but half so eloquent
To paint in words what I'll perform in deeds,
I know thou wouldst depart from hence with me!
Alm. Not for all Afric: therefore move me not.
Call. Yet hear me speak, my gentle Almeda.
Alm. No speech to that end, by your favour, sir.
Call. By Cairo runs—
Alm. No talk of running, I tell you, sir.
Call. A little further, gentle Almeda.
Alm. Well, sir, what of this?
Call. By Cairo runs to Alexandria-bay
Darotes' stream, wherein at anchor lies
A Turkish galley of my royal fleet,
Waiting my coming to the river-side,
Hoping by some means I shall be releas'd;
Which, when I come aboard, will hoist up sail,
And soon put forth into the Terrene sea,
Where, 'twixt the isles of Cyprus and of Crete,
We quickly may in Turkish seas arrive.
Then shalt thou see a hundred kings and more,
Upon their knees, all bid me welcome home.
Amongst so many crowns of burnish'd gold,
Choose which thou wilt, all are at thy command:
A thousand galleys, mann'd with Christian slaves,
I freely give thee, which shall cut the Straits,
And bring armadoes, from the coasts of Spain,
Fraughted with gold of rich America:
The Grecian virgins shall attend on thee,
Skilful in music and in amorous lays,
As fair as was Pygmalion's ivory girl
Or lovely Iö metamorphosed:

With naked negroes shall thy coach be drawn,
And, as thou rid'st in triumph through the streets,
The pavement underneath thy chariot-wheels
With Turkey-carpets will be covered,
And cloth of arras hung about the walls,
Fit objects for thy princely eye to pierce:
A hundred bassoes, cloth'd in crimson silk,
Shall ride before thee on Barbarian steeds;
And, when thou goest, a golden canopy
Enchas'd with precious stones, which shine as bright
As that fair veil that covers all the world,
When Phœbus, leaping from his hemisphere,
Descendeth downward to th' Antipodes:—
And more than this, for all I cannot tell.

Alm. How far hence lies the galley, say you?

Call. Sweet Almeda, scarce half a league from hence.

Alm. But need we not be spied going aboard?

Call. Betwixt the hollow hanging of a hill,
And crooked bending of a craggy rock,
The sails wrapt up, the mast and tacklings down,
She lies so close that none can find her out.

Alm. I like that well: but, tell me, my lord, if I should let you go, would you be as good as your word? shall I be made a king for my labour?

Call. As I am Callapine the emperor,
And by the hand of Mahomet I swear,
Thou shalt be crown'd a king, and be my mate!

Alm. Then here I swear, as I am Almeda,
Your keeper under Tamburlaine the Great,
(For that's the style and title I have yet,)
Although he sent a thousand armed men
To intercept this haughty enterprise,
Yet would I venture to conduct your grace,
And die before I brought you back again!

Call. Thanks, gentle Almeda: then let us haste,
Lest time be past, and lingering let us both.

Alm. When you will, my lord: I am ready.

Call. Even straight:—and farewell, cursed Tamburlaine!
Now go I to revenge my father's death. [*Exeunt.*

SCENE III

Enter TAMBURLAINE, ZENOCRATE, *and their three sons,* CALYPHAS, AMYRAS, *and* CELEBINUS, *with drums and trumpets.*

Tamb. Now, bright Zenocrate, the world's fair eye,
Whose beams illuminate the lamps of heaven,
Whose cheerful looks do clear the cloudy air,
And clothe it in a crystal livery,
Now rest thee here on fair Larissa-plains,
Where Egypt and the Turkish empire part
Between thy sons, that shall be emperors,
And every one commander of a world.
Zeno. Sweet Tamburlaine, when wilt thou leave these arms,
And save thy sacred person free from scathe,
And dangerous chances of the wrathful war?
Tamb. When heaven shall cease to move on both the poles,
And when the ground, whereon my soldiers march,
Shall rise aloft and touch the horned moon;
And not before, my sweet Zenocrate.
Sit up, and rest thee like a lovely queen.
So; now she sits in pomp and majesty,
When these, my sons, more precious in mine eyes
Than all the wealthy kingdoms I subdu'd,
Plac'd by her side, look on their mother's face:
But yet methinks their looks are amorous,
Not martial as the sons of Tamburlaine:
Water and air, being symbolis'd in one,
Argue their want of courage and of wit;
Their hair as white as milk, and soft as down,
(Which should be like the quills of porcupines,
As black as jet, and hard as iron or steel.)
Bewrays they are too dainty for the wars;
Their fingers made to quaver on a lute,
Their arms to hang about a lady's neck,
Their legs to dance and caper in the air,
Would make me think them bastards, not my sons,
But that I know they issu'd from thy womb,
That never look'd on man but Tamburlaine.
Zeno. My gracious lord, they have their mother's looks,
But, when they list, their conquering father's heart.
This lovely boy, the youngest of the three,

Not long ago bestrid a Scythian steed,
Trotting the ring, and tilting at a glove,
Which when he tainted with his slender rod,
He rein'd him straight, and made him so curvet
As I cried out for fear he should have faln.

Tamb. Well done, my boy! thou shalt have shield and lance,
Armour of proof, horse, helm, and curtle-axe,
And I will teach thee how to charge thy foe,
And harmless run among the deadly pikes.
If thou wilt love the wars and follow me,
Thou shalt be made a king and reign with me,
Keeping in iron cages emperors.
If thou exceed thy elder brothers' worth,
And shine in complete virtue more than they,
Thou shalt be king before them, and thy seed
Shall issue crowned from their mother's womb.

Cel. Yes, father; you shall see me, if I live,
Have under me as many kings as you,
And march with such a multitude of men
As all the world shall tremble at their view.

Tamb. These words assure me, boy, thou art my son.
When I am old and cannot manage arms,
Be thou the scourge and terror of the world.

Amy. Why may not I, my lord, as well as he,
Be term'd the scourge and terror of the world?

Tamb. Be all a scourge and terror to the world,
Or else you are not sons of Tamburlaine.

Caly. But, while my brothers follow arms, my lord,
Let me accompany my gracious mother:
They are enough to conquer all the world,
And you have won enough for me to keep.

Tamb. Bastardly boy, sprung from some coward's loins,
And not the issue of great Tamburlaine!
Of all the provinces I have subdu'd
Thou shalt not have a foot, unless thou bear
A mind courageous and invincible;
For he shall wear the crown of Persia
Whose head hath deepest scars, whose breast most wounds,
Which, being wroth, sends lightning from his eyes,
And in the furrows of his frowning brows
Harbours revenge, war, death, and cruelty;

For in a field, whose superficies
Is cover'd with a liquid purple veil,
And sprinkled with the brains of slaughter'd men,
My royal chair of state shall be advanc'd;
And he that means to place himself therein,
Must armed wade up to the chin in blood.
Zeno. My lord, such speeches to our princely sons
Dismay their minds before they come to prove
The wounding troubles angry war affords.
Cel. No, madam, these are speeches fit for us;
For, if his chair were in a sea of blood,
I would prepare a ship and sail to it,
Ere I would lose the title of a king.
Amy. And I would strive to swim through pools of blood,
Or make a bridge of murder'd carcasses,
Whose arches should be fram'd with bones of Turks,
Ere I would lose the title of a king.
Tamb. Well, lovely boys, ye shall be emperors both,
Stretching your conquering arms from east to west:—
And, sirrah, if you mean to wear a crown,
When we shall meet the Turkish deputy
And all his viceroys, snatch it from his head,
And cleave his pericranion with thy sword.
Caly. If any man will hold him, I will strike,
And cleave him to the channel with my sword.
Tamb. Hold him, and cleave him too, or I'll cleave thee;
For we will march against them presently.
Theridamas, Techelles, and Casane
Promis'd to meet me on Larissa-plains,
With hosts a-piece against this Turkish crew;
For I have sworn by sacred Mahomet
To make it parcel of my empery.
The trumpets sound; Zenocrate, they come.

Enter THERIDAMAS, *and his train, with drums and trumpets.*

Welcome Theridamas, king of Argier.
Ther. My lord, the great and mighty Tamburlaine,
Arch-monarch of the world, I offer here
My crown, myself, and all the power I have,
In all affection at thy kingly feet.
Tamb. Thanks, good Theridamas.
Ther. Under my colours march ten thousand Greeks,
And of Argier and Afric's frontier towns

Twice twenty thousand valiant men-at-arms;
All which have sworn to sack Natolia.
Five hundred brigandines are under sail,
Meet for your service on the sea, my lord,
That, launching from Argier to Tripoly,
Will quickly ride before Natolia,
And batter down the castles on the shore,

Tamb. Well said, Argier! receive thy crown again.

Enter USUMCASANE *and* TECHELLES.

Kings of Morocco and of Fez, welcome.

Usum. Magnificent and peerless Tamburlaine,
I and my neighbour king of Fez have brought,
To aid thee in this Turkish expedition,
A hundred thousand expert soldiers;
From Azamor to Tunis near the sea
Is Barbary unpeopled for thy sake,
And all the men, in armour under me,
Which with my crown, I gladly offer thee.

Tamb. Thanks, king of Morocco: take your crown again.

Tech. And, mighty Tamburlaine, our earthly god,
Whose looks make this inferior world to quake,
I here present thee with the crown of Fez,
And with an host of Moors train'd to the war,
Whose coal-black faces make their foes retire,
And quake for fear, as if infernal Jove,
Meaning to aid thee in these Turkish arms,
Should pierce the black circumference of hell,
With ugly Furies bearing fiery flags,
And millions of his strong tormenting spirits:
From strong Tesella unto Biledull
All Barbary is unpeopled for thy sake.

Tamb. Thanks, king of Fez: take here thy crown again.
Your presence, loving friends and fellow-kings,
Makes me to surfeit in conceiving joy:
If all the crystal gates of Jove's high court
Were open'd wide, and I might enter in
To see the state and majesty of heaven,
It could not more delight me than your sight.
Now will we banquet on these plains a while,
And after march to Turkey with our camp,
In number more than are the drops that fall
When Boreas rents a thousand swelling clouds;

And proud Orcanes of Natolia
With all his viceroys shall be so afraid, .
That, though the stones, as at Deucalion's flood,
Were turn'd to men, he should be overcome.
Such lavish will I make of Turkish blood,
That Jove shall send his winged messenger
To bid me sheathe my sword and leave the field;
The sun, unable to sustain the sight,
Shall hide his head in Thetis' watery lap,
And leave his steeds to fair Böotes' charge;
For half the world shall perish in this fight.
But now, my friends, let me examine ye;
How have ye spent your absent time from me?

Usum. My lord, our men of Barbary have march'd
Four hundred miles with armour on their backs,
And lain in leaguer fifteen months and more;
For, since we left you at the Soldan's court,
We have subdu'd the southern Guallatia,
And all the land unto the coast of Spain;
We kept the narrow Strait of Gibralter,
And made Canaria call us kings and lords:
Yet never did they recreate themselves,
Or cease one day from war and hot alarms;
And therefore let them rest a while, my lord.

Tamb. They shall, Casane, and 'tis time, i'faith.

Tech. And I have march'd along the river Nile
To Machda, where the mighty Christian priest,
Call'd John the Great, sits in a milk-white robe,
Whose triple mitre I did take by force,
And made him swear obedience to my crown.
From thence unto Cazates did I march,
Where Amazonians met me in the field,
With whom, being women, I vouchsaf'd a league,
And with my power did march to Zanzibar,
The western part of Afric, where I view'd
The Ethiopian sea, rivers and lakes,
But neither man nor child in all the land:
Therefore I took my course to Manico,
Where, unresisted. I remov'd my camp;
And, by the coast of Byather, at last
I came to Cubar, where the negroes dwell,
And, conquering that, made haste to Nubia.
There, having sack'd Borno, the kingly seat,

I took the king and led him bound in chains
Unto Damascus, where I stay'd before.

Tamb. Well done, Techelles!—What saith Theridamas?

Ther. I left the confines and the bounds of Afric,
And made a voyage into Europe,
Where, by the river Tyras, I subdu'd
Stoka, Podolia, and Codemia;
Then cross'd the sea and came to Oblia,
And Nigra Silva, where the devils dance,
Which, in despite of them, I set on fire.
From thence I cross'd the gulf call'd by the name
Mare Majore of the inhabitants.
Yet shall my soldiers make no period
Until Natolia kneel before your feet.

Tamb. Then will we triumph, banquet, and carouse;
Cooks shall have pensions to provide us cates,
And glut us with the dainties of the world;
Lachryma Christi and Calabrian wines
Shall common soldiers drink in quaffing bowls,
Ay, liquid gold, when we have conquer'd him,
Mingled with coral and with orient pearl.
Come, let us banquet and carouse the whiles. [*Exeunt.*

ACT II

SCENE I

Enter SIGISMUND, FREDERICK, *and* BALDWIN, *with their train.*

Sig. Now say, my lords of Buda and Bohemia,
What motion is it that inflames your thoughts,
And stirs your valours to such sudden arms?

Fred. Your majesty remembers, I am sure,
What cruel slaughter of our Christian bloods
These heathenish Turks and pagans lately made
Betwixt the city Zula and Danubius;
How through the midst of Varna and Bulgaria,
And almost to the very walls of Rome,
They have, not long since, massacred our camp.
It resteth now, then, that your majesty
Take all advantages of time and power,
And work revenge upon these infidels.

Your highness knows, for Tamburlaine's repair,
That strikes a terror to all Turkish hearts,
Natolia hath dismiss'd the greatest part
Of all his army, pitch'd against our power
Betwixt Cutheia and Orminius' mount,
And sent them marching up to Belgasar,
Acantha, Antioch, and Cæsarea,
To aid the kings of Soria and Jerusalem.
Now, then, my lord, advantage take thereof,
And issue suddenly upon the rest;
That, in the fortune of their overthrow,
We may discourage all the pagan troop
That dare attempt to war with Christians.

Sig. But calls not, then, your grace to memory
The league we lately made with King Orcanes,
Confirm'd by oath and articles of peace,
And calling Christ for record of our truths?
This should be treachery and violence
Against the grace of our profession.

Bald. No whit, my lord; for with such infidels,
In whom no faith nor true religion rests,
We are not bound to those accomplishments
The holy laws of Christendom enjoin;
But, as the faith which they profanely plight
Is not by necessary policy
To be esteem'd assurance for ourselves,
So that we vow to them should not infringe
Our liberty of arms and victory.

Sig. Though I confess the oaths they undertake
Breed little strength to our security,
Yet those infirmities that thus defame
Their faiths, their honours, and religion,
Should not give us presumption to the like.
Our faiths are sound, and must be consummate,
Religious, righteous, and inviolate.

Fred. Assure your grace, 'tis superstition
To stand so strictly on dispensive faith,
And, should we lose the opportunity
That God hath given to venge our Christians' death,
And scourge their foul blasphemous paganism,
As fell to Saul, to Balaam, and the rest,
That would not kill and curse at God's command,
So surely will the vengeance of the Highest,

And jealous anger of his fearful arm,
Be pour'd with rigour on our sinful heads,
If we neglect this offer'd victory.
Sig. Then arm, my lords, and issue suddenly,
Giving commandment to our general host,
With expedition to assail the pagan,
And take the victory our God hath given. [*Exeunt.*

SCENE II

Enter ORCANES, GAZELLUS, *and* URIBASSA, *with their train.*

Orc. Gazellus, Uribassa, and the rest,
Now will we march from proud Orminius' mount
To fair Natolia, where our neighbour kings
Expect our power and our royal presence,
T' encounter with the cruel Tamburlaine,
That nigh Larissa sways a mighty host,
And with the thunder of his martial tools
Makes earthquakes in the hearts of men and heaven.
Gaz. And now come we to make his sinews shake
With greater power than erst his pride hath felt.
An hundred kings, by scores, will bid him arms,
And hundred thousand subjects to each score:
Which, if a shower of wounding thunderbolts
Should break out of the bowels of the clouds,
And fall as thick as hail upon our heads,
In partial aid of that proud Scythian,
Yet should our courages and steeled crests,
And numbers, more than infinite, of men,
Be able to withstand and conquer him.
Uri. Methinks I see how glad the Christian king
Is made for joy of our admitted truce,
That could not but before be terrified
With unacquainted power of our host.

Enter a Messenger.

Mess. Arm, dread sovereign, and my noble lords!
The treacherous army of the Christians,
Taking advantage of your slender power,
Comes marching on us, and determines straight
To bid us battle for our dearest lives.
Orc. Traitors, villains, damned Christians!
Have I not here the articles of peace

And solemn covenants we have both confirm'd,
He by his Christ, and I by Mahomet?

Gaz. Hell and confusion light upon their heads,
That with such treason seek our overthrow,
And care so little for their prophet Christ!

Orc. Can there be such deceit in Christians,
Or treason in the fleshly heart of man,
Whose shape is figure of the highest God?
Then, if there be a Christ, as Christians say,
But in their deeds deny him for their Christ,
If he be son to everliving Jove,
And hath the power of his outstretched arm,
If he be jealous of his name and honour
As is our holy prophet Mahomet,
Take here these papers as our sacrifice
And witness of thy servant's perjury!
[*He tears to pieces the articles of peace.*
Open, thou shining veil of Cynthia,
And make a passage from th' empyreal heaven,
That he that sits on high and never sleeps,
Nor in one place is circumscriptible,
But everywhere fills every continent
With strange infusion of his sacred vigour,
May, in his endless power and purity,
Behold and venge this traitor's perjury!
Thou, Christ, that art esteem'd omnipotent,
If thou wilt prove thyself a perfect God,
Worthy the worship of all faithful hearts,
Be now reveng'd upon this traitor's soul,
And make the power I have left behind
(Too little to defend our guiltless lives)
Sufficient to discomfit and confound
The trustless force of those false Christians!—
To arms, my lords! on Christ still let us cry:
If there be Christ, we shall have victory. [*Exeunt.*

SCENE III

Alarms of battle within. Enter SIGISMUND *wounded.*

Sig. Discomfited is all the Christian host,
And God hath thunder'd vengeance from on high,
For my accurs'd and hateful perjury.
O just and dreadful punisher of sin,

Let the dishonour of the pains I feel
In this my mortal well-deserved wound
End all my penance in my sudden death!
And let this death, wherein to sin I die,
Conceive a second life in endless mercy! [*Dies.*

Enter ORCANES, GAZELLUS, URIBASSA, *with others.*

Orc. Now lie the Christians bathing in their bloods,
And Christ or Mahomet hath been my friend.
Gaz. See, here the perjur'd traitor Hungary,
Bloody and breathless for his villany!
Orc. Now shall his barbarous body be a prey
To beasts and fowls, and all the winds shall breathe
Through shady leaves of every senseless tree,
Murmurs and hisses for his heinous sin.
Now scalds his soul in the Tartarian streams,
And feeds upon the baneful tree of hell,
That Zoacum, that fruit of bitterness,
That in the midst of fire is ingraff'd,
Yet flourisheth as Flora in her pride,
With apples like the heads of damned fiends.
The devils there, in chains of quenchless flame,
Shall lead his soul, through Orcus' burning gulf,
From pain to pain, whose change shall never end.
What say'st thou yet, Gazellus, to his foil,
Which we referr'd to justice of his Christ
And to his power, which here appears as full
As rays of Cynthia to the clearest sight?
Gaz. 'Tis but the fortune of the wars, my lord,
Whose power is often prov'd a miracle.
Orc. Yet in my thoughts shall Christ be honoured,
Not doing Mahomet an injury,
Whose power had share in this our victory;
And, since this miscreant hath disgrac'd his faith,
And died a traitor both to heaven and earth,
We will both watch and ward shall keep his trunk
Amidst these plains for fowls to prey upon.
Go, Uribassa, give it straight in charge.
Uri. I will, my lord. [*Exit.*
Orc. And now, Gazellus, let us haste and meet
Our army, and our brother of Jerusalem,
Of Soria, Trebizon, and Amasia,
And happily, with full Natolian bowls

Of Greekish wine, now let us celebrate
Our happy conquest and his angry fate. [*Exeunt.*

SCENE IV

The arras is drawn, and Zenocrate *is discovered lying in her bed of state;* Tamburlaine *sitting by her; three* Pysicians *about her bed, tempering potions; her three sons* Calyphas, Amyras, *and* Celebinus; Theridamas, Techelles *and* Usumcasane.

Tamb. Black is the beauty of the brightest day;
The golden ball of heaven's eternal fire,
That danc'd with glory on the silver waves,
Now wants the fuel that inflam'd his beams;
And all with faintness, and for foul disgrace,
He binds his temples with a frowning cloud,
Ready to darken earth with endless night.
Zenocrate, that gave him light and life,
Whose eyes shot fire from their ivory bowers,
And temper'd every soul with lively heat,
Now by the malice of the angry skies,
Whose jealousy admits no second mate,
Draws in the comfort of her latest breath,
All dazzled with the hellish mists of death.
Now walk the angels on the walls of heaven,
As sentinels to warn th' immortal souls
To entertain divine Zenocrate:
Apollo, Cynthia, and the ceaseless lamps
That gently look'd upon this loathsome earth,
Shine downwards now no more, but deck the heavens
To entertain divine Zenocrate:
The crystal springs, whose taste illuminates
Refined eyes with an eternal sight,
Like tried silver run through Paradise
To entertain divine Zenocrate:
The cherubins and holy seraphins,
That sing and play before the King of Kings,
Use all their voices and their instruments
To entertain divine Zenocrate;
And, in this sweet and curious harmony,
The god that tunes this music to our souls
Holds out his hand in highest majesty
To entertain divine Zenocrate.

Then let some holy trance convey my thoughts
Up to the palace of th' empyreal heaven,
That this my life may be as short to me
As are the days of sweet Zenocrate.—
Physicians, will no physic do her good?

First Phys. My lord, your majesty shall soon perceive,
And if she pass this fit, the worst is past.

Tamb. Tell me, how fares my fair Zenocrate?

Zeno. I fare, my lord, as other empresses,
That, when this frail and transitory flesh
Hath suck'd the measure of that vital air
That feeds the body with his dated health,
Wane with enforc'd and necessary change.

Tamb. May never such a change transform my love,
In whose sweet being I repose my life!
Whose heavenly presence, beautified with health,
Gives light to Phœbus and the fixed stars;
Whose absence makes the sun and moon as dark
As when, oppos'd in one diameter,
Their spheres are mounted on the serpent's head,
Or else descended to his winding train.
Live still, my love, and so conserve my life,
Or, dying, be the author of my death.

Zeno. Live still, my lord; O, let my sovereign live!
And sooner let the fiery element
Dissolve, and make your kingdom in the sky,
Than this base earth should shroud your majesty;
For, should I but suspect your death by mine,
The comfort of my future happiness,
And hope to meet your highness in the heavens,
Turn'd to despair, would break my wretched breast,
And fury would confound my present rest.
But let me die, my love; yes, let me die;
With love and patience let your true love die:
Your grief and fury hurts my second life.
Yet let me kiss my lord before I die,
And let me die with kissing of my lord.
But, since my life is lengthen'd yet a while,
Let me take leave of these my loving sons,
And of my lords, whose true nobility
Have merited my latest memory.
Sweet sons, farewell! in death resemble me,
And in your lives your father's excellence.

Some music, and my fit will cease, my lord.

[*They call for music.*

Tamb. Proud fury, and intolerable fit,
That dares torment the body of my love,
And scourge the Scourge of the immortal God!
Now are those spheres, where Cupid us'd to sit,
Wounding the world with wonder and with love,
Sadly supplied with pale and ghastly death,
Whose darts do pierce the centre of my soul.
Her sacred beauty hath enchanted heaven;
And, had she liv'd before the siege of Troy,
Helen, whose beauty summon'd Greece to arms,
And drew a thousand ships to Tenedos,
Had not been nam'd in Homer's Iliads,—
Her name had been in every line he wrote;
Or, had those wanton poets, for whose birth
Old Rome was proud, but gaz'd a while on her,
Nor Lesbia nor Corinna had been nam'd,—
Zenocrate had been the argument
Of every epigram or elegy.

[*The music sounds—Zenocrate dies*;

What, is she dead? Techelles, draw thy sword,
And wound the earth, that it may cleave in twain,
And we descend into th' infernal vaults,
To hale the Fatal Sisters by the hair,
And throw them in the triple moat of hell,
For taking hence my fair Zenocrate.
Casane and Theridamas, to arms!
Raise cavalieros higher than the clouds,
And with the cannon break the frame of heaven;
Batter the shining palace of the sun,
And shiver all the starry firmament,
For amorous Jove hath snatch'd my love from hence,
Meaning to make her stately queen of heaven.
What god soever holds thee in his arms,
Giving thee nectar and ambrosia,
Behold me here, divine Zenocrate,
Raving, impatient, desperate, and mad,
Breaking my steeled lance, with which I burst
The rusty beams of Janus' temple-doors,
Letting out Death and tyrannising War,
To march with me under this bloody flag!
And, if thou pitiest Tamburlaine the Great,

Come down from heaven, and live with me again!

Ther. Ah, good my lord, be patient! she is dead,
And all this raging cannot make her live.
If words might serve, our voice hath rent the air;
If tears, our eyes have water'd all the earth;
If grief, our murder'd hearts have strained forth blood:
Nothing prevails, for she is dead, my lord.

Tamb. *For she is dead!* thy words do pierce my soul:
Ah, sweet Theridamas, say so no more!
Though she be dead, yet let me think she lives,
And feed my mind that dies for want of her.
Where'er her soul be, thou [*To the body*] shalt stay with me,
Embalm'd with cassia, ambergris, and myrrh,
Not lapt in lead, but in a sheet of gold,
And, till I die, thou shalt not be interr'd.
Then in as rich a tomb as Mausolus'
We both will rest, and have one epitaph
Writ in as many several languages
As I have conquer'd kingdoms with my sword.
This cursed town will I consume with fire,
Because this place bereft me of my love;
The houses, burnt, will look as if they mourn'd;
And here will I set up her statuë
And march about it with my mourning camp,
Drooping and pining for Zenocrate.

[*The arras is drawn.*

ACT III

SCENE I

Enter the Kings of Trebizon *and* Soria, *one bringing a sword and the other a sceptre; next,* Orcanes *king of Natolia, and the* King of Jerusalem *with the imperial crown; after,* Callapine; *and, after him, other* Lords *and* Almeda. Orcanes *and the* King of Jerusalem *crown* Callapine, *and the others give him the sceptre.*

Orc. Callapinus Cyricelibes, otherwise Cybelius, son and successive heir to the late mighty emperor Bajazeth, by the aid of God and his friend Mahomet, Emperor of Natolia, Jerusalem, Trebizon, Soria, Amasia, Thracia,

Ilyria, Carmania, and all the hundred and thirty kingdoms late contributory to his mighty father,—long live Callapinus, Emperor of Turkey!

Call. Thrice-worthy kings, of Natolia and the rest,
I will requite your royal gratitudes
With all the benefits my empire yields;
And, were the sinews of th' imperial seat
So knit and strengthen'd as when Bajazeth,
My royal lord and father, fill'd the throne,
Whose cursed fate hath so dismember'd it,
Then should you see this thief of Scythia,
This proud usurping king of Persia,
Do us such honour and supremacy,
Bearing the vengeance of our father's wrongs,
As all the world should blot his dignities
Out of the book of base-born infamies.
And now I doubt not but your royal cares
Have so provided for this cursed foe,
That, since the heir of mighty Bajazeth
(An emperor so honour'd for his virtues)
Revives the spirits of all true Turkish hearts,
In grievous memory of his father's shame,
We shall not need to nourish any doubt,
But that proud Fortune, who hath follow'd long
The martial sword of mighty Tamburlaine,
Will now retain her old inconstancy,
And raise our honours to as high a pitch,
In this our strong and fortunate encounter;
For so hath heaven provided my escape
From all the cruelty my soul sustain'd,
By this my friendly keeper's happy means,
That Jove, surcharg'd with pity of our wrongs,
Will pour it down in showers on our heads,
Scourging the pride of cursed Tamburlaine.

Orc. I have a hundred thousand men in arms;
Some that, in conquest of the perjur'd Christian,
Being a handful to a mighty host,
Think them in number yet sufficient
To drink the river Nile or Euphrates,
And for their power enow to win the world.

K. of Jer. And I as many from Jerusalem,
Judæa, Gaza, and Sclavonia's bounds,
That on mount Sinai, with their ensigns spread,

Look like the parti-colour'd clouds of heaven
That show fair weather to the neighbour morn.

K. of Treb. And I as many bring from Trebizon,
Chio, Famastro, and Amasia,
All bordering on the Mare-Major-sea,
Riso, Sancina, and the bordering towns
That touch the end of famous Euphrates,
Whose courages are kindled with the flames
The cursed Scythian sets on all their towns,
And vow to burn the villain's cruel heart.

K. of Sor. From Soria with seventy thousand strong,
Ta'en from Aleppo, Soldino, Tripoly,
And so unto my city of Damascus,
I march to meet and aid my neighbour kings;
All which will join against this Tamburlaine,
And bring him captive to your highness' feet.

Orc. Our battle, then, in martial manner pitch'd,
According to our ancient use, shall bear
The figure of the semicircled moon,
Whose horns shall sprinkle through the tainted air
The poison'd brains of this proud Scythian.

Call. Well, then, my noble lords, for this my friend
That freed me from the bondage of my foe,
I think it requisite and honourable
To keep my promise and to make him king,
That is a gentleman, I know, at least.

Alm. That's no matter, sir, for being a king; for Tamburlaine came up of nothing.

K. of Jer. Your majesty may choose some 'pointed time,
Performing all your promise to the full;
'Tis naught for your majesty to give a kingdom.

Call. Then will I shortly keep my promise, Almeda.

Alm. Why, I thank your majesty. [*Exeunt.*

SCENE II

Enter TAMBURLAINE *and his three* Sons, CALYPHAS, AMYRAS, *and* CELEBINUS; USUMCASANE; *four* Attendants *bearing the hearse of* ZENOCRATE, *and the drums sounding a doleful march ; the town burning.*

Tamb. So burn the turrets of this cursed town,
Flame to the highest region of the air,
And kindle heaps of exhalations,

That, being fiery meteors, may presage
Death and destruction to the inhabitants!
Over my zenith hang a blazing star,
That may endure till heaven be dissolv'd,
Fed with the fresh supply of earthly dregs,
Threatening a dearth and famine to this land!
Flying dragons, lightning, fearful thunder-claps,
Singe these fair plains, and make them seem as black
As is the island where the Furies mask,
Compass'd with Lethe, Styx, and Phlegethon,
Because my dear Zenocrate is dead!
Caly. This pillar, plac'd in memory of her,
Where in Arabian, Hebrew, Greek, is writ,
This town, being burnt by Tamburlaine the Great,
Forbids the world to build it up again.
Amy. And here this mournful streamer shall be plac'd,
Wrought with the Persian and th' Egyptian arms,
To signify she was a princess born,
And wife unto the monarch of the East.
Cel. And here this table as a register
Of all her virtues and perfections.
Tamb. And here the picture of Zenocrate,
To show her beauty which the world admir'd;
Sweet picture of divine Zenocrate,
That, hanging here, will draw the gods from heaven,
And cause the stars fix'd in the southern arc,
(Whose lovely faces never any view'd
That have not pass'd the centre's latitude,)
As pilgrims travel to our hemisphere,
Only to gaze upon Zenocrate.
Thou shalt not beautify Larissa-plains,
But keep within the circle of mine arms:
At every town and castle I besiege,
Thou shalt be set upon my royal tent;
And, when I meet an army in the field,
Those looks will shed such influence in my camp,
As if Bellona, goddess of the war,
Threw naked swords and sulphur-balls of fire
Upon the heads of all our enemies.—
And now, my lords, advance your spears again;
Sorrow no more, my sweet Casane, now:
Boys, leave to mourn; this town shall ever mourn,
Being burnt to cinders for your mother's death.

Caly. If I had wept a sea of tears for her,
It would not ease the sorrows I sustain.
Amy. As is that town, so is my heart consum'd
With grief and sorrow for my mother's death.
Cel. My mother's death hath mortified my mind,
And sorrow stops the passage of my speech.
Tamb. But now, my boys, leave off, and list to me,
That mean to teach you rudiments of war.
I'll have you learn to sleep upon the ground,
March in your armour thorough watery fens,
Sustain the scorching heat and freezing cold,
Hunger and thirst, right adjuncts of the war;
And, after this, to scale a castle-wall,
Besiege a fort, to undermine a town,
And make whole cities caper in the air:
Then next, the way to fortify your men;
In champion grounds what figure serves you best,
For which the quinque-angle form is meet,
Because the corners there may fall more flat
Whereas the fort may fittest be assail'd,
And sharpest where th' assault is desperate:
The ditches must be deep; the counterscarps
Narrow and steep; the walls made high and broad;
The bulwarks and the rampires large and strong,
With cavalieros and thick counterforts,
And room within to lodge six thousand men,
It must have privy ditches, countermines,
And secret issuings to defend the ditch;
It must have high argins and cover'd ways
To keep the bulwark-fronts from battery,
And parapets to hide the musketeers,
Casemates to place the great artillery,
And store of ordnance, that from every flank
May scour the outward curtains of the fort,
Dismount the cannon of the adverse part,
Murder the foe, and save the walls from breach.
When this is learn'd for service on the land,
By plain and easy demonstration
I'll teach you how to make the water mount,
That you may dry-foot march through lakes and pools,
Deep rivers, havens, creeks, and little seas,
And make a fortress in the raging waves,
Fenc'd with the concave of a monstrous rock,

Invincible by nature of the place.
When this is done, then are ye soldiers,
And worthy sons of Tamburlaine the Great.

Caly. My lord, but this is dangerous to be done;
We may be slain or wounded ere we learn.

Tamb. Villain, art thou the son of Tamburlaine,
And fear'st to die, or with a curtle-axe
To hew thy flesh, and make a gaping wound?
Hast thou beheld a peal of ordnance strike
A ring of pikes, mingled with shot and horse,
Whose shatter'd limbs, being toss'd as high as heaven,
Hang in the air as thick as sunny motes,
And canst thou, coward, stand in fear of death?
Hast thou not seen my horsemen charge the foe,
Shot through the arms, cut overthwart the hands,
Dying their lances with their streaming blood,
And yet at night carouse within my tent,
Filling their empty veins with airy wine,
That, being concocted, turns to crimson blood,
And wilt thou shun the field for fear of wounds?
View me, thy father, that hath conquer'd kings,
And, with his host, march'd round about the earth,
Quite void of scars and clear from any wound,
That by the wars lost not a dram of blood,
And see him lance his flesh to teach you all.

[*He cuts his arm.*

A wound is nothing, be it ne'er so deep;
Blood is the god of war's rich livery.
Now look I like a soldier, and this wound
As great a grace and majesty to me,
As if a chair of gold enamelled,
Enchas'd with diamonds, sapphires, rubies,
And fairest pearl of wealthy India,
Were mounted here under a canopy,
And I sat down, cloth'd with the massy robe
That late adorn'd the Afric potentate,
Whom I brought bound unto Damascus' walls.
Come, boys, and with your fingers search my wound,
And in my blood wash all your hands at once,
While I sit smiling to behold the sight.
Now, my boys, what think ye of a wound?

Caly. I know not what I should think of it; methinks 'tis a pitiful sight.

Cel. 'Tis nothing.—Give me a wound, father.
Amy. And me another, my lord.
Tamb. Come, sirrah, give me your arm.
Cel. Here, father, cut it bravely, as you did your own.
Tamb. It shall suffice thou dar'st abide a wound;
My boy, thou shalt not lose a drop of blood
Before we meet the army of the Turk;
But then run desperate through the thickest throngs,
Dreadless of blows, of bloody wounds, and death;
And let the burning of Larissa-walls,
My speech of war, and this my wound you see,
Teach you, my boys, to bear courageous minds,
Fit for the followers of great Tamburlaine.—
Usumcasane, now come, let us march
Towards Techelles and Theridamas,
That we have sent before to fire the towns,
The towers and cities of these hateful Turks,
And hunt that coward faint-heart runaway,
With that accursed traitor Almeda,
Till fire and sword have found them at a bay.
Usum. I long to pierce his bowels with my sword,
That hath betray'd my gracious sovereign,—
That curs'd and damned traitor Almeda.
Tamb. Then let us see if coward Callapine
Dare levy arms against our puissance,
That we may tread upon his captive neck,
And treble all his father's slaveries. [*Exeunt.*

SCENE III

Enter TECHELLES, THERIDAMAS, *and their train.*

Ther. Thus have we march'd northward from Tamburlaine,
Unto the frontier point of Soria;
And this is Balsera, their chiefest hold,
Wherein is all the treasure of the land.
Tech. Then let us bring our light artillery,
Minions, falc'nets, and sakers, to the trench,
Filling the ditches with the walls' wide breach,
And enter in to seize upon the gold.—
How say you, soldiers, shall we not?
Soldiers. Yes, my lord, yes; come, let's about it.
Ther. But stay a while; summon a parle, drum.
It may be they will yield it quietly,

Knowing two kings, the friends to Tamburlaine,
Stand at the walls with such a mighty power.

[*A parley sounded.—Captain appears on the walls, with Olympia his wife, and his son.*

Capt. What require you, my masters?
Ther. Captain, that thou yield up thy hold to us.
Capt. To you! why, do you think me weary of it?
Tech. Nay, captain, thou art weary of thy life,
If thou withstand the friends of Tamburlaine.
Ther. These pioners of Argier in Africa,
Even in the cannon's face, shall raise a hill
Of earth and faggots higher than thy fort,
And, over thy argins and cover'd ways,
Shall play upon the bulwarks of thy hold
Volleys of ordnance, till the breach be made
That with his ruin fills up all the trench;
And, when we enter in, not heaven itself
Shall ransom thee, thy wife, and family.
Tech. Captain, these Moors shall cut the leaden pipes
That bring fresh water to thy men and thee.
And lie in trench before thy castle-walls,
That no supply of victual shall come in,
Nor [any] issue forth but they shall die;
And, therefore, captain, yield it quietly.
Capt. Were you, that are the friends of Tamburlaine,
Brothers of holy Mahomet himself,
I would not yield it; therefore do your worst:
Raise mounts, batter, intrench, and undermine,
Cut off the water, all convoys that can,
Yet I am resolute: and so, farewell.

[*Captain, Olympia, and son, retire from the walls.*

Ther. Pioners, away! and where I stuck the stake,
Intrench with those dimensions I prescrib'd;
Cast up the earth towards the castle-wall,
Which, till it may defend you, labour low,
And few or none shall perish by their shot.
Pioners. We will, my lord. [*Exeunt Pioners.*
Tech. A hundred horse shall scout about the plains,
To spy what force comes to relieve the hold.
Both we, Theridamas, will intrench our men,
And with the Jacob's staff measure the height
And distance of the castle from the trench,

That we may know if our artillery
Will carry full point-plank unto their walls.

Ther. Then see the bringing of our ordnance
Along the trench into the battery,
Where we will have gabions of six foot broad,
To save our cannoneers from musket-shot;
Betwixt which shall our ordnance thunder forth,
And with the breach's fall, smoke, fire, and dust,
The crack, the echo, and the soldiers' cry,
Make deaf the air and dim the crystal sky.

Tech. Trumpets and drums, alarum presently!
And, soldiers, play the men; the hold is yours!
[*Exeunt.*

SCENE IV

Alarms within. Enter the CAPTAIN, *with* OLYMPIA, *and his* SON

Olym. Come, good my lord, and let us haste from hence,
Along the cave that leads beyond the foe:
No hope is left to save this conquer'd hold.

Capt. A deadly bullet gliding through my side,
Lies heavy on my heart; I cannot live:
I feel my liver pierc'd, and all my veins,
That there begin and nourish every part,
Mangled and torn, and all my entrails bath'd
In blood that straineth from their orifex.
Farewell, sweet wife! sweet son, farewell! I die.
[*Dies.*

Olym. Death, whither art thou gone, that both we live?
Come back again, sweet Death, and strike us both!
One minute end our days, and one sepulchre
Contain our bodies! Death, why com'st thou not?
Well, this must be the messenger for thee:
[*Drawing a dagger.*
Now, ugly Death, stretch out thy sable wings,
And carry both our souls where his remains.—
Tell me, sweet boy, art thou content to die?
These barbarous Scythians, full of cruelty,
And Moors, in whom was never pity found,
Will hew us piecemeal, put us to the wheel,
Or else invent some torture worse than that;
Therefore die by thy loving mother's hand,

Who gently now will lance thy ivory throat,
And quickly rid thee both of pain and life.
Son. Mother, despatch me, or I'll kill myself;
For think you I can live and see him dead?
Give me your knife, good mother, or strike home:
The Scythians shall not tyrannise on me:
Sweet mother, strike, that I may meet my father.
[*She stabs him, and he dies.*
Olym. Ah, sacred Mahomet, if this be sin,
Entreat a pardon of the God of heaven,
And purge my soul before it come to thee!
[*She burns the bodies of her husband and son, and then attempts to kill herself.*

Enter THERIDAMAS, TECHELLES, *and all their train.*

Ther. How now, Madam! what are you doing?
Olym. Killing myself, as I have done my son,
Whose body, with his father's, I have burnt,
Lest cruel Scythians should dismember him.
Tech. 'Twas bravely done, and like a soldier's wife.
Thou shalt with us to Tamburlaine the Great,
Who, when he hears how resolute thou wert,
Will match thee with a viceroy or a king.
Olym. My lord deceas'd was dearer unto me
Than any viceroy, king, or emperor;
And for his sake here will I end my days.
Ther. But, lady, go with us to Tamburlaine,
And thou shalt see a man greater than Mahomet,
In whose high looks is much more majesty,
Than from the concave superficies
Of Jove's vast palace, the empyreal orb,
Unto the shining bower where Cynthia sits,
Like lovely Thetis, in a crystal robe;
That treadeth fortune underneath his feet,
And makes the mighty god of arms his slave;
On whom Death and the Fatal Sisters wait
With naked swords and scarlet liveries;
Before whom, mounted on a lion's back,
Rhamnusia bears a helmet full of blood,
And strows the way with brains of slaughter'd men;
By whose proud side the ugly Furies run,
Hearkening when he shall bid them plague the world;
Over whose zenith, cloth'd in windy air,

And eagle's wings join'd to her feather'd breast,
Fame hovereth, sounding of her golden trump,
That to the adverse poles of that straight line
Which measureth the glorious frame of heaven
The name of mighty Tamburlaine is spread;
And him, fair lady, shall thy eyes behold.
Come.

Olym. Take pity of a lady's ruthful tears,
That humbly craves upon her knees to stay,
And cast her body in the burning flame
That feeds upon her son's and husband's flesh.

Tech. Madam, sooner shall fire consume us both
Than scorch a face so beautiful as this,
In frame of which Nature hath show'd more skill
Than when she gave eternal chaos form,
Drawing from it the shining lamps of heaven.

Ther. Madam, I am so far in love with you,
That you must go with us: no remedy.

Olym. Then carry me, I care not, where you will,
And let the end of this my fatal journey
Be likewise end to my accursed life.

Tech. No, madam, but the beginning of your joy:
Come willingly, therefore.

Ther. Soldiers, now let us meet the general,
Who by this time is at Natolia,
Ready to charge the army of the Turk.
The gold, the silver, and the pearl, ye got,
Rifling this fort, divide in equal shares:
This lady shall have twice so much again
Out of the coffers of our treasury. [*Exeunt.*

SCENE V

Enter CALLAPINE, ORCANES, *the* KINGS OF JERUSALEM, TREBIZON, *and* SORIA, *with their train,* ALMEDA, *and a* Messenger.

Mess. Renowmed emperor, mighty Callapine,
God's great lieutenant over all the world,
Here at Aleppo, with an host of men,
Lies Tamburlaine, this king of Persia,
(In number more than are the quivering leaves
Of Ida's forest, where your highness' hounds
With open cry pursue the wounded stag,)

Who means to girt Natolia's walls with siege,
Fire the town, and over-run the land.
Call. My royal army is as great as his,
That, from the bounds of Phrygia to the sea
Which washeth Cyprus with his brinish waves,
Covers the hills, the valleys, and the plains.
Viceroys and peers of Turkey, play the men;
Whet all your swords to mangle Tamburlaine,
His sons, his captains, and his followers:
By Mahomet, not one of them shall live!
The field wherein this battle shall be fought
For ever term the Persians' sepulchre,
In memory of this our victory.
Orc. Now he that calls himself the scourge of Jove,
The emperor of the world, and earthly god,
Shall end the warlike progress he intends,
And travel headlong to the lake of hell,
Where legions of devils (knowing he must die
Here in Natolia by your highness' hands),
All brandishing their brands of quenchless fire,
Stretching their monstrous paws, grin with their teeth,
And guard the gates to entertain his soul.
Call. Tell me, viceroys, the number of your men,
And what our army royal is esteem'd.
K. of Jer. From Palestina and Jerusalem,
Of Hebrews three score thousand fighting men
Are come, since last we show'd your majesty.
Orc. So from Arabia Desert, and the bounds
Of that sweet land whose brave metropolis
Re-edified the fair Semiramis,
Came forty thousand warlike foot and horse,
Since last we number'd to your majesty.
K. of Treb. From Trebizon in Asia the Less,
Naturalis'd Turks and stout Bithynians
Came to my bands, full fifty thousand more,
(That, fighting, know not what retreat doth mean,
Nor e'er return but with the victory,)
Since last we number'd to your majesty.
K. of Sor. Of Sorians from Halla is repair'd,
And neighbour cities of your highness' land,
Ten thousand horse, and thirty thousand foot,
Since last we number'd to your majesty;
So that the army royal is esteem'd

Six hundred thousand valiant fighting men.
Call. Then welcome, Tamburlaine, unto thy death!
Come, puissant viceroys, let us to the field
(The Persians' sepulchre), and sacrifice
Mountains of breathless men to Mahomet,
Who now, with Jove, opens the firmament
To see the slaughter of our enemies.

Enter TAMBURLAINE *with his three* sons, CALYPHUS, AMYRAS, *and* CELEBINUS; USUMCASANE, *and others.*

Tamb. How now, Casane! see, a knot of kings,
Sitting as if they were a-telling riddles!
Usum. My lord, your presence makes them pale and wan:
Poor souls, they look as if their deaths were near.
Tamb. Why, so he is, Casane; I am here:
But yet I'll save their lives, and make them slaves.—
Ye petty kings of Turkey, I am come,
As Hector did into the Grecian camp,
To overdare the pride of Græcia,
And set his warlike person to the view
Of fierce Achilles, rival of his fame:
I do you honour in the simile;
For, if I should, as Hector did Achilles,
(The worthiest knight that ever brandish'd sword,)
Challenge in combat any of you all,
I see how fearfully ye would refuse,
And fly my glove as from a scorpion.
Orc. Now thou art fearful of thy army's strength,
Thou wouldst with overmatch of person fight:
But, shepherd's issue, base-born Tamburlaine,
Think of thy end; this sword shall lance thy throat.
Tamb. Villain, the shepherd's issue (at whose birth
Heaven did afford a gracious aspect,
And join'd those stars that shall be opposite
Even till the dissolution of the world,
And never meant to make a conqueror
So famous as is mighty Tamburlaine)
Shall so torment thee, and that Callapine,
That, like a roguish runaway, suborn'd
That villain there, that slave, that Turkish dog,
To false his service to his sovereign,
As ye shall curse the birth of Tamburlaine.

Call. Rail not, proud Scythian: I shall now revenge
My father's vile abuses and mine own.
K. of Jer. By Mahomet, he shall be tied in chains,
Rowing with Christians in a brigandine
About the Grecian isles to rob and spoil,
And turn him to his ancient trade again:
Methinks the slave should make a lusty thief.
Call. Nay, when the battle ends, all we will meet,
And sit in council to invent some pain
That most may vex his body and his soul.
Tamb. Sirrah Callapine, I'll hang a clog about your neck for running away again: you shall not trouble me thus to come and fetch you.—
But as for you, viceroy[s], you shall have bits,
And, harness'd like my horses, draw my coach;
And, when ye stay, be lash'd with whips of wire:
I'll have you learn to feed on provender,
And in a stable lie upon the planks.
Orc. But, Tamburlaine, first thou shalt kneel to us,
And humbly crave a pardon for thy life.
K. of Treb. The common soldiers of our mighty host
Shall bring thee bound unto the general's tent.
K. of Sor. And all have jointly sworn thy cruel death,
Or bind thee in eternal torments' wrath.
Tamb. Well, sirs, diet yourselves; you know I shall have occasion shortly to journey you.
Cel. See, father, how Almeda the jailor looks upon us!
Tamb. Villain, traitor, damned fugitive,
I'll make thee wish the earth had swallow'd thee!
See'st thou not death within my wrathful looks?
Go, villain, cast thee headlong from a rock,
Or rip thy bowels, and rent out thy heart,
T' appease my wrath; or else I'll torture thee,
Searing thy hateful flesh with burning irons
And drops of scalding lead, while all thy joints
Be rack'd and beat asunder with the wheel;
For, if thou liv'st, not any element
Shall shroud thee from the wrath of Tamburlaine.
Call. Well in despite of thee, he shall be king.—
Come, Almeda; receive this crown of me:
I here invest thee king of Ariadan,
Bordering on Mare Roso, near to Mecca.
Orc. What! take it, man.

Alm. [*to Tamb.*] Good my lord, let me take it.

Call. Dost thou ask him leave? here; take it.

Tamb. Go to, sirrah! take your crown, and make up the half dozen. So, sirrah, now you are a king, you must give arms.

Orc. So he shall, and wear thy head in his scutcheon.

Tamb. No; let him hang a bunch of keys on his standard, to put him in remembrance he was a jailor, that, when I take him, I may knock out his brains with them, and lock you in the stable, when you shall come sweating from my chariot.

K. of Treb. Away! let us to the field, that the villain may be slain.

Tamb. Sirrah, prepare whips, and bring my chariot to my tent; for, as soon as the battle is done, I'll ride in triumph through the camp.

Enter THERIDAMAS, TECHELLES, *and their train.*

How now, ye petty kings? lo, here are bugs
Will make the hair stand upright on your heads,
And cast your crowns in slavery at their feet!—
Welcome, Theridamas and Techelles, both:
See ye this rout, and know ye this same king?

Ther. Ay, my lord; he was Callapine's keeper.

Tamb. Well now ye see he is a king. Look to him, Theridamas, when we are fighting, lest he hide his crown as the foolish king of Persia did.

K. of Sor. No, Tamburlaine; he shall not be put to that exigent, I warrant thee.

Tamb. You know not, sir.—
But now, my followers and my loving friends,
Fight as you ever did, like conquerors,
The glory of this happy day is yours.
My stern aspect shall make fair Victory,
Hovering betwixt our armies, light on me,
Loaden with laurel-wreaths to crown us all.

Tech. I smile to think how, when this field is fought
And rich Natolia ours, our men shall sweat
With carrying pearl and treasure on their backs.

Tamb. You shall be princes all, immediately.—
Come, fight, ye Turks, or yield us victory.

Orc. No; we will meet thee, slavish Tamburlaine.

[*Exeunt severally.*

ACT IV

SCENE I

Alarms within. AMYRAS *and* CELEBINUS *issue from the tent where* CALYPHAS *sits asleep.*

Amy. Now in their glories shine the golden crowns
Of these proud Turks, much like so many suns
That half dismay the majesty of heaven.
Now, brother, follow we our father's sword,
That flies with fury swifter than our thoughts,
And cuts down armies with his conquering wings.
Cel. Call forth our lazy brother from the tent,
For, if my father miss him in the field,
Wrath, kindled in the furnace of his breast,
Will send a deadly lightning to his heart.
Amy. Brother, ho! what, given so much to sleep,
You cannot leave it, when our enemies' drums
And rattling cannons thunder in our ears
Our proper ruin and our father's foil?
Caly. Away, ye fools! my father needs not me,
Nor you, in faith, but that you will be thought
More childish-valourous than manly-wise.
If half our camp should sit and sleep with me,
My father were enough to scare the foe:
You do dishonour to his majesty,
To think our helps will do him any good.
Amy. What, dar'st thou, then, be absent from the fight,
Knowing my father hates thy cowardice,
And oft hath warn'd thee to be still in field,
When he himself amidst the thickest troops
Beats down our foes, to flesh our taintless swords?
Caly. I know, sir, what it is to kill a man;
It works remorse of conscience in me.
I take no pleasure to be murderous,
Nor care for blood when wine will quench my thirst.
Cel. O cowardly boy! fie, for shame, come forth!
Thou dost dishonour manhood and thy house.
Caly. Go, go, tall stripling, fight you for us both,
And take my other toward brother here,
For person like to prove a second Mars.
'Twill please my mind as well to hear, both you

Have won a heap of honour in the field,
And left your slender carcasses behind,
As if I lay with you for company.

Amy. You will not go, then?

Caly. You say true.

Amy. Were all the lofty mounts of Zona Mundi
That fill the midst of farthest Tartary
Turn'd into pearl and proffer'd for my stay,
I would not bide the fury of my father,
When, made a victor in these haughty arms,
He comes and finds his sons have had no shares
In all the honours he propos'd for us.

Caly. Take you the honour, I will take my ease;
My wisdom shall excuse my cowardice:
I go into the field before I need!

[*Alarms within. Amyras and Celebinus run out.*

The bullets fly at random where they list;
And, should I go, and kill a thousand men,
I were as soon rewarded with a shot,
And sooner far than he that never fights;
And, should I go, and do nor harm nor good,
I might have harm, which all the good I have,
Join'd with my father's crown, would never cure.
I'll to cards.—Perdicas!

Enter PERDICAS.

Perd. Here, my lord.

Caly. Come, thou and I will go to cards to drive away the time.

Perd. Content, my lord: but what shall we play for?

Caly. Who shall kiss the fairest of the Turks' concubines first, when my father hath conquered them.

Perd. Agreed, i'faith. [*They play.*

Caly. They say I am a coward, Perdicas, and I fear as little their taratantaras, their swords, or their cannons as I do a naked lady in a net of gold, and, for fear I should be afraid, would put it off and come to bed with me.

Perd. Such a fear, my lord, would never make ye retire.

Caly. I would my father would let me be put in the front of such a battle once, to try my valour! [*Alarms within.*] What a coil they keep! I believe there will be some hurt done anon amongst them.

Enter TAMBURLAINE, THERIDAMAS, TECHELLES, USUMCASANE; AMYRAS *and* CELEBINUS *leading in* ORCANES, *and the* KINGS OF JERUSALEM, TREBIZON, *and* SORIA; *and* Soldiers.

Tamb. See now, ye slaves, my children stoops your pride,
And leads your glories sheep-like to the sword!—
Bring them, my boys, and tell me if the wars
Be not a life that may illustrate gods,
And tickle not your spirits with desire
Still to be train'd in arms and chivalry?
Amy. Shall we let go these kings again, my lord,
To gather greater numbers 'gainst our power,
That they may say, it is not chance doth this,
But matchless strength and magnanimity?
Tamb. No, no, Amyras; tempt not Fortune so:
Cherish thy valour still with fresh supplies,
And glut it not with stale and daunted foes.
But where's this coward villain, not my son,
But traitor to my name and majesty?
[*He goes in and brings Calyphas out.*
Image of sloth, and picture of a slave,
The obloquy and scorn of my renown!
How may my heart, thus fired with mine eyes,
Wounded with shame and kill'd with discontent,
Shroud any thought may hold my striving hands
From martial justice on thy wretched soul?
Ther. Yet pardon him, I pray your majesty.
Tech. and Usum. Let all of us entreat your highness' pardon.
Tamb. Stand up, ye base, unworthy soldiers!
Know ye not yet the argument of arms?
Amy. Good, my lord, let him be forgiven for once,
And we will force him to the field hereafter.
Tamb. Stand up, my boys, and I will teach ye arms,
And what the jealousy of wars must do.—
O Samarcanda, where I breathed first,
And joy'd the fire of this martial flesh,
Blush, blush, fair city, at thine honour's foil,
And shame of nature, which Jaertis' stream,
Embracing thee with deepest of his love,
Can never wash from thy distained brows!—
Here, Jove, receive his fainting soul again;
A form not meet to give that subject essence

Whose matter is the flesh of Tamburlaine,
Wherein an incorporeal spirit moves,
Made of the mould whereof thyself consists,
Which makes me valiant, proud, ambitious,
Ready to levy power against thy throne,
That I might move the turning spheres of heaven;
For earth and all this airy region
Cannot contain the state of Tamburlaine.
[*Stabs Calyphas.*
By Mahomet, thy mighty friend, I swear,
In sending to my issue such a soul,
Created of the massy dregs of earth,
The scum and tartar of the elements,
Wherein was neither courage, strength, or wit,
But folly, sloth, and damned idleness,
That hast procur'd a greater enemy
Than he that darted mountains at thy head,
Shaking the burden mighty Atlas bears,
Whereat thou trembling hidd'st thee in the air,
Cloth'd with a pitchy cloud for being seen.—
And now, ye canker'd curs of Asia,
That will not see the strength of Tamburlaine,
Although it shine as brightly as the sun,
Now you shall feel the strength of Tamburlaine,
And, by the state of his supremacy,
Approve the difference 'twixt himself and you.

Orc. Thou show'st the difference 'twixt ourselves and thee,
In this thy barbarous damned tyranny.

K. of Jer. Thy victories are grown so violent,
That shortly heaven, fill'd with the meteors
Of blood and fire thy tyrannies have made,
Will pour down blood and fire on thy head,
Whose scalding drops will pierce thy seething brains,
And, with our bloods, revenge our bloods on thee.

Tamb. Villains, these terrors, and these tyrannies
(If tyrannies war's justice ye repute),
I execute, enjoin'd me from above,
To scourge the pride of such as Heaven abhors;
Nor am I made arch-monarch of the world,
Crown'd and invested by the hand of Jove,
For deeds of bounty or nobility;
But, since I exercise a greater name,
The Scourge of God and terror of the world,

I must apply myself to fit those terms,
In war, in blood, in death, in cruelty,
And plague such peasants as resist in me
The power of Heaven's eternal majesty.—
Theridamas, Techelles, and Casane,
Ransack the tents and the pavilions
Of these proud Turks, and take their concubines,
Making them bury this effeminate brat;
For not a common soldier shall defile
His manly fingers with so faint a boy:
Then bring those Turkish harlots to my tent,
And I'll dispose them as it likes me best.—
Meanwhile, take him in.

Soldiers. We will, my lord.

[*Exeunt with the body of Calyphas.*

K. of Jer. O damned monster! nay, a fiend of hell,
Whose cruelties are not so harsh as thine,
Nor yet impos'd with such a bitter hate!

Orc. Revenge it, Rhadamanth and Æacus,
And let your hates, extended in his pains,
Expel the hate wherewith he pains our souls!

K. of Treb. May never day give virtue to his eyes,
Whose sight, compos'd of fury and of fire,
Doth send such stern affections to his heart!

K. of Sor. May never spirit, vein, or artier, feed
The cursed substance of that cruel heart;
But, wanting moisture and remorseful blood,
Dry up with anger, and consume with heat!

Tamb. Well, bark, ye dogs: I'll bridle all your tongues,
And bind them close with bits of burnish'd steel,
Down to the channels of your hateful throats;
And, with the pains my rigour shall inflict,
I'll make ye roar, that earth may echo forth
The far-resounding torments ye sustain;
As when an herd of lusty Cimbrian bulls
Run mourning round about the females' miss,
And, stung with fury of their following,
Fill all the air with troubles bellowing.
I will, with engines never exercis'd,
Conquer, sack, and utterly consume
Your cities and your golden palaces,
And, with the flames that beat against the clouds,
Incense the heavens, and make the stars to melt,

As if they were the tears of Mahomet
For hot consumption of his country's pride;
And, till by vision or by speech I hear
Immortal Jove say "Cease, my Tamburlaine,"
I will persist a terror to the world,
Making the meteors (that, like armed men,
Are seen to march upon the towers of heaven)
Run tilting round about the firmament,
And break their burning lances in the air,
For honour of my wondrous victories,—
Come, bring them in to our pavilion. [*Exeunt.*

SCENE II

Enter OLYMPIA

Olym. Distress'd Olympia, whose weeping eyes,
Since thy arrival here, beheld no sun,
But, clos'd within the compass of a tent,
Have stain'd thy cheeks, and made thee look like death,
Devise some means to rid thee of thy life,
Rather than yield to his detested suit,
Whose drift is only to dishonour thee;
And, since this earth, dew'd with thy brinish tears,
Affords no herbs whose taste may poison thee,
Nor yet this air, beat often with thy sighs,
Contagious smells and vapours to infect thee,
Nor thy close cave a sword to murder thee,
Let this invention be the instrument.

Enter THERIDAMAS.

Ther. Well met, Olympia: I sought thee in my tent,
But, when I saw the place obscure and dark,
Which with thy beauty thou wast wont to light,
Enrag'd, I ran about the fields for thee,
Supposing amorous Jove had sent his son,
The winged Hermes, to convey thee hence;
But now I find thee, and that fear is past,
Tell me, Olympia, wilt thou grant my suit?
Olym. My lord and husband's death, with my sweet son's,
(With whom I buried all affections
Save grief and sorrow, which torment my heart),
Forbids my mind to entertain a thought

That tends to love, and meditate on death,
A fitter subject for a pensive soul.
Ther. Olympia, pity him in whom thy looks
Have greater operation and more force
Than Cynthia's in the watery wilderness;
For with thy view my joys are at the full,
And ebb again as thou depart'st from me.
Olym. Ah, pity me, my lord, and draw your sword,
Making a passage for my troubled soul,
Which beats against this prison to get out,
And meet my husband and my loving son!
Ther. Nothing but still thy husband and thy son?
Leave this, my love, and listen more to me:
Thou shalt be stately queen of fair Argier;
And, cloth'd in costly cloth of massy gold,
Upon the marble turrets of my court
Sit like to Venus in her chair of state,
Commanding all thy princely eye desires;
And I will cast off arms to sit with thee,
Spending my life in sweet discourse of love.
Olym. No such discourse is pleasant in mine ears,
But that where every period ends with death,
And every line begins with death again:
I cannot love, to be an emperess.
Ther. Nay, lady, then, if nothing will prevail,
I'll use some other means to make you yield:
Such is the sudden fury of my love,
I must and will be pleas'd, and you shall yield:
Come to the tent again.
Olym. Stay, good my lord; and, will you save my honour,
I'll give your grace a present of such price
As all the world can not afford the like.
Ther. What is it?
Olym. An ointment which a cunning alchymist
Distilled from the purest balsamum
And simplest extracts of all minerals,
In which the essential form of marble stone,
Temper'd by science metaphysical,
And spells of magic from the mouths of spirits,
With which if you but 'noint your tender skin,
Nor pistol, sword, nor lance, can pierce your flesh.
Ther. Why, madam, think you to mock me thus palpably?
Olym. To prove it, I will 'noint my naked throat,

Which when you stab, look on your weapon's point,
And you shall see't rebated with the blow.

Ther. Why gave you not your husband some of it,
If you lov'd him, and it so precious?

Olym. My purpose was, my lord, to spend it so,
But was prevented by his sudden end;
And for a present easy proof hereof,
That I dissemble not, try it on me.

Ther. I will, Olympia, and will keep it for
The richest present of this eastern world.
[*She anoints her throat.*

Olym. Now stab, my lord, and mark your weapon's point,
That will be blunted if the blow be great.

Ther. Here, then, Olympia.— [*Stabs her.*
What, have I slain her? Villain, stab thyself!
Cut off this arm that murdered my love,
In whom the learned Rabbis of this age
Might find as many wondrous miracles
As in the theoria of the world!
Now hell is fairer than Elysium;
A greater lamp than that bright eye of heaven,
From whence the stars do borrow all their light,
Wanders about the black circumference;
And now the damned souls are free from pain,
For every Fury gazeth on her looks;
Infernal Dis is courting of my love,
Inventing masks and stately shows for her,
Opening the doors of his rich treasury
To entertain this queen of chastity;
Whose body shall be tomb'd with all the pomp
The treasure of my kingdom may afford.
[*Exit with the body.*

SCENE III

Enter TAMBURLAINE, *drawn in his chariot by the* KINGS OF TREBIZON *and* SORIA, *with bits in their mouths, reins in his left hand, and in his right hand a whip with which he scourgeth them;* AMYRAS, CELEBINUS, TECHELLES, THERIDAMAS, USUMCASANE; ORCANES *king of Natolia, and the* KING OF JERUSALEM, *led by with five or six common* Soldiers; *and other* Soldiers.

Tamb. Holla, ye pamper'd jades of Asia!
What, can ye draw but twenty miles a-day,

And have so proud a chariot at your heels,
And such a coachman as great Tamburlaine,
But from Asphaltis, where I conquer'd you,
To Byron here, where thus I honour you?
The horse that guide the golden eye of heaven,
And blow the morning from their nosterils,
Making their fiery gait above the clouds,
Are not so honour'd in their governor
As you, ye slaves, in mighty Tamburlaine.
The headstrong jades of Thrace Alcides tam'd,
That King Ægeus fed with human flesh,
And made so wanton that they knew their strengths,
Were not subdu'd with valour more divine
Than you by this unconquer'd arm of mine.
To make you fierce, and fit my appetite,
You shall be fed with flesh as raw as blood,
And drink in pails the strongest muscadel:
If you can live with it, then live, and draw
My chariot swifter than the racking clouds;
If not, then die like beasts, and fit for naught
But perches for the black and fatal ravens.
Thus am I right the scourge of highest Jove;
And see the figure of my dignity,
By which I hold my name and majesty!

Amy. Let me have coach, my lord, that I may ride,
And thus be drawn by these two idle kings.

Tamb. Thy youth forbids such ease, my kingly boy:
They shall to-morrow draw my chariot,
While these their fellow-kings may be refresh'd.

Orc. O thou that sway'st the region under earth,
And art a king as absolute as Jove,
Come as thou didst in fruitful Sicily,
Surveying all the glories of the land,
And as thou took'st the fair Proserpina,
Joying the fruit of Ceres' garden-plot,
For love, for honour, and to make her queen,
So, for just hate, for shame, and to subdue
This proud contemner of thy dreadful power,
Come once in fury, and survey his pride,
Haling him headlong to the lowest hell!

Ther. You majesty must get some bits for these,
To bridle their contemptuous cursing tongues,
That, like unruly never-broken jades,

Break through the hedges of their hateful mouths,
And pass their fixed bounds exceedingly.
Tech. Nay, we will break the hedges of their mouths,
And pull their kicking colts out of their pastures.
Usum. Your majesty already hath devis'd
A mean, as fit as may be, to restrain
These coltish coach-horse tongues from blasphemy.
Cel. How like you that, sir king? why speak you not?
K. of Jer. Ah, cruel brat, sprung from a tyrant's loins!
How like his cursed father he begins
To practice taunts and bitter tyrannies!
Tamb. Ay, Turk, I tell thee, this same boy is he
That must (advanc'd in higher pomp than this)
Rifle the kingdoms I shall leave unsack'd,
If Jove, esteeming me too good for earth,
Raise me, to match the fair Aldeboran,
Above the threefold astracism of heaven,
Before I conquer all the triple world.—
Now fetch me out the Turkish concubines:
I will prefer them for the funeral
They have bestow'd on my abortive son.
[*The Concubines are brought in.*
Where are my common soldiers now, that fought
So lion-like upon Asphaltis' plains?
Soldiers. Here, my lord.
Tamb. Hold ye, tall soldiers, take ye queens a-piece,—
I mean such queens as were kings' concubines;
Take them; divide them, and their jewels too,
And let them equally serve all your turns.
Soldiers. We thank your majesty.
Tamb. Brawl not, I warn you, for your lechery;
For every man that so offends shall die.
Orc. Injurious tyrant, wilt thou so defame
The hateful fortunes of thy victory,
To exercise upon such guiltless dames
The violence of thy common soldiers' lust?
Tamb. Live continent, then, ye slaves, and meet not me
With troops of harlots at your slothful heels.
Concubines. O pity us, my lord, and save our honours!
Tamb. Are ye not gone, ye villains, with your spoils?
[*The Soldiers run away with the Concubines.*
K. of Jer. O, merciless, infernal cruelty!
Tamb. Save your honours! 'twere but time indeed,

Lost long before ye knew what honour meant.
Ther. It seems they meant to conquer us, my lord,
And make us jesting pageants for their trulls.
Tamb. And now themselves shall make our pageant,
And common soliders jest with all their trulls.
Let them take pleasure soundly in their spoils,
Till we prepare our march to Babylon,
Whither we next make expedition.
Tech. Let us not be idle, then, my lord,
But presently be prest to conquer it.
Tamb. We will, Techelles.—Forward, then, ye jades!
Now crouch, ye kings of greatest Asia,
And tremble when ye hear this scourge will come
That whips down cities and controlleth crowns,
Adding their wealth and treasure to my store.
The Euxine sea, north to Natolia;
The Terrene, west; the Caspian, north north-east;
And on the south, Sinus Arabicus;
Shall all be loaden with the martial spoils
We will convey with us to Persia.
Then shall my native city Samarcanda,
And crystal waves of fresh Jaertis' stream,
The pride and beauty of her princely seat,
Be famous through the furthest continents;
For there my palace royal shall be plac'd,
Whose shining turrets shall dismay the heavens,
And cast the fame of Ilion's tower to hell:
Thorough the streets, with troops of conquer'd kings,
I'll ride in golden armour like the sun;
And in my helm a triple plume shall spring,
Spangled with diamonds, dancing in the air,
To note me emperor of the three-fold world;
Like to an almond-tree y-mounted high
Upon the lofty and celestial mount
Of ever-green Selinus, quaintly deck'd
With blooms more white than Erycina's brows,
Whose tender blossoms tremble every one
At every little breath that thorough heaven is blown.
Then in my coach, like Saturn's royal son
Mounted his shining chariot gilt with fire,
And drawn with princely eagles through the path
Pav'd with bright crystal and enchas'd with stars
When all the gods stand gazing at his pomp,

So will I ride through Samarcanda-streets,
Until my soul, dissever'd from this flesh,
Shall mount the milk-white way, and meet him there.
To Babylon, my lords, to Babylon! [*Exeunt.*

ACT V

SCENE I

Enter the GOVERNOR OF BABYLON, MAXIMUS, *and others, upon the walls.*

Gov. What saith Maximus?
Max. My lord, the breach the enemy hath made
Gives such assurance of our overthrow,
That little hope is left to save our lives,
Or hold our city from the conqueror's hands.
Then hang out flags, my lord, of humble truce,
And satisfy the people's general prayers,
That Tamburlaine's intolerable wrath
May be suppressed by our submission.
Gov. Villain, respect'st thou more thy slavish life
Than honour of thy country or thy name?
Is not my life and state as dear to me,
The city and my native country's weal,
As any thing of price with thy conceit?
Have we not hope, for all our batter'd walls,
To live secure and keep his forces out,
When this our famous lake of Limnasphaltis
Makes walls a-fresh with every thing that falls
Into the liquid substance of his stream,
More strong than are the gates of death or hell?
What faintness should dismay our courages,
When we are thus defenc'd against our foe,
And have no terror but his threatening looks?

Enter, above, a Citizen, *who kneels to the* GOVERNOR.

Cit. My lord, if ever you did deed of ruth,
And now will work a refuge to our lives,
Offer submission, hang up flags of truce,
That Tamburlaine may pity our distress,
And use us like a loving conqueror.
Though this be held his last day's dreadful siege,

Wherein he spareth neither man nor child,
Yet are there Christians of Georgia here,
Whose state he ever pitied and reliev'd,
Will get his pardon, if your grace would send.

Gov. How is my soul environed!
And this eternis'd city Babylon
Fill'd with a pack of faint-heart fugitives
That thus entreat their shame and servitude!

Enter, above, a Second Citizen.

Sec. Cit. My lord, if ever you will win our hearts,
Yield up the town, and save our wives and children;
For I will cast myself from off these walls,
Or die some death of quickest violence,
Before I bide the wrath of Tamburlaine.

Gov. Villains, cowards, traitors to our state!
Fall to the earth, and pierce the pit of hell,
That legions of tormenting spirits may vex
Your slavish bosoms with continual pains!
I care not, nor the town will never yield
As long as any life is in my breast.

Enter THERIDAMAS *and* TECHELLES, *with* Soldiers.

Ther. Thou desperate governor of Babylon,
To save thy life, and us a little labour,
Yield speedily the city to our hands,
Or else be sure thou shalt be forc'd with pains
More exquisite than ever traitor felt.

Gov. Tyrant, I turn the traitor in thy throat,
And will defend it in despite of thee.—
Call up the soldiers to defend these walls.

Tech. Yield, foolish governor; we offer more
Than ever yet we did to such proud slaves
As durst resist us till our third day's siege.
Thou seest us prest to give the last assault,
And that shall bide no more regard of parley.

Gov. Assault and spare not; we will never yield.
[*Alarms: and they scale the walls.*

Enter TAMBURLAINE, *drawn in his chariot* (*as before*) *by the* KINGS OF TREBIZON *and* SORIA; AMYRAS, CELEBINUS, USUMCASANE; ORCANES *king of Natolia, and the* KING OF JERUSALEM, *led by* Soldiers; *and others.*

Tamb. The stately buildings of fair Babylon,

Whose lofty pillars, higher than the clouds,
Were wont to guide the seaman in the deep,
Being carried thither by the cannon's force,
Now fill the mouth of Limnasphaltis' lake,
And make a bridge unto the batter'd walls.
Where Belus, Ninus, and great Alexander
Have rode in triumph, triumphs Tamburlaine,
Whose chariot-wheels have burst th' Assyrians' bones,
Drawn with these kings on heaps of carcasses.
Now in the place, where fair Semiramis,
Courted by kings and peers of Asia,
Hath trod the measures, do my soliders march;
And in the streets, where brave Assyrian dames
Have rid in pomp like rich Saturnia,
With furious words and frowning visages
My horsemen brandish their unruly blades.

Re-enter THERIDAMAS *and* TECHELLES, *bringing in the* GOVERNOR OF BABYLON

Who have ye there, my lords?
Ther. The sturdy governor of Babylon,
That made us all the labour for the town,
And us'd such slender reckoning of your majesty.
Tamb. Go, bind the villain; he shall hang in chains
Upon the ruins of this conquer'd town.—
Sirrah, the view of our vermilion tents
(Which threaten'd more than if the region
Next underneath the element of fire
Were full of comets and of blazing stars,
Whose flaming trains should reach down to the earth)
Could not affright you; no, nor I myself,
The wrathful messenger of mighty Jove,
That with his sword hath quail'd all earthly kings,
Could not persuade you to submission,
But still the ports were shut: villain, I say,
Should I but touch the rusty gates of hell,
The triple headed Cerberus would howl,
And wake black Jove to crouch and kneel to me;
But I have sent volleys of shot to you.
Yet could not enter till the breach was made.
Gov. Nor, if my body could have stopt the breach,
Shouldst thou have enter'd, cruel Tamburlaine.
'Tis not thy bloody tents can make me yield,

Nor yet thyself, the anger of the Highest;
For, though thy cannon shook the city-walls,
My heart did never quake, or courage faint.

Tamb. Well, now I'll make it quake.—Go draw him up,
Hang him in chains upon the city walls,
And let my soldiers shoot the slave to death.

Gov. Vile monster, born of some infernal hag,
And sent from hell to tryannise on earth,
Do all thy worst; nor death, nor Tamburlaine,
Torture, or pain, can daunt my dreadless mind.

Tamb. Up with him, then! his body shall be scarr'd.

Gov. But, Tamburlaine, in Limnasphaltis' lake
There lies more gold than Babylon is worth,
Which, when the city was besieg'd, I hid:
Save but my life, and I will give it thee.

Tamb. Then, for all your valour, you would save your life?
Whereabout lies it?

Gov. Under a hollow bank, right opposite
Against the western gate of Babylon.

Tamb. Go thither, some of you, and take his gold:—
[*Exeunt some Attendants.*
The rest forward with execution.
Away with him hence, let him speak no more.—
I think I make your courage something quail.—
[*Exeunt Attendants with the Governor of Babylon.*
When this is done, we'll march from Babylon,
And make our greatest haste to Persia.
These jades are broken winded and half-tir'd;
Unharness them, and let me have fresh horse.
[*Attendants unharness the Kings of Trebizon and Soria.*
So; now their best is done to honour me,
Take them and hang them both up presently.

K. of Treb. Vile tyrant! barbarous bloody Tamburlaine!

Tamb. Take them away, Theridamas; see them despatch'd.

Ther. I will, my lord.
[*Exit with the Kings of Trebizon and Soria.*

Tamb. Come, Asian viceroys; to your tasks a while,
And take such fortune as your fellows felt.

Orc. First let thy Scythian horse tear both our limbs,
Rather than we should draw thy chariot,
And, like base slaves, abject our princely minds
To vile and ignominious servitude.

K. of Jer. Rather lend me thy weapon, Tamburlaine.

That I may sheathe it in this breast of mine.
A thousand deaths could not torment our hearts
More than the thought of this doth vex our souls.

Amy. They will talk still, my lord, if you do not bridle them

Tamb. Bridle them, and let me to my coach.

[*Attendants bridle Orcanes king of Natolia, and the King of Jerusalem, and harness them to the chariot.—The Governor of Babylon appears hanging in chains on the walls.—Re-enter* THERIDAMAS.

Amy. See, now, my lord, how brave the captain hangs!

Tamb. 'Tis brave indeed, my boy:—well done!—
Shoot first, my lord, and then the rest shall follow.

Ther. Then have at him, to begin withal.

[*Theridamas shoots at the Governor.*

Gov. Yet save my life, and let this wound appease
The mortal fury of great Tamburlaine!

Tamb. No, though Asphaltis' lake were liquid gold,
And offer'd me as ransom for thy life,
Yet shouldst thou die.—Shoot at him all at once.

[*They shoot*

So, now he hangs like Bagdet's governor,
Having as many bullets in his flesh
As there be breaches in her batter'd wall.
Go now, and bind the burghers hand and foot,
And cast them headlong in the city's lake.
Tartars and Persians shall inhabit there;
And, to command the city, I will build
A citadel, that all Africa,
Which hath been subject to the Persian king,
Shall pay me tribute for in Babylon.

Tech. What shall be done with their wives and children, my lord?

Tamb. Techelles, drown them all, man, woman, and child;
Leave not a Babylonian in the town.

Tech. I will about it straight.—Come, soldiers.

[*Exit with Soldiers.*

Tamb. Now, Casane, where's the Turkish Alcoran,
And all the heaps of superstitious books
Found in the temples of that Mahomet
Whom I have thought a god? they shall be burnt.

Usum. Here they are, my lord.

Tamb. Well said! let there be a fire presently.

[*They light a fire.*

In vain, I see, men worship Mahomet:
My sword hath sent millions of Turks to hell,
Slew all his priests, his kinsmen, and his friends,
And yet I live untouch'd by Mahomet.
There is a God, full of revenging wrath,
From whom the thunder and the lightning breaks,
Whose scourge I am, and him will I obey.
So, Casane; fling them in the fire.—

[*They burn the books.*

Now, Mahomet, if thou have any power,
Come down thyself and work a miracle:
Thou art not worthy to be worshipped
That suffer'st flames of fire to burn the writ
Wherein the sum of thy religion rests:
Why send'st thou not a furious whirlwind down,
To blow thy Alcoran up to thy throne,
Where men report thou sitt'st by God himself?
Or vengeance on the head of Tamburlaine
That shakes his sword against thy majesty,
And spurns the abstracts of thy foolish laws?—
Well, soldiers, Mahomet remains in hell;
He cannot hear the voice of Tamburlaine:
Seek out another godhead to adore;
The God that sits in heaven, if any god,
For he is God alone, and none but he.

Re-enter TECHELLES.

Tech. I have fulfill'd your highness' will, my lord:
Thousands of men, drown'd in Asphaltis' lake,
Have made the water swell above the banks,
And fishes, fed by human carcasses,
Amaz'd, swim up and down upon the waves,
As when they swallow assafœtida,
Which makes them fleet aloft and gasp for air.

Tamb. Well, then, my friendly lords, what now remains.
But that we leave sufficient garrison,
And presently depart to Persia,
To triumph after all our victories?

Ther. Ay, good my lord, let us in haste to Persia;
And let this captain be remov'd the walls
To some high hill about the city here.

Tamb. Let it be so;—about it, soldiers;—
But stay; I feel myself distemper'd suddenly.

Tech. What is it dares distemper Tamburlaine?

Tamb. Something, Techelles; but I know not what.—
But, forth, ye vassals! whatsoe'er it be,
Sickness or death can never conquer me.
[*Exeunt.*

SCENE II

Enter CALLAPINE, KING OF AMASIA, a Captain, *and train, with drums and trumpets.*

Call. King of Amasia, now our mighty host
Marcheth in Asia Major, where the streams
Of Euphrates and Tigris swiftly run;
And here may we behold great Babylon,
Circled about with Limnasphaltis' lake,
Where Tamburlaine with all his army lies,
Which being faint and weary with the siege,
We may lie ready to encounter him
Before his host be full from Babylon,
And so revenge our latest grievous loss,
If God or Mahomet send any aid.

K. of Ama. Doubt not, my lord, but we shall conquer him:
The monster that hath drunk a sea of blood,
And yet gapes still for more to quench his thirst,
Our Turkish swords shall headlong send to hell;
And that vile carcass, drawn by warlike kings,
The fowls shall eat; for never sepulchre
Shall grace this base-born tyrant Tamburlaine.

Call. When I record my parents' slavish life,
Their cruel death, mine own captivity,
My viceroys' bondage under Tamburlaine,
Methinks I could sustain a thousand deaths,
To be reveng'd of all his villany.—
Ah, sacred Mahomet, thou that hast seen
Millions of Turks perish by Tamburlaine,
Kingdoms made waste, brave cities sack'd and burnt,
And but one host is left to honour thee,
Aid thy obedient servant Callapine,
And make him, after all these overthrows,
To triumph over cursed Tamburlaine!

K. of Ama. Fear not, my lord: I see great Mahomet,
Clothed in purple clouds, and on his head
A chaplet brighter than Apollo's crown,

Marching about the air with armed men,
To join with you against this Tamburlaine.

Capt. Renowned general, mighty Callapine,
Though God himself and holy Mahomet
Should come in person to resist your power,
Yet might your mighty host encounter all,
And pull proud Tamburlaine upon his knees
To sue for mercy at your highness' feet.

Call. Captain, the force of Tamburlaine is great,
His fortune greater, and the victories
Wherewith he hath so sore dismay'd the world
Are greatest to discourage all our drifts;
Yet, when the pride of Cynthia is at full,
She wanes again; and so shall his, I hope;
For we have here the chief selected men
Of twenty several kingdoms at the least;
Nor ploughman, priest, nor merchant, stays at home;
All Turkey is in arms with Callapine;
And never will we sunder camps and arms
Before himself or his be conquered:
This is the time that must eternise me
For conquering the tyrant of the world.
Come, soldiers, let us lie in wait for him,
And, if we find him absent from his camp,
Or that it be rejoin'd again at full,
Assail it, and be sure of victory. [*Exeunt.*

SCENE III

Enter THERIDAMAS, TECHELLES, *and* USUMCASANE.

Ther. Weep, heavens, and vanish into liquid tears!
Fall, stars that govern his nativity,
And summon all the shining lamps of heaven
To cast their bootless fires to the earth,
And shed their feeble influence in the air;
Muffle your beauties with eternal clouds;
For Hell and Darkness pitch their pitchy tents,
And Death, with armies of Cimmerian spirits,
Gives battle 'gainst the heart of Tamburlaine!
Now, in defiance of that wonted love
Your sacred virtues pour'd upon his throne,
And made his state an honour to the heavens,
These cowards invisibly assail his soul,

And threaten conquest on our sovereign;
But, if he die, your glories are disgrac'd,
Earth droops, and says that hell in heaven is plac'd!

Tech. O, then, ye powers that sway eternal seats,
And guide this massy substance of the earth,
If you retain desert of holiness,
As your supreme estates instruct our thoughts,
Be not inconstant, careless of your fame,
Bear not the burden of your enemies' joys,
Triumphing in his fall whom you advanc'd;
But, as his birth, life, health, and majesty
Were strangely blest and governed by heaven,
So honour, heaven (till heaven dissolved be,)
His birth, his life, his health, and majesty!

Usum. Blush, heaven, to lose the honour of thy name,
To see thy footstool set upon thy head;
And let no baseness in thy haughty breast
Sustain a shame of such inexcellence,
To see the devils mount in angels' thrones,
And angels dive into the pools of hell!
And, though they think their painful date is out,
And that their power is puissant as Jove's,
Which makes them manage arms against thy state,
Yet make them feel the strength of Tamburlaine
(Thy instrument and note of majesty)
Is greater far than they can thus subdue;
For, if he die, thy glory is disgrac'd,
Earth droops, and says that hell in heaven is plac'd!

Enter TAMBURLAINE, *drawn in his chariot* (*as before*) *by* ORCANES *king of Natolia, and the* KING OF JERUSALEM, AMYRAS, CELEBINUS, *and* Physicians.

Tamb. What daring god torments my body thus,
And seeks to conquer mighty Tamburlaine?
Shall sickness prove me now to be a man,
That have been term'd the terror of the world?
Techelles and the rest, come, take your swords,
And threaten him whose hand afflicts my soul:
Come, let us march against the powers of heaven,
And set black streamers in the firmament,
To signify the slaughter of the gods.
Ah, friends, what shall I do? I cannot stand.
Come, carry me to war against the gods,

That thus envy the health of Tamburlaine.
Ther. Ah, good my lord, leave these impatient words,
Which add much danger to your malady!
Tamb. Why, shall I sit and languish in this pain?
No, strike the drums, and, in revenge of this,
Come, let us charge our spears, and pierce his breast
Whose shoulders bear the axis of the world,
That, if I perish, heaven and earth may fade.
Theridamas, haste to the court of Jove;
Will him to send Apollo hither straight,
To cure me, or I'll fetch him down myself.
Tech. Sit still, my gracious lord; this grief will cease,
And cannot last, it is so violent.
Tamb. Not last, Techelles! no, for I shall die.
See, where my slave, the ugly monster Death,
Shaking and quivering, pale and wan for fear,
Stands aiming at me with his murdering dart,
Who flies away at every glance I give,
And, when I look away, comes stealing on!—
Villain, away, and hie thee to the field!
I and mine army come to load thy bark
With souls of thousand mangled carcasses.—
Look, where he goes! but, see, he comes again,
Because I stay! Techelles, let us march,
And weary Death with bearing souls to hell.
First Phy. Pleaseth your majesty to drink this potion,
Which will abate the fury of your fit,
And cause some milder spirits govern you.
Tamb. Tell me what think you of my sickness now?
First Phy. I view'd your urine, and the hypostasis,
Thick and obscure, doth make your danger great:
Your veins are full of accidental heat,
Whereby the moisture of your blood is dried:
The humidum and calor, which some hold
Is not a parcel of the elements,
But of a substance more divine and pure,
Is almost clean extinguished and spent;
Which, being the cause of life, imports your death:
Besides, my lord, this day is critical,
Dangerous to those whose crisis is as yours:
Your artiers, which alongst the veins convey
The lively spirits which the heart engenders,
Are parch'd and void of spirit, that the soul,

Wanting those organons by which it moves,
Cannot endure, by argument of art.
Yet, if your majesty may escape this day,
No doubt but you shall soon recover all.

Tamb. Then will I comfort all my vital parts,
And live, in spite of death, above a day.

[*Alarms within.*

Enter a Messenger.

Mes. My lord, young Callapine, that lately fled from your majesty, hath now gathered a fresh army, and, hearing your absence in the field, offers to set upon us presently.

Tamb. See, my physicians, now, how Jove hath sent
A present medicine to recure my pain!
My looks shall make them fly; and, might I follow,
There should not one of all the villain's power
Live to give offer of another fight.

Usum. I joy, my lord, your highness is so strong,
That can endure so well your royal presence,
Which only will dismay the enemy.

Tamb. I know it will, Casane.—Draw, you slaves!
In spite of death, I will go show my face.

[*Alarms. Exit Tamburlaine with all the rest (except the Physicians), and re-enter presently.*

Tamb. Thus are the villain cowards fled for fear,
Like summer's vapours vanish'd by the sun;
And, could I but a while pursue the field,
That Callapine should be my slave again.
But I perceive my martial strength is spent:
In vain I strive and rail against those powers
That mean t' invest me in a higher throne,
As much too high for this disdainful earth.
Give me a map; then let me see how much
Is left for me to conquer all the world.
That these, my boys, may finish all my wants.

[*One brings a map.*

Here I began to march towards Persia,
Along Armenia and the Caspian Sea,
And thence unto Bithynia, where I took
The Turk and his great empress prisoners.
Then march'd I into Egypt and Arabia;
And here, not far from Alexandria,
Whereas the Terrene and the Red Sea meet.

Being distant less than full a hundred leagues,
I meant to cut a channel to them both,
That men might quickly sail to India.
From thence to Nubia near Borno-lake,
And so along the Æthiopian sea,
Cutting the tropic line of Capricorn,
I conquer'd all as far as Zanzibar.
Then, by the northern part of Africa,
I came at last to Græcia, and from thence
To Asia, where I stay against my will;
Which is from Scythia, where I first began,
Backward[s] and forwards near five thousand leagues.
Look here, my boys; see, what a world of ground
Lies westward from the midst of Cancer's line
Unto the rising of this earthly globe,
Whereas the sun, declining from our sight,
Begins the day with our Antipodes!
And shall I die, and this unconquered?
Lo, here, my sons, are all the golden mines,
Inestimable drugs and precious stones,
More worth than Asia and the world beside;
And from th'Antarctic Pole eastward behold
As much more land, which never was descried,
Wherein are rocks of pearl that shine as bright
As all the lamps that beautify the sky!
And shall I die, and this unconquered?
Here, lovely boys; what death forbids my life,
That let your lives command in spite of death.

Amy. Alas, my lord, how should our bleeding hearts,
Wounded and broken with your highness' grief,
Retain a thought of joy or spark of life?
Your soul gives essence to our wretched subjects,
Whose matter is incorporate in your flesh.

Cel. Your pains do pierce our souls; no hope survives,
For by your life we entertain our lives.

Tamb. But, sons, this subject, not of force enough
To hold the fiery spirit it contains,
Must part, imparting his impressions
By equal portions into both your breasts;
My flesh, divided in your precious shapes,
Shall still retain my spirit, though I die,
And live in all your seeds immortally.—
Then now remove me, that I may resign

My place and proper title to my son.—
First, take my scourge and my imperial crown,
And mount my royal chariot of estate,
That I may see thee crown'd before I die.—
Help me, my lords, to make my last remove.
[*They assist Tamburlaine to descend from the chariot.*
Ther. A woful change, my lord, that daunts our thoughts
More than the ruin of our proper souls!
Tamb. Sit up, my son, let me see how well
Thou wilt become thy father's majesty.
Amy. With what a flinty bosom should I joy
The breath of life and burden of my soul,
If not resolv'd into resolved pains,
My body's mortified lineaments
Should exercise the motions of my heart,
Pierc'd with the joy of any dignity!
O father, if the unrelenting ears
Of Death and Hell be shut against my prayers,
And that the spiteful influence of Heaven
Deny my soul fruition of her joy,
How should I step, or stir my hateful feet
Against the inward powers of my heart,
Leading a life that only strives to die,
And plead in vain unpleasing sovereignty?
Tamb. Let not thy love exceed thine honour, son,
Nor bar thy mind that magnanimity
That nobly must admit necessity.
Sit up, my boy, and with these silken reins
Bridle the steeled stomachs of these jades.
Ther. My lord, you must obey his majesty,
Since fate commands and proud necessity.
Amy. Heavens witness me with what a broken heart
[*Mounting the chariot.*
And damned spirit I ascend this seat,
And send my soul, before my father die,
His anguish and his burning agony!
[*They crown Amyras.*
Tamb. Now fetch the hearse of fair Zenocrate;
Let it be plac'd by this my fatal chair,
And serve as parcel of my funeral.
Usum. Then feels your majesty no sovereign ease,
Nor may our hearts, all drown'd in tears of blood,
Joy any hope of your recovery?

Tamb. Casane, no; the monarch of the earth,
And eyeless monster that torments my soul,
Cannot behold the tears ye shed for me,
And therefore still augments his cruelty.
Tech. Then let some god oppose his holy power
Against the wrath and tyranny of Death,
That his tear-thirsty and unquenched hate
May be upon himself reverberate!
[*They bring in the hearse of Zenocrate.*
Tamb. Now, eyes, enjoy your latest benefit,
And, when my soul hath virtue of your sight,
Pierce through the coffin and the sheet of gold,
And glut your longings with a heaven of joy.
So, reign, my son; scourge and control those slaves,
Guiding thy chariot with thy father's hand.
As precious is the charge thou undertak'st
As that which Clymene's brain-sick son did guide,
When wandering Phœbe's ivory cheeks were scorch'd,
And all the earth, like Ætna, breathing fire:
Be warn'd by him, then learn with awful eye
To sway a throne as dangerous as his;
For, if thy body thrive not full of thoughts
As pure and fiery as Phyteus' beams,
The nature of these proud rebelling jades
Will take occasion by the slenderest hair,
And draw thee piecemeal, like Hippolytus,
Through rocks more steep and sharp than Caspian cliffs:
The nature of thy chariot will not bear
A guide of baser temper than myself,
More than heaven's coach the pride of Phaeton.
Farewell, my boys! my dearest friends, farewell!
My body feels, my soul doth weep to see
Your sweet desires depriv'd my company,
For Tamburlaine, the scourge of God, must die.
[*Dies.*
Amy. Meet heaven and earth, and here let all things end,
For earth hath spent the pride of all her fruit,
And heaven consum'd his choicest living fire!
Let earth and heaven his timeless death deplore,
For both their worths will equal him no more!
[*Exeunt.*

THE TRAGICAL HISTORY OF DOCTOR FAUSTUS

FROM THE QUARTO OF 1604

DRAMATIS PERSONÆ

THE POPE.
CARDINAL OF LORRAIN.
THE EMPEROR OF GERMANY.
DUKE OF VANHOLT.
FAUSTUS.
VALDES, } *friends to* FAUSTUS.
CORNELIUS, } *friends to* FAUSTUS.
WAGNER, *servant to* FAUSTUS.
CLOWN.
ROBIN.
RALPH.
VINTNER.
HORSE-COURSER.
A KNIGHT.
AN OLD MAN.
SCHOLARS, FRIARS, *and* ATTENDANTS.

DUCHESS OF VANHOLT.

LUCIFER.
BELZEBUB.
MEPHISTOPHILIS.
GOOD ANGEL.
EVIL ANGEL.
THE SEVEN DEADLY SINS.
DEVILS.
SPIRITS *in the shapes of* ALEXANDER THE GREAT, *of his* PARAMOUR *and of* HELEN.
CHORUS.

Enter Chorus.

Chorus. Not marching now in fields of Thrasymene,
Where Mars did mate the Carthaginians;
Nor sporting in the dalliance of love,
In courts of kings where state is overturn'd;
Nor in the pomp of proud audacious deeds,
Intends our Muse to vaunt her heavenly verse:
Only this, gentlemen,—we must perform
The form of Faustus' fortunes, good or bad:
To patient judgments we appeal our plaud,
And speak for Faustus in his infancy.
Now is he born, his parents base of stock,
In Germany, within a town call'd Rhodes:
Of riper years, to Wertenberg he went,
Whereas his kinsmen chiefly brought him up.
So soon he profits in divinity,

The fruitful plot of scholarism grac'd,
That shortly he was grac'd with doctor's name,
Excelling all whose sweet delight disputes
In heavenly matters of theology;
Till swoln with cunning, of a self-conceit,
His waxen wings did mount above his reach,
And melting heavens conspir'd his overthrow;
For, falling to a devilish exercise,
And glutted now with learning's golden gifts,
He surfeits upon cursed necromancy;
Nothing so sweet as magic is to him,
Which he prefers before his chiefest bliss:
And this the man that in his study sits. [*Exit.*

FAUSTUS *discovered in his study.*

Faust. Settle thy studies, Faustus, and begin
To sound the depth of that thou wilt profess:
Having commenc'd, be a divine in show,
Yet level at the end of every art,
And live and die in Aristotle's works.
Sweet Analytics, 'tis thou hast ravish'd me!
Bene disserere est finis logices.
Is, to dispute well, logic's chiefest end?
Affords this art no greater miracle?
Then read no more; thou hast attain'd the end:
A greater subject fitteth Faustus' wit:
Bid ὂν καὶ μὴ ὂν farewell, Galen come,
Seeing, *Ubi desinit philosophus, ibi incipit medicus:*
Be a physician, Faustus; heap up gold,
And be eternis'd for some wondrous cure:
Summum bonum medicinæ sanitas,
The end of physic is our body's health.
Why, Faustus, hast thou not attain'd that end?
Is not thy common talk found aphorisms?
Are not thy bills hung up as monuments,
Whereby whole cities have escap'd the plague,
And thousand desperate maladies been eas'd?
Yet art thou still but Faustus, and a man.
Couldst thou make men to live eternally,
Or, being dead, raise them to life again,
Then this profession were to be esteem'd.
Physic, farewell! Where is Justinian? [*Reads.*

Si una eademque res legatur duobus, alter rem, alter valorem, rei, etc.
A pretty case of paltry legacies! [*Reads.*
Exhæreditare filium non potest pater, nisi, etc.
Such is the subject of the institute,
And universal body of the Church:
His study fits a mercenary drudge,
Who aims at nothing but external trash;
Too servile and illiberal for me.
When all is done, divinity is best:
Jerome's Bible, Faustus; view it well. [*Reads.*
Stipendium peccati mors est. Ha! *Stipendium, etc.*
The reward of sin is death: that's hard. [*Reads.*
Si peccasse negamus, fallimur, et nulla est in nobis veritas ;
If we say that we have no sin, we deceive ourselves, and there's no truth in us. Why, then, belike we must sin, and so consequently die:
Ay, we must die an everlasting death.
What doctrine call you this, *Che sera, sera,*
What will be, shall be? Divinity, adieu!
These metaphysics of magicians,
And necromantic books are heavenly;
Lines, circles, scenes, letters, and characters;
Ay, these are those that Faustus most desires.
O, what a world of profit and delight,
Of power, of honour, of omnipotence,
Is promis'd to the studious artisan!
All things that move between the quiet poles
Shall be at my command: emperors and kings
Are but obeyed in their several provinces,
Nor can they raise the wind, or rend the clouds;
But his dominion that exceeds in this,
Stretcheth as far as doth the mind of man;
A sound magician is a mighty god:
Here, Faustus, try thy brains to gain a deity.

Enter WAGNER.

Wagner, commend me to my dearest friends,
The German Valdes and Cornelius;
Request them earnestly to visit me.
Wag. I will, sir. [*Exit.*
Faust. Their conference will be a greater help to me
Than all my labours, plod I ne'er so fast.

Enter Good Angel *and* Evil Angel.

G. Ang. O, Faustus, lay thy damned book aside,
And gaze not on it, lest it tempt thy soul,
And heap God's heavy wrath upon thy head!
Read, read the Scriptures:—that is blasphemy.
E. Ang. Go forward, Faustus, in that famous art
Wherein all Nature's treasury is contain'd:
Be thou on earth as Jove is in the sky,
Lord and commander of these elements.
[*Exeunt Angels.*
Faust. How am I glutted with conceit of this!
Shall I make spirits fetch me what I please,
Resolve me of all ambiguities,
Perform what desperate enterprise I will?
I'll have them fly to India for gold,
Ransack the ocean for orient pearl,
And search all corners of the new-found world
For pleasant fruits and princely delicates;
I'll have them read me strange philosophy,
And tell the secrets of all foreign kings;
I'll have them wall all Germany with brass,
And make swift Rhine circle fair Wertenberg;
I'll have them fill the public schools with silk,
Wherewith the students shall be bravely clad;
I'll levy soldiers with the coin they bring,
And chase the Prince of Parma from our land,
And reign sole king of all our provinces;
Yea, stranger engines for the brunt of war,
Than was the fiery keel at Antwerp's bridge,
I'll make my servile spirits to invent.

Enter VALDES *and* CORNELIUS.

Come, German Valdes and Cornelius,
And make me blest with your sage conference.
Valdes, sweet Valdes, and Cornelius,
Know that your words have won me at the last
To practise magic and concealed arts:
Yet not your words only, but mine own fantasy,
That will receive no object for my head,
But ruminates on necromantic skill.
Philosophy is odious and obscure;
Both law and physic are for petty wits;

Divinity is basest of the three,
Unpleasant, harsh, contemptible, and vile:
'Tis magic, magic, that hath ravish'd me.
Then, gentle friends, aid me in this attempt;
And I, that have with concise syllogisms
Gravell'd the pastors of the German church,
And made the flowering pride of Wertenberg
Swarm to my problems, as the infernal spirits
On sweet Musæus when he came to hell,
Will be as cunning as Agrippa was,
Whose shadow made all Europe honour him.

Vald. Faustus, these books, thy wit, and our experience,
Shall make all nations to canonise us.
As Indian Moors obey their Spanish lords,
So shall the subjects of every element
Be always serviceable to us three;
Like lions shall they guard us when we please;
Like Almain rutters with their horsemen's staves
Or Lapland giants, trotting by our sides;
Sometimes like women, or unwedded maids,
Shadowing more beauty in their airy brows
Than have the white breasts of the queen of love:
From Venice shall they drag huge argosies,
And from America the golden fleece
That yearly stuffs old Philip's treasury;
If learned Faustus will be resolute.

Faust. Valdes, as resolute am I in this
As thou to live: therefore object it not.

Corn. The miracles that magic will perform
Will make thee vow to study nothing else.
He that is grounded in astrology,
Enrich'd with tongues, well seen in minerals,
Hath all the principles magic doth require:
Then doubt not, Faustus, but to be renowm'd,
And more frequented for this mystery
Than heretofore the Delphian oracle.
The spirits tell me they can dry the sea,
And fetch the treasure of all foreign wrecks,
Ay, all the wealth that our forefathers hid
Within the massy entrails of the earth:
Then tell me, Faustus, what shall we three want?

Faust. Nothing, Cornelius. O, this cheers my soul!
Come, show me some demonstrations magical,

That I may conjure in some lusty grove,
And have these joys in full possession.

Vald. Then haste thee to some solitary grove,
And bear wise Bacon's and Albertus' works,
The Hebrew Psalter, and New Testament;
And whatsoever else is requisite
We will inform thee ere our conference cease.

Corn. Valdes, first let him know the words of art;
And then, all other ceremonies learn'd,
Faustus may try his cunning by himself.

Vald. First I'll instruct thee in the rudiments,
And then wilt thou be perfecter than I.

Faust, Then come and dine with me, and, after meat,
We'll canvass every quiddity thereof;
For, ere I sleep, I'll try what I can do:
This night I'll conjure, though I die therefore.

[*Exeunt.*

Enter two Scholars.

First Schol. I wonder what's become of Faustus, that was wont to make our schools ring with *sic probo.*

Sec. Schol. That shall we know, for see, here comes his boy.

Enter WAGNER

First Schol. How now, sirrah! where's thy master?

Wag. God in heaven knows.

Sec. Schol. Why, dost not thou know?

Wag. Yes, I know; but that follows not.

First Schol. Go to, sirrah! leave your jesting, and tell us where he is.

Wag. That follows not necessary by force of argument, that you, being licentiate, should stand upon 't: therefore acknowledge your error, and be attentive.

Sec. Schol. Why, didst thou not say thou knewest?

Wag. Have you any witness on't?

First Schol. Yes, sirrah, I heard you.

Wag. Ask my fellow if I be a thief.

Sec. Schol. Well, you will not tell us?

Wag. Yes, sir, I will tell you; yet, if you were not dunces, you would never ask me such a question, for is not he *corpus naturale?* and is not that *mobile?* then wherefore should you ask me such a question? But that I am by nature phlegmatic, slow to wrath, and prone to lechery (to love, I would say), it were not for you to come within forty foot of the place of execution, although I do not doubt to see you both hanged the next sessions. Thus having triumphed over you, I will set my countenance like a precisian, and begin to speak thus:—Truly, my dear brethren, my master is within at dinner, with Valdes and Cornelius, as this wine, if it could speak, it would inform your worships: and so, the Lord bless you, preserve you, and keep you, my dear brethren, my dear brethren! [*Exit.*

First Schol. Nay, then, I fear he is fallen into that damned art for which they two are infamous through the world.

Sec. Schol. Were he a stranger, and not allied to me, yet should I grieve for him. But, come, let us go and inform the Rector, and see if he by his grave counsel can reclaim him.

First Schol. O, but I fear me nothing can reclaim him!

Sec. Schol. Yet let us try what we can do. [*Exeunt.*

Enter FAUSTUS *to conjure.*

Faust. Now that the gloomy shadow of the earth,
Longing to view Orion's drizzling look,
Leaps from th' antarctic world unto the sky,
And dims the welkin with her pitchy breath,
Faustus, begin thine incantations,
And try if devils will obey thy hest,
Seeing thou hast pray'd and sacrific'd to them.
Within this circle is Jehovah's name,
Forward and backward anagrammatis'd,
Th' abbreviated names of holy saints,
Figures of every adjunct to the heavens,
And characters of signs and erring stars,
By which the spirits are enforc'd to rise:
Then fear not, Faustus, but be resolute,
And try the uttermost magic can perform.—
Sint mihi dei Acherontis propitii! Valeat numen triplex Jehovæ! Ignei, aërii, aquatani spiritus, salvete! Orientis princeps Belzebub, inferni ardentis monarcha, et Demogorgon, propitiamus vos, ut appareat et surgat Mephistophilis; quid tu moraris: per Jehovam, Gehennam, et consecratam aquam quam nunc spargo, signumque crucis quod nunc facio, et per vota nostra, ipse nunc surgat nobis dicatus Mephistophilis!

Enter MEPHISTOPHILIS.

I charge thee to return, and change thy shape;
Thou art too ugly to attend on me:
Go, and return an old Franciscan friar;
That holy shape becomes a devil best.
[*Exit Mephistophilis.*
I see there's virtue in my heavenly words:
Who would not be proficient in this art?
How pliant is this Mephistophilis,
Full of obedience and humility!
Such is the force of magic and my spells:
No, Faustus, thou art conjuror laureat,
That canst command great Mephistophilis:
Quin regis Mephistophilis fratris imagine.

Re-enter MEPHISTOPHILIS *like a Franciscan friar.*

Meph. Now, Faustus, what wouldst thou have me do?
Faust. I charge thee wait upon me whilst I live,
To do whatever Faustus shall command,
Be it to make the moon drop from her sphere,
Or the ocean to overwhelm the world.
Meph. I am a servant to great Lucifer,
And may not follow thee without his leave:
No more than he commands must we perform.
Faust. Did not he charge thee to appear to me?
Meph. No, I came now hither of mine own accord.
Faust. Did not my conjuring speeches raise thee? speak.
Meph. That was the cause, but yet *per accidens* ;
For, when we hear one rack the name of God,
Abjure the Scriptures and his Saviour Christ,
We fly, in hope to get his glorious soul;
Nor will we come, unless he use such means
Whereby he is in danger to be damn'd.
Therefore the shortest cut for conjuring
Is stoutly to abjure the Trinity,
And pray devoutly to the prince of hell.
Faust. So Faustus hath
Already done; and holds this principle,
There is no chief but only Belzebub;
To whom Faustus doth dedicate himself.
This word " damnation " terrifies not him,
For he confounds hell in Elysium:

His ghost be with the old philosophers!
But, leaving these vain trifles of men's souls,
Tell me what is that Lucifer thy lord?
Meph. Arch-regent and commander of all spirits.
Faust. Was not that Lucifer an angel once?
Meph. Yes, Faustus, and most dearly lov'd of God.
Faust. How comes it, then, that he is prince of devils?
Meph. O, by aspiring pride and insolence;
For which God threw him from the face of heaven.
Faust. And what are you that live with Lucifer?
Meph. Unhappy spirits that fell with Lucifer,
Conspir'd against our God with Lucifer,
And are for ever damn'd with Lucifer.
Faust. Where are you damn'd?
Meph. In hell.
Faust. How comes it, then, that thou art out of hell?
Meph. Why, this is hell, nor am I out of it.
Think'st thou that I, who saw the face of God,
And tasted the eternal joys of heaven,
Am not tormented with ten thousand hells,
In being depriv'd of everlasting bliss?
O, Faustus, leave these frivolous demands,
Which strike a terror to my fainting soul!
Faust. What, is great Mephistophilis so passionate
For being deprived of the joys of heaven?
Learn thou of Faustus manly fortitude,
And scorn those joys thou never shalt possess.
Go bear these tidings to great Lucifer:
Seeing Faustus hath incurr'd eternal death
By desperate thoughts against Jove's deity,
Say, he surrenders up to him his soul,
So he will spare him four-and-twenty years,
Letting him live in all voluptuousness;
Having thee ever to attend on me,
To give me whatsoever I shall ask,
To tell me whatsoever I demand,
To slay mine enemies, and aid my friends,
And always be obedient to my will.
Go and return to mighty Lucifer,
And meet me in my study at midnight,
And then resolve me of thy master's mind.
Meph. I will, Faustus. [*Exit.*
Faust. Had I as many souls as there be stars

I'd give them all for Mephistophilis.
By him I'll be great emperor of the world,
And make a bridge thorough the moving air,
To pass the ocean with a band of men;
I'll join the hills that bind the Afric shore,
And make that land continent to Spain,
And both contributory to my crown:
The Emperor shall not live but by my leave,
Nor any potentate of Germany.
Now that I have obtained what I desire,
I'll live in speculation of this art,
Till Mephistophilis return again. [*Exit.*

Enter WAGNER *and* Clown.

Wag. Sirrah boy, come hither.

Clown. How, boy! swowns, boy! I hope you have seen many boys with such pickadevaunts as I have: boy, quotha!

Wag. Tell me, sirrah, hast thou any comings in?

Clown. Ay, and goings out too; you may see else.

Wag. Alas, poor slave! see how poverty jesteth in his nakedness! the villain is bare and out of service, and so hungry, that I know he would give his soul to the devil for a shoulder of mutton, though it were blood-raw.

Clown. How! my soul to the devil for a shoulder of mutton, though 'twere blood-raw! not so, good friend: by'r lady, I had need have it well roasted, and good sauce to it, if I pay so dear.

Wag. Well, wilt thou serve me, and I'll make thee go like *Qui mihi discipulus?*

Clown. How, in verse?

Wag. No, sirrah; in beaten silk and staves-acre.

Clown. How, how, knaves-acre! ay, I thought that was all the land his father left him. Do you hear? I would be sorry to rob you of your living.

Wag. Sirrah, I say in staves-acre.

Clown. Oho, oho, staves-acre! why, then, belike, if I were your man, I should be full of vermin.

Wag. So thou shalt, whether thou beest with me or no. But, sirrah, leave your jesting, and bind yourself presently unto me for seven years, or I'll turn all the lice about thee into familiars, and they shall tear thee in pieces.

Clown. Do you hear, sir? you may save that labour; they

are too familiar with me already: swowns, they are as bold with my flesh as if they had paid for my meat and drink.

Wag. Well, do your hear, sirrah? hold, take these guilders. [*Gives money*.

Clown. Gridirons! what be they?

Wag. Why, French crowns.

Clown. Mass, but for the name of French crowns, a man were as good have as many English counters. And what should I do with these?

Wag. Why, now, sirrah, thou art at an hour's warning, whensoever and wheresoever the devil shall fetch thee.

Clown. No, no; here, take your gridirons again.

Wag. Truly, I'll none of them.

Clown. Truly, but you shall.

Wag. Bear witness I gave them him.

Clown. Bear witness I give them you again.

Wag. Well, I will cause two devils presently to fetch thee away.—Baliol and Belcher!

Clown. Let your Baliol and your Belcher come here, and I'll knock them, they were never so knocked since they were devils: say I should kill one of them, what would folks say? "Do ye see yonder tall fellow in the round slop? he has killed the devil." So I should be called Kill-devil all the parish over.

Enter two Devils; *and the* Clown *runs up and down crying*.

Wag. Baliol and Belcher,—spirits, away! [*Exeunt Devils*.

Clown. What, are they gone? a vengeance on them! they have vile long nails. There was a he-devil and a she-devil: I'll tell you how you shall know them; all he-devils has horns, and all she-devils has clifts and cloven feet.

Wag. Well, sirrah, follow me.

Clown. But, do you hear? if I should serve you, would you teach me to raise up Banios and Belcheos?

Wag. I will teach thee to turn thyself to anything, to a dog, or a cat, or a mouse, or a rat, or anything.

Clown. How! a Christian fellow to a dog, or a cat, a mouse, or a rat! no, no, sir; if you turn me into anything, let it be in the likeness of a little pretty frisking flea, that I may be here and there and everywhere: O, I'll tickle the pretty wenches' plackets! I'll be amongst them, i'faith.

Wag. Well, sirrah, come.
Clown. But, do you hear, Wagner?
Wag. How!—Baliol and Belcher!
Clown. O Lord! I pray, sir, let Banio and Belcher go sleep.
Wag. Villain, call me Master Wagner, and let thy left eye be diametarily fixed upon my right heel, with *quasi vestigias nostras insistere.* [*Exit.*
Clown. God forgive me, he speaks Dutch fustian.
Well, I'll follow him; I'll serve him, that's flat. [*Exit.*

FAUSTUS *discovered in his study.*

Faust. Now, Faustus, must
Thou needs be damn'd, and canst thou not be sav'd:
What boots it, then, to think of God or heaven?
Away with such vain fancies, and despair;
Despair in God, and trust in Belzebub:
Now go not backward; no, Faustus, be resolute:
Why waver'st thou? O, something soundeth in mine ears,
"Abjure this magic, turn to God again!"
Ay, and Faustus will turn to God again.
To God? he loves thee not;
The god thou serv'st is thine own appetite,
Wherein is fix'd the love of Belzebub:
To him I'll build an altar and a church,
And offer lukewarm blood of new-born babes.

Enter Good Angel *and* Evil Angel.

G. Ang. Sweet Faustus, leave that execrable art.
Faust. Contrition, prayer, repentance—what of them?
G. Ang. O, they are means to bring thee unto heaven!
E. Ang. Rather illusions, fruits of lunacy,
That make men foolish that do trust them most.
G. Ang. Sweet Faustus, think of heaven and heavenly things.
E. Ang. No, Faustus; think of honour and of wealth.
[*Exeunt Angels.*
Faust. Of wealth!
Why, the signiory of Embden shall be mine.
When Mepistophilis shall stand by me,
What god can hurt thee, Faustus? thou art safe:
Cast no more doubts.—Come, Mephistophilis,
And bring glad tidings from great Lucifer;—

Is't not midnight?—come, Mephistophilis,
Veni, veni Mephistophile!

Enter MEPHISTOPHILIS.

Now tell me what says Lucifer, thy lord?
Meph. That I shall wait on Faustus whilst I live,
So he will buy my service with his soul.
Faust. Already Faustus hath hazarded that for thee.
Meph. But, Faustus, thou must bequeath it solemnly,
And write a deed of gift with thine own blood;
For that security craves great Lucifer.
If thou deny it, I will back to hell.
Faust. Stay, Mephistophilis, and tell me, what good will my soul do thy lord?
Meph. Enlarge his kingdom.
Faust. Is that the reason why he tempts us thus?
Meph. *Solamen miseris socios habuisse doloris.*
Faust. Why, have you any pain that torture others?
Meph. As great as have the human souls of men.
But, tell me, Faustus, shall I have thy soul?
And I will be thy slave, and wait on thee,
And give thee more than thou hast wit to ask.
Faust. Ay, Mephistophilis, I give it thee.
Meph. Then, Faustus, stab thy arm courageously,
And bind thy soul, that at some certain day
Great Lucifer may claim it as his own;
And then be thou as great as Lucifer.
Faust. [*Stabbing his arm*] Lo, Mephistophilis, for love of thee,
I cut mine arm, and with my proper blood
Assure my soul to be great Lucifer's,
Chief lord and regent of perpetual night!
View here the blood that trickles from mine arm,
And let it be propitious for my wish.
Meph. But, Faustus, thou must
Write it in manner of a deed of gift.
Faust. Ay, so I will [*Writes*]. But, Mephistophilis,
My blood congeals, and I can write no more.
Meph. I'll fetch thee fire to dissolve it straight. [*Exit.*
Faust. Why might the staying of my blood portend?
Is it unwilling I should write this bill?
Why streams it not, that I may write afresh?
Faustus gives to thee his soul: ah, there it stay'd!

Why shouldst thou not? is not thy soul thine own?
Then write again, *Faustus gives to thee his soul.*

Re-enter MEPHISTOPHILIS *with a chafer of coals.*

Meph. Here's fire; come, Faustus, set it on.
Faust. So, now the blood begins to clear again;
Now will I make an end immediately. [*Writes.*
Meph. O, what will not I do to obtain his soul! [*Aside.*
Faust. *Consummatum est;* this bill is ended,
And Faustus hath bequeathed his soul to Lucifer.
But what is this inscription on mine arm?
Homo, fuge: whither should I fly?
If unto God, he'll throw thee down to hell.
My senses are deceiv'd; here's nothing writ:—
I see it plain; here in this place is writ,
Homo, fuge: yet shall not Faustus fly.
Meph. I'll fetch him somewhat to delight his mind.
[*Aside, and then exit.*

Re-enter MEPHISTOPHILIS *with* Devils, *who give crowns and rich apparel to* FAUSTUS, *dance, and then depart.*

Faust. Speak, Mephistophilis, what means this show?
Meph. Nothing, Faustus, but to delight thy mind withal,
And to show thee what magic can perform.
Faust. But may I raise up spirits when I please?
Meph. Ay, Faustus, and do greater things than these.
Faust. Then there's enough for a thousand souls.
Here, Mephistophilis, receive this scroll,
A deed of gift of body and of soul:
But yet conditionally that thou perform
All articles prescrib'd between us both.
Meph. Faustus, I swear by hell and Lucifer
To effect all promises between us made!
Faust. Then hear me read them. [*Reads*] *On these conditions following. First that Faustus may be a spirit in form and substance. Secondly, that Mephistophilis shall be his servant, and at his command. Thirdly, that Mephistophilis shall do for him, and bring him whatsoever. Fourthly, that he shall be in his chamber or house invisible. Lastly, that he shall appear to the said John Faustus, at all times, in what form or shape soever he please. I, John Faustus, of Wertenberg, Doctor, by these presents, do give both body and soul to Lucifer prince of the east, and his minister*

Mephistophilis; and furthermore grant unto them, that, twenty-four years being expired, the articles above-written inviolate, full power to fetch or carry the said John Faustus, body and soul, flesh, blood, or goods, into their habitation wheresoever. By me, John Faustus.

Meph. Speak, Faustus, do you deliver this as your deed?
Faust. Ay, take it, and the devil give thee good on't!
Meph. Now, Faustus, ask what thou wilt.
Faust. First will I question with thee about hell.
Tell me, where is the place that men call hell?
Meph. Under the heavens.
Faust. Ay, but whereabout?
Meph. Within the bowels of these elements,
Where we are tortur'd and remain for ever:
Hell hath no limits, nor is circumscrib'd
In one self place; for where we are is hell,
And where hell is, there must we ever be:
And, to conclude, when all the world dissolves,
And every creature shall be purified,
All places shall be hell that are not heaven.
Faust. Come, I think hell's a fable.
Meph. Ay, think so still, till experience change thy mind.
Faust. Why, think'st thou, then, that Faustus shall be damn'd?
Meph. Ay, of necessity, for here's the scroll
Wherein thou hast given thy soul to Lucifer.
Faust. Ay, and body too: but what of that?
Think'st thou that Faustus is so fond to imagine
That, after this life, there is any pain?
Tush, these are trifles and mere old wives' tales.
Meph. But, Faustus, I am an instance to prove the contrary,
For I am damn'd, and am now in hell.
Faust. How! now in hell!
Nay, an this be hell, I'll willingly be damn'd here:
What! walking, disputing, etc.
But, leaving off this, let me have a wife,
The fairest maid in Germany;
For I am wanton and lascivious,
And cannot live without a wife.
Meph. How! a wife!
I prithee, Faustus, talk not of a wife.
Faust. Nay, sweet Mephistophilis, fetch me one, for I will have one.

Meph. Well, thou wilt have one? Sit there till I come: I'll fetch thee a wife in the devil's name. [*Exit.*

Re-enter MEPHISTOPHILIS *with a* Devil *drest like a* Woman, *with fireworks.*

Meph. Tell me, Faustus, how dost thou like thy wife?
Faust. A plague on her for a hot whore!
Meph. Tut, Faustus,
Marriage is but a ceremonial toy;
If thou lovest me, think no more of it.
I'll cull thee out the fairest courtesans,
And bring them every morning to thy bed:
She whom thine eye shall like, thy heart shall have,
Be she as chaste as was Penelope,
As wise as Saba, or as beautiful
As was bright Lucifer before his fall.
Hold, take this book, peruse it thoroughly: [*Gives book.*
The iterating of these lines brings gold;
The framing of this circle on the ground
Brings whirlwinds, tempests, thunder, and lightning;
Pronounce this thrice devoutly to thyself,
And men in armour shall appear to thee,
Ready to execute what thou desir'st.

Faust. Thanks, Mephistophilis: yet fain would I have a book wherein I might behold all spells and incantations, that I might raise up spirits when I please.

Meph. Here they are in this book. [*Turns to them.*

Faust. Now would I have a book where I might see all characters and planets of the heavens, that I might know their motions and dispositions.

Meph. Here they are too. [*Turns to them.*

Faust. Nay, let me have one book more,—and then I have done,—wherein I might see all plants, herbs, and trees, that grow upon the earth.

Meph. Here they be.

Faust. O, thou art deceived.

Meph. Tut, I warrant thee. [*Turns to them.*

Faust. When I behold the heavens, then I repent,
And curse thee, wicked Mephistophilis,
Because thou hast depriv'd me of those joys.
Meph. Why, Faustus,
Thinkest thou heaven is such a glorious thing?

I tell thee, 'tis not half so fair as thou,
Or any man that breathes on earth.
Faust. How prov'st thou that?
Meph. 'Twas made for man, therefore is man more excellent.
Faust. If it were made for man, 'twas made for me:
I will renounce this magic and repent.

Enter Good Angel *and* Evil Angel.

G. Ang. Faustus, repent; yet God will pity thee.
E. Ang. Thou art a spirit; God cannot pity thee.
Faust. Who buzzeth in mine ears I am a spirit?
Be I a devil, yet God may pity me;
Ay, God will pity me, if I repent.
E. Ang. Ay, but Faustus never shall repent.
[*Exeunt Angels.*
Faust. My heart's so harden'd, I cannot repent:
Scarce can I name salvation, faith, or heaven,
But fearful echoes thunder in mine ears,
"Faustus, thou art damn'd!" then swords, and knives,
Poison, guns, halters, and envenom'd steel
Are laid before me to despatch myself;
And long ere this I should have slain myself,
Had not sweet pleasure conquer'd deep despair.
Have not I made blind Homer sing to me
Of Alexander's love and Œnon's death?
And hath not he, that built the walls of Thebes
With ravishing sound of his melodious harp,
Made music with my Mephistophilis?
Why should I die, then, or basely despair!
I am resolv'd; Faustus shall ne'er repent.—
Come, Mephistophilis, let us dispute again,
And argue of divine astrology.
Tell me, are there many heavens above the moon?
Are all celestial bodies but one globe,
As is the substance of this centric earth?
Meph. As are the elements, such are the spheres,
Mutually folded in each other's orb,
And, Faustus,
All jointly move upon one axletree,
Whose terminus is term'd the world's wide pole;
Nor are the names of Saturn, Mars, or Jupiter
Feign'd, but are erring stars.

Faust. But, tell me, have they all one motion, both *situ et tempore?*

Meph. All jointly move from east to west in twenty-four hours upon the poles of the world; but differ in their motion upon the poles of the zodiac.

Faust. Tush,
These slender trifles Wagner can decide:
Hath Mephistophilis no greater skill?
Who knows not the double motion of the planets?
The first is finish'd in a natural day;
The second thus; as Saturn in thirty years; Jupiter in twelve; Mars in four; the Sun, Venus, and Mercury in a year; the Moon in twenty-eight days. Tush, these are freshmen's suppositions. But, tell me, hath every sphere a dominion or *intelligentia?*

Meph. Ay.

Faust. How many heavens or spheres are there?

Meph. Nine; the seven planets, the firmament, and the empyreal heaven.

Faust. Well resolve me in this question; why have we not conjunctions, oppositions, aspects, eclipses, all at one time, but in some years we have more, in some less?

Meph. Per inæqualem motum respectu totius.

Faust. Well, I am answered. Tell me who made the world?

Meph. I will not.

Faust. Sweet Mephistophilis, tell me.

Meph. Move me not, for I will not tell thee.

Faust. Villain, have I not bound thee to tell me anything?

Meph. Ay, that is not against our kingdom; but this is. Think thou on hell, Faustus, for thou art damned.

Faust. Think, Faustus, upon God that made the world.

Meph. Remember this. [*Exit.*

Faust. Ay, go, accursed spirit, to ugly hell!
'Tis thou hast damn'd distressed Faustus' soul
Is't not too late?

Re-enter Good Angel *and* Evil Angel.

E. Ang. Too late.

G. Ang. Never too late, if Faustus can repent,

E. Ang. If thou repent, devils shall tear thee in pieces.

G. Ang. Repent, and they shall never raze thy skin.

[*Exeunt Angels.*

Faust. Ah, Christ, my Saviour,
Seek to save distressed Faustus' soul!

Enter LUCIFER, BELZEBUB, *and* MEPHISTOPHILIS.

Luc. Christ cannot save thy soul, for he is just:
There's none but I have interest in the same.
Faust. O, who art thou that look'st so terrible?
Luc. I am Lucifer,
And this is my companion-prince in hell.
Faust. O, Faustus, they are come to fetch away thy soul!
Luc. We come to tell thee thou dost injure us;
Thou talk'st of Christ, contrary to thy promise:
Thou shouldst not think of God: think of the devil,
And of his dam too.
Faust. Nor will I henceforth: pardon me in this,
And Faustus vows never to look to heaven,
Never to name God, or to pray to Him,
To burn his Scriptures, slay his ministers,
And make my spirits pull his churches down.
Luc. Do so, and we will highly gratify thee.
Faustus, we are come from hell to show thee some pastime: sit down, and thou shalt see all the Seven Deadly Sins appear in their proper shapes.
Faust. That sight will be as pleasing unto me,
As Paradise was to Adam, the first day
Of his creation.
Luc. Talk not of Paradise nor creation; but mark this show: talk of the devil, and nothing else.—Come away!

Enter the Seven Deadly Sins.

Now, Faustus, examine them of their several names and dispositions.
Faust. What art thou, the first?
Pride. I am Pride. I disdain to have any parents. I am like to Ovid's flea; I can creep into every corner of a wench; sometimes, like a perriwig, I sit upon her brow; or, like a fan of feathers, I kiss her lips; indeed, I do—what do I not? But, fie, what a scent is here! I'll not speak another word, except the ground were perfumed, and covered with cloth of arras.
Faust. What art thou, the second?
Covet. I am Covetousness, begotten of an old churl, in an old leathern bag: and, might I have my wish, I would

desire that this house and all the people in it were turned to gold, that I might lock you up in my good chest: O, my sweet gold!

Faust. What art thou, the third?

Wrath. I am Wrath. I had neither father nor mother: I leapt out of a lion's mouth when I was scarce half an hour old; and ever since I have run up and down the world with this case of rapiers, wounding myself when I had nobody to fight withal. I was born in hell; and look to it, for some of you shall be my father.

Faust. What art thou, the fourth?

Envy. I am Envy, begotten of a chimney-sweeper and an oyster-wife. I cannot read, and therefore wish all books were burnt. I am lean with seeing others eat. O, that there would come a famine through all the world, that all might die, and I live alone! then thou shouldst see how fat I would be. But must thou sit, and I stand? come down, with a vengeance!

Faust. Away, envious rascal!—What art thou, the fifth?

Glut. Who I, sir? I am Gluttony. My parents are all dead, and the devil a penny they have left me, but a bare pension, and that is thirty meals a day, and ten bevers,—a small trifle to suffice nature. O, I come of a royal parentage! my grandfather was a Gammon of Bacon, my grandmother a Hogshead of Claret-wine; my godfathers were these, Peter Pickle-herring and Martin Martlemas-beef; O, but my godmother, she was a jolly gentlewoman, and well-beloved in every good town and city; her name was Mistress Margery March-beer. Now, Faustus, thou hast heard all my progeny; wilt thou bid me to supper?

Faust. No, I'll see thee hanged: thou wilt eat up all my victuals.

Glut. Then the devil choke thee!

Faust. Choke thyself, glutton!—What art thou, the sixth?

Sloth. I am Sloth. I was begotten on a sunny bank, where I have lain ever since; and you have done me great injury to bring me from thence: let me be carried thither again by Gluttony and Lechery. I'll not speak another word for a king's ransom.

Faust. What are you, Mistress Minx, the seventh and last?

Lechery. Who I, sir? I am one that loves an inch of raw mutton better than an ell of fried stock-fish; and the first letter of my name begins with L.

Faust. Away, to hell, to hell! [*Exeunt the Sins.*
Luc. Now, Faustus, how dost thou like this?
Faust. O, this feeds my soul!
Luc. Tut, Faustus, in hell is all manner of delight.
Faust. O, might I see hell, and return again,
How happy were I then!
Luc. Thou shalt; I will send for thee at midnight.
In meantime take this book, peruse it throughly,
And thou shalt turn thyself into what shape thou wilt.
Faust. Great thanks, mighty Lucifer!
This will I keep as chary as my life.
Luc. Farewell, Faustus, and think on the devil.
Faust. Farewell, great Lucifer.
[*Exeunt Lucifer and Belzebub.*
Come, Mephistophilis. [*Exeunt.*

Enter Chorus.

Chor. Learned Faustus,
To know the secrets of astronomy
Graven in the book of Jove's high firmament,
Did mount himself to scale Olympus' top,
Being seated in a chariot burning bright,
Drawn by the strength of yoky dragons' necks.
He now is gone to prove cosmography,
And, as I guess, will first arrive in Rome,
To see the Pope and manner of his court,
And take some part of holy Peter's feast,
That to this day is highly solemnis'd. [*Exit.*

Enter FAUSTUS *and* MEPHISTOPHILIS.

Faust. Having now, my good Mephistophilis,
Pass'd with delight the stately town of Trier,
Environ'd round with airy mountain-tops,
With walls of flint, and deep-entrenched lakes,
Not to be won by any conquering prince;
From Paris next, coasting the realm of France,
We saw the river Maine fall into Rhine,
Whose banks are set with groves of fruitful vines;
Then up to Naples, rich Campania,
Whose buildings fair and gorgeous to the eye,
The streets straight forth, and pav'd with finest brick,
Quarter the town in four equivalents:
There saw we learned Maro's golden tomb,

The way he cut, an English mile in length,
Thorough a rock of stone, in one night's space;
From thence to Venice, Padua, and the rest,
In one of which a sumptuous temple stands,
That threats the stars with her aspiring top.
Thus hitherto hath Faustus spent his time:
But tell me now what resting-place is this?
Hast thou, as erst I did command,
Conducted me within the walls of Rome?

Meph. Faustus, I have; and, because we will not be unprovided, I have taken up his Holiness' privy-chamber for our use.

Faust. I hope his Holiness will bid us welcome.

Meph. Tut, 'tis no matter, man; we'll be bold with his good cheer.
And now, my Faustus, that thou mayst perceive
What Rome containeth to delight thee with,
Know that this city stands upon seven hills
That underprop the groundwork of the same:
Just through the midst runs flowing Tiber's stream
With winding banks that cut it in two parts;
Over the which four stately bridges lean,
That make safe passage to each part of Rome:
Upon the bridge call'd Ponte Angelo
Erected is a castle passing strong,
Within whose walls such store of ordnance are,
And double cannons fram'd of carved brass,
As match the days within one complete year;
Besides the gates, and high pyramides,
Which Julius Cæsar brought from Africa.

Faust. Now, by the kingdoms of infernal rule,
Of Styx, of Acheron, and the fiery lake
Of ever-burning Phlegethon, I swear
That I do long to see the monuments
And situation of bright-splendent Rome:
Come, therefore, let's away.

Meph. Nay, Faustus, stay: I know you'd fain see the Pope,
And take some part of holy Peter's feast,
Where thou shalt see a troop of bald-pate friars,
Whose *summum bonum* is in belly-cheer.

Faust. Well, I'm content to compass then some sport,
And by their folly make us merriment.
Then charm me, that I

May be invisible, to do what I please,
Unseen of any whilst I stay in Rome.
[*Mephistophilis charms him.*

Meph. So, Faustus; now
Do what thou wilt, thou shalt not be discern'd.

Sound a Sonnet. Enter the POPE *and the* CARDINAL OF LORRAIN *to the banquet, with* Friars *attending.*

Pope. My lord of Lorrain, will't please you draw near?

Faust. Fall to, and the devil choke you, an you spare!

Pope. How now! who's that which spake?—Friars, look about.

First Friar. Here's nobody, if it like your Holiness.

Pope. My lord, here is a dainty dish was sent me from the Bishop of Milan.

Faust. I thank you, sir. [*Snatches the dish.*

Pope. How now! who's that which snatched the meat from me? will no man look?—My lord, this dish was sent me from the Cardinal of Florence.

Faust. You say true; I'll ha't. [*Snatches the dish.*

Pope. What, again!—My lord, I'll drink to your grace.

Faust. I'll pledge your grace. [*Snatches the cup.*

C. of Lor. My lord, it may be some ghost, newly crept out of Purgatory, come to beg a pardon of your Holiness.

Pope. It may be so.—Friars, prepare a dirge to lay the fury of this ghost.—Once again, my lord, fall to.
[*The Pope crosses himself.*

Faust. What, are you crossing of yourself?
Well, use that trick no more, I would advise you.
[*The Pope crosses himself again.*
Well, there's the second time. Aware the third;
I give you fair warning.
[*The Pope crosses himself again, and Faustus hits him a box of the ear; and they all run away.*
Come on, Mephistophilis; what shall we do?

Meph. Nay, I know not: we shall be cursed with bell, book, and candle.

Faust. How! bell, book, and candle,—candle, book, and bell,—
Forward and backward, to curse Faustus to hell!
Anon you shall hear a hog grunt, a calf bleat, and an ass bray,
Because it is Saint Peter's holiday.

Re-enter all the Friars *to sing the Dirge.*

First Friar. Come, brethren, let's about our business with good devotion.

They sing.

Cursed be he that stole away his Holiness' meat from the table!
maledicat Dominus!
Cursed be he that struck his Holiness a blow on the face!
maledicat Dominus!
Cursed be he that took Friar Sandelo a blow on the pate!
maledicat Dominus!
Cursed be he that disturbeth our holy dirge! maledicat Dominus!
Cursed be he that took away his Holiness' wine! maledicat Dominus!

Et omnes Sancti! Amen!

[*Mephistophilis and Faustus beat the Friars, and fling fireworks among them; and so exeunt.*

Enter Chorus.

Chor. When Faustus had with pleasure ta'en the view
Of rarest things, and royal courts of kings,
He stay'd his course, and so returned home;
Where such as bear his absence but with grief,
I mean his friends and near'st companions,
Did gratulate his safety with kind words,
And in their conference of what befell,
Touching his journey through the world and air,
They put forth questions of astrology,
Which Faustus answer'd with such learned skill
As they admir'd and wonder'd at his wit.
Now is his fame spread forth in every land:
Amongst the rest the Emperor is one,
Carolus the Fifth, at whose palace now
Faustus is feasted 'mongst his noblemen.
What there he did, in trial of his art,
I leave untold, your eyes shall see perform'd. [*Exit.*

Enter Robin *the Ostler, with a book in his hand.*

Robin. O, this is admirable! here I ha' stolen one of Doctor Faustus' conjuring books, and, i'faith, I mean to search some circles for my own use. Now will I make all the maidens in our parish dance at my pleasure, stark naked, before me; and so by that means I shall see more than e'er I felt or saw yet.

Enter RALPH, *calling* ROBIN.

Ralph. Robin, prithee, come away; there's a gentleman tarries to have his horse, and he would have his things rubbed and made clean: he keeps such a chafing with my mistress about it; and she has sent me to look thee out; prithee, come away.

Robin. Keep out, keep out, or else you are blown up, you are dismembered, Ralph: keep out, for I am about a roaring piece of work.

Ralph. Come, what doest thou with that same book? thou canst not read?

Robin. Yes, my master and mistress shall find that I can read, he for his forehead, she for her private study; she's born to bear with me, or else my art fails.

Ralph. Why, Robin, what book is that?

Robin. What book! why, the most intolerable book for conjuring that e'er was invented by any brimstone devil.

Ralph. Canst thou conjure with it?

Robin. I can do all these things easily with it; first, I can make thee drunk with ippocras at any tavern in Europe for nothing; that's one of my conjuring works.

Ralph. Our Master Parson says that's nothing.

Robin. True, Ralph: and more, Ralph, if thou hast any mind to Nan Spit, our kitchen-maid, then turn her and wind her to thy own use, as often as thou wilt, and at midnight.

Ralph. O, brave, Robin! shall I have Nan Spit, and to mine own use? On that condition I'll feed thy devil with horse-bread as long as he lives, of free cost.

Robin. No more, sweet Ralph: let's go and make clean our boots, which lie foul upon our hands, and then to our conjuring in the devil's name. [*Exeunt.*

Enter ROBIN *and* RALPH *with a silver goblet.*

Robin. Come, Ralph: did not I tell thee, we were for ever made by this Doctor Faustus' book? *ecce, signum!* here's a simple purchase for horse-keepers: our horses shall eat no hay as long as this lasts.

Ralph. But, Robin, here comes the Vintner.

Robin. Hush! I'll gull him supernaturally.

Enter Vintner.

Drawer, I hope all is paid; God be with you!—Come, Ralph.

Vint. Soft, sir; a word with you. I must yet have a goblet paid from you, ere you go.

Robin. I a goblet, Ralph, I a goblet!—I scorn you; and you are but a, etc. I a goblet! search me.

Vint. I mean so, sir, with your favour. [*Searches Robin.*

Robin. How say you now?

Vint. I must say somewhat to your fellow.—You, sir!

Robin. Me, sir! me, sir! search your fill. [*Vintner searches him.*] Now, sir, you may be ashamed to burden honest men with a matter of truth.

Vint. Well, one of you hath this goblet about you.

Robin. You lie, drawer, 'tis afore me [*Aside*].—Sirrah you, I'll teach you to impeach honest men;—stand by;— I'll scour you for a goblet;—stand aside you had best, I charge you in the name of Belzebub.—Look to the goblet, Ralph [*Aside to Ralph*].

Vint. What mean you, sirrah?

Robin. I'll tell you what I mean. [*Reads from a book*] *Sanctobulorum Periphrasticon*—nay, I'll tickle you, Vintner. —Look to the goblet, Ralph [*Aside to Ralph*].—[*Reads*] *Polypragmos Belseborams framanto pacostiphos tostu, Mephistophilis,* etc.

Enter MEPHISTOPHILIS, *sets squibs at their backs, and then exit. They run about.*

Vint. O, nomine Domini! what meanest thou, Robin? thou hast no goblet.

Ralph. Peccatum peccatorum!—Here's thy goblet, good Vintner. [*Gives the goblet to Vintner, who exit.*

Robin. Misericordia pro nobis! what shall I do? Good devil, forgive me now, and I'll never rob thy library more.

Re-enter MEPHISTOPHILIS.

Meph. Monarch of hell, under whose black survey
Great potentates do kneel with awful fear,
Upon whose altars thousand souls do lie,
How am I vexed with these villains' charms?
From Constantinople am I hither come,
Only for pleasure of these damned slaves.

Robin. How, from Constantinople! you have had a great journey: will you take sixpence in your purse to pay for your supper, and be gone?

Meph. Well, villains, for your presumption, I transform thee into an ape, and thee into a dog; and so be gone! [*Exit.*

Robin. How, into an ape! that's brave: I'll have fine sport with the boys; I'll get nuts and apples enow.

Ralph. And I must be a dog.

Robin. I'faith, thy head will never be out of the pottage-pot. [*Exeunt.*

Enter EMPEROR, FAUSTUS, *and a* Knight, *with* Attendants.

Emp. Master Doctor Faustus, I have heard strange report of thy knowledge in the black art, how that none in my empire nor in the whole world can compare with thee for the rare effects of magic: they say thou hast a familiar spirit, by whom thou canst accomplish what thou list. This, therefore, is my request, that thou let me see some proof of thy skill, that mine eyes may be witnesses to confirm what mine ears have heard reported: and here I swear to thee, by the honour of mine imperial crown, that, whatever thou doest, thou shalt be no ways prejudiced or endamaged.

Knight. I'faith, he looks much like a conjurer. [*Aside.*

Faust. My gracious sovereign, though I must confess myself far inferior to the report men have published, and nothing answerable to the honour of your imperial majesty, yet, for that love and duty binds me thereunto, I am content to do whatsoever your majesty shall command me.

Emp. Then, Doctor Faustus, mark what I shall say.
As I was sometime solitary set
Within my closet, sundry thoughts arose
About the honour of mine ancestors,
How they had won by prowess such exploits,
Got such riches, subdu'd so many kingdoms,
As we that do succeed, or they that shall
Hereafter possess our throne, shall
(I fear me) ne'er attain to that degree
Of high renown and great authority:
Amongst which kings is Alexander the Great,
Chief spectacle of the world's pre-eminence,
The bright shining of whose glorious acts

Lightens the world with his reflecting beams,
As when I hear but motion made of him,
It grieves my soul I never saw the man:
If, therefore, thou, by cunning of thine art,
Canst raise this man from hollow vaults below,
Where lies entomb'd this famous conqueror,
And bring with him his beauteous paramour,
Both in their right shapes, gesture, and attire
They us'd to wear during their time of life,
Thou shalt both satisfy my just desire,
And give me cause to praise thee whilst I live.

Faust. My gracious lord, I am ready to accomplish your request, so far forth as by art and power of my spirit I am able to perform.

Knight. I'faith, that's just nothing at all. [*Aside.*

Faust. But, if it like your grace, it is not in my ability to present before your eyes the true substantial bodies of those two deceased princes, which long since are consumed to dust.

Knight. Ay, marry, Master Doctor, now there's a sign of grace in you, when you will confess the truth. [*Aside.*

Faust. But such spirits as can lively resemble Alexander and his paramour shall appear before your grace, in that manner that they best lived in, in their most flourishing estate; which I doubt not shall sufficiently content your imperial majesty.

Emp. Go to, Master Doctor; let me see them presently.

Knight. Do you hear, Master Doctor? you bring Alexander and his paramour before the Emperor!

Faust. How then, sir?

Knight. I'faith, that's as true as Diana turned me to a stag.

Faust. No, sir; but, when Actæon died, he left the horns for you.—Mephistophilis, be gone. [*Exit Mephistophilis.*

Knight. Nay, an you go to conjuring, I'll be gone. [*Exit.*

Faust. I'll meet with you anon for interrupting me so.—Here they are, my gracious lord.

Re-enter MEPHISTOPHILIS *with* Spirits *in the shapes of* ALEXANDER *and his* Paramour.

Emp. Master Doctor, I heard this lady, while she lived, had a wart or mole in her neck: how shall I know whether it be so or no?

Faust. Your highness may boldly go and see.

Emp. Sure, these are no spirits, but the true substantial bodies of those two deceased princes. [*Exeunt Spirits.*

Faust. Wilt please your highness now to send for the knight that was so pleasant with me here of late?

Emp. One of you call him forth. [*Exit Attendant.*

Re-enter the Knight *with a pair of horns on his head.*

How now, sir knight! why, I had thought thou hadst been a bachelor, but now I see thou hast a wife, that not only gives thee horns, but makes thee wear them. Feel on thy head.

Knight. Thou damned wretch and execrable dog,
Bred in the concave of some monstrous rock,
How dar'st thou thus abuse a gentleman?
Villain, I say, undo what thou hast done!

Faust. O, not so fast, sir! there's no haste: but, good, are you remembered how you crossed me in my conference with the Emperor? I think I have met with you for it.

Emp. Good Master Doctor, at my entreaty release him: he hath done penance sufficient.

Faust. My gracious lord, not so much for the injury he offered me here in your presence, as to delight you with some mirth, hath Faustus worthily requited this injurious knight; which being all I desire, I am content to release him of his horns:—and, sir knight, hereafter speak well of scholars.—Mephistophilis, transform him straight. [*Mephistophilis removes the horns.*]—Now, my good lord, having done my duty, I humbly take my leave.

Emp. Farewell, Master Doctor: yet, ere you go,
Expect from me a bounteous reward.
[*Exeunt Emperor, Knight, and attendants.*

Faust. Now, Mephistophilis, the restless course
That time doth run with calm and silent foot,
Shortening my days and thread of vital life,
Calls for the payment of my latest years:
Therefore, sweet Mephistophilis, let us
Make haste to Wertenberg,

Meph. What, will you go on horse-back or on foot?

Faust. Nay, till I'm past this fair and pleasant green,
I'll walk on foot.

Enter a Horse-courser.

Horse-c. I have been all this day seeking one Master Fustian: mass, see where he is!—God save you Master Doctor!

Faust. What, horse-courser! you are well met.

Horse-c. Do you hear, sir? I have brought you forty dollars for your horse.

Faust. I cannot sell him so: if thou likest him for fifty, take him.

Horse-c. Alas, sir, I have no more!—I pray you, speak for me.

Meph. I pray you, let him have him: he is an honest fellow, and he has a great charge, neither wife nor child.

Faust. Well, come, give me your money [*Horse-courser gives Faustus the money*]: my boy will deliver him to you. But I must tell you one thing before you have him; ride him not into the water, at any hand.

Horse-c. Why, sir, will he not drink of all waters?

Faust. O, yes, he will drink of all waters; but ride him not into the water; ride him over hedge or ditch, or where thou wilt, but not into the water.

Horse-c. Well, sir.—Now am I made man for ever: I'll not leave my horse for forty: if he had but the quality of hey-ding-ding, hey-ding-ding, I'd make a brave living on him: he has a buttock as slick as an eel [*Aside*].—Well, God b'wi'ye, sir: your boy will deliver him me: but, hark you, sir; if my horse be sick or ill at ease if I bring his water to you, you'll tell me what it is?

Faust. Away, you villain! what, dost think I am a horse-doctor? [*Exit Horse-courser.*
What art thou, Faustus, but a man condemn'd to die?
Thy fatal time doth draw to final end;
Despair doth drive distrust into my thoughts:
Confound these passions with a quiet sleep:
Tush, Christ did call the thief upon the Cross;
Then rest thee, Faustus, quiet in conceit.
[*Sleeps in his chair.*

Re-enter Horse-courser, *all wet, crying.*

Horse-c. Alas, alas! Doctor Fustian, quotha? mass, Doctor Lopus was never such a doctor: has given me a purgation, has purged me of forty dollars; I shall never see them more. But yet, like an ass as I was, I would not be ruled by him, for he bade me I should ride him into no water: now I, thinking my horse had had some rare quality that he would not have had me know of, I, like a venturous youth, rid him into the deep pond at the town's end. I was no sooner in the middle of the pond, but my horse vanished away, and I sat upon a bottle of hay, never so near drowning in my life. But I'll seek out my doctor, and have my forty dollars again, or I'll make it the dearest horse!—O, yonder is his snipper-snapper. Do you hear? you, hey-pass, where's your master?

Meph. Why, sir, what would you? you cannot speak with him.

Horse-c. But I will speak with him.

Meph. Why, he's fast asleep: come some other time.

Horse-c. I'll speak with him now, or I'll break his glass-windows about his ears.

Meph. I tell thee, he has not slept this eight nights.

Horse-c. An he have not slept this eight weeks, I'll speak with him.

Meph. See, where he is, fast asleep.

Horse-c. Ay, this is he.—God save you, Master Doctor, Master Doctor, Master Doctor Fustian! forty dollars, forty dollars for a bottle of hay!

Meph. Why, thou seest he hears thee not.

Horse-c. So-ho, ho! so-ho, ho! [*Hollows in his ear.*] No, will you not wake? I'll make you wake ere I go. [*Pulls Faustus by the leg, and pulls it away.*] Alas, I am undone! what shall I do?

Faust. O, my leg, my leg!—Help, Mephistophilis! call the officers.—My leg, my leg!

Meph. Come, villain, to the constable.

Horse-c. O Lord, sir, let me go, and I'll give you forty dollars more!

Meph. Where be they?

Horse-c. I have none about me: come to my ostry, and I'll give them you.

Meph. Be gone quickly. [*Horse-courser runs away.*

Faust. What, is he gone? farewell he! Faustus has his leg again, and the Horse-courser, I take it, a bottle of hay for his labour: well, this trick shall cost him forty dollars more.

Enter WAGNER.

How now, Wagner! what's the news with thee?

Wag. Sir, the Duke of Vanholt doth earnestly entreat your company.

Faust. The Duke of Vanholt! an honourable gentleman, to whom I must be no niggard of my cunning.—Come, Mephistophilis, let's away to him. [*Exeunt.*

Enter the DUKE OF VANHOLT, *the* DUCHESS, *and* FAUSTUS.

Duke. Believe me, Master Doctor, this merriment hath much pleased me.

Faust. My gracious lord, I am glad it contents you so well. —But it may be, madam, you take no delight in this. I have heard that great-bellied women do long for some dainties or other: what is it, madam? tell me, and you shall have it.

Duchess. Thanks, good Master Doctor: and, for I see your courteous intent to pleasure me, I will not hide from you the thing my heart desires; and, were it now summer, as it is January and the dead time of the winter, I would desire no better meat than a dish of ripe grapes.

Faust. Alas, madam, that's nothing!—Mephistophilis, be gone. [*Exit Mephistophilis.*] Were it a greater thing than this, so it would content you, you should have it.

Re-enter MEPHISTOPHILIS *with grapes.*

Here they be, madam: wilt please you taste on them?

Duke. Believe me, Master Doctor, this makes me wonder above the rest, that being in the dead time of winter and in the month of January, how you should come by these grapes.

Faust. If it like your grace, the year is divided into two circles over the whole world, that, when it is here winter with us, in the contrary circle it is summer with them, as in India, Saba, and farther countries in the east; and by means of a swift spirit that I have, I had them brought hither, as you see.—How do you like them, madam? be they good?

Duchess. Believe me, Master Doctor, they be the best grapes that e'er I tasted in my life before.

Faust. I am glad they content you so, madam.

Duke. Come, madam, let us in, where you must well reward this learned man for the great kindness he hath showed to you.

Duchess. And so I will, my lord; and, whilst I live, rest beholding for this courtesy.

Faust. I humbly thank your grace.

Duke. Come, Master Doctor, follow us, and receive your reward. [*Exeunt.*

Enter WAGNER.

Wag. I think my master means to die shortly,
For he hath given to me all his goods:
And yet, methinks, if that death were near,
He would not banquet, and carouse, and swill
Amongst the students, as even now he doth,
Who are at supper with such belly-cheer
As Wagner ne'er beheld in all his life.
See, where they come! belike the feast is ended. [*Exit.*

Enter FAUSTUS *with two or three* Scholars, *and* MEPHISTOPHILIS.

First Schol. Master Doctor Faustus, since our conference about fair ladies, which was the beautifulest in all the world, we have determined with ourselves that Helen of Greece was the admirablest lady that ever lived: therefore, Master Doctor, if you will do us that favour, as to let us see that peerless dame of Greece, whom all the world admires for majesty, we should think ourselves much beholding unto you.

Faust. Gentlemen,
For that I know your friendship is unfeign'd,
And Faustus' custom is not to deny
The just requests of those that wish him well,
You shall behold that peerless dame of Greece,
No otherways for pomp and majesty
Than when Sir Paris cross'd the seas with her,
And brought the spoils to rich Dardania.
Be silent, then, for danger is in words.
[*Music sounds, and Helen passeth over the stage.*

Sec. Schol. Too simple is my wit to tell her praise,
Whom all the world admires for majesty.

Third Schol. No marvel though the angry Greeks pursu'd
With ten years' war the rape of such a queen,
Whose heavenly beauty passeth all compare.

First Schol. Since we have seen the pride of Nature's works,

And only paragon of excellence,
Let us depart; and for this glorious deed
Happy and blest be Faustus evermore!
Faust. Gentlemen, farewell: the same I wish to you.
[*Exeunt Scholars.*

Enter an Old Man.

Old Man. Ah, Doctor Faustus, that I might prevail
To guide thy steps unto the way of life,
By which sweet path thou mayst attain the goal
That shall conduct thee to celestial rest!
Break heart, drop blood, and mingle it with tears,
Tears falling from repentant heaviness
Of thy most vile and loathsome filthiness,
The stench whereof corrupts the inward soul
With such flagitious crimes of heinous sin
As no commiseration may expel,
But mercy, Faustus, of thy Saviour sweet,
Whose blood alone must wash away thy guilt.
Faust. Where art thou, Faustus? wretch, what hast thou done?
Damn'd art thou, Faustus, damn'd; despair and die!
Hell calls for right, and with a roaring voice
Says, "Faustus, come; thine hour is come;"
And Faustus will come to do thee right.
[*Mephistophilis gives him a dagger.*
Old Man. Ah, stay, good Faustus, stay thy desperate steps!
I see an angel hovers o'er thy head,
And, with a vial full of precious grace,
Offers to pour the same into thy soul:
Then call for mercy, and avoid despair.
Faust. Ah, my sweet friend, I feel
Thy words to comfort my distressed soul!
Leave me a while to ponder on my sins.
Old Man. I go, sweet Faustus; but with heavy cheer,
Fearing the ruin of thy hopeless soul. [*Exit.*
Faust. Accursed Faustus, where is mercy now?
I do repent; and yet I do despair:
Hell strives with grace for conquest in my breast:
What shall I do to shun the snares of death?
Meph. Thou traitor, Faustus, I arrest thy soul
For disobedience to my sovereign lord:
Revolt, or I'll in piece-meal tear thy flesh.

Faust. Sweet Mephistophilis, entreat thy lord
To pardon my unjust presumption,
And with my blood again I will confirm
My former vow I made to Lucifer.
Meph. Do it, then, quickly, with unfeigned heart,
Lest greater danger do attend thy drift.
Faust. Torment, sweet friend, that base and crooked age,
That durst dissuade me from thy Lucifer,
With greatest torments that our hell affords.
Meph. His faith is great; I cannot touch his soul;
But what I may afflict his body with
I will attempt, which is but little worth.
Faust. One thing, good servant, let me crave of thee,
To glut the longing of my heart's desire,—
That I might have unto my paramour
That heavenly Helen which I saw of late,
Whose sweet embracings may extinguish clean
Those thoughts that do dissuade me from my vow,
And keep mine oath I made to Lucifer.
Meph. Faustus, this, or what else thou shalt desire,
Shall be perform'd in twinkling of an eye.

Re-enter HELEN.

Faust. Was this the face that launch'd a thousand ships?
And burnt the topless towers of Ilium?—
Sweet Helen, make me immortal with a kiss.—
[*Kisses her.*
Her lips suck forth my soul: see, where it flies!—
Come, Helen, come, give me my soul again.
Here will I dwell, for heaven is in these lips,
And all is dross that is not Helena.
I will be Paris, and for love of thee,
Instead of Troy, shall Wertenberg be sack'd;
And I will combat with weak Menelaus,
And wear thy colours on my plumed crest;
Yea, I will wound Achilles in the heel,
And then return to Helen for a kiss.
O, thou art fairer than the evening air
Clad in the beauty of a thousand stars;
Brighter art thou than flaming Jupiter
When he appear'd to hapless Semele;
More lovely than the monarch of the sky

In wanton Arethusa's azur'd arms;
And none but thou shalt be my paramour! [*Exeunt.*

Enter the Old Man.

Old Man. Accursed Faustus, miserable man,
That from thy soul exclud'st the grace of heaven,
And fly'st the throne of his tribunal-seat!

Enter Devils.

Satan begins to sift me with his pride:
As in this furnace God shall try my faith,
My faith, vile hell, shall triumph over thee,
Ambitious fiends, see how the heavens smile
At your repulse, and laugh your state to scorn!
Hence, hell! for hence I fly unto my God.
[*Exeunt—on one side, Devils, on the other, Old Man.*

Enter FAUSTUS, *with* Scholars.

Faust. Ah, gentlemen!

First Schol. What ails Faustus?

Faust. Ah, my sweet chamber-fellow, had I lived with thee, then had I lived still! but now I die eternally. Look, comes he not? comes he not?

Sec. Schol. What means Faustus?

Third Schol. Belike he is grown into some sickness by being over-solitary.

First Schol. If it be so, we'll have physicians to cure him.—'Tis but a surfeit; never fear, man.

Faust. A surfeit of deadly sin, that hath damned both body and soul.

Sec. Schol. Yet, Faustus, look up to heaven; remember God's mercies are infinite.

Faust. But Faustus' offence can ne'er be pardoned: the serpent that tempted Eve may be saved, but not Faustus. Ah, gentlemen, hear me with patience, and tremble not at my speeches! Though my heart pants and quivers to remember that I have been a student here these thirty years, O, would I had never seen Wertenberg, never read book! and what wonders I have done, all Germany can witness, yea, all the world; for which Faustus hath lost both Germany and the world, yea, heaven itself, heaven, the seat of God, the throne of the blessed, the kingdom of joy; and must remain in hell for ever, hell, ah, hell, for ever! Sweet friends, what shall become of Faustus, being in hell for ever?

Third Schol. Yet, Faustus, call on God.

Faust. On God, whom Faustus hath abjured! on God, whom Faustus hath blasphemed! Ah, my God, I would weep! but the devil draws in my tears. Gush forth blood, instead of tears! yea, life and soul! O, he stays my tongue! I would lift up my hands; but see, they hold them, they hold them!

All. Who, Faustus?

Faust. Lucifer and Mephistophilis. Ah, gentlemen, I gave them my soul for my cunning!

All. God forbid!

Faust. God forbade it, indeed; but Faustus hath done it: for vain pleasure of twenty-four years hath Faustus lost eternal joy and felicity. I writ them a bill with mine own blood: the date is expired; the time will come, and he will fetch me.

First Schol. Why did not Faustus tell us of this before, that divines might have prayed for thee?

Faust. Oft have I thought to have done so; but the devil threatened to tear me in pieces, if I named God, to fetch both body and soul, if I once gave ear to divinity: and now 'tis too late. Gentlemen, away, lest you perish with me.

Sec. Schol. O, what shall we do to save Faustus?

Faust. Talk not of me, but save yourselves, and depart.

Third Schol. God will strengthen me; I will stay with Faustus.

First Schol. Tempt not God, sweet friend; but let us into the next room, and there pray for him.

Faust. Ay, pray for me, pray for me; and what noise soever ye hear, come not unto me, for nothing can rescue me.

Sec. Schol. Pray thou, and we will pray that God may have mercy upon thee.

Faust. Gentlemen, farewell: if I live till morning, I'll visit you; if not, Faustus is gone to hell.

All. Faustus, farewell.

[*Exeunt Scholars.—The clock strikes eleven.*

Faust. Ah, Faustus.
Now hast thou but one bare hour to live,
And then thou must be damn'd perpetually!
Stand still, you ever-moving spheres of heaven,
That time may cease, and midnight never come;

Fair Nature's eye, rise, rise again, and make
Perpetual day; or let this hour be but
A year, a month, a week, a natural day,
That Faustus may repent and save his soul!
O lente, lente currite, noctis equi!
The stars move still, time runs, the clock will strike,
The devil will come, and Faustus must be damn'd.
O, I'll leap up to my God!—Who pulls me down?—
See, see, where Christ's blood streams in the firmament!
One drop would save my soul, half a drop: ah, my Christ!—
Ah, rend not my heart for naming of my Christ!
Yet will I call on him: O, spare me, Lucifer!—
Where is it now? 'tis gone: and see, where God
Stretcheth out his arm, and bends his ireful brows!
Mountains and hills, come, come, and fall on me,
And hide me from the heavy wrath of God!
No, no!
Then will I headlong run into the earth:
Earth, gape! O, no, it will not harbour me!
You stars that reign'd at my nativity,
Whose influence hath allotted death and hell,
Now draw up Faustus, like a foggy mist,
Into the entrails of yon labouring clouds,
That, when you vomit forth into the air,
My limbs may issue from your smoky mouths,
So that my soul may but ascend to heaven!
[*The clock strikes the half-hour.*
Ah, half the hour is past! 'twill all be past anon.
O God,
If thou wilt not have mercy on my soul,
Yet for Christ's sake, whose blood hath ransom'd me,
Impose some end to my incessant pain;
Let Faustus live in hell a thousand years,
A hundred thousand, and at last be sav'd!
O, no end is limited to damned souls!
Why wert thou not a creature wanting soul?
Or why is this immortal that thou hast?
Ah, Pythagoras' metempsychosis, were that true,
This soul should fly from me, and I be chang'd
Unto some brutish beast! all beasts are happy,
For, when they die,
Their souls are soon dissolv'd in elements;

But mine must live still to be plagu'd in hell.
Curs'd be the parents that engender'd me!
No, Faustus, curse thyself, curse Lucifer
That hath depriv'd thee of the joys of heaven.
[*The clock strikes twelve.*
O, it strikes, it strikes! Now, body, turn to air,
Or Lucifer will bear thee quick to hell!
[*Thunder and lightning.*
O soul, be chang'd into little water-drops,
And fall into the ocean, ne'er be found!

Enter Devils.

My God, my God, look not so fierce on me!
Adders and serpents, let me breathe a while!
Ugly hell, gape not! come not, Lucifer!
I'll burn my books!—Ah, Mephistophilis!
[*Exeunt Devils with Faustus.*

Enter Chorus.

Chor. Cut is the branch that might have grown full straight,
And burned is Apollo's laurel-bough,
That sometime grew within this learned man.
Faustus is gone: regard his hellish fall,
Whose fiendful fortune may exhort the wise,
Only to wonder at unlawful things,
Whose deepness doth entice such forward wits
To practise more than heavenly power permits.
[*Exit.*

Terminat hora diem; terminat auctor opus.

THE JEW OF MALTA

TO MY WORTHY FRIEND, MASTER THOMAS HAMMON, OF GRAY'S INN, ETC.

THIS play, composed by so worthy an author as Master Marlowe, and the part of the Jew presented by so unimitable an actor as Master Alleyn, being in this later age commended to the stage; as I ushered it unto the court, and presented it to the Cock-pit, with these Prologues and Epilogues here inserted, so now being newly brought to the press, I was loath it should be published without the ornament of an Epistle; making choice of you unto whom to devote it; than whom (of all those gentlemen and acquaintance within the compass of my long knowledge) there is none more able to tax ignorance, or attribute right to merit. Sir, you have been pleased to grace some of mine own works with your courteous patronage: I hope this will not be the worse accepted, because commended by me; over whom none can claim more power or privilege than yourself. I had no better a new year's gift to present you with; receive it therefore as a continuance of that inviolable obligement, by which he rests still engaged, who, as he ever hath, shall always remain,

Tuissimus,

THO. HEYWOOD.

THE PROLOGUE SPOKEN AT COURT

GRACIOUS and great, that we so boldly dare
('Mongst other plays that now in fashion are)
To present this, writ many years agone,
And in that age thought second unto none,
We humbly crave your pardon. We pursue
The story of a rich and famous Jew

Who liv'd in Malta: you shall find him still,
In all his projects, a sound Machiavill;
And that's his character. He that hath past
So many censures is now come at last
To have your princely ears: grace you him; then
You crown the action, and renown the pen.

EPILOGUE SPOKEN AT COURT

It is our fear, dread sovereign, we have bin
Too tedious; neither can't be less than sin
To wrong your princely patience: if we have,
Thus low dejected, we your pardon crave;
And, if aught here offend your ear or sight,
We only act and speak what others write.

THE PROLOGUE TO THE STAGE

AT THE COCK-PIT

We know not how our play may pass this stage,
But by the best of poets in that age
The Malta-Jew had being and was made;
And he then by the best of actors play'd:
In *Hero and Leander* one did gain
A lasting memory; in Tamburlaine,
This Jew, with others many, th' other wan
The attribute of peerless, being a man
Whom we may rank with (doing no one wrong)
Proteus for shapes, and Roscius for a tongue,—
So could he speak, so vary; nor is't hate
To merit in him who doth personate
Our Jew this day; nor is it his ambition
To exceed or equal, being of condition
More modest: this is all that he intends,
(And that too at the urgence of some friends,)
To prove his best, and, if none here gainsay it,
The part he hath studied, and intends to play it.

EPILOGUE TO THE STAGE

AT THE COCK-PIT

In graving with Pygmalion to contend,
Or painting with Apelles, doubtless the end
Must be disgrace: our actor did not so,—
He only aim'd to go, but not out-go.
Nor think that this day any prize was play'd;
Here were no bets at all, no wagers laid:
All the ambition that his mind doth swell,
Is but to hear from you (by me) 'twas well.

DRAMATIS PERSONÆ

FERNEZE, *governor of Malta.*
LODOWICK, *his son.*
SELIM CALYMATH, *son to the* GRAND SEIGNIOR.
MARTIN DEL BOSCO, *vice-admiral of Spain.*
MATHIAS, *a gentleman.*
JACOMO, BARNARDINE, *friars.*
BARABAS, *a wealthy Jew.*
ITHAMORE, *a slave.*
PILIA-BORZA, *a bully, attendant to* BELLAMIRA.
TWO MERCHANTS.
THREE JEWS.
KNIGHTS, BASSOES, OFFICERS, GUARD, SLAVES, MESSENGER, *and* CARPENTERS.

KATHARINE, *mother to* MATHIAS.
ABIGAIL, *daughter to* BARABAS.
BELLAMIRA, *a courtesan.*
ABBESS.
NUN.

MACHIAVEL as Prologue-speaker.

Scene, Malta.

Enter MACHIAVEL.

Mach. Albeit the world think Machiavel is dead,
Yet was his soul but flown beyond the Alps;
And, now the Guise is dead, is come from France,
To view this land, and frolic with his friends.
To some perhaps my name is odious;
But such as love me, guard me from their tongues,
And let them know that I am Machiavel,
And weigh not men, and therefore not men's words.
Admir'd I am of those that hate me most:
Though some speak openly against my books,
Yet will they read me, and thereby attain
To Peter's chair; and, when they cast me off,
Are poison'd by my climbing followers.

I count religion but a childish toy,
And hold there is no sin but ignorance.
Birds of the air will tell of murders past!
I am asham'd to hear such fooleries.
Many will talk of title to a crown:
What right had Cæsar to the empery?
Might first made kings, and laws were then most sure
When, like the Draco's, they were writ in blood.
Hence comes it that a strong built citadel
Commands much more than letters can import:
Which maxim had Phalaris observ'd,
H'ad never bellow'd, in a brazen bull,
Of great ones' envy: o' the poor petty wights
Let me be envied and not pitied.
But whither am I bound! I come not, I,
To read a lecture here in Britain,
But to present the tragedy of a Jew,
Who smiles to see how full his bags are cramm'd;
Which money was not got without my means.
I crave but this,—grace him as he deserves,
And let him not be entertain'd the worse
Because he favours me. [*Exit.*

ACT I

BARABAS *discovered in his counting house, with heaps of gold before him.*

Bara. So that of thus much that return was made;
And of the third part of the Persian ships
There was the venture summ'd and satisfied.
As for those Samnites, and the men of Uz,
That brought my Spanish oils and wines of Greece,
Here have I purs'd their paltry silverlings.
Fie, what a trouble 'tis to count this trash!
Well fare the Arabians, who so richly pay
The things they traffic for with wedge of gold,
Whereof a man may easily in a day
Tell that which may maintain him all his life.
The needy groom, that never finger'd groat,
Would make a miracle of thus much coin;
But he whose steel-barr'd coffers are cramm'd full,

And all his life-time hath been tired,
Wearying his fingers' ends with telling it,
Would in his age be loath to labour so,
And for a pound to sweat himself to death.
Give me the merchants of the Indian mines,
That trade in metal of the purest mould;
The wealthy Moor, that in the eastern rocks
Without control can pick his riches up,
And in his house heap pearl like pebble stones,
Receive them free, and sell them by the weight!
Bags of fiery opals, sapphires, amethysts,
Jacinths, hard topaz, grass-green emeralds,
Beauteous rubies, sparkling diamonds,
And seld-seen costly stones of so great price,
As one of them, indifferently rated,
And of a carat of this quantity,
May serve, in peril of calamity,
To ransom great kings from captivity.
This is the ware wherein consists my wealth;
And thus methinks should men of judgment frame
Their means of traffic from the vulgar trade,
And, as their wealth increaseth, so inclose
Infinite riches in a little room.
But now how stands the wind?
Into what corner peers my halcyon's bill?
Ha! to the east? yes. See how stand the vanes—
East and by south: why, then, I hope my ships
I sent for Egypt and the bordering isles
Are gotten up by Nilus' winding banks;
Mine argosy from Alexandria,
Loaden with spice and silks, now under sail,
Are smoothly gliding down by Candy-shore
To Malta, through our Mediterranean sea.—
But who comes here?

Enter a Merchant-seaman.

How now!

Merch. Barabas, thy ships are safe,
Riding in Malta-road; and all the merchants
With other merchandise are safe arriv'd,
And have sent me to know whether yourself
Will come and custom them.

Bara. The ships are safe thou say'st, and richly fraught?

Merch. They are.
Bara. Why, then, go bid them come ashore,
And bring with them their bills of entry:
I hope our credit in the custom-house
Will serve as well as I were present there.
Go send 'em threescore camels, thirty mules,
And twenty waggons, to bring up the ware.
But art thou master in a ship of mine,
And is thy credit not enough for that?
Merch. The very custom barely comes to more
Than many merchants of the town are worth,
And therefore far exceeds my credit, sir.
Bara. Go tell 'em the Jew of Malta sent thee, man:
Tush, who amongst 'em knows not Barabas?
Merch. I go.
Bara. So, then, there's somewhat come.—
Sirrah, which of my ships art thou master of?
Merch. Of the Speranza, sir.
Bara. And saw'st thou not
Mine argosy at Alexandria?
Thou couldst not come from Egypt, or by Caire,
But at the entry there into the sea,
Where Nilus pays his tribute to the main,
Thou needs must sail by Alexandria.
Merch. I neither saw them, nor inquir'd of them:
But this we heard some of our seamen say,
They wonder'd how you durst with so much wealth
Trust such a crazed vessel, and so far.
Bara. Tush, they are wise! I know her and her strength.
But go, go thou thy ways, discharge thy ship,
And bid my factor bring his loading in.
[*Exit Merchant.*
And yet I wonder at this argosy.

Enter a Second Merchant.

Sec. Merch. Thine argosy from Alexandria,
Know, Barabas, doth ride in Malta road,
Laden with riches, and exceeding store
Of Persian silks, of gold, and orient pearl.
Bara. How chance you came not with those other ships
That sail'd by Egypt?
Sec. Merch. Sir, we saw 'em not.
Bara. Belike they coasted round by Candy-shore

About their oils or other businesses.
But 'twas ill done of you to come so far
Without the aid or conduct of their ships.
Sec. Merch. Sir, we were wafted by a Spanish fleet,
That never left us till within a league,
That had the galleys of the Turk in chase.
Bara. O, they were going up to Sicily.
Well, go,
And bid the merchants and my men despatch,
And come ashore, and see the fraught discharg'd.
Sec. Merch. I go. [*Exit.*
Bara. Thus trolls our fortune in by land and sea,
And thus are we on every side enrich'd:
These are the blessings promis'd to the Jews,
And herein was old Abraham's happiness:
What more may heaven do for earthly man
Than thus to pour out plenty in their laps,
Ripping the bowels of the earth for them,
Making the sea their servants, and the winds
To drive their substance with successful blasts?
Who hateth me but for my happiness?
Or who is honour'd now but for his wealth?
Rather had I, a Jew, be hated thus,
Than pitied in a Christian poverty;
For I can see no fruits in all their faith,
But malice, falsehood, and excessive pride,
Which methinks fits not their profession.
Haply some hapless man hath conscience,
And for his conscience lives in beggary.
They say we are a scatter'd nation:
I cannot tell; but we have scambled up
More wealth by far than those that brag of faith:
There's Kirriah Jairim, the great Jew of Greece.
Obed in Bairseth, Nones in Portugal,
Myself in Malta, some in Italy,
Many in France, and wealthy every one;
Ay, wealthier far than any Christian.
I must confess we come not to be kings:
That's not our fault: alas, our number's few!
And crowns come either by succession,
Or urg'd by force; and nothing violent,
Oft have I heard tell, can be permanent.
Give us a peaceful rule; make Christians kings,

That thirst so much for principality.
I have no charge, nor many children,
But one sole daughter, whom I hold as dear
As Agamemnon did his Iphigen;
And all I have is hers.—But who comes here?

Enter three Jews.

First Jew. Tush, tell not me; 'twas done of policy.
Sec. Jew. Come, therefore, let us go to Barabas;
For he can counsel best in these affairs:
And here he comes.
Bara. Why, how now, countrymen!
Why flock you thus to me in multitudes?
What accident's betided to the Jews?
First Jew. A fleet of warlike galleys, Barabas,
Are come from Turkey, and lie in our road:
And they this day sit in the council-house
To entertain them and their embassy.
Bara. Why, let 'em come, so they come not to war;
Or let 'em war, so we be conquerors.—
Nay, let 'em combat, conquer, and kill all.
So they spare me, my daughter, and my wealth. [*Aside.*
First Jew. Were it for confirmation of a league,
They would not come in warlike manner thus.
Sec. Jew. I fear their coming will afflict us all.
Bara. Fond men, what dream you of their multitudes?
What need they treat of peace that are in league?
The Turks and those of Malta are in league:
Tut, tut, there is some other matter in't.
First Jew. Why, Barabas, they come for peace or war.
Bara. Haply for neither, but to pass along,
Towards Venice, by the Adriatic sea,
With whom they have attempted many times,
But never could effect their stratagem.
Third Jew. And very wisely said; it may be so.
Sec. Jew. But there's a meeting in the senate-house,
And all the Jews in Malta must be there.
Bara. Hum,—all the Jews in Malta must be there!
Ay, like enough: why, then, let every man
Provide him, and be there for fashion-sake.
If anything shall there concern our state,
Assure yourselves I'll look—unto myself. [*Aside.*
First Jew. I know you will.—Well, brethren, let us go.

Sec. Jew. Let's take our leaves.—Farewell, good Barabas.
Bara. Do so. Farewell, Zaareth; farewell, Temainte.
[*Exeunt Jews.*
And, Barabas, now search this secret out;
Summon thy senses, call thy wits together:
These silly men mistake the matter clean,
Long to the Turk did Malta contribute;
Which tribute all in policy, I fear,
The Turk has let increase to such a sum
As all the wealth of Malta cannot pay;
And now by that advantage thinks, belike,
To seize upon the town; ay, that he seeks.
Howe'er the world go, I'll make sure for one,
And seek in time to intercept the worst,
Warily guarding that which I ha' got:
Ego mihimet sum semper proximus :
Why, let 'em enter, let 'em take the town. [*Exit.*

Enter FERNEZE *governor of Malta,* Knights, *and* Officers; *met by* CALYMATH, *and* Bassoes *of the* Turk.

Fern. Now, bassoes, what demand you at our hands?
First Bas. Know, knights of Malta, that we came from Rhodes,
From Cyprus, Candy, and those other isles
That lie betwixt the Mediterranean seas.
Fern. What's Cyprus, Candy, and those other isles
To us or Malta? what at our hands demand ye?
Cal. The ten years' tribute that remains unpaid.
Fern. Alas, my lord, the sum is over-great!
I hope your highness will consider us.
Cal. I wish, grave governor, 'twere in my power
To favour you; but 'tis my father's cause.
Wherein I may not, nay, I dare not dally.
Fern. Then give us leave, great Selim Calymath.
Cal. Stand all aside, and let the knights determine;
And send to keep our galleys under sail,
For happily we shall not tarry here.—
Now, governor, how are you resolv'd?
Fern. Thus; since your hard conditions are such
That you will needs have ten years' tribute past,
We may have time to make collection
Amongst the inhabitants of Malta for't.
First Bas. That's more than is in our commission.
Cal. What, Callapine! a little courtesy:

Let's know their time; perhaps it is not long;
And 'tis more kingly to obtain by peace
Than to enforce conditions by constraint.—
What respite ask you, governor?

Fern. But a month.

Cal. We grant a month; but see you keep your promise.
Now launch our galleys back again to sea,
Where we'll attend the respite you have ta'en,
And for the money send our messenger.
Farewell, great governor, and brave knights of Malta.

Fern. And all good fortune wait on Calymath!
[*Exeunt Calymath and Bassoes.*
Go one and call those Jews of Malta hither:
Were they not summon'd to appear to-day?

First Off. They were, my lord; and here they come.

Enter BARABAS *and three* Jews.

First Knight. Have you determin'd what to say to them?

Fern. Yes; give me leave:—and, Hebrews, now come near.
From the Emperor of Turkey is arriv'd
Great Selim Calymath, his highness' son,
To levy of us ten years' tribute past:
Now, then, here know that it concerneth us.

Bara. Then, good my lord, to keep your quiet still,
Your lordship shall do well to let them have it.

Fern. Soft, Barabas! there's more 'longs to't than so.
To what this ten years' tribute will amount,
That we have cast, but cannot compass it
By reason of the wars, that robb'd our store;
And therefore are we to request your aid.

Bara. Alas, my lord, we are no soldiers!
And what's our aid against so great a prince?

First Knight. Tut, Jew, we know thou art no soldier:
That art a merchant and a money'd man,
And 'tis thy money, Barabas, we seek.

Bara. How, my lord! my money!

Fern. Thine and the rest;
For, to be short, amongst you't must be had.

First Jew. Alas, my lord, the most of us are poor!

Fern. Then let the rich increase your portions.

Bara. Are strangers with your tribute to be tax'd?

Sec. Knight. Have strangers leave with us to get their wealth?

Then let them with us contribute.

Bara. How! equally?

Fern. No, Jew, like infidels;
For through our sufferance of your hateful lives,
Who stand accursed in the sight of heaven,
These taxes and afflictions are befall'n,
And therefore thus we are determined.
Read there the articles of our decrees.

Officer. [reads] *First, the tribute-money of the Turks shall all be levied amongst the Jews, and each of them to pay one half of his estate.*

Bara. How! half his estate!—I hope you mean not mine. [*Aside.*

Fern. Read on.

Officer. [reads] *Secondly, he that denies to pay, shall straight become a Christian.*

Bara. How! a Christian!—Hum,—what's here to do? [*Aside.*

Officer. [reads] *Lastly, he that denies this, shall absolutely lose all he has.*

Three Jews. O my lord, we will give half!

Bara. O earth-mettled villains, and no Hebrews born!
And will you basely thus submit yourselves
To leave your goods to their arbitrement?

Fern. Why, Barabas, wilt thou be christened?

Bara. No, governor, I will be no convertite.

Fern. Then pay thy half.

Bara. Why, know you what you did by this device?
Half of my substance is a city's wealth.
Governor, it was not got so easily;
Nor will I part so slightly therewithal.

Fern. Sir, half is the penalty of our decree;
Either pay that, or we will seize on all.

Bara. *Corpo di Dio!* stay: you shall have half;
Let me be us'd but as my brethren are.

Fern. No, Jew, thou hast denied the articles,
And now it cannot be recall'd.

[*Exeunt Officers, on a sign from Ferneze.*

Bara. Will you, then, steal my goods?
Is theft the ground of your religion?

Fern. No, Jew; we take particularly thine,
To save the ruin of a multitude:
And better one want for a common good,

Than many perish for a private man:
Yet, Barabas, we will not banish thee,
But here in Malta, where thou gott'st thy wealth,
Live still; and, if thou canst, get more.

Bara. Christians, what or how can I multiply?
Of naught is nothing made.

First Knight. From naught at first thou cam'st to little wealth,
From little unto more, from more to most:
If your first curse fall heavy on thy head,
And make thee poor and scorn'd of all the world,
'Tis not our fault, but thy inherent sin.

Bara. What, bring you Scripture to confirm your wrongs?
Preach me not out of my possessions.
Some Jews are wicked, as all Christians are;
But say the tribe that I descended of
Were all in general cast away for sin,
Shall I be tried for their transgression?
The man that dealeth righteously shall live;
And which of you can charge me otherwise?

Fern. Out, wretched Barabas!
Sham'st thou not thus to justify thyself,
As if we knew not thy profession?
If thou rely upon thy righteousness,
Be patient, and thy riches will increase.
Excess of wealth is cause of covetousness;
And covetousness, O, 'tis a monstrous sin!

Bara. Ay, but theft is worse: tush! take not from me, then,
For that is theft; and, if you rob me thus,
I must be forc'd to steal, and compass more.

First Knight. Grave governor, list not to his exclaims:
Convert his mansion to a nunnery;
His house will harbour many holy nuns.

Fern. It shall be so.

Re-enter Officers.

Now, officers, have you done?

First Off. Ay, my lord, we have seiz'd upon the goods
And wares of Barabas, which, being valu'd,
Amount to more than all the wealth in Malta:
And of the other we have seiz'd half.

Fern. Then we'll take order for the residue.

Bara. Well, then, my lord, say, are you satisfied?

You have my goods, my money, and my wealth,
My ships, my store, and all that I enjoy'd;
And, having all, you can request no more,
Unless your unrelenting flinty hearts
Suppress all pity in your stony breasts,
And now shall move you to bereave my life.

Fern. No, Barabas; to stain our hands with blood
Is far from us and our profession.

Bara. Why, I esteem the injury far less,
To take the lives of miserable men
Than be the causers of their misery.
You have my wealth, the labour of my life,
The comfort of mine age, my children's hope;
And therefore ne'er distinguish of the wrong.

Fern. Content thee, Barabas; thou hast naught but right.

Bara. Your extreme right does me exceeding wrong:
But take it to you, i' the devil's name!

Fern. Come, let us in, and gather of these goods
The money for this tribute of the Turk.

First Knight. 'Tis necessary that be look'd unto;
For, if we break our day, we break the league,
And that will prove but simple policy.
[*Exeunt all except Barabas and the three Jews.*

Bara. Ay, policy! that's their profession,
And not simplicity, as they suggest.—
The plagues of Egypt, and the curse of heaven,
Earth's barrenness, and all men's hatred,
Inflict upon them, thou great *Primus Motor!*
And here upon my knees, striking the earth,
I ban their souls to everlasting pains,
And extreme tortures of the fiery deep,
That thus have dealt with me in my distress!

First Jew. O, yet be patient, gentle Barabas!

Bara. O silly brethren, born to see this day,
Why stand you thus unmov'd with my laments?
Why weep you not to think upon my wrongs?
Why pine not I, and die in this distress?

First Jew. Why, Barabas, as hardly can we brook
The cruel handling of ourselves in this:
Thou seest they have taken half our goods.

Bara. Why did you yield to their extortion?
You were a multitude, and I but one;
And of me only have they taken all.

First Jew. Yet, brother Barabas, remember Job.
Bara. What tell you me of Job? I wot his wealth
Was written thus; he had seven thousand sheep,
Three thousand camels, and two hundred yoke
Of labouring oxen, and five hundred
She asses: but for every one of those,
Had they been valu'd at indifferent rate,
I had at home, and in mine argosy,
And other ships that came from Egypt last,
As much as would have bought his beasts and him,
And yet have kept enough to live upon;
So that not he, but I, may curse the day,
Thy fatal birthday, forlorn Barabas;
And henceforth wish for an eternal night,
That clouds of darkness may inclose my flesh,
And hide these extreme sorrows from mine eyes;
For only I have toil'd to inherit here
The months of vanity, and loss of time,
And painful nights, have been appointed me.
Sec. Jew. Good Barabas, be patient.
Bara. Ay, I pray, leave me in my patience. You, that
Were ne'er possess'd of wealth, are pleas'd with want;
But give him liberty at least to mourn,
That in a field, amidst his enemies,
Doth see his soldiers slain, himself disarm'd,
And know no means of his recovery:
Ay, let me sorrow for this sudden chance;
'Tis in the trouble of my spirit I speak:
Great injuries are not so soon forgot.
First Jew. Come, let us leave him; in his ireful mood
Our words will but increase his ecstasy.
Sec. Jew. On, then: but, trust me, 'tis a misery
To see a man in such affliction.—
Farewell, Barabas.
Bara. Ay, fare you well. [*Exeunt three Jews.*
See the simplicity of these base slaves,
Who, for the villains have no wit themselves,
Think me to be a senseless lump of clay,
That will with every water wash to dirt!
No, Barabas is born to better chance,
And fram'd of finer mould than common men,
That measure naught but by the present time.
A reaching thought will search his deepest wits,

And casts with cunning for the time to come;
For evils are apt to happen every day.

Enter ABIGAIL.

But whither wends my beauteous Abigail?
O, what has made my lovely daughter sad?
What, woman! moan not for a little loss;
Thy father has enough in store for thee.
Abig. Not for myself, but aged Barabas,
Father, for thee lamenteth Abigail:
But I will learn to leave these fruitless tears;
And, urg'd thereto with my afflictions,
With fierce exclaims run to the senate-house,
And in the senate reprehend them all,
And rent their hearts with tearing of my hair,
Till they reduce the wrongs done to my father.
Bara. No, Abigail; things past recovery
Are hardly cur'd with exclamations:
Be silent, daughter; sufferance breeds ease,
And time may yield us an occasion,
Which on the sudden cannot serve the turn.
Besides, my girl, think me not all so fond
As negligently to forego so much
Without provision for thyself and me:
Ten thousand portagues, besides great pearls,
Rich costly jewels, and stones infinite,
Fearing the worst of this before it fell,
I closely hid.
Abig. Where, father?
Bara. In my house, my girl.
Abig. Then shall they ne'er be seen of Barabas;
For they have seiz'd upon thy house and wares.
Bara. But they will give me leave once more, I trow,
To go into my house.
Abig. That may they not;
For there I left the governor placing nuns,
Displacing me; and of thy house they mean
To make a nunnery, where none but their own sect
Must enter in; men generally barr'd.
Bara. My gold, my gold, and all my wealth is gone!—
You partial heavens, have I deserv'd this plague?
What, will you thus oppose me, luckless stars,
To make me desperate in my poverty?

And, knowing me impatient in distress,
Think me so mad as I will hang myself,
That I may vanish o'er the earth in air,
And leave no memory that e'er I was?
No, I will live; nor loathe I this my life:
And, since you leave me in the ocean thus
To sink or swim, and put me to my shifts,
I'll rouse my senses, and awake myself.—
Daughter, I have it: thou perceiv'st the plight
Wherein these Christians have oppressed me:
Be rul'd by me, for in extremity
We ought to make bar of no policy.

Abig. Father, whate'er it be, to injure them
That have so manifestly wronged us,
What will not Abigail attempt?

Bara. Why, so.
Then thus: thou told'st me they have turn'd my house
Into a nunnery, and some nuns are there?

Abig. I did.

Bara. Then, Abigail, there must my girl
Entreat the abbess to be entertain'd.

Abig. How! as a nun?

Bara. Ay, daughter; for religion
Hides many mischiefs from suspicion.

Abig. Ay, but, father, they will suspect me there.

Bara. Let 'em suspect; but be thou so precise
As they may think it done of holiness:
Entreat 'em fair, and give them friendly speech,
And seem to them as if thy sins were great,
Till thou hast gotten to be entertain'd.

Abig. Thus, father, shall I much dissemble.

Bara. Tush!
As good dissemble that thou never mean'st,
As first mean truth and then dissemble it:
A counterfeit profession is better
Than unseen hypocrisy.

Abig. Well, father, say I be entertain'd,
What then shall follow?

Bara. This shall follow then.
There have I hid, close underneath the plank
That runs along the upper-chamber floor,
The gold and jewels which I kept for thee:—
But here they come: be cunning, Abigail.

Abig. Then, father, go with me.
Bara. No, Abigail, in this
It is not necessary I be seen;
For I will seem offended with thee for't:
Be close, my girl, for this must fetch my gold.
[*They retire.*

Enter FRIAR JACOMO, FRIAR BARNARDINE, Abbess, *and a* Nun.

Friar Jac. Sisters,
We now are almost at the new-made nunnery.
Abb. The better; for we love not to be seen:
'Tis thirty winters long since some of us
Did stray so far amongst the multitude.
Friar Jac. But, madam, this house
And waters of this new-made nunnery
Will much delight you.
Abb. It may be so.—But who comes here?
[*Abigail comes forward.*
Abig. Grave abbess, and you happy virgins' guide,
Pity the state of a distressed maid!
Abb. What art thou, daughter?
Abig. The hopeless daughter of a hapless Jew,
The Jew of Malta, wretched Barabas,
Sometime the owner of a goodly house,
Which they have now turn'd to a nunnery.
Abb. Well, daughter, say, what is thy suit with us?
Abig. Fearing the afflictions which my father feels
Proceed from sin or want of faith in us,
I'd pass away my life in penitence,
And be a novice in your nunnery,
To make atonement for my labouring soul.
Friar Jac. No doubt, brother, but this proceedeth of the spirit.
Friar Barn. Ay, and of a moving spirit too, brother: but come,
Let us entreat she may be entertain'd.
Abb. Well, daughter, we admit you for a nun.
Abig. First let me as a novice learn to frame
My solitary life to your strait laws,
And let me lodge where I was wont to lie:
I do not doubt, by your divine precepts
And mine own industry, but to profit much.

Bara. As much, I hope, as all I hid is worth. [*Aside.*
Abb. Come, daughter, follow us.
Bara. [*coming forward*] Why, how now, Abigail!
What mak'st thou 'mongst these hateful Christians?
Friar Jac. Hinder her not, thou man of little faith,
For she has mortified herself.
Bara. How! mortified!
Friar Jar. And is admitted to the sisterhood.
Bara. Child of perdition, and thy father's shame!
What wilt thou do among these hateful fiends?
I charge thee on my blessing that thou leave
These devils and their damned heresy!
Abig. Father, give me—
Bara. Nay, back, Abigail——
And think upon the jewels and the gold;
The board is marked thus that covers it.—
[*Aside to Abigail in a whisper.*
Away, accursed, from thy father's sight!
Friar Jac. Barabas, although thou art in misbelief,
And wilt not see thine own afflictions,
Yet let thy daughter be no longer blind.
Bara. Blind friar, I reck not thy persuasions,—
The board is marked thus that covers it—
[*Aside to Abigail in a whisper.*
For I had rather die than see her thus.—
Wilt thou forsake me too in my distress,
Seduced daughter?—Go, forget not.—
[*Aside to her in a whisper.*
Becomes it Jews to be so credulous?—
To-morrow early I'll be at the door.—
[*Aside to her in a whisper.*
No, come not at me; if thou wilt be damn'd,
Forget me, see me not; and so, be gone!—
Farewell; remember to-morrow morning.—
[*Aside to her in a whisper.*
Out, out, thou wretch!
[*Exit, on one side, Barabas. Exeunt, on the other side, Friars, Abbess, Nun, and Abigail: and, as they are going out,*

Enter MATHIAS.

Math. Who's this? fair Abigail, the rich Jew's daughter,
Become a nun! her father's sudden fall

Has humbled her, and brought her down to this:
Tut, she were fitter for a tale of love,
Than to be tired out with orisons;
And better would she far become a bed,
Embraced in a friendly lover's arms,
Than rise at midnight to a solemn mass.

Enter LODOWICK.

Lod. Why, how now, Don Mathias! in a dump?
Math. Believe me, noble Lodowick, I have seen
The strangest sight, in my opinion,
That ever I beheld.
Lod. What was't, I prithee?
Math. A fair young maid, scarce fourteen years of age,
The sweetest flower in Cytherea's field,
Cropt from the pleasures of the fruitful earth,
And strangely metamorphos'd [to a] nun.
Lod. But say, what was she?
Math. Why, the rich Jew's daughter.
Lod. What, Barabas, whose goods were lately seiz'd?
Is she so fair?
Math. And matchless beautiful.
As, had you seen her, 'twould have mov'd your heart,
Though countermin'd with walls of brass, to love,
Or, at the least, to pity.
Lod. An if she be so fair as you report,
'Twere time well spent to go and visit her:
How say you? shall we?
Math. I must and will, sir; there's no remedy.
Lod. And so will I too, or it shall go hard.
Farewell, Mathias.
Math. Farewell, Lodowick. [*Exeunt severally.*

ACT II

Enter BARABAS, *with a light.*

Bara. Thus, like the sad presaging raven, that tolls
The sick man's passport in her hollow beak,
And in the shadow of the silent night
Doth shake contagion from her sable wings,
Vex'd and tormented runs poor Barabas

With fatal curses towards these Christians.
The incertain pleasures of swift-footed time
Have ta'en their flight, and left me in despair;
And of my former riches rests no more
But bare remembrance; like a soldier's scar,
That has no further comfort for his maim.—
O Thou, that with a fiery pillar ledd'st
The sons of Israel through the dismal shades,
Light Abraham's offspring; and direct the hand
Of Abigail this night! or let the day
Turn to eternal darkness after this!—
No sleep can fasten on my watchful eyes,
Nor quiet enter my distemper'd thoughts,
Till I have answer of my Abigail.

Enter ABIGAIL *above.*

Abig. Now have I happily espied a time
To search the plank my father did appoint;
And here, behold, unseen, where I have found
The gold, the pearls, and jewels, which he hid.

Bara. Now I remember those old women's words,
Who in my wealth would tell me winter's tales,
And speak of spirits and ghosts that glide by night
About the place where treasure hath been hid:
And now methinks that I am one of those;
For, whilst I live, here lives my soul's sole hope,
And, when I die, here shall my spirit walk.

Abig. Now that my father's fortune were so good
As but to be about this happy place!
'Tis not so happy: yet, when we parted last,
He said he would attend me in the morn.
Then, gentle Sleep, where'er his body rests,
Give charge to Morpheus that he may dream
A golden dream, and of the sudden wake,
Come and receive the treasure I have found.

Bara. Bueno para todos mi ganado no era:
As good go on, as sit so sadly thus.—
But stay: what star shines yonder in the east?
The loadstar of my life, if Abigail.—
Who's there?

Abig. Who's that?

Bara. Peace, Abigail! 'tis I.

Abig. Then, father, here receive thy happiness.

Bara. Hast thou't?
Abig. Here. [*Throws down bags*] Hast thou't?
There's more, and more, and more.
Bara. O my girl,
My gold, my fortune, my felicity,
Strength to my soul, death to mine enemy;
Welcome the first beginner of my bliss!
O Abigail, Abigail, that I had thee here too!
Then my desires were fully satisfied:
But I will practise thy enlargement thence:
O girl! O gold! O beauty! O my bliss!
[*Hugs the bags.*
Abig. Father, it draweth towards midnight now,
And 'bout this time the nuns begin to wake;
To shun suspicion, therefore, let us part.
Bara. Farewell, my joy, and by my fingers take
A kiss from him that sends it from his soul.
[*Exit Abigail above.*
Now, Phœbus, ope the eye-lids of the day,
And, for the raven, wake the morning lark,
That I may hover with her in the air,
Singing o'er these, as she does o'er her young.
Hermoso placer de los dineros. [*Exit.*

Enter FERNEZE, MARTIN DEL BOSCO, Knights, *and* Officers.

Fern. Now, captain, tell us whither thou art bound?
Whence is thy ship that anchors in our road?
And why thou cam'st ashore without our leave?
Bosco. Governor of Malta, hither am I bound;
My ship, the Flying Dragon, is of Spain,
And so am I; Del Bosco is my name,
Vice-admiral unto the Catholic King.
First Knight. 'Tis true, my lord; therefore entreat him well.
Bosco. Our fraught is Grecians, Turks, and Afric Moors;
For late upon the coast of Corsica,
Because we vail'd not to the Turkish fleet,
Their creeping galleys had us in the chase:
But suddenly the wind began to rise,
And then we luff'd and tack'd, and fought at ease:
Some have we fir'd, and many have we sunk;
But one amongst the rest became our prize:

The captain's slain; the rest remain our slaves,
Of whom we would make sale in Malta here.

Fern. Martin del Bosco, I have heard of thee:
Welcome to Malta, and to all of us!
But to admit a sale of these thy Turks,
We may not, nay, we dare not give consent,
By reason of a tributary league.

First Knight. Del Bosco, as thou lov'st and honour'st us,
Persuade our governor against the Turk:
This truce we have is but in hope of gold,
And with that sum he craves might we wage war.

Bosco. Will knights of Malta be in league with Turks,
And buy it basely too for sums of gold?
My lord, remember that, to Europe's shame,
The Christian Isle of Rhodes, from whence you came,
Was lately lost, and you were stated here
To be at deadly enmity with Turks.

Fern. Captain, we know it; but our force is small.

Bosco. What is the sum that Calymath requires?

Fern. A hundred thousand crowns.

Bosco. My lord and king hath title to this isle,
And he means quickly to expel you hence;
Therefore be rul'd by me, and keep the gold:
I'll write unto his majesty for aid,
And not depart until I see you free.

Fern. On this condition shall thy Turks be sold.—
Go, officers, and set them straight in show.—
[*Exeunt Officers.*

Bosco, thou shalt be Malta's general;
We and our warlike knights will follow thee
Against these barbarous misbelieving Turks.

Bosco. So shall you imitate those you succeed;
For, when their hideous force environ'd Rhodes,
Small though the number was that kept the town,
They fought it out, and not a man surviv'd
To bring the hapless news to Christendom.

Fern. So will we fight it out; come, let's away.
Proud daring Calymath, instead of gold,
We'll send thee bullets wrapt in smoke and fire:
Claim tribute where thou wilt, we are resolv'd—
Honour is bought with blood, and not with gold.
[*Exeunt.*

Enter Officers, *with* ITHAMORE *and other* Slaves.

First Off. This is the market-place; here let 'em stand:
Fear not their sale, for they'll be quickly bought.

Sec. Off. Every one's price is written on his back,
And so much must they yield, or not be sold.

First Off. Here comes the Jew: had not his goods been seiz'd,
He'd give us present money for them all.

Enter BARABAS.

Bara. In spite of these swine-eating Christians,
(Unchosen nation, never circumcis'd,
Poor villains, such as were ne'er thought upon
Till Titus and Vespasian conquer'd us,)
Am I become as wealthy as I was.
They hop'd my daughter would ha' been a nun;
But she's at home, and I have bought a house
As great and fair as is the governor's:
And there, in spite of Malta, will I dwell,
Having Ferneze's hand; whose heart I'll have,
Ay, and his son's too, or it shall go hard.
I am not of the tribe of Levi, I,
That can so soon forget an injury.
We Jews can fawn like spaniels when we please;
And when we grin we bite; yet are our looks
As innocent and harmless as a lamb's.
I learn'd in Florence how to kiss my hand,
Heave up my shoulders when they call me dog,
And duck as low as any bare-foot friar;
Hoping to see them starve upon a stall,
Or else be gather'd for in our synagogue,
That, when the offering-basin comes to me,
Even for charity I may spit into't.—
Here comes Don Lodowick, the governor's son,
One that I love for his good father's sake.

Enter LODOWICK

Lod. I hear the wealthy Jew walked this way:
I'll seek him out, and so insinuate,
That I may have a sight of Abigail,
For Don Mathias tells me she is fair.

Bara. Now will I show myself to have more of the serpent than the dove; that is, more knave than fool. [*Aside.*

Lod. Yond' walks the Jew: now for fair Abigail.
Bara. Ay, ay, no doubt but she's at your command. [*Aside.*
Lod. Barabas, thou know'st I am the governor's son.
Bara. I would you were his father too, sir! that's all the harm I wish you.—The slave looks like a hog's cheek new singed. [*Aside.*
Lod. Whither walk'st thou, Barabas?
Bara. No further: 'tis a custom held with us,
That when we speak with Gentiles like to you,
We turn into the air to purge ourselves;
For unto us the promise doth belong.
Lod. Well, Barabas, canst help me to a diamond?
Bara. O, sir, your father had my diamonds:
Yet I have one left that will serve your turn.—
I mean my daughter; but, ere he shall have her,
I'll sacrifice her on a pile of wood:
I ha' the poison of the city for him,
And the white leprosy. [*Aside.*
Lod. What sparkle does it give without a foil?
Bara. The diamond that I talk of ne'er was foil'd:—
But, when he touches it, it will be foil'd.— [*Aside.*
Lord Lodowick, it sparkles bright and fair.
Lod. Is it square or pointed? pray, let me know.
Bara. Pointed it is, good sir,—but not for you. [*Aside.*
Lod. I like it much the better.
Bara. So do I too.
Lod. How shows it by night?
Bara. Outshines Cynthia's rays:—
You'll like it better far o' nights than days. [*Aside.*
Lod. And what's the price?
Bara. Your life, an if you have it [*Aside*].—O my lord,
We will not jar about the price: come to my house,
And I will give't your honour—with a vengeance. [*Aside.*
Lod. No, Barabas, I will deserve it first.
Bara. Good sir,
Your father has deserv'd it at my hands,
Who, of mere charity and Christian ruth,
To bring me to religious purity,
And, as it were, in catechising sort,
To make me mindful of my mortal sins,

Against my will, and whether I would or no,
Seiz'd all I had, and thrust me out of doors,
And made my house a place for nuns most chaste.

Lod. No doubt your soul shall reap the fruit of it.

Bara. Ay, but, my lord, the harvest is far off:
And yet I know the prayers of those nuns
And holy friars, having money for their pains,
Are wondrous;—and indeed do no man good;— [*Aside.*
And, seeing they are not idle, but still doing,
'Tis likely they in time may reap some fruit,
I mean, in fullness of perfection.

Lod. Good Barabas, glance not at our holy nuns.

Bara. No, but I do it through a burning zeal,—
Hoping ere long to set the house a-fire;
For, though they do a while increase and multiply,
I'll have a saying to that nunnery.— [*Aside.*
As for the diamond, sir, I told you of,
Come home, and there's no price shall make us part,
Even for your honourable father's sake,—
It shall go hard but I will see your death.— [*Aside.*
But now I must be gone to buy a slave.

Lod. And, Barabas, I'll bear thee company.

Bara. Come, then; here's the market place.—
What's the price of this slave? two hundred crowns! do the Turks weigh so much?

First Off. Sir, that's his price.

Bara. What, can he steal, that you demand so much?
Belike he has some new trick for a purse;
An if he has, he is worth three hundred plates,
So that, being bought, the town seal might be got
To keep him for his life-time from the gallows:
The sessions-day is critical to thieves,
And few or none escape but by being purg'd.

Lod. Rat'st thou this Moor but at two hundred plates?

First Off. No more, my lord.

Bara. Why should this Turk be dearer than that Moor?

First Off. Because he is young, and has more qualities.

Bara. What, hast the philosopher's stone? an thou hast, break my head with it, I'll forgive thee.

Slave. No, sir; I can cut and shave.

Bara. Let me see, sirrah; are you not an old shaver?

Slave. Alas, sir, I am a very youth!

Bara. A youth! I'll buy you, and marry you to Lady Vanity, if you do well.

Slave. I will serve you, sir.

Bara. Some wicked trick or other: it may be, under colour of shaving, thou'lt cut my throat for my goods. Tell me, hast thou thy health well?

Slave. Ay, passing well.

Bara. So much the worse: I must have one that's sickly, an't be but for sparing victuals: 'tis not a stone of beef a day will maintain you in these chops.—Let me see one that's somewhat leaner.

First Off. Here's a leaner; how like you him?

Bara. Where wast thou born?

Itha. In Thrace; brought up in Arabia.

Bara. So much the better; thou art for my turn.
An hundred crowns? I'll have him; there's the coin.
[*Gives money.*

First Off. Then mark him, sir, and take him hence.

Bara. Ay, mark him, you were best; for this is he
That by my help shall do much villany.— [*Aside.*
My lord, farewell.—Come, sirrah; you are mine.—
As for the diamond, it shall be yours:
I pray, sir, be no stranger at my house;
All that I have shall be at your command.

Enter Mathias *and* Katharine.

Math. What make the Jew and Lodowick so private?
I fear me 'tis about fair Abigail. [*Aside.*

Bara. [*to Lod.*] Yonder comes Don Mathias; let us stay:
He loves my daughter, and she holds him dear;
But I have sworn to frustrate both their hopes,
And be reveng'd upon the—governor. [*Aside.*
[*Exit Lodowick.*

Kath. This Moor is comeliest, is he not? speak, son.

Math. No, this is the better, mother, view this well.

Bara. Seem not to know me here before your mother,
Lest she mistrust the match that is in hand:
When you have brought her home, come to my house;
Think of me as thy father; son, farewell.

Math. But wherefore talk'd Don Lodowick with you?

Bara. Tush, man! we talk'd of diamonds, not of Abigail.

Kath. Tell me, Mathias, is not that the Jew?

Bara. As for the comment on the Maccabees,
I have it, sir, and 'tis at your command.

Math. Yes, madam, and my talk with him was
About the borrowing of a book or two.
Kath. Converse not with him; he is cast off from heaven.—
Thou hast thy crowns, fellow.—Come, let's away.
Math. Sirrah Jew, remember the book.
Bara. Marry, will I, sir.
[*Exeunt Katharine and Mathias.*
First Off. Come, I have made a reasonable market; let's away. [*Exeunt Officers with Slaves.*
Bara. Now let me know thy name, and therewithal
Thy birth, condition, and profession.
Itha. Faith, sir, my birth is but mean; my name's
Ithamore; my profession what you please.
Bara. Hast thou no trade? then listen to my words,
And I will teach [thee] that shall stick by thee:
First, be thou void of these affections,
Compassion, love, vain hope, and heartless fear;
Be mov'd at nothing, see thou pity none,
But to thyself smile when the Christians moan.
Itha. O, brave, master! I worship your nose for this.
Bara. As for myself, I walk abroad o' nights,
And kill sick people groaning under walls:
Sometimes I go about and poison wells;
And now and then, to cherish Christian thieves,
I am content to lose some of my crowns,
That I may, walking in my gallery,
See 'em go pinion'd along by my door.
Being young, I studied physic, and began
To practise first upon the Italian;
There I enrich'd the priests with burials,
And always kept the sexton's arms in ure
With digging graves and ringing dead men's knells:
And, after that, was I an engineer,
And in the wars 'twixt France and Germany,
Under the pretence of helping Charles the Fifth,
Slew friend and enemy with my stratagems:
Then, after that, was I an usurer,
And with extorting, cozening, forfeiting,
And tricks belonging unto brokery,
I fill'd the gaols with bankrupts in a year,
And with young orphans planted hospitals;
And every moon made some or other mad,
And now and then one hang himself for grief,

Pinning upon his breast a long great scroll
How I with interest tormented him.
But mark how I am blest for plaguing them;—
I have as much coin as will buy the town.
But tell me now, how hast thou spent thy time?

Itha. Faith, master.
In setting Christian villages on fire,
Chaining of eunuchs, binding galley slaves.
One time I was an hostler at an inn,
And in the night time secretly would I steal
To travellers' chambers, and there cut their throats.
Once at Jerusalem, where the pilgrims kneel'd,
I strewed powder on the marble stones,
And therewithal their knees would rankle so,
That I have laugh'd a-good to see the cripples
Go limping home to Christendom on stilts.

Bara. Why, this is something: make account of me
As of thy fellow; we are villains both;
Both circumcised; we hate Christians both:
Be true and secret; thou shalt want no gold.
But stand aside; here comes Don Lodowick.

Enter LODOWICK

Lod. O, Barabas, well met;
Where is the diamond you told me of?

Bara. I have it for you, sir: please you walk in with me.—
What, ho, Abigail! open the door, I say!

Enter ABIGAIL, *with letters.*

Abig. In good time, father; here are letters come
From Ormus, and the post stays here within.

Bara. Give me the letters.—Daughter, do you hear?
Entertain Lodowick, the governor's son,
With all the courtesy you can afford,
Provided that you keep your maidenhead——
Use him as if he were a Philistine;
Dissemble, swear, protest, vow love to him:
He is not of the seed of Abraham.— [*Aside to her.*
I am a little busy, sir; pray, pardon me.—
Abigail, bid him welcome for my sake.

Abig. For your sake and his own he's welcome hither.

Bara. Daughter, a word more: kiss him, speak him fair,
And like a cunning Jew so cast about,

That ye be both made sure ere you come out.
[*Aside to her.*
Abig. O father, Don Mathias is my love! [*Aside to him.*
Bara. I know it: yet, I say, make love to him;
Do, it is requisite it should be so.— [*Aside to her.*
Nay, on my life, it is my factor's hand;
But go you in, I'll think upon the account.
[*Exeunt Abigail and Lodowick into the house.*
The account is made, for Lodovico dies.
My factor sends me word that a merchant's fled
That owes me for a hundred tun of wine:
I weigh it thus much [*snapping his fingers*]! I have wealth enough;
For now by this has he kiss'd Abigail,
And she vows love to him, and he to her.
As sure as heaven rain'd manna for the Jews,
So sure shall he and Don Mathias die:
His father was my chiefest enemy.

Enter MATHIAS.

Whither goes Don Mathias? stay a while.
Math. Whither, but to my fair love Abigail?
Bara. Thou know'st, and heaven can witness it is true,
That I intend my daughter shall be thine.
Math. Ay, Barabas, or else thou wrong'st me much.
Bara. O, heaven forbid I should have such a thought!
Pardon me though I weep: the governor's son
Will, whether I will or no, have Abigail;
He sends her letters, bracelets, jewels, rings.
Math. Does she receive them?
Bara. She! no, Mathias, no, but sends them back;
And, when he comes, she locks herself up fast;
Yet through the key-hole will he talk to her,
While she runs to the window looking out
When you should come and hale him from the door.
Math. O treacherous Lodowick!
Bara. Even now, as I came home, he slipt me in,
And I am sure he is with Abigail.
Math. I'll rouse him thence.
Bara. Not for all Malta; therefore sheatne your sword;
If you love me, no quarrels in my house;
But steal you in, and seem to see him not:
I'll give him such a warning ere he goes,

As he shall have small hopes of Abigail.
Away, for here they come.

Re-enter LODOWICK *and* ABIGAIL.

Math. What, hand in hand! I cannot suffer this.
Bara. Mathias, as thou lov'st me, not a word.
Math. Well, let it pass; another time shall serve.
[*Exit into the house.*
Lod. Barabas, is not that the widow's son?
Bara. Ay, and take heed, for he hath sworn your death.
Lod. My death! what, is the base-born peasant mad?
Bara. No, no; but happily he stands in fear
Of that which you, I think, ne'er dream upon,—
My daughter here, a paltry silly girl.
Lod. Why, loves she Don Mathias?
Bara. Doth she not with her smiling answer you?
Abig. He has my heart; I smile against my will. [*Aside.*
Lod. Barabas, thou know'st I have lov'd thy daughter long.
Bara. And so has she done you, even from a child.
Lod. And now I can no longer hold my mind.
Bara. Nor I the affection that I bear to you.
Lod. This is thy diamond; tell me, shall I have it?
Bara. Win it, and wear it; it is yet unsoil'd.
O, but I know your lordship would disdain
To marry with the daughter of a Jew:
And yet I'll give her many a golden cross,
With Christian posies round about the ring.
Lod. 'Tis not thy wealth, but her that I esteem;
Yet crave I thy consent.
Bara. And mine you have; yet let me talk to her.—
This offspring of Cain, this Jebusite,
That never tasted of the Passover,
Nor e'er shall see the land of Canaan,
Nor our Messias that is yet to come;
This gentle maggot, Lodowick, I mean,
Must be deluded: let him have thy hand,
But keep thy heart till Don Mathias comes.
[*Aside to her.*
Abig. What, shall I be betroth'd to Lodowick?
Bara. It's no sin to deceive a Christian;
For they themselves hold it a principle,
Faith is not to be held with heretics:
But all are heretics that are not Jews;

This follows well, and therefore, daughter, fear not.
[*Aside to her.*
I have entreated her, and she will grant.
Lod. Then, gentle Abigail, plight thy faith to me.
Abig. I cannot choose, seeing my father bids:
Nothing but death shall part my love and me.
Lod. Now have I that for which my soul hath long'd.
Bara. So have not I; but yet I hope I shall. [*Aside.*
Abig. O wretched Abigail, what hast thou done? [*Aside.*
Lod. Why on the sudden is your colour chang'd?
Abig. I know not: but farewell; I must be gone.
Bara. Stay her, but let her not speak one word more.
Lod. Mute o' the sudden! here's a sudden change.
Bara. O, muse not at it; 'tis the Hebrews' guise,
That maidens new-betrothed should weep a while:
Trouble her not; sweet Lodowick, depart:
She is thy wife, and thou shalt be mine heir.
Lod. O, is't the custom? then I am resolv'd:
But rather let the brightsome heavens be dim,
And nature's beauty choke with stifling clouds,
Than my fair Abigail should frown on me.—
There comes the villain; now I'll be reveng'd.

Re-enter MATHIAS.

Bara. Be quiet, Lodowick; it is enough
That I have made thee sure to Abigail.
Lod. Well, let him go. [*Exit.*
Bara. Well, but for me, as you went in at doors
You had been stabb'd: but not a word on't now;
Here must no speeches pass, nor swords be drawn.
Math. Suffer me, Barabas, but to follow him.
Bara. No; so shall I, if any hurt be done,
Be made an accessary of your deeds:
Revenge it on him when you meet him next.
Math. For this I'll have his heart.
Bara. Do so. Lo, here I give thee Abigail!
Math. What greater gift can poor Mathias have?
Shall Lodowick rob me of so fair a love?
My life is not so dear as Abigail.
Bara. My heart misgives me, that, to cross your love,
He's with your mother; therefore after him.
Math. What, is he gone unto my mother?
Bara. Nay, if you will, stay till she comes herself.

Math. I cannot stay; for, if my mother come,
She'll die with grief. [*Exit.*
Abig. I cannot take my leave of him for tears.
Father, why have you thus incens'd them both?
Bara. What's that to thee?
Abig. I'll make 'em friends again.
Bara. You'll make 'em friends! are there not Jews enow in Malta,
But thou must dote upon a Christian?
Abig. I will have Don Mathias; he is my love.
Bara. Yes, you shall have him.—Go, put her in.
Itha. Ay, I'll put her in. [*Puts in Abigail.*
Bara. Now tell me, Ithamore, how lik'st thou this?
Itha. Faith, master, I think by this
You purchase both their lives: is it not so?
Bara. True; and it shall be cunningly perform'd.
Itha. O, master, that I might have a hand in this!
Bara. Ay, so thou shalt; 'tis thou must do the deed:
Take this, and bear it to Mathias straight.
[*Giving a letter.*
And tell him that it comes from Lodowick.
Itha. 'Tis poison'd, is it not?
Bara. No, no; and yet it might be done that way:
It is a challenge feign'd from Lodowick.
Itha. Fear not; I will so set his heart a-fire,
That he shall verily think it comes from him.
Bara. I cannot choose but like thy readiness:
Yet be not rash, but do it cunningly.
Itha. As I behave myself in this, employ me hereafter.
Bara. Away, then! [*Exit Ithamore.*
So; now will I go in to Lodowick,
And, like a cunning spirit, feign some lie,
Till I have set 'em both at enmity. [*Exit.*

ACT III

Enter BELLAMIRA.

Bell. Since this town was besieg'd, my gain grows cold:
The time has been, that but for one bare night
A hundred ducats have been freely given;
But now against my will I must be chaste:

And yet I know my beauty doth not fail.
From Venice merchants, and from Padua
Were wont to come rare-witted gentlemen,
Scholars I mean, learned and liberal;
And now, save Pilia-Borza, comes there none,
And he is very seldom from my house;
And here he comes.

Enter PILIA-BORZA.

Pilia. Hold thee, wench, there's something for thee to spend.
[*Showing a bag of silver.*

Bell. 'Tis silver; I disdain it.

Pilia. Ay, but the Jew has gold,
And I will have it, or it shall go hard.

Bell. Tell me, how cam'st thou by this?

Pilia. Faith, walking the back-lanes, through the gardens, I chanced to cast mine eye up to the Jew's counting-house, where I saw some bags of money, and in the night I clambered up with my hooks; and, as I was taking my choice, I heard a rumbling in the house; so I took only this, and run my way.—But here's the Jew's man.

Bell. Hide the bag.

Enter ITHAMORE.

Pilia. Look not towards him, let's away. Zoons, what a looking thou keepest! thou'lt betray's anon.
[*Exeunt Bellamira and Pilia-Borza.*

Itha. O, the sweetest face that ever I beheld! I know she is a courtesan by her attire: now would I give a hundred of the Jew's crowns that I had such a concubine.
Well, I have deliver'd the challenge in such sort,
As meet they will, and fighting die,—brave sport!
[*Exit.*

Enter MATHIAS.

Math. This is the place: now Abigail shall see
Whether Mathias holds her dear or no.

Enter LODOWICK.

What, dares the villain write in such base terms?
[*Looking at a letter.*

Lod. I did it; and revenge it, if thou dar'st! [*They fight.*

Enter BARABAS *above.*

Bara. O, bravely fought! and yet they thrust not home.
Now, Lodovico! now, Mathias!—So; [*Both fall.*
So, now they have show'd themselves to be tall fellows.
[*Cries within*] Part 'em, part 'em!
Bara. Ay, part 'em now they are dead. Farewell, farewell!
[*Exit above.*

Enter FERNEZE, KATHARINE, *and* Attendants.

Fern. What sight is this? my Lodovico slain!
These arms of mine shall be thy sepulchre.
Kath. Who is this? my son Mathias slain!
Fern. O Lodowick, hadst thou perish'd by the Turk,
Wretched Ferneze might have veng'd thy death!
Kath. Thy son slew mine, and I'll revenge his death.
Fern. Look, Katharine, look! thy son gave mine these wounds.
Kath. O, leave to grieve me! I am griev'd enough.
Fern. O, that my sighs could turn to lively breath,
And these my tears to blood, that he might live!
Kath. Who made them enemies?
Fern. I know not; and that grieves me most of all.
Kath. My son lov'd thine.
Fern. And so did Lodowick him.
Kath. Lend me that weapon that did kill my son,
And it shall murder me.
Fern. Nay, madam, stay; that weapon was my son's,
And on that rather should Ferneze die.
Kath. Hold; let's inquire the causers of their deaths,
That we may venge their blood upon their heads.
Fern. Then take them up, and let them be interr'd
Within one sacred monument of stone;
Upon which altar I will offer up
My daily sacrifice of sighs and tears,
And with my prayers pierce impartial heavens,
Till they [reveal] the causers of our smarts,
Which forc'd their hands divide united hearts.
Come, Katharine; our losses equal are;
Then of true grief let us take equal share.
[*Exeunt with the bodies.*

Enter ITHAMORE.

Itha. Why, was there ever seen such villany,
So neatly plotted, and so well perform'd?
Both held in hand, and flatly both beguil'd?

Enter ABIGAIL.

Abig. Why, how now, Ithamore! why laugh'st thou so?
Itha. O mistress! ha, ha, ha!
Abig. Why, what ail'st thou?
Itha. O, my master!
Abig. Ha!
Itha. O mistress, I have the bravest, gravest, secret, subtle, bottle-nosed knave to my master, that ever gentleman had!
Abig. Say, knave, why rail'st upon my father thus?
Itha. O, my master has the bravest policy!
Abig. Wherein?
Itha. Why, know you not?
Abig. Why, no.
Itha. Know you not of Mathia[s'] and Don Lodowick['s] disaster?
Abig. No: what was it?
Itha. Why, the devil invented a challenge, my master writ it, and I carried it, first to Lodowick, and *imprimis* to Mathia[s];
And then they met, [and,] as the story says,
In doleful wise they ended both their days.
Abig. And was my father furtherer of their deaths?
Itha. Am I Ithamore?
Abig. Yes.
Itha. So sure did your father write, and I carry the challenge.
Abig. Well, Ithamore, let me request thee this:
Go to the new-made nunnery, and inquire
For any of the friars of Saint Jaques,
And say, I pray them come and speak with me.
Itha. I pray, mistress, will you answer me to one question?
Abig. Well, sirrah, what is't?
Itha. A very feeling one: have not the nuns fine sport with the friars now and then?
Abig. Go to, Sirrah Sauce! is this your question? get ye gone,
Itha. I will, forsooth, mistress. [*Exit.*

Abig. Hard-hearted father, unkind Barabas!
Was this the pursuit of thy policy,
To make me show them favour severally,
That by my favour they should both be slain?
Admit thou lov'dst not Lodowick for his sire,
Yet Don Mathias ne'er offended thee:
But thou wert set upon extreme revenge,
Because the prior dispossess'd thee once,
And couldst not venge it but upon his son;
Nor on his son but by Mathias' means;
Nor on Mathias but by murdering me:
But I perceive there is no love on earth,
Pity in Jews, nor piety in Turks.—
But here comes cursed Ithamore with the friar.

Re-enter ITHAMORE *with* FRIAR JACOMO.

Friar Jac. Virgo, salve.
Itha. When duck you?
Abig. Welcome, grave friar.—Ithamore, be gone.
[*Exit Ithamore.*
Know, holy sir, I am bold to solicit thee.
Friar Jac. Wherein?
Abig. To get me be admitted for a nun.
Friar Jac. Why, Abigail, it is not yet long since
That I did labour thy admission,
And then thou didst not like that holy life.
Abig. Then were my thoughts so frail and unconfirm'd
As I was chain'd to follies of the world:
But now experience, purchased with grief,
Has made me see the difference of things.
My sinful soul, alas, hath pac'd too long
The fatal labyrinth of misbelief,
Far from the sun that gives eternal life!
Friar Jac. Who taught thee this?
Abig. The abbess of the house,
Whose zealous admonition I embrace:
O, therefore, Jacomo, let me be one,
Although unworthy, of that sisterhood!
Friar Jac. Abigail, I will: but see thou change no more,
For that will be most heavy to thy soul.
Abig. That was my father's fault.
Friar Jac. Thy father's! how?
Abig. Nay, you shall pardon me.—O Barabas,

Though thou deservest hardly at my hands,
Yet never shall these lips bewray thy life! [*Aside.*

Friar Jac. Come, shall we go?

Abig. My duty waits on you. [*Exeunt.*

Enter BARABAS, *reading a letter.*

Bara. What, Abigail become a nun again!
False and unkind! what, hast thou lost thy father?
And, all unknown and unconstrain'd of me,
Art thou again got to the nunnery?
Now here she writes, and wills me to repent:
Repentance! *Spurca!* what pretendeth this?
I fear she knows—'tis so—of my device
In Don Mathias' and Lodovico's deaths:
If so, 'tis time that it be seen into;
For she that varies from me in belief,
Gives great presumption that she loves me not,
Or, loving, doth dislike of something done.—
But who comes here?

Enter ITHAMORE.

O Ithamore, come near;
Come near, my love; come near, thy master's life,
My trusty servant, nay, my second self;
For I have now no hope but even in thee,
And on that hope my happiness is built.
When saw'st thou Abigail?

Itha. To-day.

Bara. With whom?

Itha. A friar.

Bara. A friar! false villain, he hath done the deed.

Itha. How, sir!

Bara. Why, made mine Abigail a nun.

Itha. That's no lie; for she sent me for him.

Bara. O unhappy day!
False, credulous, inconstant Abigail!
But let 'em go: and, Ithamore, from hence
Ne'er shall she grieve me more with her disgrace;
Ne'er shall she live to inherit aught of mine,
Be bless'd of me, nor come within my gates,
But perish underneath my bitter curse,
Like Cain by Adam for his brother's death.

Itha. O master—

Bara. Ithamore, entreat not for her; I am mov'd,
And she is hateful to my soul and me:
And, 'less thou yield to this that I entreat,
I cannot think but that thou hat'st my life.
Itha. Who, I, master? why, I'll run to some rock,
And throw myself headlong into the sea;
Why, I'll do anything for your sweet sake.
Bara. O trusty Ithamore! no servant, but my friend!
I here adopt thee for mine only heir:
All that I have is thine when I am dead;
And, whilst I live, use half; spend as myself;
Here, take my keys,—I'll give 'em thee anon;
Go buy thee garments; but thou shalt not want:
Only know this, that thus thou art to do—
But first go fetch me in the pot of rice
That for our supper stands upon the fire.
Itha. I hold my head, my master's hungry [*Aside*].—
I go, sir. [*Exit.*
Bara. Thus every villain ambles after wealth,
Although he ne'er be richer than in hope.—
But, husht!

Re-enter ITHAMORE *with the pot.*

Itha. Here 'tis, master.
Bara. Well said, Ithamore! What, hast thou brought
The ladle with thee too?
Itha. Yes, sir; the proverb says, he that eats with the devil had need of a long spoon; I have brought you a ladle.
Bara. Very well, Ithamore; then now be secret;
And, for thy sake, whom I so dearly love,
Now shalt thou see the death of Abigail,
That thou mayst freely live to be my heir.
Itha. Why, master, will you poison her with a mess of rice-porridge? that will preserve life, make her round and plump, and batten more than you are aware.
Bara. Ay, but, Ithamore, seest thou this?
It is a precious powder that I bought
Of an Italian, in Ancona, once,
Whose operation is to bind, infect,
And poison deeply, yet not appear
In forty hours after it is ta'en.
Itha. How, master?

Bara. Thus, Ithamore:
This even they use in Malta here,—'tis call'd
Saint Jaques' Even,—and then, I say, they use
To send their alms unto the nunneries:
Amongst the rest, bear this, and set it there:
There's a dark entry where they take it in,
Where they must neither see the messenger,
Nor make inquiry who hath sent it them.
Itha. How so?
Bara. Belike there is some ceremony in't.
There, Ithamore, must thou go place this pot:
Stay; let me spice it first.
Itha. Pray, do, and let me help you, master.
Pray, let me taste first.
Bara. Prithee, do. [*Ithamore tastes.*] What say'st thou now?
Itha. Troth, master, I'm loath such a pot of pottage should be spoiled.
Bara. Peace, Ithamore! 'tis better so than spar'd.
[*Puts the powder into the pot.*
Assure thyself thou shalt have broth by the eye:
My purse, my coffer, and myself is thine.
Itha, Well, master, I go.
Bara. Stay; first let me stir it, Ithamore.
As fatal be it to her as the draught
Of which great Alexander drunk, and died;
And with her let it work like Borgia's wine,
Whereof his sire the Pope was poisoned!
In few, the blood of Hydra, Lerna's bane,
The juice of hebon, and Cocytus' breath,
And all the poisons of the Stygian pool,
Break from the fiery kingdom, and in this
Vomit your venom, and envenom her
That, like a fiend, hath left her father thus!
Itha. What a blessing has he given't! was ever pot of rice-porridge so sauced? [*Aside*].—What shall I do with it?
Bara. O my sweet Ithamore, go set it down;
And come again as soon as thou hast done,
For I have other business for thee,
Itha. Here's a drench to poison a whole stable of Flanders mares: I'll carry't to the nuns with a powder.
Bara. And the horse-pestilence to boot: away!
Itha. I am gone:

Pay me my wages, for my work is done.
[*Exit with the pot.*

Bara. I'll pay thee with a vengeance, Ithamore! [*Exit*

Enter FERNEZE, MARTIN DEL BOSCO, Knights, *and* BASSO.

Fern. Welcome, great basso: how fares Calymath?
What wind drives you thus into Malta-road?
Bas. The wind that bloweth all the world besides,
Desire of gold.
Fern. Desire of gold, great sir!
That's to be gotten in the Western Inde:
In Malta are no golden minerals.
Bas. To you of Malta thus saith Calymath:
The time you took for respite is at hand
For the performance of your promise pass'd;
And for the tribute money I am sent.
Fern. Basso, in brief, shalt have no tribute here,
Nor shall the heathens live upon our spoil:
First will we raze the city-walls ourselves,
Lay waste the island, hew the temples down,
And, shipping off our goods to Sicily,
Open an entrance for the wasteful sea,
Whose billows, beating the resistless banks,
Shall overflow it with their refluence.
Bas. Well, governor, since thou hast broke the league
By flat denial of the promis'd tribute,
Talk not of razing down your city-walls;
You shall not need trouble yourselves so far,
For Selim Calymath shall come himself,
And with brass bullets batter down your towers,
And turn proud Malta to a wilderness,
For these intolerable wrongs of yours:
And so farewell.
Fern. Farewell. [*Exit* BASSO
And now, you men of Malta, look about,
And let's provide to welcome Calymath:
Close your port-cullis, charge your basilisks,
And, as you profitably take up arms,
So now courageously encounter them,
For by this answer broken is the league,
And naught is to be look'd for now but wars,
And naught to us more welcome is than wars. [*Exeunt.*

Enter Friar Jacomo *and* Friar Barnardine.

Friar Jac. O brother, brother, all the nuns are sick,
And physic will not help them! they must die.
Friar Barn. The abbess sent for me to be confess'd:
O, what a sad confession will there be!
Friar Jac. And so did fair Maria send for me:
I'll to her lodging; hereabouts she lies. [*Exit.*

Enter Abigail.

Friar Barn. What, all dead, save only Abigail!
Abig. And I shall die too, for I feel death coming.
Where is the friar that convers'd with me?
Friar Barn. O, he is gone to see the other nuns.
Abig. I sent for him; but, seeing you are come,
Be you my ghostly father: and first know,
That in this house I liv'd religiously,
Chaste, and devout, much sorrowing for my sins;
But, ere I came—
Friar Barn. What then?
Abig. I did offend high heaven so grievously
As I am almost desperate for my sins;
And one offence torments me more than all.
You knew Mathias and Don Lodowick?
Friar Barn. Yes; what of them?
Abig. My father did contract me to 'em both;
First to Don Lodowick: him I never lov'd;
Mathias was the man that I held dear,
And for his sake did I become a nun.
Friar Barn. So: say how was their end?
Abig. Both, jealous of my love, envied each other;
And by my father's practice, which is there
[*Gives writing.*
Set down at large, the gallants were both slain.
Friar Barn. O, monstrous villany!
Abig. To work my peace, this I confess to thee:
Reveal it not; for then my father dies.
Friar Barn. Know that confession must not be reveal'd;
The canon-law forbids it, and the priest
That makes it known, being degraded first,
Shall be condemn'd, and then sent to the fire.
Abig. So I have heard; pray, therefore, keep it close.
Death seizeth on my heart: ah, gentle friar,

Convert my father that he may be sav'd,
And witness that I die a Christian! [*Dies.*

Friar Barn. Ay, and a virgin too; that grieves me most.
But I must to the Jew, and exclaim on him,
And make him stand in fear of me.

Re-enter FRIAR JACOMO.

Friar Jac. O brother, all the nuns are dead! let's bury them.

Friar Barn. First help to bury this; then go with me,
And help me to exclaim against the Jew.

Friar Jac. Why, what has he done?

Friar Barn. A thing that makes me tremble to unfold.

Friar Jac. What, has he crucified a child?

Friar Barn. No, but a worse thing: 'twas told me in shrift;
Thou know'st 'tis death, an if it be reveal'd.
Come, let's away. [*Exeunt.*

ACT IV

Enter BARABAS *and* ITHAMORE. *Bells within.*

Bara. There is no music to a Christian's knell:
How sweet the bells ring, now the nuns are dead,
That sound at other times like tinkers' pans!
I was afraid the poison had not wrought,
Or, though it wrought, it would have done no good,
For every year they swell, and yet they live:
Now all are dead, not one remains alive.

Itha. That's brave, master: but think you it will not be known?

Bara. How can it, if we two be secret?

Itha. For my part, fear you not.

Bara. I'd cut thy throat, if I did.

Itha. And reason too.
But here's a royal monastery hard by;
Good master, let me poison all the monks.

Bara. Thou shalt not need; for, now the nuns are dead,
They'll die with grief.

Itha. Do you not sorrow for your daughter's death?

Bara. No, but I grieve because she liv'd so long,
An Hebrew born, and would become a Christian:
Cazzo, diabolo!

Itha. Look, look, master; here come two religious caterpillars.

Enter FRIAR JACOMO *and* FRIAR BARNARDINE.

Bara. I smelt 'em ere they came.
Itha. God-a-mercy, nose! Come, let's begone.
Friar Barn. Stay, wicked Jew; repent, I say, and stay.
Friar Jac. Thou hast offended, therefore must be damn'd
Bara. I fear they know we sent the poison'd broth.
Itha. And so do I, master; therefore speak 'em fair.
Friar Barn. Barabas, thou hast——
Friar Jac. Ay, that thou hast——
Bara. True, I have money; what though I have?
Friar Barn. Thou art a——
Friar Jac. Ay, that thou art, a——
Bara. What needs all this? I know I am a Jew.
Friar Barn. Thy daughter——
Friar Jac. Ay, thy daughter——
Bara. O, speak not of her! then I die with grief.
Friar Barn. Remember that——
Friar Jac. Ay, remember that——
Bara. I must needs say that I have been a great usurer.
Friar Barn. Thou hast committed——
Bara. Fornication: but that was in another country;
And besides the wench is dead.
Friar Barn. Ay, but, Barabas,
Remember Mathias and Don Lodowick.
Bara. Why, what of them?
Friar Barn. I will not say that by a forged challenge they met.
Bara. She has confess'd, and we are both undone,
My bosom intimates! but I must dissemble.—
[*Aside to Ithamore.*
O holy friars, the burden of my sins
Lie heavy on my soul! then, pray you, tell me,
Is't not too late now to turn Christian?
I have been zealous in the Jewish faith,
Hard-hearted to the poor, a covetous wretch,
That would for lucre's sake have sold my soul;
A hundred for a hundred I have ta'en;
And now for store of wealth may I compare
With all the Jews in Malta: but what is wealth?
I am a Jew, and therefore am I lost.

Would penance serve for this my sin,
I could afford to whip myself to death,—
Itha. And so could I; but penance will not serve.
Bara. To fast, to pray, and wear a shirt of hair,
And on my knees creep to Jerusalem.
Cellars of wine, and sollars full of wheat,
Warehouses stuff'd with spices and with drugs,
Whole chests of gold in bullion and in coin,
Besides, I know not how much weight in pearl,
Orient and round, have I within my house;
At Alexandria merchandise untold;
But yesterday two ships went from this town,
Their voyage will be worth ten thousand crowns;
In Florence, Venice, Antwerp, London, Seville,
Frankfort, Lubeck, Moscow, and where not,
Have I debts owing; and, in most of these,
Great sums of money lying in the banco;
All this I'll give to some religious house,
So I may be baptiz'd, and live therein.
Friar Jac. O good Barabas, come to our house!
Friar Barn. O, no, good Barabas, come to our house!
And Barabas, you know——
Bara. I know that I have highly sinn'd:
You shall convert me, you shall have all my wealth.
Friar Jac. O Barabas, their laws are strict!
Bara. I know they are; and I will be with you.
Friar Jac. They wear no shirts, and they go barefoot too.
Bara. Then 'tis not for me; and I am resolv'd
You shall confess me, and have all my goods.
Friar Jac. Good Barabas, come to me.
Bara. You see I answer him, and yet he stays;
Rid him away, and go you home with me.
Friar Jac. I'll be with you to-night.
Bara. Come to my house at one o'clock this night.
Friar Jac. You hear your answer, and you may be gone.
Friar Barn. Why, go, get you away.
Friar Jac. I will not go for thee.
Friar Barn. Not! then I'll make thee go.
Friar Jac. How! dost call me rogue? [*They fight*
Itha. Part 'em, master, part 'em.
Bara. This is mere frailty: brethren, be content.—
Friar Barnardine, go you with Ithamore:
You know my mind; let me alone with him.

Friar Jac. Why does he go to thy house? let him be gone.
Bara. I'll give him something, and so stop his mouth.
[*Exit Ithamore with Friar Barnardine.*
I never heard of any man but he
Malign'd the order of the Jacobins;
But do you think that I believe his words?
Why, brother, you converted Abigail;
And I am bound in charity to requite it,
And so I will. O Jacomo, fail not, but come.
Friar Jac. But, Barabas, who shall be your godfathers?
For presently you shall be shriv'd.
Bara. Marry, the Turk shall be one of my godfathers,
But not a word to any of your covent.
Friar Jac. I warrant thee, Barabas. [*Exit.*
Bara. So, now the fear is past, and I am safe;
For he that shriv'd her is within my house:
What, if I murder'd him ere Jacomo comes?
Now I have such a plot for both their lives,
As never Jew nor Christian knew the like:
One turn'd my daughter, therefore he shall die;
The other knows enough to have my life,
Therefore 'tis not requisite he should live.
But are not both these wise men, to suppose
That I will leave my house, my goods, and all,
To fast and be well whipt? I'll none of that.
Now, Friar Barnardine, I come to you:
I'll feast you, lodge you, give you fair words,
And, after that, I and my trusty Turk—
No more, but so: it must and shall be done.

Enter ITHAMORE.

Ithamore, tell me, is the friar asleep?
Itha. Yes; and I know not what the reason is,
Do what I can, he will not strip himself,
Nor go to bed, but sleeps in his own clothes:
I fear me he mistrusts what we intend.
Bara. No; 'tis an order which the friars use:
Yet, if he knew our meanings, could he scape?
Itha. No, none can hear him, cry he ne'er so loud.
Bara. Why, true; therefore did I place him there:
The other chambers open towards the street.
Itha. You loiter, master; wherefore stay we thus?
O, how I long to see him shake his heels!

Bara. Come on, sirrah:
Off with your girdle; make a handsome noose.—
[*Ithamore takes off his girdle, and ties a noose on it.*
Friar, awake! [*They put the noose round the Friar's neck.*
Friar Barn. What, do you mean to strangle me?
Itha. Yes, 'cause you use to confess.
Bara. Blame not us, but the proverb,—Confess and be hanged.—Pull hard.
Friar Barn. What, will you have my life?
Bara. Pull hard, I say.—You would have had my goods.
Itha. Ay, and our lives too:—therefore pull amain.
[*They strangle the Friar.*
'Tis neatly done, sir; here's no print at all.
Bara. Then is it as it should be. Take him up.
Itha. Nay, master, be ruled by me a little. [*Takes the body, sets it upright against the wall, and puts a staff in its hand.*] So, let him lean upon his staff; excellent! he stands as if he were begging of bacon.
Bara. Who would not think but that this friar liv'd?
What time o' night is't now, sweet Ithamore?
Itha. Towards one.
Bara. Then will not Jacomo be long from hence. [*Exeunt.*

Enter FRIAR JACOMO.

Friar Jac. This is the hour wherein I shall proceed;
O happy hour, wherein I shall convert
An infidel, and bring his gold into our treasury!
But soft! is not this Barnardine? it is;
And, understanding I should come this way,
Stands here o' purpose, meaning me some wrong,
And intercept my going to the Jew.—
Barnardine!
Wilt thou not speak? thou think'st I see thee not;
Away, I'd wish thee, and let me go by:
No, wilt thou not? nay, then, I'll force my way;
And, see, a staff stands ready for the purpose
As thou lik'st that, stop me another time!
[*Takes the staff, and strikes down the body.*

Enter BARABAS *and* ITHAMORE.

Bara. Why, how now, Jacomo! what hast thou done?
Friar Jac. Why, stricken him that would have struck at me.
Bara. Who is it? Barnardine! now, out, alas, he is slain!

Itha. Ay, master, he's slain; look how his brains drop out on's nose.

Friar Jac. Good sirs, I have done't: but nobody knows it but you two; I may escape.

Bara. So might my man and I hang with you for company.

Itha. No; let us bear him to the magistrates.

Friar Jac. Good Barabas, let me go.

Bara. No, pardon me; the law must have his course:
I must be forc'd to give in evidence,
That, being importun'd by this Barnardine
To be a Christian, I shut him out,
And there he sate: now I, to keep my word,
And give my goods and substance to your house,
Was up thus early, with intent to go
Unto your friary, because you stay'd.

Itha. Fie upon 'em! master, will you turn Christian, when holy friars turn devils and murder one another?

Bara. No; for this example I'll remain a Jew:
Heaven bless me! what, a friar a murderer!
When shall you see a Jew commit the like?

Itha. Why, a Turk could ha' done no more.

Bara. To-morrow is the sessions; you shall to it.—
Come, Ithamore, let's help to take him hence.

Friar Jac. Villains, I am a sacred person; touch me not.

Bara. The law shall touch you; we'll but lead you, we:
'Las, I could weep at your calamity!—
Take in the staff too, for that must be shown:
Law wills that each particular be known. [*Exeunt.*

Enter BELLAMIRA *and* PILIA-BORZA.

Bell. Pilia-Borza, didst thou meet with Ithamore?

Pilia. I did.

Bell. And didst thou deliver my letter?

Pilia. I did.

Bell. And what thinkest thou? will he come?

Pilia. I think so: and yet I cannot tell; for, at the reading of the letter, he looked like a man of another world.

Bell. Why so?

Pilia. That such a base slave as he should be saluted by such a tall man as I am, from such a beautiful dame as you.

Bell. And what said he?

Pilia. Not a wise word; only gave me a nod, as who should

say, "Is it even so?" and so I left him, being driven to a non-plus at the critical aspect of my terrible countenance.

Bell. And where didst meet him?

Pilia. Upon mine own free-hold, within forty foot of the gallows, conning his neck-verse, I take it, looking of a friar's execution; whom I saluted with an old hempen proverb, *Hodie tibi, cras mihi,* and so I left him to the mercy of the hangman: but, the exercise being done, see where he comes.

Enter ITHAMORE.

Itha. I never knew a man take his death so patiently as this friar; he was ready to leap off ere the halter was about his neck; and, when the hangman had put on his hempen tippet, he made such haste to his prayers, as if he had had another cure to serve. Well, go whither he will, I'll be none of his followers in haste: and, now I think on't, going to the execution, a fellow met me with a muschatoes like a raven's wing, and a dagger with a hilt like a warming pan; and he gave me a letter from one Madam Bellamira, saluting me in such sort as if he had meant to make clean my boots with his lips; the effect was, that I should come to her house: I wonder what the reason is; it may be she sees more in me than I can find in myself; for she writes further, that she loves me ever since she saw me; and who would not requite such love? Here's her house; and here she comes; and now would I were gone! I am not worthy to look upon her.

Pilia. This is the gentleman you writ to.

Itha. Gentleman! he flouts me: what gentry can be in a poor Turk of tenpence? I'll be gone. [*Aside.*

Bell. Is't not a sweet-faced youth, Pilia?

Itha. Again, sweet youth! [*Aside*]—Did not you, sir, bring the sweet youth a letter?

Pilia. I did, sir, and from this gentlewoman, who, as myself and the rest of the family, stand or fall at your service.

Bell. Though woman's modesty should hale me back,
I can withhold no longer: welcome, sweet love.

Itha. Now am I clean, or rather foully, out of the way. [*Aside.*

Bell. Whither so soon?

Itha. I'll go steal some money from my master to make me

handsome [*Aside*].—Pray, pardon me; I must go see a ship discharged.

Bell. Canst thou be so unkind to leave me thus?

Pilia. An ye did but know how she loves you, sir!

Itha. Nay, I care not how much she loves me.— Sweet Bellamira, would I had my master's wealth for thy sake!

Pilia. And you can have it, sir, an if you please.

Itha. If 'twere above ground, I could, and would have it; but he hides and buries it up, as partridges do their eggs, under the earth.

Pilia. And is't not possible to find it out?

Itha. By no means possible.

Bell. What shall we do with this base villain, then?
[*Aside to Pilia-Borza.*

Pilia. Let me alone; do but you speak him fair.—
[*Aside to her.*
But you know some secrets of the Jew,
Which, if they were reveal'd, would do him harm.

Itha. Ay, and such as—go to, no more! I'll make him send me half he has, and glad he scapes so too: pen and ink: I'll write unto him; we'll have money straight.

Pilia. Send for a hundred crowns at least.

Itha. Ten hundred thousand crowns.—[*writing*] *Master Barabas,*—

Pilia. Write not so submissively, but threatening him.

Itha. [*writing*] *Sirrah Barabas, send me a hundred crowns.*

Pilia. Put in two hundred at least.

Itha. [*writing*] *I charge thee send me three hundred by this bearer, and this shall be your warrant: if you do not—no more, but so.*

Pilia. Tell him you will confess.

Itha. [*writing*] *Otherwise I'll confess all.*—Vanish, and return in a twinkle.

Pilia. Let me alone; I'll use him in his kind.

Itha. Hang him, Jew! [*Exit Pilia-Borza with the letter.*

Bell. Now, gentle Ithamore, lie in my lap.—
Where are my maids? provide a running banquet;
Send to the merchant, bid him bring me silks;
Shall Ithamore, my love, go in such rags?

Itha. And bid the jeweller come hither too.

Bell. I have no husband; sweet, I'll marry thee.

Itha. Content: but we will leave this paltry land,

And sail from hence to Greece, to lovely Greece;—
I'll be thy Jason, thou my golden fleece;—
Where painted carpets o'er the meads are hurl'd,
And Bacchus' vineyards overspread the world;
Where woods and forests go in goodly green;—
I'll be Adonis, thou shalt be Love's Queen;—
The meads, the orchards, and the primrose-lanes,
Instead of sedge and reed, bear sugar-canes:
Thou in those groves, by Dis above,
Shalt live with me, and be my love.

Bell. Whither will I not go with gentle Ithamore?

Re-enter PILIA-BORZA.

Itha. How now! hast thou the gold?

Pilia. Yes.

Itha. But came it freely? did the cow give down her milk freely?

Pilia. At reading of the letter, he stared and stamped, and turned aside: I took him by the beard, and looked upon him thus; told him he were best to send it: then he hugged and embraced me.

Itha. Rather for fear than love.

Pilia. Then, like a Jew, he laughed and jeered, and told me he loved me for your sake, and said what a faithful servant you had been.

Itha. The more villain he to keep me thus: here's goodly 'parel, is there not?

Pilia. To conclude, he gave me ten crowns.
[*Delivers the money to Ithamore.*

Itha. But ten? I'll not leave him worth a grey groat. Give me a ream of paper: we'll have a kingdom of gold for't.

Pilia. Write for five hundred crowns.

Itha. [*writing*] *Sirrah Jew, as you love your life, send me five hundred crowns, and give the bearer a hundred.*—Tell him I must have't.

Pilia. I warrant, you worship shall have't.

Itha. And, if he ask why I demand so much, tell him I scorn to write a line under a hundred crowns.

Pilia. You'd make a rich poet, sir. I am gone.
[*Exit with the letter.*

Itha. Take thou the money; spend it for my sake.

Bell. 'Tis not thy money, but thyself I weigh:
Thus Bellamira esteems of gold; [*Throws it aside.*

But thus of thee. [*Kisses him.*

Itha. That kiss again!—She runs division of my lips.
What an eye she casts on me! it twinkles like a star. [*Aside.*

Bell. Come, my dear love, let's in and sleep together.

Itha. O, that ten thousand nights were put in one, that we might sleep seven years together afore we wake!

Bell. Come, amorous wag, first banquet, and then sleep. [*Exeunt.*

Enter BARABAS, *reading a letter.*

Bara. Barabas, send me three hundred crowns ;—
Plain Barabas! O, that wicked courtesan!
He was not wont to call me Barabas;—
Or else I will confess ;—ay, there it goes:
But, if I get him, *coupe de gorge* for that.
He sent a shaggy, tatter'd, staring slave,
That, when he speaks, draws out his grisly beard,
And winds it twice or thrice about his ear;
Whose face has been a grind-stone for men's swords;
His hands are hack'd, some fingers cut quite off,
Who, when he speaks, grunts like a hog, and looks
Like one that is employ'd in catzery
And cross-biting; such a rogue
As is the husband to a hundred whores;
And I by him must send three hundred crowns.
Well, my hope is, he will not stay there still;
And, when he comes—O, that he were but here!

Enter PILIA-BORZA.

Pilia. Jew, I must ha' more gold.

Bara. Why, want'st thou any of thy tale?

Pilia. No; but three hundred will not serve his turn.

Bara. Not serve his turn, sir!

Pilia. No, sir; and therefore I must have five hundred more.

Bara. I'll rather——

Pilia. O, good words, sir, and send it you were best! see, there's his letter. [*Gives letter.*

Bara. Might he not as well come as send? pray, bid him come and fetch it: what he writes for you, ye shall have straight.

Pilia. Ay, and the rest too, or else——

Bara. I must make this villain away [*Aside*].—Please you

dine with me, sir — and you shall be most heartily poisoned. [*Aside.*

Pilia. No, God-a-mercy. Shall I have these crowns?

Bara. I cannot do it; I have lost my keys.

Pilia. O, if that be all, I can pick ope your locks.

Bara. Or climb up to my counting-house window: you know my meaning.

Pilia. I know enough, and therefore talk not to me of your counting-house. The gold! or know, Jew, it is in my power to hang thee.

Bara. I am betray'd.— [*Aside.*
'Tis not five hundred crowns that I esteem;
I am not mov'd at that: this angers me,
That he, who knows I love him as myself,
Should write in this imperious vein. Why, sir,
You know I have no child, and unto whom
Should I leave all, but unto Ithamore?

Pilia. Here's many words, but no crowns: the crowns!

Bara. Commend me to him, sir, most humbly,
And unto your good mistress as unknown.

Pilia. Speak, shall I have 'em, sir?

Bara. Sir, here they are.— [*Gives money.*
O, that I should part with so much gold!— [*Aside.*
Here, take 'em, fellow, with as good a will——
As I would see thee hang'd [*Aside*]. O, love stops my breath!
Never lov'd man servant as I do Ithamore.

Pilia. I know it, sir.

Bara. Pray, when, sir, shall I see you at my house?

Pilia. Soon enough to your cost, sir. Fare you well. [*Exit.*

Bara. Nay, to thine own cost, villain, if thou com'st!
Was ever Jew tormented as I am?
To have a shag-rag knave to come [force from me]
Three hundred crowns, and then five hundred crowns!
Well; I must seek a means to rid 'em all,
And presently; for in his villany
He will tell all he knows, and I shall die for't.
I have it:
I will in some disguise go see the slave,
And how the villain revels with my gold. [*Exit.*

Enter BELLAMIRA, ITHAMORE, *and* PILIA-BORZA.

Bell. I'll pledge thee, love, and therefore drink it off.
Itha. Say'st thou me so? have at it! and do you hear? [*Whispers to her.*
Bell. Go to, it shall be so.
Itha. Of that condition I will drink it up:
Here's to thee.
Bell. Nay, I'll have all or none.
Itha. There, if thou lov'st me, do not leave a drop.
Bell. Love thee! fill me three glasses.
Itha. Three and fifty dozen: I'll pledge thee.
Pilia. Knavely spoke, and like a knight-at-arms.
Itha. Hey, *Rivo Castiliano!* a man's a man.
Bell. Now to the Jew.
Itha. Ha! to the Jew; and send me money he were best.
Pilia. What wouldst thou do, if he should send thee none?
Itha. Do nothing: but I know what I know; he's a murderer.
Bell. I had not thought he had been so brave a man.
Itha. You knew Mathias and the governor's son; he and I killed 'em both, and yet never touched 'em.
Pilia. O, bravely done!
Itha. I carried the broth that poisoned the nuns; and he and I, snicle hand too fast, strangled a friar.
Bell. You two alone?
Itha. We two; and 'twas never known, nor never shall be for me.
Pilia. This shall with me unto the governor. [*Aside to Bellamira.*
Bell. And fit it should: but first let's ha' more gold.— [*Aside to Pilia-Borza.*
Come, gentle Ithamore, lie in my lap.
Itha. Love me little, love me long: let music rumble,
Whilst I in thy incony lap do tumble.

Enter BARABAS, *disguised as a French musician, with a lute, and a nosegay in his hat.*

Bell. A French musician!—Come, let's hear your skill.
Bara. Must tuna my lute for sound, twang, twang, first.
Itha. Wilt drink, Frenchman? here's to thee with a——Pox on this drunken hiccup!
Bara. Gramercy, monsieur.

Bell. Prithee, Pilia-Borza, bid the fiddler give me the posy in his hat there.

Pilia. Sirrah, you must give my mistress your posy.

Bara. *A votre commandement, madame.* [*Giving nosegay.*

Bell. How sweet, my Ithamore, the flowers smell!

Itha. Like thy breath, sweetheart; no violet like 'em.

Pilia. Foh! methinks they stink like a hollyhock.

Bara. So, now I am reveng'd upon 'em all:
The scent thereof was death; I poison'd it. [*Aside.*

Itha. Play, fiddler, or I'll cut your cat's guts into chitterlings.

Bara. *Pardonnez moi,* be no in tune yet: so, now, now all be in.

Itha. Give him a crown, and fill me out more wine.

Pilia. There's two crowns for thee: play. [*Giving money.*

Bara. How liberally the villain gives me mine own gold!
[*Aside, and then plays.*

Pilia. Methinks he fingers very well.

Bara. So did you when you stole my gold. [*Aside.*

Pilia. How swift he runs!

Bara. You run swifter when you threw my gold out of my window. [*Aside.*

Bell. Musician, hast been in Malta long?

Bara. Two, three, four month, madam.

Itha. Dost not know a Jew, one Barabas?

Bara. Very mush: monsieur, you no be his man?

Pilia. His man!

Itha. I scorn the peasant: tell him so.

Bara. He knows it already. [*Aside.*

Itha. 'Tis a strange thing of that Jew, he lives upon pickled grasshoppers and sauced mushrooms.

Bara. What a slave's this! the governor feeds not as I do.
[*Aside.*

Itha. He never put on clean shirt since he was circumcised.

Bara. O rascal! I change myself twice a-day. [*Aside.*

Itha. The hat he wears, Judas left under the elder when he hanged himself.

Bara. 'Twas sent me for a present from the Great Cham.
[*Aside.*

Pilia. A nasty slave he is.—Whither now, fiddler?

Bara. *Pardonnez moi, monsieur ;* me be no well.

Pilia. Farewell, fiddler [*Exit Barabas*]. One letter more to the Jew.

Bell. Prithee, sweet love, one more, and write it sharp.
Itha. No, I'll send by word of mouth now.—Bid him deliver thee a thousand crowns, by the same token that the nuns loved rice, that Friar Barnardine slept in his own clothes; any of 'em will do it.
Pilia. Let me alone to urge it, now I know the meaning.
Itha. The meaning has a meaning. Come, let's in:
To undo a Jew is charity, and not sin. [*Exeunt.*

ACT

Enter FERNEZE, Knights, MARTIN DEL BOSCO, *and* Officers.

Fern. Now, gentlemen, betake you to your arms,
And see that Malta be well fortified;
And it behoves you to be resolute;
For Calymath, having hover'd here so long,
Will win the town, or die before the walls.
First Knight. And die he shall: for we will never yield.

Enter BELLAMIRA *and* PILIA-BORZA.

Bell. O, bring us to the governor!
Fern. Away with her! she is a courtesan.
Bell. Whate'er I am, yet, governor, hear me speak:
I bring thee news by whom thy son was slain:
Mathias did it not; it was the Jew.
Pilia. Who, besides the slaughter of these gentlemen,
Poison'd his own daughter and the nuns,
Strangled a friar, and I know not what
Mischief beside.
Fern. Had we but proof of this——
Bell. Strong proof, my lord: his man's now at my lodging.
That was his agent; he'll confess it all.
Fern. Go fetch him straight [*Exeunt Officers*]. I always fear'd that Jew.

Re-enter Officers *with* BARABAS *and* ITHAMORE.

Bara. I'll go alone; dogs, do not hale me thus.
Itha. Nor me neither; I cannot out-run you, constable.—O, my belly!

Bara. One dram of powder more had made all sure:
What a damn'd slave was I! [*Aside.*
Fern. Make fires, heat irons, let the rack be fetched.
First Knight. Nay, stay, my lord; 't may be he will confess.
Bara. Confess! what mean you, lords? who should confess?
Fern. Thou and thy Turk; 'twas you that slew my son.
Itha. Guilty, my lord, I confess. Your son and Mathias were both contracted unto Abigail: [he] forged a counterfeit challenge.
Bara. Who carried that challenge?
Itha. I carried it, I confess; but who writ it? marry, even he that strangled Barnardine, poisoned the nuns and his own daughter.
Fern. Away with him! his sight is death to me.
Bara. For what, you men of Malta? hear me speak.
She is a courtesan, and he a thief.
And he my bondman: let me have law;
For none of this can prejudice my life.
Fern. Once more, away with him!—You shall have law.
Bara. Devils, do your worst!—I['ll] live in spite of you.— [*Aside.*
As these have spoke, so be it to their souls!—
I hope the poison'd flowers will work anon. [*Aside.*
[*Exeunt Officers with Barabas and Ithamore; Bellamira, and Pilia-Borza.*

Enter KATHARINE.

Kath. Was my Mathias murder'd by the Jew?
Ferneze, 'twas thy son that murder'd him.
Fern. Be patient, gentle madam; it was he;
He forg'd the daring challenge made them fight.
Kath. Where is the Jew? where is that murderer?
Fern. In prison, till the law has pass'd on him.

Re-enter First Officer.

First Off. My lord, the courtesan and her man are dead;
So is the Turk and Barabas the Jew.
Fern. Dead?
First Off. Dead, my lord, and here they bring his body.
Bosco. This sudden death of his is very strange.

Re-enter Officers, *carrying* BARABAS *as dead.*

Fern. Wonder not at it, sir; the heavens are just;

Their deaths were like their lives; then think not of 'em.—
Since they are dead, let them be buried:
For the Jew's body, throw that o'er the walls,
To be a prey for vultures and wild beasts.—
So, now away and fortify the town.

[*Exeunt all, leaving Barabas on the floor.*

Bara. [*rising*] What, all alone! well fare, sleepy drink!
I'll be reveng'd on this accursed town;
For by my means Calymath shall enter in:
I'll help to slay their children and their wives,
To fire the churches, pull their houses down,
Take my goods too, and seize upon my lands.
I hope to see the governor a slave,
And, rowing in a galley, whipt to death.

Enter CALYMATH, Bassoes, *and* Turks.

Caly. Whom have we there? a spy?
Bara. Yes, my good lord, one that can spy a place
Where you may enter, and surprise the town:
My name is Barabas; I am a Jew.
Caly. Art thou that Jew whose goods we heard were sold
For tribute money?
Bara. The very same, my lord:
And since that time they have hir'd a slave, my man,
To accuse me of a thousand villanies:
I was imprisoned, but scap'd their hands.
Caly. Didst break prison?
Bara. No, no:
I drank of poppy and cold mandrake juice;
And being asleep, belike they thought me dead,
And threw me o'er the walls: so, or how else,
The Jew is here, and rests at your command.
Caly. 'Twas bravely done: but tell me, Barabas,
Canst thou, as thou report'st, make Malta ours?
Bara. Fear not, my lord; for here, against the trench,
The rock is hollow, and of purpose digg'd,
To make a passage for the running streams
And common channels of the city.
Now, whilst you give assault unto the walls,
I'll lead five hundred soldiers through the vault,
And rise with them i' the middle of the town,
Open the gates for you to enter in;
And by this means the city is your own.

Caly. If this be true, I'll make thee governor.
Bara. And, if it be not true, then let me die.
Caly. Thou'st doom'd thyself.—Assault it presently.
[*Exeunt.*

Alarums within. *Enter* CALYMATH, Bassoes, Turks, *and* BARABAS; *with* FERNEZE *and* Knights *prisoners.*

Caly. Now vail your pride, you captive Christians,
And kneel for mercy to your conquering foe:
Now where's the hope you had of haughty Spain?
Ferneze, speak; had it not been much better
To keep thy promise than be thus surpris'd?
Fern. What should I say? we are captives, and must yield.
Caly. Ay, villains, you must yield, and under Turkish yokes
Shall groaning bear the burden of our ire:—
And, Barabas, as erst we promis'd thee,
For thy desert we make thee governor;
Use them at thy discretion.
Bara. Thanks, my lord.
Fern. O fatal day, to fall into the hands
Of such a traitor and unhallow'd Jew!
What greater misery could heaven inflict?
Caly. 'Tis our command:—and, Barabas, we give,
To guard thy person, these our Janizaries:
Entreat them well, as we have used thee,—
And now, brave bassoes, come; we'll walk about
The ruin'd town, and see the wreck we made.—
Farewell, brave Jew, farewell, great Barabas!
Bara. May all good fortune follow Calymath!
[*Exeunt Calymath and Bassoes.*
And now, as entrance to our safety,
To prison with the governor and these
Captains, his consorts and confederates.
Fern. O villain! heaven will be reveng'd on thee.
Bara. Away! no more; let him not trouble me.
[*Exeunt Turks with Ferneze and Knights.*
Thus hast thou gotten, by thy policy,
No simple place, no small authority:
I now am governor of Malta; true,—
But Malta hates me, and, in hating me,
My life's in danger; and what boots it thee,
Poor Barabas, to be the governor,
Whenas thy life shall be at their command?

No, Barabas, this must be look'd into;
And, since by wrong thou gott'st authority,
Maintain it bravely by firm policy;
At least, unprofitably lose it not;
For he that liveth in authority,
And neither gets him friends nor fills his bags,
Lives like the ass that Æsop speaketh of,
That labours with a load of bread and wine,
And leaves it off to snap on thistle tops:
But Barabas will be more circumspect.
Begin betimes; Occasion's bald behind:
Slip not thine opportunity, for fear too late
Thou seek'st for much, but canst not compass it.—
Within here!

Enter FERNEZE, *with a* Guard.

Fern. My lord?
Bara. Ay, *lord;* thus slaves will learn.
Now, governor,—stand by there, wait within,—
[*Exeunt Guard*
This is the reason that I sent for thee:
Thou seest thy life and Malta's happiness
Are at my arbitrement; and Barabas
At his discretion may dispose of both:
Now tell me, governor, and plainly too,
What think'st thou shall become of it and thee?
Fern. This, Barabas; since things are in thy power,
I see no reason but of Malta's wreck,
Nor hope of thee but extreme cruelty:
Nor fear I death, nor will I flatter thee.
Bara. Governor, good words; be not so furious.
'Tis not thy life which can avail me aught;
Yet you do live, and live for me you shall:
And as for Malta's ruin, think you not
'Twas slender policy for Barabas
To dispossess himself of such a place?
For sith, as once you said, within this isle,
In Malta here, that I have got my goods,
And in this city still have had success,
And now at length am grown your governor,
Yourselves shall see it shall not be forgot;
For, as a friend not known but in distress,
I'll rear up Malta, now remediless.

Fern. Will Barabas recover Malta's loss?
Will Barabas be good to Christians?
Bara. What wilt thou give me, governor, to procure
A dissolution of the slavish bands
Wherein the Turk hath yok'd your land and you?
What will you give me if I render you
The life of Calymath, surprise his men,
And in an out-house of the city shut
His soldiers, till I have consum'd 'em all with fire?
What will you give him that procureth this?
Fern. Do but bring this to pass which thou pretendest,
Deal truly with us as thou intimatest,
And I will send amongst the citizens,
And by my letetrs privately procure
Great sums of money for thy recompense:
Nay, more, do this, and live thou governor still.
Bara. Nay, do thou this, Ferneze, and be free:
Governor, I enlarge thee; live with me;
Go walk about the city, see thy friends:
Tush, send not letters to 'em; go thyself,
And let me see what money thou canst make:
Here is my hand that I'll set Malta free;
And thus we cast it: to a solemn feast
I will invite young Selim Calymath,
Where be thou present, only to perform
One stratagem that I'll impart to thee,
Wherein no danger shall betide thy life,
And I will warrant Malta free for ever.
Fern. Here is my hand; believe me, Barabas,
I will be there, and do as thou desirest.
When is the time?
Bara. Governor, presently;
For Calymath, when he hath view'd the town,
Will take his leave, and sail toward Ottoman.
Fern. Then will I, Barabas, about this coin,
And bring it with me to thee in the evening.
Bara. Do so; but fail not: now farewell, Ferneze:—
[*Exit Ferneze.*

And thus far roundly goes the business:
Thus, loving neither, will I live with both,
Making a profit of my policy;
And he from whom my most advantage comes,
Shall be my friend.

This is the life we Jews are us'd to lead;
And reason too, for Christians do the like.
Well, now about effecting this device;
First, to surprise great Selim's soldiers,
And then to make provision for the feast,
That at one instant all things may be done:
My policy detests prevention.
To what event my secret purpose drives,
I know; and they shall witness with their lives. [*Exeunt.*

Enter CALYMATH *and* Bassoes.

Caly. Thus have we view'd the city, seen the sack,
And caus'd the ruins to be new-repair'd,
Which with our bombards' shot and basilisk[s]
We rent in sunder at our entry:
And, now I see the situation,
And how secure this conquer'd island stands,
Environ'd with the Mediterranean sea,
Strong countermin'd with other petty isles,
And, toward Calabria, back'd by Sicily
(Where Syracusian Dionysius reign'd),
Two lofty turrets that command the town,
I wonder how it could be conquered thus.

Enter a Messenger.

Mess. From Barabas, Malta's governor, I bring
A message unto mighty Calymath:
Hearing his sovereign was bound for sea,
To sail to Turkey, to great Ottoman,
He humbly would entreat your majesty
To come and see his homely citadel,
And banquet with him ere thou leav'st the isle.
Caly. To banquet with him in his citadel!
I fear me, messenger, to feast my train
Within a town of war so lately pillag'd
Will be too costly and too troublesome:
Yet would I gladly visit Barabas,
For well has Barabas deserv'd of us.
Mess. Selim, for that, thus saith the governor,—
That he hath in [his] store a pearl so big,
So precious, and withal so orient,
As, be it valu'd but indifferently,
The price thereof will serve to entertain

Selim and all his soldiers for a month;
Therefore he humbly would entreat your highness
Not to depart till he has feasted you.

Caly. I cannot feast my men in Malta-walls,
Except he place his tables in the streets.

Mess. Know, Selim, that there is a monastery
Which standeth as an out-house to the town;
There will he banquet them; but thee at home,
With all thy bassoes and brave followers.

Caly. Well, tell the governor we grant his suit;
We'll in this summer-evening feast with him.

Mess. I shall, my lord. [*Exit.*

Caly. And now, bold bassoes, let us to our tents,
And meditate how we may grace us best,
To solemnise our governor's great feast. [*Exeunt.*

Enter FERNEZE, Knights, *and* MARTIN DEL BOSCO.

Fern. In this, my countrymen, be rul'd by me:
Have special care that no man sally forth
Till you shall hear a culverin discharg'd
By him that bears the linstock, kindled thus;
Then issue out and come to rescue me,
For happily I shall be in distress,
Or you released of this servitude.

First Knight. Rather than thus to live as Turkish thralls,
What will we not adventure?

Fern. On, then; be gone.

Knights. Farewell, grave governor.
[*Exeunt, on one side, Knights and Martin Del Bosco; on the other, Ferneze.*

Enter, above, BARABAS, *with a hammer, very busy; and* Carpenters.

Bara. How stand the cords? how hang these hinges? fast?
Are all the cranes and pulleys sure?

First Carp. All fast.

Bara. Leave nothing loose, all levell'd to my mind.
Why, now I see that you have art, indeed:
There, carpenters, divide that gold amongst you;
[*Giving money.*
Go, swill in bowls of sack and muscadine;
Down to the cellar, taste of all my wines.

First Carp. We shall, my lord, and thank you.
[*Exeunt Carpenters.*

Bara. And, if you like them, drink your fill and die;
For, so I live, perish may all the world!
Now, Selim Calymath, return me word
That thou wilt come, and I am satisfied.

Enter Messenger.

Now, sirrah; what, will he come?

Mess. He will; and has commanded all his men
To come ashore, and march through Malta-streets,
That thou mayst feast them in thy citadel.

Bara. Then now are all things as my wish would have 'em;
There wanteth nothing but the governor's pelf;
And see, he brings it.

Enter FERNEZE.

Now governor, the sum?

Fern. With free consent, a hundred thousand pounds.

Bara. Pounds say'st thou, governor? well, since it is no more,
I'll satisfy myself with that; nay, keep it still,
For, if I keep not promise, trust not me:
And, governor, now partake my policy,
First, for his army, they are sent before,
Enter'd the monastery, and underneath
In several places are field-pieces pitch'd,
Bombards, whole barrels full of gunpowder,
That on the sudden shall dissever it,
And batter all the stones about their ears,
Whence none can possibly escape alive:
Now, as for Calymath and his consorts,
Here have I made a dainty gallery,
The floor whereof, this cable being cut,
Doth fall asunder, so that it doth sink
Into a deep pit past recovery.
Here, hold that knife; and, when thou seest he comes,
[*Throws down a knife.*
And with his bassoes shall be blithely set,
A warning-piece shall be shot off from the tower,
To give thee knowledge when to cut the cord,
And fire the house. Say, will not this be brave?

Fern. O, excellent! here, hold thee, Barabas;
I trust thy word; take what I prromis'd thee.
Bara. No, governor; I'll satisfy thee first;
Thou shalt not live in doubt of anything.
Stand close, for here they come. [*Ferneze retires.*
Why, is not this
A kingly kind of trade, to purchase towns
By treachery, and sell 'em by deceit?
Now tell me, worldlings, underneath the sun
If greater falsehood ever has been done?

Enter CALYMATH *and* Bassoes.

Caly. Come, my companion-bassoes: see, I pray,
How busy Barabas is there above
To entertain us in his gallery:
Let us salute him.—Save thee, Barabas!
Bara. Welcome, great Calymath!
Fern. How the slave jeers at him! [*Aside.*
Bara. Will't please thee, mighty Selim Calymath,
To ascend our homely stairs?
Caly. Ay, Barabas.—
Come, bassoes, ascend.
Fern. [*coming forward*] Stay, Calymath;
For I will show thee greater courtesy
Than Barabas would have afforded thee.
Knight. [*within*] Sound a charge there!
[*A charge sounded within: Ferneze cuts the cord; the floor of the gallery gives way, and Barabas falls into a cauldron placed in a pit.*

Enter Knights *and* MARTIN DEL BOSCO.

Caly. How now! what means this?
Bara. Help, help me, Christians, help!
Fern. See, Calymath! this was devis'd for thee.
Caly. Treason, treason! bassoes, fly!
Fern. No, Selim, do not fly:
See his end first, and fly then if thou canst.
Bara. O, help me, Selim! help me, Christians!
Governor, why stand you all so pitiless?
Fern. Should I in pity of thy plaints or thee,
Accursed Barabas, base Jew, relent?

No, thus I'll see thy treachery repaid,
But wish thou hadst behav'd thee otherwise.

Bara. You will not help me, then?

Fern. No, villain, no.

Bara. And, villains, know you cannot help me now.—
Then, Barabas, breathe forth thy latest fate,
And in the fury of thy torments strive
To end thy life with resolution.—
Know, governor, 'twas I that slew thy son,—
I fram'd the challenge that did make them meet:
Know, Calymath, I aim'd thy overthrow:
And, had I but escap'd this stratagem,
I would have brought confusion on you all,
Damn'd Christian dogs, and Turkish infidels!
But now begins the extremity of heat
To pinch me with intolerable pangs:
Die, life! fly, soul! tongue, curse thy fill, and die!
[*Dies.*

Caly. Tell me, you Christians, what doth this portend?

Fern. This train he laid to have entrapp'd thy life;
Now, Selim, note the unhallow'd deeds of Jews;
Thus he determin'd to have handled thee,
But I have rather chose to save thy life.

Caly. Was this the banquet he prepar'd for us?
Let's hence, lest further mischief be pretended.

Fern. Nay, Selim, stay; for, since we have thee here,
We will not let thee part so suddenly:
Besides, if we should let thee go, all's one,
For with thy galleys couldst thou not get hence,
Without fresh men to rig and furnish them.

Caly. Tush, governor, take thou no care for that;
My men are all aboard,
And do attend my coming there by this.

Fern. Why, heard'st thou not the trumpet sound a charge?

Caly. Yes, what of that?

Fern. Why, then the house was fir'd,
Blown up, and all thy soldiers massacred.

Caly. O, monstrous treason!

Fern. A Jew's courtesy;
For he that did by treason work our fall,
By treason hath deliver'd thee to us:
Know, therefore, till thy father hath made good
The ruins done to Malta and to us,

Thou canst not part; for Malta shall be freed,
Or Selim ne'er return to Ottoman.

Caly. Nay, rather, Christians, let me go to Turkey,
In person there to mediate your peace:
To keep me here will naught advantage you.

Fern. Content thee, Calymath, here thou must stay,
And live in Malta prisoner; for come all the world
To rescue thee, so will we guard us now,
As sooner shall they drink the ocean dry,
Than conquer Malta, or endanger us.
So, march away; and let due praise begin
Neither to Fate nor Fortune, but to Heaven. [*Exeunt.*

EDWARD THE SECOND

DRAMATIS PERSONÆ

KING EDWARD THE SECOND.
PRINCE EDWARD, *his son, afterwards* KING EDWARD THE THIRD.
KENT, *brother to* KING EDWARD THE SECOND.
GAVESTON.
ARCHBISHOP OF CANTERBURY.
BISHOP OF COVENTRY.
BISHOP OF WINCHESTER.
WARWICK.
LANCASTER.
PEMBROKE.
ARUNDEL.
LEICESTER.
BERKELEY.
MORTIMER *the elder.*
MORTIMER *the younger, his nephew.*
SPENSER *the elder.*
SPENSER *the younger, his son.*
BALDOCK.
BEAUMONT.
TRUSSEL.
GURNEY.
MATREVIS.
LIGHTBORN.
SIR JOHN OF HAINAULT.
LEVUNE.
RICE AP HOWEL.
ABBOT.
MONKS.
HERALD.
LORDS, POOR MEN, JAMES, MOWER, CHAMPION, MESSENGERS, SOLDIERS, *and* ATTENDANTS.

QUEEN ISABELLA, *wife to* KING EDWARD THE SECOND.
NIECE *to* KING EDWARD THE SECOND, *daughter to the* DUKE OF GLOCESTER.
LADIES.

Enter GAVESTON, *reading a letter.*

Gav. My father is deceas'd. Come, Gaveston,
And share the kingdom with thy dearest friend.
Ah, words that make me surfeit with delight!
What greater bliss can hap to Gaveston
Than live and be the favourite of a king!
Sweet prince, I come! these, these thy amorous lines
Might have enforc'd me to have swum from France,
And, like Leander, gasp'd upon the sand,
So thou wouldst smile, and take me in thine arms.
The sight of London to my exil'd eyes
Is as Elysium to a new-come soul:
Not that I love the city or the men,
But that it harbours him I hold so dear,—
The king, upon whose bosom let me lie,
And with the world be still at enmity.

What need the arctic people love star-light,
To whom the sun shines both by day and night?
Farewell base stooping to the lordly peers!
My knee shall bow to none but to the king.
As for the multitude, that are but sparks,
Rak'd up in embers of their poverty,—
Tanti,—I'll fawn first on the wind,
That glanceth at my lips, and flieth away.

Enter three Poor Men.

But how now! what are these?
Poor Men. Such as desire your worship's service.
Gav. What canst thou do?
First P. Man. I can ride.
Gav. But I have no horses.—What art thou?
Sec. P. Man. A traveller.
Gav. Let me see; thou wouldst do well
To wait at my trencher, and tell me lies at dinner-time;
And, as I like your discoursing, I'll have you.—
And what art thou?
Third P. Man. A soldier, that hath serv'd against the Scot.
Gav. Why, there are hospitals for such as you:
I have no war; and therefore, sir, be gone.
Third P. Man. Farewell, and perish by a soldier's hand,
That wouldst reward them with an hospital!
Gav. Ay, ay, these words of his move me as much
As if a goose should play the porcupine,
And dart her plumes, thinking to pierce my breast.
But yet it is no pain to speak men fair;
I'll flatter these, and make them live in hope.— [*Aside.*
You know that I came lately out of France,
And yet I have not view'd my lord the king:
If I speed well, I'll entertain you all.
All. We thank your worship.
Gav. I have some business: leave me to myself.
All. We will wait here about the court.
Gav. Do. [*Exeunt Poor Men.*
These are not men for me;
I must have wanton poets, pleasant wits,
Musicians, that with touching of a string
May draw the pliant king which way I please:
Music and poetry is his delight;
Therefore I'll have Italian masks by night,

Sweet speeches, comedies, and pleasing shows;
And in the day, when he shall walk abroad,
Like sylvan nymphs my pages shall be clad;
My men, like satyrs grazing on the lawns,
Shall with their goat-feet dance an antic hay;
Sometime a lovely boy in Dian's shape,
With hair that gilds the water as it glides,
Crownets of pearl about his naked arms,
And in his sportful hands an olive-tree,
To hide those parts which men delight to see,
Shall bathe him in a spring; and there, hard by,
One like Actæon, peeping through the grove,
Shall by the angry goddess be transform'd,
And running in the likeness of an hart,
By yelping hounds pull'd down, shall seem to die:
Such things as these best please his majesty.—
Here comes my lord the king, and the nobles,
From the parliament. I'll stand aside. [*Retires.*

Enter KING EDWARD, KENT, LANCASTER, *the elder* MORTIMER, *the younger* MORTIMER, WARWICK, PEMBROKE, *and* Attendants.

K. Edw. Lancaster!
Lan. My lord?
Gav. That Earl of Lancaster do I abhor. [*Aside.*
K. Edw. Will you not grant me this?—In spite of them
I'll have my will; and these two Mortimers,
That cross me thus, shall know I am displeased. [*Aside.*
E. Mor. If you love us, my lord, hate Gaveston.
Gav. That villain Mortimer! I'll be his death. [*Aside.*
Y. Mor. Mine uncle here, this earl, and I myself,
Were sworn to your father at his death,
That he should ne'er return into the realm:
And know, my lord, ere I will break my oath,
This sword of mine, that should offend your foes,
Shall sleep within the scabbard at thy need,
And underneath thy banners march who will,
For Mortimer will hang his armour up.
Gav. Mort dieu! [*Aside.*
K. Edw. Well, Mortimer, I'll make thee rue these words:
Beseems it thee to contradict thy king?
Frown'st thou thereat, aspiring Lancaster?
The sword shall plane the furrows of thy brows,

And hew these knees that now are grown so stiff.
I will have Gaveston; and you shall know
What danger 'tis to stand against your king.

Gav. Well done, Ned! [*Aside.*

Lan. My lord, why do you thus incense your peers,
That naturally would love and honour you,
But for that base and obscure Gaveston?
Four earldoms have I, besides Lancaster,—
Derby, Salisbury, Lincoln, Leicester;
These will I sell, to give my soldiers pay,
Ere Gaveston shall stay within the realm:
Therefore, if he be come, expel him straight.

Kent. Barons and earls, your pride hath made me mute;
But now I'll speak, and to the proof, I hope.
I do remember, in my father's days,
Lord Percy of the North, being highly mov'd,
Brav'd Mowberay in presence of the king;
For which, had not his highness lov'd him well,
He should have lost his head; but with his look
Th' undaunted spirit of Percy was appeas'd,
And Mowberay and he were reconcil'd:
Yet dare you brave the king unto his face.—
Brother, revenge it, and let these their heads
Preach upon poles, for trespass of their tongues.

War. O, our heads!

K. Edw. Ay, yours; and therefore I would wish you grant.

War. Bridle thy anger, gentle Mortimer.

Y. Mor. I cannot, nor I will not; I must speak.—
Cousin, our hands I hope shall fence our heads,
And strike off his that makes you threaten us.—
Come, uncle, let us leave the brain-sick king,
And henceforth parley with our naked swords.

E Mor. Wiltshire hath men enough to save our heads.

War. All Warwickshire will leave him for my sake.

Lan. And northward Lancaster hath many friends.—
Adieu, my lord; and either change your mind,
Or look to see the throne, where you should sit,
To float in blood, and at thy wanton head
The glozing head of thy base minion thrown.

[*Exeunt all except King Edward, Kent, Gaveston, and attendants.*

K. Edw. I cannot brook these haughty menaces:
Am I a king, and must be over-rul'd!—

Brother, display my ensigns in the field:
I'll bandy with the barons and the earls,
And either die or live with Gaveston.

Gav. I can no longer keep me from my lord.
[*Comes forward.*

K. Edw. What, Gaveston! welcome! Kiss not my hand:
Embrace me, Gaveston, as I do thee.
Why shouldst thou kneel? know'st thou not who I am?
Thy friend, thyself, another Gaveston:
Not Hylas was more mourned of Hercules
Than thou hast been of me since thy exile.

Gav. And, since I went from hence, no soul in hell
Hath felt more torment than poor Gaveston.

K. Edw. I know it.—Brother, welcome home my friend.—
Now let the treacherous Mortimers conspire,
And that high-minded Earl of Lancaster:
I have my wish, in that I joy thy sight;
And sooner shall the sea o'erwhelm my land
Than bear the ship that shall transport thee hence.
I here create thee Lord High-chamberlain,
Chief Secretary to the state and me,
Earl of Cornwall, King and Lord of Man.

Gav. My lord, these titles far exceed my worth.

Kent. Brother, the least of these may well suffice
For one of greater birth than Gaveston.

K. Edw. Cease, brother, for I cannot brook these words.—
Thy worth, sweet friend, is far above my gifts:
Therefore, to equal it, receive my heart.
If for these dignities thou be envied,
I'll give thee more; for, but to honour thee,
Is Edward pleas'd with kingly regiment.
Fear'st thou thy person? thou shalt have a guard:
Wantest thou gold? go to my treasury:
Wouldst thou be lov'd and fear'd? receive my seal,
Save or condemn, and in our name command
What so thy mind affects, or fancy likes.

Gav. It shall suffice me to enjoy your love;
Which whiles I have, I think myself as great
As Cæsar riding in the Roman street,
With captive kings at his triumphant car.

Enter the BISHOP OF COVENTRY.

K. Edw. Whither goes my Lord of Coventry so fast?

Bish. of Cov. To celebrate your father's exequies.
But is that wicked Gaveston return'd?
K. Edw. Ay, priest, and lives to be reveng'd on thee,
That wert the only cause of his exile.
Gav. 'Tis true; and, but for reverence of these robes,
Thou shouldst not plod one foot beyond this place.
Bish. of Cov. I did no more than I was bound to do:
And, Gaveston, unless thou be reclaim'd,
As then I did incense the parliament,
So will I now, and thou shalt back to France.
Gav. Saving your reverence, you must pardon me.
K. Edw. Throw off his golden mitre, rend his stole,
And in the channel christen him anew.
Kent. Ah, brother, lay not violent hands on him!
For he'll complain unto the see of Rome.
Gav. Let him complain unto the see of hell:
I'll be reveng'd on him for my exile.
K. Edw. No, spare his life, but seize upon his goods:
Be thou lord bishop, and receive his rents,
And make him serve thee as thy chaplain:
I give him thee; here, use him as thou wilt.
Gav. He shall to prison, and there die in bolts.
K. Edw. Ay, to the Tower, the Fleet, or where thou wilt.
Bish. of Cov. For this offence be thou accurs'd of God!
K. Edw. Who's there? Convey this priest to the Tower.
Bish. of Cov. True, true.
K. Edw. But, in the meantime, Gaveston, away,
And take possession of his house and goods.
Come, follow me, and thou shalt have my guard
To see it done, and bring thee safe again.
Gav. What should a priest do with so fair a house?
A prison may beseem his holiness. [*Exeunt.*

Enter, on one side, the elder MORTIMER, *and the younger* MORTIMER; *on the other,* WARWICK, *and* LANCASTER.

War. 'Tis true, the bishop is in the Tower,
And goods and body given to Gaveston.
Lan. What, will they tyrannise upon the church?
Ah, wicked king! accursed Gaveston!
This ground, which is corrupted with their steps,
Shall be their timeless sepulchre or mine.
Y. Mor. Well, let that peevish Frenchman guard him sure:
Unless his breast be sword-proof, he shall die.

E. Mor. How now! why droops the Earl of Lancaster?
Y. Mor. Wherefore is Guy of Warwick discontent?
Lan. That villain Gaveston is made an earl.
E. Mor. An earl!
War. Ay, and besides Lord-chamberlain of the realm,
And Secretary too, and Lord of Man.
E. Mor. We may not nor we will not suffer this.
Y. Mor. Why post we not from hence to levy men?
Lan. "My Lord of Cornwall" now at every word;
And happy is the man whom he vouchsafes,
For vailing of his bonnet, one good look.
Thus, arm in arm, the king and he doth march:
Nay, more, the guard upon his lordship waits,
And all the court begins to flatter him.
War. Thus leaning on the shoulder of the king,
He nods, and scorns, and smiles at those that pass.
E. Mor. Doth no man take exceptions at the slave?
Lan. All stomach him, but none dare speak a word.
Y. Mor. Ah, that bewrays their baseness, Lancaster!
Were all the earls and barons of my mind,
We'd hale him from the bosom of the king,
And at the court-gate hang the peasant up,
Who, swoln with venom of ambitious pride,
Will be the ruin of the realm and us.
War. Here comes my Lord of Canterbury's grace.
Lan. His countenance bewrays he is displeas'd.

Enter the ARCHBISHOP OF CANTERBURY, *and an* Attendant.

Archb. of Cant. First were his sacred garments rent and torn;
Then laid they violent hands upon him; next,
Himself imprison'd, and his goods asseiz'd:
This certify the Pope: away, take horse.
[*Exit Attendant.*
Lan. My lord, will you take arms against the king?
Archb. of Cant. What need I? God himself is up in arms
When violence is offer'd to the church.
Y. Mor. Then will you join with us, that be his peers,
To banish or behead that Gaveston?
Archb. of Cant. What else, my lords? for it concerns me near;
The bishoprick of Coventry is his.

Enter QUEEN ISABELLA.

Y. Mor. Madam, whither walks your majesty so fast?
Q. Isab. Unto the forest, gentle Mortimer,
To live in grief and baleful discontent;
For now my lord the king regards me not,
But dotes upon the love of Gaveston:
He claps his cheeks, and hangs about his neck,
Smiles in his face, and whispers in his ears;
And, when I come, he frowns, as who should say,
"Go whither thou wilt, seeing I have Gaveston."
E. Mor. Is it not strange that he is thus bewitch'd?
Y. Mor. Madam, return unto the court again:
That sly inveigling Frenchman we'll exile,
Or lose our lives; and yet, ere that day come,
The king shall lose his crown; for we have power,
And courage too, to be reveng'd at full.
Archb. of Cant. But yet lift not your swords against the king.
Lan. No; but we will lift Gaveston from hence.
War. And war must be the means, or he'll stay still.
Q. Isab. Then let him stay; for, rather than my lord
Shall be oppress'd by civil mutinies,
I will endure a melancholy life,
And let him frolic with his minion.
Archb. of Cant. My lords, to ease all this, but hear me speak:
We and the rest, that are his counsellors,
Will meet, and with a general consent
Confirm his banishment with our hands and seals.
Lan. What we confirm the king will frustrate.
Y. Mor. Then may we lawfully revolt from him.
War. But say, my lord, where shall this meeting be?
Archb. of Cant. At the New Temple.
Y. Mor. Content.
Archb. of Cant. And, in the meantime, I'll entreat you all
To cross to Lambeth, and there stay with me.
Lan. Come, then, let's away.
Y. Mor. Madam, farewell.
Q. Isab. Farewell, sweet Mortimer, and, for my sake,
Forbear to levy arms against the king.
Y. Mor. Ay, if words will serve; if not, I must. [*Exeunt.*

Enter GAVESTON *and* KENT.

Gav. Edmund, the mighty prince of Lancaster,
That hath more earldoms than an ass can bear,
And both the Mortimers, two goodly men,
With Guy of Warwick, that redoubted knight,
Are gone towards Lambeth: there let them remain.
[*Exeunt.*

Enter LANCASTER, WARWICK, PEMBROKE, *the elder* MORTIMER, *the younger* MORTIMER, *the* ARCHBISHOP OF CANTERBURY, *and* Attendants.

Lan. Here is the form of Gaveston's exile;
May it please your lordship to subscribe your name.
Archb. of Cant. Give me the paper.
[*He subscribes, as the others do after him.*
Lan. Quick, quick, my lord; I long to write my name.
War. But I long more to see him banish'd hence.
Y. Mor. The name of Mortimer shall fright the king,
Unless he be declin'd from that base peasant.

Enter KING EDWARD, GAVESTON, *and* KENT.

K. Edw. What, are you mov'd that Gaveston sits here?
It is our pleasure; we will have it so.
Lan. Your grace doth well to place him by your side,
For nowhere else the new earl is so safe.
E. Mor. What man of noble birth can brook this sight?
Quam male conveniunt!—
See, what a scornful look the peasant casts!
Pem. Can kingly lions fawn on creeping ants?
War. Ignoble vassal, that, like Phaeton,
Aspir'st unto the guidance of the sun!
Y. Mor. Their downfall is at hand, their forces down:
We will not thus be fac'd and over-peer'd.
K. Edw. Lay hands on that traitor Mortimer!
E. Mor. Lay hands on that traitor Gaveston!
Kent. Is this the duty that you owe your king?
War. We know our duties; let him know his peers.
K. Edw. Whither will you bear him? stay, or ye shall die.
E. Mor. We are no traitors; therefore threaten not.
Gav. No, threaten not, my lord, but pay them home.
Were I a king—
Y. Mor. Thou, villain! wherefore talk'st thou of a king,

That hardly art a gentleman by birth?
K. Edw. Were he a peasant, being my minion,
I'll make the proudest of you stoop to him.
Lan. My lord—you may not thus disparage us.—
Away, I say, with hateful Gaveston!
E. Mor. And with the Earl of Kent that favours him.

[*Attendants remove Gaveston and Kent.*

K. Edw. Nay, then, lay violent hands upon your king:
Here, Mortimer, sit thou in Edward's throne;
Warwick and Lancaster, wear you my crown.
Was ever king thus over-rul'd as I?
Lan. Learn, then, to rule us better, and the realm.
Y. Mor. What we have done, our heart-blood shall maintain.
War. Think you that we can brook this upstart['s] pride?
K. Edw. Anger and wrathful fury stops my speech.
Archb. of Cant. Why are you mov'd? be patient, my lord,
And see what we your counsellors have done.
Y. Mor. My lords, now let us all be resolute,
And either have our wills, or lose our lives.
K. Edw. Meet you for this, proud over-daring peers!
Ere my sweet Gaveston shall part from me,
This isle shall fleet upon the ocean,
And wander to the unfrequented Inde.
Archb. of Cant. You know that I am legate to the Pope:
On your allegiance to the see of Rome,
Subscribe, as we have done, to his exile.
Y. Mor. Curse him, if he refuse; and then may we
Depose him, and elect another king.
K. Edw. Ay, there it goes! but yet I will not yield:
Curse me, depose me, do the worst you can.
Lan. Then linger not, my lord, but do it straight.
Archb. of Cant. Remember how the bishop was abus'd:
Either banish him that was the cause thereof,
Or I will presently discharge these lords
Of duty and allegiance due to thee.
K. Edw. It boots me not to threat; I must speak fair:
The legate of the Pope will be obey'd.— [*Aside.*
My lord, you shall be Chancellor of the realm;
Thou, Lancaster, High-Admiral of our fleet;
Young Mortimer and his uncle shall be earls;
And you, Lord Warwick, President of the North;

And thou of Wales. If this content you not,
Make several kingdoms of this monarchy,
And share it equally amongst you all,
So I may have some nook or corner left,
To frolic with my dearest Gaveston.

Archb. of Cant. Nothing shall alter us; we are resolv'd.

Lan. Come, come, subscribe.

Y. Mor. Why should you love him whom the world hates so?

K. Edw. Because he loves me more than all the world.
Ah, none but rude and savage-minded men
Would seek the ruin of my Gaveston!
You that be noble-born should pity him.

War. You that are princely-born should shake him off:
For shame, subscribe, and let the lown depart.

E. Mor. Urge him, my lord.

Archb. of Cant. Are you content to banish him the realm?

K. Edw. I see I must, and therefore am content:
Instead of ink, I'll write it with my tears. [*Subscribes.*

Y. Mor. The king is love-sick for his minion.

K. Edw. 'Tis done: and now, accursed hand, fall off!

Lan. Give it me: I'll have it publish'd in the streets.

Y. Mor. I'll see him presently despatch'd away.

Archb. of Cant. Now is my heart at ease.

War. And so is mine.

Pem. This will be good news to the common sort.

E. Mor. Be it or no, he shall not linger here.
[*Exeunt all except King Edward.*

K. Edw. How fast they run to banish him I love!
They would not stir, were it to do me good.
Why should a king be subject to a priest?
Proud Rome, that hatchest such imperial grooms,
With these thy superstitious taper-lights,
Wherewith thy antichristian churches blaze,
I'll fire thy crazed buildings, and enforce
The papal towers to kiss the lowly ground,
With slaughter'd priests make Tiber's channel swell,
And banks rais'd higher with their sepulchres!
As for the peers, that back the clergy thus,
If I be king, not one of them shall live.

Re-enter GAVESTON.

Gav. My lord, I hear it whisper'd everywhere,

That I am banish'd and must fly the land.
K. Edw. 'Tis true, sweet Gaveston: O, were it false!
The legate of the Pope will have it so,
And thou must hence, or I shall be depos'd.
But I will reign to be reveng'd of them;
And therefore, sweet friend, take it patiently.
Live where thou wilt, I'll send thee gold enough;
And long thou shalt not stay; or, if thou dost,
I'll come to thee; my love shall ne'er decline.
Gav. Is all my hope turn'd to this hell of grief?
K. Edw. Rend not my heart with thy too-piercing words:
Thou from this land, I from myself am banish'd.
Gav. To go from hence grieves not poor Gaveston;
But to forsake you, in whose gracious looks
The blessedness of Gaveston remains;
For nowhere else seeks he felicity.
K. Edw. And only this torments my wretched soul,
That, whether I will or no, thou must depart.
Be governor of Ireland in my stead,
And there abide till fortune call thee home.
Here, take my picture, and let me wear thine:
[*They exchange pictures.*
O, might I keep thee here, as I do this,
Happy were I! but now most miserable.
Gav. 'Tis something to be pitied of a king.
K. Edw. Thou shalt not hence; I'll hide thee, Gaveston.
Gav. I shall be found, and then 'twill grieve me more.
K. Edw. Kind words and mutual talk makes our grief greater:
Therefore, with dumb embracement, let us part.
Stay, Gaveston; I cannot leave thee thus.
Gav. For every look, my love drops down a tear:
Seeing I must go, do not renew my sorrow.
K. Edw. The time is little that thou hast to stay,
And, therefore, give me leave to look my fill.
But, come, sweet friend; I'll bear thee on thy way.
Gav. The peers will frown.
K. Edw. I pass not for their anger. Come, let's go:
O, that we might as well return as go!

Enter QUEEN ISABELLA.

Q. Isab. Whither goes my lord?
K. Edw. Fawn not on me, French strumpet; get thee gone!

Q. Isab. On whom but on my husband should I fawn?
Gav. On Mortimer; with whom, ungentle queen,—
I say no more—judge you the rest, my lord.
Q. Isab. In saying this, thou wrong'st me, Gaveston:
Is't not enough that thou corrupt'st my lord,
And art a bawd to his affections,
But thou must call mine honour thus in question?
Gav. I mean not so; your grace must pardon me.
K. Edw. Thou art too familiar with that Mortimer,
And by thy means is Gaveston exil'd:
But I would wish thee reconcile the lords,
Or thou shalt ne'er be reconcil'd to me.
Q. Isab. Your highness knows, it lies not in my power.
K. Edw. Away, then! touch me not.—Come, Gaveston.
Q. Isab. Villain, 'tis thou that robb'st me of my lord.
Gav. Madam, 'tis you that rob me of my lord.
K. Edw. Speak not unto her: let her droop and pine.
Q. Isab. Wherein, my lord, have I deserv'd these words?
Witness the tears that Isabella sheds,
Witness this heart, that sighing for thee breaks,
How dear my lord is to poor Isabel!
K. Edw. And witness heaven how dear thou art to me:
There weep; for, till my Gaveston be repeal'd,
Assure thyself thou com'st not in my sight.
[*Exeunt King Edward and Gaveston.*
Q. Isab. O miserable and distressed queen!
Would, when I left sweet France, and was embarked,
That charming Circe, walking on the waves,
Had chang'd my shape! or at the marriage-day
The cup of Hymen had been full of poison!
Or with those arms, that twin'd about my neck,
I had been stifled, and not liv'd to see
The king my lord thus to abandon me!
Like frantic Juno, will I fill the earth
With ghastly murmur of my sighs and cries;
For never doted Jove on Ganymede
So much as he on cursed Gaveston:
But that will more exasperate his wrath;
I must entreat him, I must speak him fair,
And be a means to call home Gaveston:
And yet he'll ever dote on Gaveston;
And so am I for ever miserable.

Re-enter LANCASTER, WARWICK, PEMBROKE, *the elder* MORTIMER, *and the younger* MORTIMER.

Lan. Look, where the sister of the king of France
Sits wringing of her hands and beats her breast!
War. The king, I fear, hath ill entreated her.
Pem. Hard is the heart that injures such a saint.
Y. Mor. I know 'tis 'long of Gaveston she weeps.
E. Mor. Why, he is gone.
Y. Mor. Madam, how fares your grace?
Q. Isab. Ah, Mortimer, now breaks the king's hate forth,
And he confesseth that he loves me not!
Y. Mor. Cry quittance, madam, then, and love not him.
Q. Isab. No, rather will I die a thousand deaths:
And yet I love in vain; he'll ne'er love me.
Lan. Fear ye not, madam; now his minion's gone,
His wanton humour will be quickly left.
Q. Isab. O, never, Lancaster! I am enjoin'd
To sue unto you all for his repeal:
This wills my lord, and this must I perform,
Or else be banish'd from his highness' presence.
Lan. For his repeal? Madam, he comes not back,
Unless the sea cast up his shipwreck'd body.
War. And to behold so sweet a sight as that,
There's none here but would run his horse to death.
Y. Mor. But, madam, would you have us call him home?
Q. Isab. Ay, Mortimer, for, till he be restor'd,
The angry king hath banish'd me the court;
And, therefore, as thou lov'st and tender'st me,
Be thou my advocate unto these peers.
Y. Mor. What, would you have me plead for Gaveston?
E. Mor. Plead for him he that will, I am resolv'd.
Lan. And so am I, my lord: dissuade the queen.
Q. Isab. O, Lancaster, let him dissuade the king!
For 'tis against my will he should return.
War. Then speak not for him; let the peasant go.
Q. Isab. 'Tis for myself I speak, and not for him.
Pem. No speaking will prevail; and therefore cease.
Y. Mor. Fair queen, forbear to angle for the fish
Which, being caught, strikes him that takes it dead;
I mean that vile torpedo, Gaveston,
That now, I hope, floats on the Irish seas.
Q. Isab. Sweet Mortimer, sit down by me a while,

And I will tell thee reasons of such weight
As thou wilt soon subscribe to his repeal.
Y. Mor. It is impossible: but speak your mind.
Q. Isab. Then thus;—but none shall hear it but ourselves.
[*Talks to Y. Mor. apart.*
Lan. My lords, albeit the queen win Mortimer,
Will you be resolute and hold with me?
E. Mor. Not I, against my nephew.
Pem. Fear not; the queen's words cannot alter him.
War. No? do but mark how earnestly she pleads!
Lan. And see how coldly his looks make denial!
War. She smiles: now, for my life, his mind is chang'd!
Lan. I'll rather lose his friendship, I, than grant.
Y. Mor. Well, of necessity it must be so.—
My lords, that I abhor base Gaveston
I hope your honours make no question,
And therefore, though I plead for his repeal,
'Tis not for his sake, but for our avail;
Nay, for the realm's behoof, and for the king's.
Lan. Fie, Mortimer, dishonour not thyself!
Can this be true, 'twas good to banish him?
And is this true, to call him home again?
Such reasons make white black, and dark night day.
Y. Mor. My lord of Lancaster, mark the respect.
Lan. In no respect can contraries be true.
Q. Isab. Yet, good my lord, hear what he can allege.
War. All that he speaks is nothing; we are resolv'd.
Y. Mor. Do you not wish that Gaveston were dead?
Pem. I would he were!
Y. Mor. Why, then, my lord, give me but leave to speak.
E. Mor. But, nephew, do not play the sophister.
Y. Mor. This which I urge is of a burning zeal
To mend the king and do our country good.
Know you not Gaveston hath store of gold,
Which may in Ireland purchase him such friends
As he will front the mightiest of us all?
And whereas he shall live and be belov'd,
'Tis hard for us to work his overthrow.
War. Mark you but that, my lord of Lancaster.
Y. Mor. But, were he here, detested as he is,
How easily might some base slave be suborn'd
To greet his lordship with a poniard,
And none so much as blame the murderer,

But rather praise him for that brave attempt,
And in the chronicle enrol his name
For purging of the realm of such a plague!

Pem. He saith true.

Lan. Ay, but how chance this was not done before?

Y. Mor. Because, my lords, it was not thought upon.
Nay, more, when he shall know it lies in us
To banish him, and then to call him home,
'Twill make him vail the top flag of his pride,
And fear to offend the meanest nobleman.

E. Mor. But how if he do not, nephew?

Y. Mor. Then may we with some colour rise in arms;
For, howsoever we have borne it out,
'Tis treason to be up against the king;
So shall we have the people of our side,
Which, for his father's sake, lean to the king,
But cannot brook a night-grown mushroom,
Such a one as my Lord of Cornwall is,
Should bear us down of the nobility:
And, when the commons and the nobles join,
'Tis not the king can buckler Gaveston;
We'll pull him from the strongest hold he hath.
My lords, if to perform this I be slack,
Think me as base a groom as Gaveston.

Lan. On that condition Lancaster will grant.

War. And so will Pembroke and I.

E. Mor. And I.

Y. Mor. In this I count me highly gratified,
And Mortimer will rest at your command.

Q. Isab. And when this favour Isabel forgets,
Then let her live abandon'd and forlorn.—
But see, in happy time, my lord the king,
Having brought the Earl of Cornwall on his way,
Is new return'd. This news will glad him much:
Yet not so much as me; I love him more
Than he can Gaveston: would he lov'd me
But half so much! then were I treble-blest.

Re-enter KING EDWARD, *mourning.*

K. Edw. He's gone, and for his absence thus I mourn:
Did never sorrow go so near my heart
As doth the want of my sweet Gaveston;
And, could my crown's revenue bring him back,

I would freely give it to his enemies,
And think I gain'd, having bought so dear a friend.
Q. Isab. Hark, how he harps upon his minion!
K. Edw. My heart is as an anvil unto sorrow,
Which beats upon it like the Cyclops' hammers,
And with the noise turns up my giddy brain,
And makes me frantic for my Gaveston.
Ah, had some bloodless Fury rose from hell,
And with my kingly sceptre struck me dead,
When I was forc'd to leave my Gaveston!
Lan. Diablo, what passions call you these?
Q. Isab. My gracious lord, I come to bring you news.
K. Edw. That you have parled with your Mortimer?
Q. Isab. That Gaveston, my lord, shall be repeal'd.
K. Edw. Repeal'd! the news is too sweet to be true.
Q. Isab. But will you love me, if you find it so?
K. Edw. If it be so, what will not Edward do?
Q. Isab. For Gaveston, but not for Isabel.
K. Edw. For thee, fair queen, if thou lov'st Gaveston;
I'll hang a golden tongue about thy neck,
Seeing thou hast pleaded with so good success.
Q. Isab. No other jewels hang about my neck
Than these, my lord; nor let me have more wealth
Than I may fetch from this rich treasury.
O, how a kiss revives poor Isabel!
K. Edw. Once more receive my hand; and let this be
A second marriage 'twixt thyself and me.
Q. Isab. And may it prove more happy than the first!
My gentle lord, bespeak these nobles fair,
That wait attendance for a gracious look,
And on their knees salute your majesty.
K. Edw. Courageous Lancaster, embrace thy king;
And, as gross vapours perish by the sun,
Even so let hatred with thy sovereign's smile:
Live thou with me as my companion.
Lan. This salutation overjoys my heart.
K. Edw. Warwick shall be my chiefest counsellor:
These silver hairs will more adorn my court
Than gaudy silks or rich embroidery.
Chide me, sweet Warwick, if I go astray.
War. Slay me, my lord, when I offend your grace.
K. Edw. In solemn triumphs and in public shows
Pembroke shall bear the sword before the king.

Pem. And with this sword Pembroke will fight for you.
K. Edw. But wherefore walks young Mortimer aside?
Be thou commander of our royal fleet;
Or, if that lofty office like thee not,
I make thee here Lord Marshal of the realm.
Y. Mor. My lord, I'll marshal so your enemies,
As England shall be quiet, and you safe.
K. Edw. And as for you, Lord Mortimer of Chirke,
Whose great achievements in our foreign war
Deserve no common place nor mean reward,
Be you the general of the levied troops
That now are ready to assail the Scots.
E. Mor. In this your grace hath highly honour'd me,
For with my nature war doth best agree.
Q. Isab. Now is the king of England rich and strong,
Having the love of his renowned peers.
K. Edw. Ay, Isabel, ne'er was my heart so light.—
Clerk of the crown, direct our warrant forth,
For Gaveston, to Ireland!

Enter BEAUMONT *with warrant.*

Beaumont, fly
As fast as Iris or Jove's Mercury.
Beau. It shall be done, my gracious lord. [*Exit.*
K. Edw. Lord Mortimer, we leave you to your charge.
Now let us in, and feast it royally.
Against our friend the Earl of Cornwall comes
We'll have a general tilt and tournament;
And then his marriage shall be solemnis'd;
For wot you not that I have made him sure
Unto our cousin, the Earl of Glocester's heir?
Lan. Such news we hear, my lord.
K. Edw. That day, if not for him, yet for my sake,
Who in the triumph will be challenger,
Spare for no cost; we will requite your love.
War. In this or aught your highness shall command us.
K. Edw. Thanks, gentle Warwick. Come, let's in and revel.
[*Exeunt all except the elder Mortimer and the younger Mortimer.*
E. Mor. Nephew, I must to Scotland; thou stay'st here.
Leave now to oppose thyself against the king:
Thou seest by nature he is mild and calm;
And, seeing his mind so dotes on Gaveston,

Let him without controlment have his will.
The mightiest kings have had their minions;
Great Alexander lov'd Hephæstion,
The conquering Hercules for Hylas wept,
And for Patroclus stern Achilles droop'd:
And not kings only, but the wisest men;
The Roman Tully lov'd Octavius,
Grave Socrates wild Alcibiades.
Then let his grace, whose youth is flexible,
And promiseth as much as we can wish,
Freely enjoy that vain light-headed earl;
For riper years will wean him from such toys.

Y. Mor. Uncle, his wanton humour grieves not me;
But this I scorn, that one so basely-born
Should by his sovereign's favour grow so pert,
And riot it with the treasure of the realm,
While soldiers mutiny for want of pay.
He wears a lord's revenue on his back,
And, Midas-like, he jets it in the court,
With base outlandish cullions at his heels,
Whose proud fantastic liveries make such show
As if that Proteus, god of shapes, appear'd.
I have not seen a dapper Jack so brisk:
He wears a short Italian hooded cloak,
Larded with pearl, and in his Tuscan cap
A jewel of more value than the crown.
While other walk below, the king and he,
From out a window, laugh at such as we,
And flout our train, and jest at our attire.
Uncle, 'tis this that makes me impatient.

E. Mor. But, nephew, now you see the king is chang'd.

Y. Mor. Then so am I, and live to do him service:
But, whiles I have a sword, a hand, a heart,
I will not yield to any such upstart.
You know my mind: come, uncle, let's away, [*Exeunt.*

Enter the younger SPENSER *and* BALDOCK.

Bald. Spenser,
Seeing that our lord the Earl of Glocester's dead,
Which of the nobles dost thou mean to serve?

Y. Spen. Not Mortimer, nor any of his side,
Because the king and he are enemies.
Baldock, learn this of me: a factious lord

Shall hardly do himself good, much less us;
But he that hath the favour of a king
May with one word advance us while we live.
The liberal Earl of Cornwall is the man
On whose good fortune Spenser's hope depends.

Bald. What, mean you, then, to be his follower?

Y. Spen. No, his companion; for he loves me well,
And would have once preferr'd me to the king.

Bald. But he is banish'd; there's small hope of him.

Y. Spen. Ay, for a while; but, Baldock, mark the end.
A friend of mine told me in secrecy
That he's repeal'd and sent for back again;
And even now a post came from the court
With letters to our lady from the king;
And, as she read, she smil'd; which makes me think
It is about her lover Gaveston.

Bald. 'Tis like enough; for, since he was exil'd,
She neither walks abroad nor comes in sight.
But I had thought the match had been broke off,
And that his banishment had chang'd her mind.

Y. Spen. Our lady's first love is not wavering;
My life for thine, she will have Gaveston.

Bald. Then hope I by her means to be preferr'd,
Having read unto her since she was a child.

Y. Spen. Then, Baldock, you must cast the scholar off,
And learn to court it like a gentleman.
'Tis not a black coat and a little band,
A velvet-cap'd cloak, fac'd before with serge,
And smelling to a nosegay all the day,
Or holding of a napkin in your hand,
Or saying a long grace at a table's end,
Or making low legs to a nobleman,
Or looking downward, with your eye-lids close,
And saying, "Truly, an't may please your honour,"
Can get you any favour with great men:
You must be proud, bold, pleasant, resolute,
And now and then stab, as occasion serves.

Bald. Spenser, thou know'st I hate such formal toys,
And use them but of mere hypocrisy.
Mine old lord, whiles he liv'd, was so precise,
That he would take exceptions at my buttons,
And, being like pins' heads, blame me for the bigness;
Which made me curate-like in mine attire,

Though inwardly licentious enough,
And apt for any kind of villany.
I am none of these common pedants, I,
That cannot speak without *propterea quod.*

Y. Spen. But one of those that saith *quando-quidem,*
And hath a special gift to form a verb.

Bald. Leave off this jesting; here my lady comes.

Enter KING EDWARD'S Niece.

Niece. The grief for his exile was not so much
As is the joy of his returning home.
This letter came from my sweet Gaveston:
What need'st thou, love, thus to excuse thyself?
I know thou couldst not come and visit me. [*Reads.*
I will not long be from thee, though I die;—
This argues the entire love of my lord;— [*Reads.*
When I forsake thee, death seize on my heart!—
But stay thee here where Gaveston shall sleep.
[*Puts the letter into her bosom.*
Now to the letter of my lord the king:
He wills me to repair unto the court,
And meet my Gaveston: why do I stay,
Seeing that he talks thus of my marriage day?—
Who's there? Baldock!
See that my coach be ready; I must hence.

Bald. It shall be done, madam.

Niece. And meet me at the park-pale presently.
[*Exit Baldock.*
Spenser, stay you, and bear me company,
For I have joyful news to tell thee of;
My lord of Cornwall is a-coming over,
And will be at the court as soon as we.

Y. Spen. I knew the king would have him home again.

Niece. If all things sort out, as I hope they will,
Thy service, Spenser, shall be thought upon.

Y. Spen. I humbly thank your ladyship.

Niece. Come, lead the way: I long till I am there. [*Exeunt.*

Enter KING EDWARD, QUEEN ISABELLA, KENT, LANCASTER, *the younger* MORTIMER, WARWICK, PEMBROKE, *and* Attendants.

K. Edw. The wind is good; I wonder why he stays:
I fear me he is wreck'd upon the sea.

Great celebration which all the knights will arrive bringing their coats of Arms.

Q. Isab. Look, Lancaster, how passionate he is,
And still his mind runs on his minion!
Lan. My lord,—
K. Edw. How now! what news? is Gaveston arriv'd?
Y. Mor. Nothing but Gaveston! what means your grace?
You have matters of more weight to think upon:
The King of France sets foot in Normandy.
K. Edw. A trifle! we'll expel him when we please.
But tell me, Mortimer, what's thy device
Against the stately triumph we decreed?
Y. Mor. A homely one, my lord, not worth the telling.
K. Edw. Pray thee, let me know it.
Y. Mor. But, seeing you are so desirous, thus it is;
A lofty cedar tree, fair flourishing,
On whose top branches kingly eagles perch,
And by the bark a canker creeps me up,
And gets unto the highest bough of all;
The motto, *Æque tandem.*
K. Edw. And what is yours, my Lord of Lancaster?
Lan. My lord, mine's more obscure than Mortimer's.
Pliny reports, there is a flying-fish
Which all the other fishes deadly hate,
And therefore, being pursu'd, it takes the air:
No sooner is it up, but there's a fowl
That seizeth it: this fish, my lord, I bear;
The motto this, *Undique mors est.*

Cancer or canker = Gaveston open insults.

Kent. Proud Mortimer! ungentle Lancaster!
Is this the love you bear your sovereign?
Is this the fruit your reconcilement bears?
Can you in words make show of amity,
And in your shields display your rancorous minds?
What call you this but private libelling
Against the Earl of Cornwall and my brother?
Q. Isab. Sweet husband, be content; they all love you.
K. Edw. They love me not that hate my Gaveston.
I am that cedar; shake me not too much;
And you the eagles; soar ye ne'er so high,
I have the jesses that will pull you down;
And *Æque tandem* shall that canker cry
Unto the proudest peer of Britainy.
Thou that compar'st him to a flying-fish.
And threaten'st death whether he rise or fall,
'Tis not the hugest monster of the sea,

Nor foulest harpy, that shall swallow him.
Y. Mor. If in his absence thus he favours him,
What will he do whenas he shall be present?
Lan. That shall we see: look, where his lordship comes!

Enter GAVESTON.

K. Edw. My Gaveston!
Welcome to Tynmouth! welcome to thy friend!
Thy absence made me droop and pine away;
For, as the lovers of fair Danaë,
When she was lock'd up in a brazen tower,
Desir'd her more, and wax'd outrageous,
So did it sure with me: and now thy sight
Is sweeter far than was thy parting hence
Bitter and irksome to my sobbing heart.
Gav. Sweet lord and king, your speech preventeth mine;
Yet have I words left to express my joy:
The shepherd, nipt with biting winter's rage,
Frolics not more to see the painted spring
Than I do to behold your majesty.
K. Edw. Will none of you salute my Gaveston?
Lan. Salute him! yes.—Welcome, Lord Chamberlain!
Y. Mor. Welcome is the good Earl of Cornwall!
War. Welcome, Lord Governor of the Isle of Man!
Pem. Welcome, Master Secretary!
Kent. Brother, do you hear them?
K. Edw. Still will these earls and barons use me thus?
Gav. My lord, I cannot brook these injuries.
Q. Isab. Ay me, poor soul, when these begin to jar! [*Aside.*
K. Edw. Return it to their throats; I'll be thy warrant.
Gav. Base, leaden earls, that glory in your birth,
Go sit at home, and eat your tenants' beef;
And come not here to scoff at Gaveston,
Whose mounting thoughts did never creep so low
As to bestow a look on such as you.
Lan. Yet I disdain not to do this for you.
[*Draws his sword, and offers to stab Gaveston.*
K. Edw. Treason! treason! where's the traitor?
Pem. Here, here!
K. Edw. Convey hence Gaveston; they'll murder him.
Gav. The life of thee shall salve this foul disgrace.
Y. Mor. Villain, thy life! unless I miss mine aim.
[*Wounds Gaveston.*

openly insult Gaveston.

drag him out only to save him.

Q. Isab. Ah, furious Mortimer, what hast thou done.
Y. Mor. No more than I would answer, were he slain.
[*Exit Gaveston with Attendants.*
K. Edw. Yes, more than thou canst answer, though he live:
Dear shall you both aby this riotous deed:
Out of my presence! come not near the court.
Y. Mor. I'll not be barr'd the court for Gaveston.
Lan. We'll hale him by the ears unto the block.
K. Edw. Look to your own heads; his is sure enough.
War. Look to your own crown, if you back him thus.
Kent. Warwick, these words do ill beseem thy years.
K. Edw. Nay, all of them conspire to cross me thus:
But, if I live, I'll tread upon their heads
That think with high looks thus to tread me down.
Come, Edmund, let's away, and levy men:
'Tis war that must abate these barons' pride.
[*Exeunt King Edward, Queen Isabella, and Kent.*
War. Let's to our castles, for the king is mov'd.
Y. Mor. Mov'd may he be, and perish in his wrath!
Lan. Cousin, it is no dealing with him now;
He means to make us stoop by force of arms:
And therefore let us jointly here protest
To prosecute that Gaveston to the death.
Y. Mor. By heaven, the abject villain shall not live!
War. I'll have his blood, or die in seeking it.
Pem. The like oath Pembroke takes.
Lan. And so doth Lancaster.
Now send our heralds to defy the king;
And make the people swear to put him down.

Enter a Messenger.

Y. Mor. Letters! from whence?
Mes. From Scotland, my lord. [*Giving letters to Mortimer.*
Lan. Why, how now, cousin! how fare all our friends?
Y. Mor. My uncle's taken prisoner by the Scots.
Lan. We'll have him ransom'd, man: be of good cheer.
Y. Mor. They rate his ransom at five thousand pound.
Who should defray the money but the king,
Seeing he is taken prisoner in his wars?
I'll to the king.
Lan. Do, cousin, and I'll bear thee company.
War. Meantime my Lord of Pembroke and myself
Will to Newcastle here, and gather head.

Y. Mor. About it, then, and we will follow you.
Lan. Be resolute and full of secrecy.
War. I warrant you. [*Exit with Pembroke.*
Y. Mor. Cousin, an if he will not ransom him,
I'll thunder such a peal into his ears
As never subject did unto his king.
Lan. Content; I'll bear my part.—Hollo! who's there?

Enter Guard.

Y. Mor. Ay, marry, such a guard as this doth well.
Lan. Lead on the way.
Guard. Whither will your lordships?
Y. Mor. Whither else but to the king?
Guard. His highness is dispos'd to be alone.
Lan. Why, so he may; but we will speak to him.
Guard. You may not in, my lord.
Y. Mor. May we not?

Enter King Edward *and* Kent.

K. Edw. How now!
What noise is this? who have we there? is't you? [*Going.*
Y. Mor. Nay, stay, my lord; I come to bring you news;
Mine uncle's taken prisoner by the Scots.
K. Edw. Then ransom him.
Lan. 'Twas in your wars; you should ransom him.
Y. Mor. And you shall ransom him, or else—
Kent. What, Mortimer, you will not threaten him?
K. Edw. Quiet yourself; you shall have the broad seal,
To gather for him th[o]roughout the realm.
Lan. Your minion Gaveston hath taught you this.
Y. Mor. My lord, the family of the Mortimers
Are not so poor, but, would they sell their land,
'Twould levy men enough to anger you.
We never beg, but use such prayers as these.
K. Edw. Shall I still be haunted thus?
Y. Mor. Nay, now you are here alone, I'll speak my mind.
Lan. And so will I; and then, my lord, farewell.
Y. Mor. The idle triumphs, masks, lascivious shows,
And prodigal gifts bestow'd on Gaveston,
Have drawn thy treasury dry, and made thee weak;
The murmuring commons, overstretched, break.
Lan. Look for rebellion, look to be depos'd:
Thy garrisons are beaten out of France,

And, lame and poor, lie groaning at the gates;
The wild Oneil, with swarms of Irish kerns,
Lives uncontroll'd within the English pale;
Unto the walls of York the Scots make road,
And, unresisted, drive away rich spoils.

Y. Mor. The haughty Dane commands the narrow seas,
While in the harbour ride thy ships unrigg'd.

Lan. What foreign prince sends thee ambassadors?

Y. Mor. Who loves thee, but a sort of flatterers?

Lan. Thy gentle queen, sole sister to Valois,
Complains that thou hast left her all forlorn.

Y. Mor. Thy court is naked, being bereft of those
That make a king seem glorious to the world,
I mean the peers, whom thou shouldst dearly love;
Libels are cast again thee in the street;
Ballads and rhymes made of thy overthrow.

Lan. The northern borderers, seeing their houses burnt,
Their wives and children slain, run up and down,
Cursing the name of thee and Gaveston.

Y. Mor. When wert thou in the field with banner spread?
But once; and then thy soldiers march'd like players,
With garish robes, not armour; and thyself,
Bedaub'd with gold, rode laughing at the rest,
Nodding and shaking of thy spangled crest,
Where women's favours hung like labels down.

Lan. And thereof came it that the fleering Scots,
To England's high disgrace, have made this jig;
Maids of England, sore may you mourn,
For your lemans you have lost at Bannocksbourn,—
With a heave and a ho!
What weeneth the king of England
So soon to have won Scotland!—
With a rombelow!

Y. Mor. Wigmore shall fly, to set my uncle free.

Lan. And, when 'tis gone, our swords shall purchase more.
If you be mov'd, revenge it as you can:
Look next to see us with our ensigns spread.
[*Exit with Y. Mortimer.*

K. Edw. My swelling heart for very anger breaks:
How oft have I been baited by these peers,
And dare not be reveng'd, for their power is great!
Yet, shall the crowing of these cockerels
Affright a lion? Edward, unfold thy paws,

And let their lives'-blood slake thy fury's hunger.
If I be cruel and grow tyrannous,
Now let them thank themselves, and rue too late.
Kent. My lord, I see your love to Gaveston
Will be the ruin of the realm and you,
For now the wrathful nobles threaten wars;
And therefore, brother, banish him for ever.
K. Edw. Art thou an enemy to my Gaveston?
Kent. Ay; and it grieves me that I favour'd him.
K. Edw. Traitor, be gone! whine thou with Mortimer.
Kent. So will I, rather than with Gaveston.
K. Edw. Out of my sight, and trouble me no more!
Kent. No marvel though thou scorn thy noble peers,
When I thy brother am rejected thus.
K. Edw. Away! [*Exit Kent.*
Poor Gaveston, thou hast no friend but me!
Do what they can, we'll live in Tynmouth here;
And, so I walk with him about the walls,
What care I though the earls begirt us round?
Here comes she that is cause of all these jars.

Enter QUEEN ISABELLA, *with* EDWARD'S Niece, *two* Ladies, GAVESTON, BALDOCK, *and the younger* SPENSER.

Q. Isab. My lord, 'tis thought the earls are up in arms.
K. Edw. Ay, and 'tis likewise thought you favour 'em.
Q. Isab. Thus do you still suspect me without cause.
Niece. Sweet uncle, speak more kindly to the queen.
Gav. My lord, dissemble with her; speak her fair.
K. Edw. Pardon me, sweet; I forgot myself.
Q. Isab. Your pardon is quickly got of Isabel.
K. Edw. The younger Mortimer is grown so brave,
That to my face he threatens civil wars.
Gav. Why do you not commit him to the Tower?
K. Edw. I dare not, for the people love him well.
Gav. Why, then, we'll have him privily made away.
K. Edw. Would Lancaster and he had both carous'd
A bowl of poison to each other's health!
But let them go, and tell me what are these.
Niece. Two of my father's servants whilst he liv'd:
May't please your grace to entertain them now.
K. Edw. Tell me, where wast thou born? what is thine arms?
Bald. My name is Baldock, and my gentry

Edward is totally isolated – surrounded by military & personal enemies even his own brother.

I fetch'd from Oxford, not from heraldry.
K. Edw. The fitter art thou, Baldock, for my turn.
Wait on me, and I'll see thou shalt not want.
Bald. I humbly thank your majesty.
K. Edw. Knowest thou him, Gaveston?
Gav. Ay, my lord;
His name is Spenser; he is well allied:
For my sake let him wait upon your grace;
Scarce shall you find a man of more desert.
K. Edw. Then, Spenser, wait upon me for his sake:
I'll grace thee with a higher style ere long.
Y. Spen. No greater titles happen unto me
Than to be favour'd of your majesty!
K. Edw. Cousin, this day shall be your marriage feast:—
And, Gaveston, think that I love thee well,
To wed thee to our niece, the only heir
Unto the Earl of Glocester late deceas'd.
Gav. I know, my lord, many will stomach me;
But I respect neither their love nor hate.
K. Edw. The headstrong barons shall not limit me;
He that I list to favour shall be great.
Come, let's away; and, when the marriage ends,
Have at the rebels and their complices! [*Exeunt.*

Enter KENT, LANCASTER, *the younger* MORTIMER, WARWICK, PEMBROKE, *and others.*

Kent. My lords, of love to this our native land,
I come to join with you, and leave the king;
And in your quarrel, and the realm's behoof,
Will be the first that shall adventure life.
Lan. I fear me, you are sent of policy,
To undermine us with a show of love.
War. He is your brother; therefore have we cause
To cast the worst, and doubt of your revolt.
Kent. Mine honour shall be hostage of my truth:
If that will not suffice, farewell, my lords.
Y. Mor. Stay, Edmund: never was Plantagenet
False of his word; and therefore trust we thee.
Pem. But what's the reason you should leave him now?
Kent. I have inform'd the Earl of Lancaster.
Lan. And it sufficeth. Now, my lords, know this,
That Gaveston is secretly arriv'd,
And here in Tynmouth frolics with the king.

Let us with these our followers scale the walls,
And suddenly surprise them unawares.
Y. Mor. I'll give the onset.
War And I'll follow thee.
Y. Mor. This tatter'd ensign of my ancestors,
Which swept the desert shore of that Dead Sea
Whereof we got the name of Mortimer,
Will I advance upon this castle ['s] walls—
Drums, strike alarum, raise them from their sport,
And ring aloud the knell of Gaveston!
Lan. None be so hardy as to touch the king;
But neither spare you Gaveston nor his friends.
[*Exeunt.*

Enter, severally, KING EDWARD *and the younger* SPENSER.

K. Edw. O, tell me, Spenser, where is Gaveston?
Y. Spen. I fear me he is slain, my gracious lord.
K. Edw. No, here he comes; now let them spoil and kill.

Enter QUEEN ISABELLA, KING EDWARD'S Niece, GAVESTON, *and* Nobles.

Fly, fly, my lords; the earls have got the hold;
Take shipping, and away to Scarborough:
Spenser and I will post away by land.
Gav. O, stay, my lord! they will not injure you.
K. Edw. I will not trust them. Gaveston, away!
Gav. Farewell, my lord.
K. Edw. Lady, farewell.
Niece. Farewell, sweet uncle, till we meet again.
K. Edw. Farewell, sweet Gaveston; and farewell, niece.
Q. Isab. No farewell to poor Isabel thy queen?
K. Edw. Yes, yes, for Mortimer your lover's sake.
Q. Isab. Heavens can witness, I love none but you.
[*Exeunt all except Queen Isabella.*
From my embracements thus he breaks away.
O, that mine arms could close this isle about,
That I might pull him to me where I would!
Or that these tears, that drizzle from mine eyes,
Had power to mollify his stony heart,
That, when I had him, we might never part!

Enter LANCASTER, WARWICK, *the younger* MORTIMER, *and others. Alarums within.*

Lan. I wonder how he scap'd.
Y. Mor. Who's this? the queen!
Q. Isab. Ay, Mortimer, the miserable queen,
Whose pining heart her inward sighs have blasted,
And body with continual mourning wasted:
These hands are tir'd with haling of my lord
From Gaveston, from wicked Gaveston;
And all in vain; for, when I speak him fair,
He turns away, and smiles upon his minion.
Y. Mor. Cease to lament, and tell us where's the king?
Q. Isab. What would you with the king? is't him you seek?
Lan. No, madam, but that cursed Gaveston:
Far be it from the thought of Lancaster
To offer violence to his sovereign!
We would but rid the realm of Gaveston:
Tell us where he remains, and he shall die.
Q. Isab. He's gone by water unto Scarborough:
Pursue him quickly, and he cannot scape;
The king hath left him, and his train is small.
War. Forslow no time, sweet Lancaster; let's march.
Y. Mor. How comes it that the king and he is parted?
Q. Isab. That this your army, going several ways,
Might be of lesser force, and with the power
That he intendeth presently to raise,
Be easily suppress'd: therefore be gone.
Y. Mor. Here in the river rides a Flemish hoy:
Let's all aboard, and follow him amain.
Lan. The wind that bears him hence will fill our sails;
Come, come, aboard! 'tis but an hour's sailing.
Y. Mor. Madam, stay you within this castle here.
Q. Isab. No, Mortimer; I'll to my lord the king.
Y. Mor. Nay, rather sail with us to Scarborough.
Q. Isab. You know the king is so suspicious
As, if he hear I have but talk'd with you,
Mine honour will be call'd in question;
And therefore, gentle Mortimer, be gone.
Y. Mor. Madam, I cannot stay to answer you:
But think of Mortimer as he deserves.
[*Exeunt all except Queen Isabella.*
Q. Isab. So well hast thou deserv'd, sweet Mortimer,

growing Affair between Queen Isabella & Mortimer which develops later on

As Isabel could live with thee for ever.
In vain I look for love at Edward's hand,
Whose eyes are fix'd on none but Gaveston.
Yet once more I'll importune him with prayers:
If he be strange, and not regard my words,
My son and I will over into France,
And to the king my brother there complain
How Gaveston hath robb'd me of his love:
But yet, I hope, my sorrows will have end,
And Gaveston this blessed day be slain. [*Exit.*

Enter GAVESTON, *pursued.*

Gav. Yet, lusty lords, I have escap'd your hands,
Your threats, your 'larums, and your hot pursuits;
And, though divorced from King Edward's eyes,
Yet liveth Pierce of Gaveston unsurpris'd,
Breathing in hope (malgrado all your beards,
That muster rebels thus against your king)
To see his royal sovereign once again.

Enter WARWICK, LANCASTER, PEMBROKE, *the younger* MORTIMER, Soldiers, JAMES *and other* Attendants *of* PEMBROKE.

War. Upon him, soldiers! take away his weapons!
Y. Mor. Thou proud disturber of thy country's peace,
Corrupter of thy king, cause of these broils,
Base flatterer, yield! and, were it not for shame,
Shame and dishonour to a soldier's name,
Upon my weapon's point here shouldst thou fall,
And welter in thy gore.
Lan. Monster of men,
That, like the Greekish strumpet, train'd to arms
And bloody wars so many valiant knights,
Look for no other fortune, wretch, than death!
Kind Edward is not here to buckler thee.
War. Lancaster, why talk'st thou to the slave?—
Go, soldiers, take him hence; for, by my sword,
His head shall off.—Gaveston, short warning
Shall serve thy turn: it is our country's cause
That here severely we will execute
Upon thy person.—Hang him at a bough.
Gav. My lord,—
War. Soldiers, have him away.—

But, for thou wert the favourite of a king,
Thou shalt have so much honour at our hands.
Gav. I thank you all, my lords: then I perceive
That heading is one, and hanging is the other,
And death is all.

Enter ARUNDEL.

Lan. How now, my Lord of Arundel!
Arun. My lords, King Edward greets you all by me.
War. Arundel, say your message.
Arun. His majesty, hearing that you had taken Gaveston,
Entreateth you by me, yet but he may
See him before he dies; for why, he says,
And sends you word, he knows that die he shall;
And, if you gratify his grace so far,
He will be mindful of the courtesy.
War. How now!
Gav. Renowmed Edward, how thy name
Revives poor Gaveston!
War. No, it needeth not:
Arundel, we will gratify the king
In other matters; he must pardon us in this.—
Soldiers, away with him!
Gav. Why, my Lord of Warwick,
Will not these delays beget my hopes?
I know it, lords, it is this life you aim at,
Yet grant King Edward this.
Y. Mor. Shalt thou appoint
What we shall grant?—Soldiers, away with him!—
Thus we'll gratify the king;
We'll send his head by thee; let him bestow
His tears on that, for that is all he gets
Of Gaveston, or else his senseless trunk.
Lan. Not so, my lord, lest he bestow more cost
In burying him than he hath ever earn'd.
Arun. My lords, it is his majesty's request,
And in the honour of a king he swears,
He will but talk with him, and send him back.
War. When, can you tell? Arundel, no; we wot,
He that the care of his realm remits,
And drives his nobles to these exigents
For Gaveston, will, if he seize him once,
Violate any promise to possess him.

Arun. Then, if you will not trust his grace in keep,
My lords, I will be pledge for his return.
Y. Mor. 'Tis honourable in thee to offer this;
But, for we know thou art a noble gentleman,
We will not wrong thee so,
To make away a true man for a thief.
Gav. How mean'st thou, Mortimer? that is over-base.
Y. Mor. Away, base groom, robber of kings' renown!
Question with thy companions and thy mates.
Pem. My Lord Mortimer, and you, my lords, each one,
To gratify the king's request therein,
Touching the sending of this Gaveston,
Because his majesty so earnestly
Desires to see the man before his death,
I will upon mine honour undertake
To carry him, and bring him back again;
Provided this, that you, my Lord of Arundel,
Will join with me.
War. Pembroke, what wilt thou do?
Cause yet more bloodshed? is it not enough
That we have taken him, but must we now
Leave him on "Had I wist," and let him go?
Pem. My lords, I will not over-woo your honours:
But, if you dare trust Pembroke with the prisoner,
Upon mine oath, I will return him back.
Arun. My Lord of Lancaster, what say you in this?
Lan. Why, I say, let him go on Pembroke's word.
Pem. And you, Lord Mortimer?
Y. Mor. How say you, my Lord of Warwick?
War. Nay, do your pleasures: I know how 'twill prove.
Pem. Then give him me.
Gav. Sweet sovereign, yet I come
To see thee ere I die!
War. Yet not perhaps,
If Warwick's wit and policy prevail. [*Aside.*
Y. Mor. My Lord of Pembroke, we deliver him you:
Return him on your honour.—Sound, away!
[*Exeunt all except Pembroke, Arundel, Gaveston, James and other attendants of Pembroke.*
Pem. My lord, you shall go with me:
My house is not far hence; out of the way
A little; but our men shall go along.
We that have pretty wenches to our wives,

All takes place in Yorkshire.

Sir, must not come so near to balk their lips.
Arun. 'Tis very kindly spoke, my Lord of Pembroke:
Your honour hath an adamant of power
To draw a prince.
Pem. So, my lord.—Come, hither, James:
I do commit this Gaveston to thee;
Be thou this night his keeper; in the morning
We will discharge thee of thy charge: be gone.
Gav. Unhappy Gaveston, whither go'st thou now?
[*Exit with James and other Attendants of Pembroke.*
Horse-boy. My lord, we'll quickly be at Cobham. [*Exeunt.*

Enter GAVESTON *mourning,* JAMES *and other* Attendants *of* PEMBROKE.

Gav. O treacherous Warwick, thus to wrong thy friend!
James. I see it is your life these arms pursue.
Gav. Weaponless must I fall, and die in bands?
O, must this day be period of my life,
Centre of all my bliss? And ye be men,
Speed to the king.

Enter WARWICK *and* Soldiers.

War. My Lord of Pembroke's men,
Strive you no longer: I will have that Gaveston.
James. Your lordship doth dishonour to yourself,
And wrong our lord, your honourable friend.
War. No, James, it is my country's cause I follow.—
Go, take the villain: soldiers, come away;
We'll make quick work.—Commend me to your master,
My friend, and tell him that I watch'd it well.—
Come, let thy shadow parley with King Edward.
Gav. Treacherous earl, shall not I see the king?
War. The king of heaven perhaps, no other king.—
Away! [*Exeunt Warwick and Soldiers with Gaveston.*
James. Come, fellows: it booted not for us to strive:
We will in haste go certify our lord. [*Exeunt.*

Enter KING EDWARD, *the younger* SPENSER, BALDOCK, Noblemen *of the king's side, and* Soldiers *with drums and fifes.*

K. Edw. I long to hear an answer from the barons
Touching my friend, my dearest Gaveston.

Drag of Gaveston & kill him.

Ah, Spenser, not the riches of my realm
Can ransom him! ah, he is mark'd to die!
I know the malice of the younger Mortimer;
Warwick I know is rough, and Lancaster
Inexorable; and I shall never see
My lovely Pierce, my Gaveston again:
The barons overbear me with their pride.

Y. Spen. Were I King Edward, England's sovereign,
Son to the lovely Eleanor of Spain,
Great Edward Longshanks' issue, would I bear
These braves, this rage, and suffer uncontroll'd
These barons thus to beard me in my land,
In mine own realm? My lord, pardon my speech:
Did you retain your father's magnanimity,
Did you regard the honour of your name,
You would not suffer thus your majesty
Be counterbuff'd of your nobility.
Strike off their heads, and let them preach on poles:
No doubt, such lessons they will teach the rest,
As by their preachments they will profit much,
And learn obedience to their lawful king.

K. Edw. Yea, gentle Spenser, we have been too mild,
Too kind to them; but now have drawn our sword,
And, if they send me not my Gaveston,
We'll steel it on their crest[s], and poll their tops.

Bald. This haught resolve becomes your majesty,
Not to be tied to their affection,
As though your highness were a school-boy still.
And must be aw'd and govern'd like a child.

Enter the elder SPENSER *with his truncheon, and* Soldiers.

E. Spen. Long live my sovereign, the noble Edward,
In peace triumphant, fortunate in wars!

K. Edw. Welcome, old man: com'st thou in Edward's aid?
Then tell thy prince of whence and what thou art.

E. Spen. Lo, with a band of bowmen and of pikes,
Brown bills and targeteers, four hundred strong,
Sworn to defend King Edward's royal right,
I come in person to your majesty,
Spenser, the father of Hugh Spenser there,
Bound to your highness everlastingly
For favours done, in him, unto us all.

K. Edw. Thy father, Spenser?
Y. Spen. True, an it like your grace,
That pours, in lieu of all your goodness shown,
His life, my lord, before your princely feet.
K. Edw. Welcome ten thousand times, old man, again!
Spenser, this love, this kindness to thy king,
Argues thy noble mind and disposition.
Spenser, I here create thee Earl of Wiltshire,
And daily will enrich thee with our favour,
That, as the sunshine, shall reflect o'er thee.
Beside, the more to manifest our love,
Because we hear Lord Bruce doth sell his land,
And that the Mortimers are in hand withal,
Thou shalt have crowns of us t'outbid the barons;
And, Spenser, spare them not, but lay it on.—
Soldiers, a largess, and thrice-welcome all!
Y. Spen. My lord, here comes the queen.

Enter QUEEN ISABELLA, PRINCE EDWARD, *and* LEVUNE.

K. Edw. Madam, what news?
Q. Isab. News of dishonour, lord, and discontent.
Our friend Levune, faithful and full of trust,
Informeth us, by letters and by words,
That Lord Valois our brother, King of France,
Because your highness hath been slack in homage,
Hath seized Normandy into his hands:
These be the letters, this the messenger.
K. Edw. Welcome, Levune.—Tush, Sib, if this be all,
Valois and I will soon be friends again.—
But to my Gaveston: shall I never see,
Never behold thee now!—Madam, in this matter
We will employ you and your little son;
You shall go parley with the King of France.—
Boy, see you bear you bravely to the king,
And do your message with a majesty.
P. Edw. Commit not to my youth things of more weight
Than fits a prince so young as I to bear;
And fear not, lord and father,—heaven's great beams
On Atlas' shoulder shall not lie more safe
Than shall your charge committed to my trust.
Q. Isab. Ah, boy, this towardness makes thy mother fear
Thou are not mark'd to many days on earth!

K. Edw. Madam, we will that you with speed be shipp'd,
And this our son; Levune shall follow you
With all the haste we can despatch him hence.
Choose of our lords to bear you company;
And go in peace; leave us in wars at home.
Q. Isab. Unnatural wars, where subjects brave their king:
God end them once!—My lord, I take my leave,
To make my preparation for France.
[*Exit with Prince Edward.*

Enter ARUNDEL.

K. Edw. What, Lord Arundel, dost thou come alone?
Arun. Yea, my good lord, for Gaveston is dead.
K. Edw. Ah, traitors, have they put my friend to death?
Tell me, Arundel, died he ere thou cam'st,
Or didst thou see my friend to take his death?
Arun. Neither, my lord; for, as he was surpris'd,
Begirt with weapons and with enemies round,
I did your highness' message to them all,
Demanding him of them, entreating rather,
And said, upon the honour of my name,
That I would undertake to carry him
Unto your highness, and to bring him back.
K. Edw. And, tell me, would the rebels deny me that?
Y. Spen. Proud recreants!
K. Edw. Yea, Spenser, traitors all!
Arun. I found them at the first inexorable;
The Earl of Warwick would not bide the hearing,
Mortimer hardly; Pembroke and Lancaster
Spake least; and when they flatly had denied,
Refusing to receive me pledge for him,
The Earl of Pembroke mildly thus bespake;
"My lords, because our sovereign sends for him,
And promiseth he shall be safe return'd,
I will this undertake, to have him hence,
And see him re-deliver'd to your hands."
K. Edw. Well, and how fortunes [it] that he came not?
Y. Spen. Some treason or some villany was cause.
Arun. The Earl of Warwick seiz'd him on his way;
For, being deliver'd unto Pembroke's men,
Their lord rode home, thinking his prisoner safe;
But, ere he came, Warwick in ambush lay,
And bare him to his death; and in a trench

Strake off his head, and march'd unto the camp.
Y. Spen. A bloody part, flatly 'gainst law of arms!
K. Edw. O, shall I speak, or shall I sigh and die!
Y. Spen. My lord, refer your vengeance to the sword
Upon these barons; hearten up your men;
Let them not unreveng'd murder your friends:
Advance your standard, Edward, in the field,
And march to fire them from their starting-holes.
K. Edw. [*kneeling.*] By earth, the common mother of us all,
By heaven, and all the moving orbs thereof,
By this right hand, and by my father's sword,
And all the honours 'longing to my crown,
I will have heads and lives for him as many
As I have manors, castles, towns, and towers!— [*Rises.*
Treacherous Warwick! traitorous Mortimer!
If I be England's king, in lakes of gore
Your headless trunks, your bodies will I trail,
That you may drink your fill, and quaff in blood,
And stain my royal standard with the same,
That so my bloody colours may suggest
Remembrance of revenge immortally
On your accursed traitorous progeny,
You villains that have slain my Gaveston!—
And in this place of honour and of trust,
Spenser, sweet Spenser, I adopt thee here;
And merely of our love we do create thee
Earl of Glocester and Lord Chamberlain,
Despite of times, despite of enemies.
Y. Spen. My lord, here's in a messenger from the barons
Desires access unto your majesty.
K. Edw. Admit him near.

Enter Herald *with his coat of arms.*

Her. Long live King Edward, England's lawful lord!
K. Edw. So wish not they, I wis, that sent thee hither:
Thou com'st from Mortimer and his complices:
A ranker rout of rebels never was.
Well, say thy message.
Her. The barons, up in arms, by me salute
Your highness with long life and happiness;
And bid me say, as plainer to your grace,
That if without effusion of blood
You will this grief have ease and remedy,

That from your princely person you remove
This Spenser, as a putrifying branch
That deads the royal vine, whose golden leaves
Empale your princely head, your diadem;
Whose brightness such pernicious upstarts dim,
Say they, and lovingly advise your grace
To cherish virtue and nobility,
And have old servitors in high esteem,
And shake off smooth dissembling flatterers:
This granted, they, their honours, and their lives,
Are to your highness vow'd and consecrate.

Y. Spen. Ah, traitors, will they still display their pride?

K. Edw. Away! tarry no answer, but be gone!—
Rebels, will they appoint their sovereign
His sports, his pleasures, and his company?—
Yet, ere thou go, see how I do divorce
[*Embraces young Spenser.*
Spenser from me. Now get thee to thy lords,
And tell them I will come to chastise them
For murdering Gaveston: hie thee, get thee gone!
Edward, with fire and sword, follows at thy heels.
[*Exit Herald.*
My lord[s], perceive you how these rebels swell?—
Soldiers, good hearts! defend your sovereign's right,
For, now, even now, we march to make them stoop.
Away!

[*Exeunt. Alarums, excursions, a great fight, and a retreat sounded, within.*

Re-enter KING EDWARD, *the elder* SPENSER, *the younger* SPENSER, BALDOCK, *and* Noblemen *of the king's side.*

K. Edw. Why do we sound retreat? upon them, lords!
This day I shall pour vengeance with my sword
On those proud rebels that are up in arms,
And do confront and countermand their king.

Y. Spen. I doubt it not, my lord; right will prevail.

E. Spen. 'Tis not amiss, my liege, for either part
To breathe a while; our men, with sweat and dust
All chok'd well near, begin to faint for heat;
And this retire refresheth horse and man.

Y. Spen. Here come the rebels.

Enter the younger MORTIMER, LANCASTER, WARWICK, PEMBROKE, *and others.*

Y. Mor. Look, Lancaster, yonder is Edward
Among his flatterers.
Lan. And there let him be,
Till he pay dearly for their company.
War. And shall, or Warwick's sword shall smite in vain.
K. Edw. What, rebels, do you shrink and sound retreat?
Y. Mor. No, Edward, no; thy flatterers faint and fly.
Lan. Thou'd best betimes forsake them and their trains,
For they'll betray thee, traitors as they are.
Y. Spen. Traitor on thy face, rebellious Lancaster!
Pem. Away, base upstart! brav'st thou nobles thus?
E. Spen. A noble attempt and honourable deed,
Is it not, trow ye, to assemble aid
And levy arms against your lawful king?
K. Edw. For which, ere long, their heads shall satisfy
T' appease the wrath of their offended king.
Y. Mor. Then, Edward, thou wilt fight it to the last,
And rather bathe thy sword in subjects' blood
Than banish that pernicious company?
K. Edw. Ay, traitors all, rather than thus be brav'd,
Make England's civil towns huge heaps of stones,
And ploughs to go about our palace-gates.
War. A desperate and unnatural resolution!—
Alarum to the fight!
Saint George for England, and the barons' right!
K. Edw. Saint George for England, and King Edward's
right! [*Alarums. Exeunt the two parties severally.*

Battle occurs.

Enter KING EDWARD *and his followers, with the* Barons *and* KENT *captive.*

Captives

K. Edw. Now, lusty lords, now not by chance of war,
But justice of the quarrel and the cause,
Vail'd is your pride: methinks you hang the heads;
But we'll advance them, traitors: now 'tis time
To be aveng'd on you for all your braves,
And for the murder of my dearest friend,
To whom right well you knew our soul was knit,
Good Pierce of Gaveston, my sweet favourite:
Ah, rebels, recreants, you made him away!

Kent. Brother, in regard of thee and of thy land,
Did they remove that flatterer from thy throne.
K. Edw. So, sir, you have spoke: away, avoid our presence!
[*Exit Kent*.
Accursed wretches, was't in regard of us,
When we had sent our messenger to request
He might be spar'd to come to speak with us,
And Pembroke undertook for his return,
That thou, proud Warwick, watch'd the prisoner,
Poor Pierce, and headed him 'gainst law of arms?
For which thy head shall overlook the rest
As much as thou in rage outwent'st the rest.
War. Tyrant, I scorn thy threats and menaces;
It is but temporal that thou canst inflict.
Lan. The worst is death; and better die to live
Than live in infamy under such a king.
K. Edw. Away with them, my lord of Winchester!
These lusty leaders, Warwick and Lancaster,
I charge you roundly, off with both their heads!
Away!
War. Farewell, vain world!
Lan. Sweet Mortimer, farewell!
Y. Mor. England, unkind to thy nobility,
Groan for this grief! behold how thou art maim'd!
K. Edw. Go, take that haughty Mortimer to the Tower;
There see him safe bestow'd; and, for the rest,
Do speedy execution on them all.
Be gone!
Y. Mor. What, Mortimer, can ragged stony walls
Immure thy virtue that aspires to heaven?
No, Edward, England's scourge, it may not be;
Mortimer's hope surmounts his fortune far.
[*The captive Barons are led off*.
K. Edw. Sound, drums and trumpets! March with me, my friends.
Edward this day hath crown'd him king anew.
[*Exeunt all except the younger Spenser, Levune, and Baldock*.
Y. Spen. Levune, the trust that we repose in thee
Begets the quiet of King Edward's land:
Therefore be gone in haste, and with advice
Bestow that treasure on the lords of France,
That, therewith all enchanted, like the guard

That suffer'd Jove to pass in showers of gold
To Danaë, all aid may be denied
To Isabel the queen, that now in France
Makes friends, to cross the seas with her young son,
And step into his father's regiment.

Levune. That's it these barons and the subtle queen
Long levell'd at.

Bal. Yea, but, Levune, thou seest,
These barons lay their heads on blocks together:
What they intend, the hangman frustrates clean.

Levune. Have you no doubt, my lords, I'll clap so close
Among the lords of France with England's gold,
That Isabel shall make her plaints in vain,
And France shall be obdurate with her tears.

Y. Spen. Then make for France amain; Levune, away!
Proclaim King Edward's wars and victories. [*Exeunt.*

London

Enter KENT.

Kent. Fair blows the wind for France: blow, gentle gale,
Till Edmund be arriv'd for England's good!
Nature, yield to my country's cause in this!
A brother? no, a butcher of thy friends!
Proud Edward, dost thou banish me thy presence?
But I'll to France, and cheer the wronged queen,
And certify what Edward's looseness is.
Unnatural king, to slaughter nobleman
And cherish flatterers! Mortimer, I stay
Thy sweet escape. Stand gracious, gloomy night,
To his device!

Enter the younger MORTIMER *disguised.*

Y. Mor. Holla! who walketh there?
Is't you, my lord?

Kent. Mortimer, 'tis I.
But hath thy potion wrought so happily?

Y. Mor. It hath, my lord: the warders all asleep,
I thank them, gave me leave to pass in peace.
But hath your grace got shipping unto France?

Kent. Fear it not. [*Exeunt.*

Enter QUEEN ISABELLA *and* PRINCE EDWARD.

in France

Q. Isab. Ah, boy, our friends do fail us all in France!
The lords are cruel, and the king unkind.

attempting to get the support of French king.

What shall we do?

P. Edw. Madam, return to England,
And please my father well; and then a fig
For all my uncle's friendship here in France!
I warrant you, I'll win his highness quickly;
'A loves me better than a thousand Spensers.

Q. Isab. Ah, boy, thou art deceiv'd, at least in this,
To think that we can yet be tun'd together!
No, no, we jar too far.—Unkind Valois!
Unhappy Isabel, when France rejects,
Whither, O, whither dost thou bend thy steps?

Enter SIR JOHN OF HAINAULT.

Sir J. Madam, what cheer?

Q. Isab. Ah, good Sir John of Hainault,
Never so cheerless nor so far distrest!

Sir J. I hear, sweet lady, of the king's unkindness:
But droop not, madam; noble minds contemn
Despair. Will your grace with me to Hainault,
And there stay time's advantage with your son?—
How say you, my lord! will you go with your friends,
And shake off all our fortunes equally?

P. Edw. So pleaseth the queen my mother, me it likes:
The king of England, nor the court of France,
Shall have me from my gracious mother's side,
Till I be strong enough to break a staff;
And then have at the proudest Spenser's head!

Sir J. Well said, my lord!

Q. Isab. O my sweet heart, how do I moan thy wrongs,
Yet triumph in the hope of thee, my joy!—
Ah, sweet Sir John, even to the utmost verge
Of Europe, or the shore of Tanais,
Will we with thee to Hainault—so we will:
The marquis is a noble gentleman;
His grace, I dare presume, will welcome me.—
But who are these?

Enter KENT *and the younger* MORTIMER.

Kent. Madam, long may you live
Much happier than your friends in England do!

Q. Isab. Lord Edmund and Lord Mortimer alive!
Welcome to France! the news was here, my lord,
That you were dead, or very near your death.

Y. Mor. Lady, the last was truest of the twain:
But Mortimer, reserv'd for better hap,
Hath shaken off the thraldom of the Tower,
And lives t' advance your standard, good my lord.
P. Edw. How mean you, and the king my father lives?
No, my Lord Mortimer, not I, I trow.
Q. Isab. Not, son! why not? I would it were no worse!—
But, gentle lords, friendless we are in France.
Y. Mor. Monsieur Le Grand, a noble friend of yours,
Told us, at our arrival, all the news,—
How hard the nobles, how unkind the king
Hath show'd himself: but, madam, right makes room
Where weapons want; and, though a many friends
Are made away, as Warwick, Lancaster,
And others of our part and faction,
Yet have we friends, assure your grace, in England,
Would cast up caps, and clap their hands for joy,
To see us there, appointed for our foes.
Kent. Would all were well, and Edward well reclaim'd,
For England's honour, peace, and quietness!
Y. Mor. But by the sword, my lord, 't must be deserv'd:
The king will ne'er forsake his flatterers.
Sir J. My lords of England, sith th' ungentle king
Of France refuseth to give aid of arms
To this distressed queen, his sister, here,
Go you with her to Hainault: doubt ye not
We will find comfort, money, men, and friends,
Ere long to bid the English king a base.—
How say, young prince, what think you of the match?
P. Edw. I think King Edward will outrun us all.
Q. Isab. Nay, son, not so; and you must not discourage
Your friends that are so forward in your aid.
Kent. Sir John of Hainault, pardon us, I pray:
These comforts that you give our woful queen
Bind us in kindness all at your command.
Q. Isab. Yea, gentle brother:—and the God of heaven
Prosper your happy motion, good Sir John!
Y. Mor. This noble gentleman, forward in arms,
Was born, I see, to be our anchor-hold.—
Sir John of Hainault, be it thy renown,
That England's queen and nobles in distress
Have been by thee restor'd and comforted.
Sir J. Madam, along; and you, my lord[s], with me,

That England's peers may Hainault's welcome see.
[*Exeunt.*

Enter King Edward, Arundel, *the elder* Spenser, *the younger* Spenser, *and others.*

K. Edw. Thus, after many threats of wrathful war,
Triumpheth England's Edward with his friends,
And triumph Edward with his friends uncontroll'd!—
My Lord of Glocester, do you hear the news?
Y. Spen. What news, my lord?
K. Edw. Why, man, they say there is great execution
Done through the realm.—My Lord of Arundel,
You have the note, have you not?
Arun. From the Lieutenant of the Tower, my lord.
K. Edw. I pray, let us see it. [*Takes the note from Arundel.*]
—What have we there?—
Read it, Spenser.
[*Gives the note to young Spenser, who reads their names.*
Why, so: they bark'd apace a month ago;
Now, on my life, they'll neither bark nor bite.
Now, sirs, the news from France? Gloster, I trow,
The lords of France love England's gold so well
As Isabella gets no aid from thence.
What now remains? have you proclaim'd, my lord,
Reward for them can bring in Mortimer?
Y. Spen. My lord, we have; and, if he be in England,
'A will be had ere long, I doubt it not.
K. Edw. If, dost thou say? Spenser, as true as death,
He is in England's ground: our port-masters
Are not so careless of their king's command.

Enter a Messenger.

How now! what news with thee? from whence come these?
Mess. Letters, my lord, and tidings forth of France:
To you, my Lord of Glocester, from Levune.
[*Gives letters to young Spenser.*
K. Edw. Read.
Y. Spen. [reading.] *My duty to your honour promised, etc., I have, according to instructions in that behalf, dealt with the King of France and his lords, and effected that the queen, all discontented and discomforted, is gone: whither, if you ask,*

with Sir John of Hainault, brother to the marquis, into Flanders. With them are gone Lord Edmund and the Lord Mortimer, having in their company divers of your nation, and others; and, as constant report goeth, they intend to give King Edward battle in England, sooner than he can look for them. This is all the news of import.

Your honour's in all service, Levune.

K. Edw. Ah, villains, hath that Mortimer escap'd?
With him is Edmund gone associate?
And will Sir John of Hainault lead the round?
Welcome, o' God's name, madam, and your son!
England shall welcome you and all your rout.
Gallop apace, bright Phœbus, through the sky;
And, dusky Night, in rusty iron car,
Between you both shorten the time, I pray,
That I may see that most desired day,
When we may meet these traitors in the field!
Ah, nothing grieves me, but my little boy
Is thus misled to countenance their ills!
Come, friends, to Bristow, there to make us strong:
And, winds, as equal be to bring them in,
As you injurious were to bear them forth! [*Exeunt.*

Enter QUEEN ISABELLA, PRINCE EDWARD, KENT, *the younger* MORTIMER, *and* SIR JOHN OF HAINAULT.

Q. Isab. Now, lords, our loving friends and countrymen,
Welcome to England all, with prosperous winds!
Our kindest friends in Belgia have we left,
To cope with friends at home; a heavy case
When force to force is knit, and sword and glaive
In civil broils make kin and countrymen
Slaughter themselves in others, and their sides
With their own weapons gor'd! But what's the help?
Misgovern'd kings are cause of all this wreck;
And, Edward, thou art one among them all,
Whose looseness hath betray'd thy land to spoil,
Who made the channel overflow with blood
Of thine own people: patron shouldst thou be;
But thou—

Y. Mor. Nay, madam, if you be a warrior,
You must not grow so passionate in speeches.—
Lords, sith that we are, by sufferance of heaven,
Arriv'd and armed in this prince's right,

Here for our country's cause swear we to him
All homage, fealty, and forwardness;
And for the open wrongs and injuries
Edward hath done to us, his queen, and land,
We come in arms to wreck it with the sword;
That England's queen in peace may repossess
Her dignities and honours; and withal
We may remove these flatterers from the king
That havock England's wealth and treasury.
Sir J. Sound trumpets, my lord, and forward let us march.
Edward will think we come to flatter him.
Kent. I would he never had been flatter'd more! [*Exeunt.*

Enter KING EDWARD, BALDOCK, *and the younger* SPENSER.

Y. Spen. Fly, fly, my lord! the queen is overstrong;
Her friends do multiply, and yours do fail.
Shape we our course to Ireland, there to breathe.
K. Edw. What, was I born to fly and run away,
And leave the Mortimers conquerors behind?
Give me my horse, and let's reinforce our troops.
And in this bed of honour die with fame.
Bald. O, no, my lord! this princely resolution
Fits not the time: away! we are pursu'd. [*Exeunt.*

Enter KENT, *with a sword and target.*

Kent. This way he fled; but I am come too late.
Edward, alas, my heart relents for thee!
Proud traitor, Mortimer, why dost thou chase
Thy lawful king, thy sovereign, with thy sword?
Vile wretch, and why hast thou, of all unkind,
Borne arms against thy brother and thy king?
Rain showers of vengeance on my cursed head,
Thou God, to whom in justice it belongs
To punish this unnatural revolt!
Edward, this Mortimer aims at thy life:
O, fly him, then! But, Edmund, calm this rage;
Dissemble, or thou diest; for Mortimer
And Isabel do kiss, while they conspire:
And yet she bears a face of love, forsooth:
Fie on that love that hatcheth death and hate!
Edmund, away! Bristow to Longshanks' blood
Is false; be not found single for suspect:
Proud Mortimer pries near into thy walks.

Enter QUEEN ISABELLA, PRINCE EDWARD, *the younger* MORTIMER, *and* SIR JOHN OF HAINAULT.

Q. Isab. Successful battles gives the God of kings
To them that fight in right, and fear his wrath.
Since, then, successfully we have prevail'd,
Thanked be heaven's great architect, and you!
Ere farther we proceed, my noble lords,
We here create our well-beloved son,
Of love and care unto his royal person,
Lord Warden of the realm; and, sith the Fates
Have made his father so infortunate,
Deal you, my lords, in this, my loving lords,
As to your wisdoms fittest seems in all.

Kent. Madam, without offence if I may ask
How will you deal with Edward in his fall?

P. Edw. Tell me, good uncle, what Edward do you mean?

Kent. Nephew, your father; I dare not call him king.

Y. Mor. My Lord of Kent, what needs these questions?
'Tis not in her controlment nor in ours;
But as the realm and parliament shall please,
So shall your brother be disposed of.—
I like not this relenting mood in Edmund:
Madam, 'tis good to look to him betimes.
[*Aside to the Queen.*

Q. Isab. My lord, the Mayor of Bristow knows our mind.

Y. Mor. Yea, madam; and they scape not easily
That fled the field.

Q. Isab. Baldock is with the king:
A goodly chancellor, is he not, my lord?

Sir J. So are the Spensers, the father and the son.

Y. Mor. This Edward is the ruin of the realm.

Enter RICE AP HOWEL *with the elder* SPENSER *prisoner, and* Attendants.

Rice. God save Queen Isabel and her princely son!
Madam, the Mayor and citizens of Bristow,
In sign of love and duty to this presence,
Present by me this traitor to the state,
Spenser, the father to that wanton Spenser,
That, like the lawless Catiline of Rome,
Revell'd in England's wealth and treasury.

Isab. We thank you all.

Y. Mor. Your loving care in this
Deserveth princely favours and rewards.
But where's the king and the other Spenser fled?
Rice. Spenser the son, created Earl of Glocester,
Is with that smooth-tongu'd scholar Baldock gone,
And shipp'd but late for Ireland with the king.
Y. Mor. Some whirlwind fetch them back, or sink them all!—
[*Aside.*
They shall be started thence, I doubt it not.
P. Edw. Shall I not see the king my father yet?
Kent. Unhappy Edward, chas'd from England's bounds!
[*Aside.*
Sir J. Madam, what resteth? why stand you in a muse?
Q. Isab. I rue my lord's ill-fortune: but, alas,
Care of my country call'd me to this war!
Y. Mor. Madam, have done with care and sad complaint:
Your king hath wrong'd your country and himself,
And we must seek to right it as we may.—
Meanwhile have hence this rebel to the block.
Your lordship cannot privilege your head.
E. Spen. Rebel is he that fights against his prince:
So fought not they that fought in Edward's right.
Y. Mor. Take him away; he prates.
[*Exeunt Attendants with the elder Spenser.*
You, Rice ap Howel,
Shall do good service to her majesty,
Being of countenance in your country here,
To follow these rebellious runagates.—
We in mean while, madam, must take advice.
How Baldock, Spenser, and their complices,
May in their fall be follow'd to their end. [*Exeunt.*

Enter the Abbot, Monks, KING EDWARD, *the younger* SPENSER, *and* BALDOCK (*the three latter disguised*).

Abbot. Have you no doubt, my lord; have you no fear:
As silent and as careful we will be
To keep your royal person safe with us,
Free from suspect, and fell invasion
Of such as have your majesty in chase,
Yourself, and those your chosen company,
As danger of this stormy time requires.
K. Edw. Father, thy face should harbour no deceit.
O, hadst thou ever been a king, thy heart,
Pierc'd deeply with the sense of my distress,

Could not but take compassion of my state!
Stately and proud in riches and in train,
Whilom I was, powerful and full of pomp:
But what is he whom rule and empery
Have not in life or death made miserable?—
Come, Spenser,—come, Baldock,—come, sit down by me;
Make trial now of that philosophy
That in our famous nurseries of arts
Thou suck'dst from Plato and from Aristotle.—
Father, this life contemplative is heaven:
O, that I might this life in quiet lead!
But we, alas, are chas'd!—and you, my friends,
Your lives and my dishonour they pursue.—
Yet, gentle monks, for treasure, gold, nor fee,
Do you betray us and our company.

First Monk. Your grace may sit secure, if none but we
Do wot of your abode.

Y. Spen. Not one alive: but shrewdly I suspect
A gloomy fellow in a mead below;
'A gave a long look after us, my lord;
And all the land, I know, is up in arms,
Arms that pursue our lives with deadly hate.

Bald. We were embark'd for Ireland; wretched we,
With awkward winds and with sore tempests driven,
To fall on shore, and here to pine in fear
Of Mortimer and his confederates!

K. Edw. Mortimer! who talks of Mortimer?
Who wounds me with the name of Mortimer,
That bloody man?—Good father, on thy lap
Lay I this head, laden with mickle care.
O, might I never ope these eyes again,
Never again lift up this drooping head,
O, never more lift up this dying heart!

Y. Spen. Look up, my lord.—Baldock, this drowsiness
Betides no good; here even we are betray'd.

Enter, with Welsh hooks, RICE AP HOWEL, *a* Mower, *and* LEICESTER.

Mow. Upon my life, these be the men ye seek.

Rice. Fellow, enough.—My lord, I pray, be short;
A fair commission warrants what we do.

Leices. The queen's commission, urg'd by Mortimer:
What cannot gallant Mortimer with the queen?—

Alas, see where he sits, and hopes unseen
T'escape their hands that seek to reave his life!
Too true it is, *Quem dies vidit veniens superbum,*
Hunc dies vidit fugiens jacentem.
But, Leicester, leave to grow so passionate.—
Spenser and Baldock, by no other names,
I arrest you of high treason here.
Stand not on titles, but obey th' arrest:
'Tis in the name of Isabel the queen.—
My lord, why droop you thus?

K. Edw. O day, the last of all my bliss on earth!
Centre of all misfortune! O my stars,
Why do you lour unkindly on a king?
Comes Leicester, then, in Isabella's name,
To take my life, my company from me?
Here, man, rip up this panting breast of mine,
And take my heart in rescue of my friends.

Rice. Away with them!

Y. Spen. It may become thee yet
To let us take our farewell of his grace.

Abbot. My heart with pity earns to see this sight;
A king to bear these words and proud commands! [*Aside.*

K. Edw. Spenser, ah, sweet Spenser, thus, then, must we part?

Y. Spen. We must, my lord; so will the angry heavens.

K. Edw. Nay, so will hell and cruel Mortimer:
The gentle heavens have not to do in this.

Bald. My lord, it is in vain to grieve or storm.
Here humbly of your grace we take our leaves:
Our lots are cast; I fear me, so is thine.

K. Edw. In heaven we may, in earth ne'er shall we meet:—
And, Leicester, say, what shall become of us?

Leices. Your majesty must go to Killingworth.

K. Edw. Must! it is somewhat hard when kings must go.

Leices. Here is a litter ready for your grace,
That waits your pleasure, and the day grows old.

Rice. As good be gone, as stay and be benighted.

K. Edw. A litter hast thou? lay me in a hearse,
And to the gates of hell convey me hence;
Let Pluto's bells ring out my fatal knell,
And hags howl for my death at Charon's shore;
For friends hath Edward none but these,
And these must die under a tyrant's sword.

Rice. My lord, be going: care not for these;
For we shall see them shorter by the heads.

K. Edw. Well, that shall be shall be: part we must;
Sweet Spenser, gentle Baldock, part we must.—
Hence, feigned weeds! unfeigned are my woes.—
[*Throwing off his disguise.*
Father, farewell.—Leicester, thou stay'st for me;
And go I must.—Life, farewell, with my friends!
[*Exeunt King Edward and Leicester.*

Y. Spen. O, is he gone? is noble Edward gone?
Parted from hence, never to see us more!
Rend, sphere of heaven! and, fire, forsake thy orb!
Earth, melt to air! gone is my sovereign,
Gone, gone, alas, never to make return!

Bald. Spenser, I see our souls are fleeted hence;
We are depriv'd the sunshine of our life.
Make for a new life, man; throw up thy eyes
And heart and hand to heaven's immortal throne;
Pay nature's debt with cheerful countenance,
Reduce we all our lessons unto this,—
To die, sweet Spenser, therefore live we all;
Spenser, all live to die, and rise to fall.

Rice. Come, come, keep these preachments till you come to the place appointed. You, and such as you are, have made wise work in England. Will your lordships away?

Mow. Your worship I trust will remember me?

Rice. Remember thee, fellow! what else? Follow me to the town. [*Exeunt.*

Enter KING EDWARD, LEICESTER, *the* BISHOP OF WINCHESTER, *and* TRUSSEL.

Leices. Be patient, good my lord, cease to lament;
Imagine Killingworth Castle were your court,
And that you lay for pleasure here a space,
Not of compulsion or necessity.

K. Edw. Leicester, if gentle words might comfort me,
Thy speeches long ago had eas'd my sorrows,
For kind and loving hast thou always been.
The griefs of private men are soon allay'd;
But not of kings. The forest deer, being struck,
Runs to an herb that closeth up the wounds;
But when the imperial lion's flesh is gor'd,

He rends and tears it with his wrathful paw,
[And], highly scorning that the lowly earth
Should drink his blood, mounts up into the air:
And so it fares with me, whose dauntless mind
Th' ambitious Mortimer would seek to curb,
And that unnatural queen, false Isabel,
That thus hath pent and mew'd me in a prison
For such outrageous passions cloy my soul,
As with the wings of rancour and disdain
Full often am I soaring up to heaven,
To plain me to the gods against them both.
But when I call to mind I am a king,
Methinks I should revenge me of the wrongs,
That Mortimer and Isabel have done.
But what are kings, when regiment is gone,
But perfect shadows in a sunshine day?
My nobles rule; I bear the name of king;
I wear the crown; but am controll'd by them,
By Mortimer, and my unconstant queen,
Who spots my nuptial bed with infamy;
Whilst I am lodg'd within this cave of care,
Where sorrow at my elbow still attends,
To company my heart with sad laments,
That bleeds within me for this strange exchange.
But tell me, must I now resign my crown,
To make usurping Mortimer a king?

Bish. of Win. Your grace mistakes; it is for England's good,
And princely Edward's right, we crave the crown.

K. Edw. No, 'tis for Mortimer, not Edward's head
For he's a lamb, encompassed by wolves,
Which in a moment will abridge his life.
But, if proud Mortimer do wear this crown,
Heavens turn it to a blaze of quenchless fire!
Or, like the snaky wreath of Tisiphon,
Engirt the temples of his hateful head!
So shall not England's vine be perished,
But Edward's name survive, though Edward dies.

Leices. My lord, why waste you thus the time away?
They stay your answer: will you yield your crown?

K. Edw. Ah, Leicester, weigh how hardly I can brook
To lose my crown and kingdom without cause;
To give ambitious Mortimer my right,
That, like a mountain, overwhelms my bliss;

In which extreme my mind here murder'd is!
But what the heavens appoint I must obey.—
Here, take my crown; the life of Edward too:
[*Taking off the crown.*
Two kings in England cannot reign at once.
But stay a while: let me be king till night,
That I may gaze upon this glittering crown;
So shall my eyes receive their last content,
My head, the latest honour due to it,
And jointly both yield up their wished right.
Continue ever, thou celestial sun;
Let never silent night possess this clime;
Stand still, you watches of the element;
All times and seasons, rest you at a stay,
That Edward may be still fair England's king!
But day's bright beams doth vanish fast away,
And needs I must resign my wished crown.
Inhuman creatures, nurs'd with tiger's milk,
Why gape you for your sovereign's overthrow?
My diadem, I mean, and guiltless life.
See, monsters, see! I'll wear my crown again.
[*Putting on the crown.*
What, fear you not the fury of your king?—
But, hapless Edward, thou art fondly led;
They pass not for thy frowns as late they did,
But seek to make a new-elected king;
Which fills my mind with strange despairing thoughts,
Which thoughts are martyred with endless torments;
And in this torment comfort find I none,
But that I feel the crown upon my head;
And therefore let me wear it yet a while.

Trus. My lord, the parliament must have present news;
And therefore say, will you resign or no?
[*The King rageth.*

K. Edw. I'll not resign, but, whilst I live, [be king].
Traitors, be gone, and join you with Mortimer.
Elect, conspire, install, do what you will:
Their blood and yours shall seal these treacheries.

Bish. of Win. This answer we'll return; and so, farewell.
[*Going with Trussel.*

Leices. Call them again, my lord, and speak them fair;
For, if they go, the prince shall lose his right.

K. Edw. Call thou them back; I have no power to speak.

Leices. My lord, the king is willing to resign.
Bish. of Win. If he be not, let him choose.
K. Edw. O, would I might! but heavens and earth conspire
To make me miserable. Here, receive my crown.
Receive it? no, these innocent hands of mine
Shall not be guilty of so foul a crime;
He of you all that most desires my blood,
And will be call'd the murderer of a king,
Take it. What, are you mov'd? pity you me?
Then send for unrelenting Mortimer,
And Isabel, whose eyes being turn'd to steel
Will sooner sparkle fire than shed a tear.
Yet stay; for, rather than I'll look on them,
Here, here! [*Gives the crown.*]—Now, sweet God of heaven,
Make me despise this transitory pomp,
And sit for aye enthronised in heaven!
Come, death, and with thy fingers close my eyes,
Or, if I live, let me forget myself!
Bish. of Win. My lord,—
K. Edw. Call me not lord; away, out of my sight!
Ah, pardon me! grief makes me lunatic.
Let not that Mortimer protect my son;
More safety is there in a tiger's jaws
Than his embracements. Bear this to the queen,
Wet with my tears, and dried again with sighs:
[*Gives a handkerchief.*
If with the sight thereof she be not mov'd,
Return it back, and dip it in my blood.
Commend me to my son, and bid him rule
Better than I: yet how have I transgress'd,
Unless it be with too much clemency?
Trus. And thus, most humbly do we take our leave.
K. Edw. Farewell.
[*Exeunt the Bishop of Winchester and Trussel with the crown.*
I know the next news that they bring
Will be my death; and welcome shall it be:
To wretched men death is felicity.
Leices. Another post! what news brings he?

Enter BERKELEY, *who gives a paper to* LEICESTER.

K. Edw. Such news as I expect.—Come, Berkeley, come,
And tell thy message to my naked breast.

Berk. My lord, think not a thought so villanous
Can harbour in a man of noble birth.
To do your highness service and devoir,
And save you from your foes, Berkeley would die.
Leices. My lord, the council of the queen commands
That I resign my charge.
K. Edw. And who must keep me now? Must you, my lord?
Berk. Ay, my most gracious lord; so 'tis decreed.
K. Edw. [*Taking the paper.*] By Mortimer, whose name is written here!
Well may I rent his name that rends my heart. [*Tears it.*
This poor revenge hath something eas'd my mind:
So may his limbs be torn as is this paper!
Hear me, immortal Jove, and grant it too!
Berk. Your grace must hence with me to Berkeley straight.
K. Edw. Whither you will: all places are alike,
And every earth is fit for burial.
Leices. Favour him, my lord, as much as lieth in you
Berk. Even so betide my soul as I use him!
K. Edw. Mine enemy hath pitied my estate,
And that's the cause that I am now remov'd.
Berk. And thinks your grace that Berkeley will be cruel?
K. Edw. I know not; but of this am I assur'd,
That death ends all, and I can die but once.—
Leicester, farewell.
Leices. Not yet, my lord; I'll bear you on your way.
[*Exeunt.*

Enter QUEEN ISABELLA *and the younger* MORTIMER.

Y. Mor. Fair Isabel, now have we our desire;
The proud corrupters of the light-brain'd king
Have done their homage to the lofty gallows,
And he himself lies in captivity.
Be rul'd by me, and we will rule the realm:
In any case take heed of childish fear,
For now we hold an old wolf by the ears,
That, if he slip, will seize upon us both,
And gripe the sorer, being grip'd himself.
Think therefore, madam, it imports us much
To erect your son with all the speed we may,
And that I be protector over him:
For our behoof will bear the greater sway
Whenas a king's name shall be under-writ.

Q. Isab. Sweet Mortimer, the life of Isabel,
Be thou persuaded that I love thee well;
And therefore, so the prince my son be safe,
Whom I esteem as dear as these mine eyes,
Conclude against his father what thou wilt,
And I myself will willingly subscribe.
Y. Mor. First would I hear news that he were depos'd,
And then let me alone to handle him.

Enter Messenger.

Letters! from whence?
Mess. From Killingworth, my lord.
Q. Isab. How fares my lord the king?
Mess. In health, madam, but full of pensiveness.
Q. Isab. Alas, poor soul, would I could ease his grief!

Enter the BISHOP OF WINCHESTER *with the crown.*

Thanks, gentle Winchester.—
Sirrah, be gone. [*Exit Messenger.*
Bish. of Win. The king hath willingly resign'd his crown.
Q. Isab. O, happy news! send for the prince my son.
Bish. of Win. Further, or this letter was seal'd, Lord Berkeley came,
So that he now is gone from Killingworth;
And we have heard that Edmund laid a plot
To set his brother free; no more but so.
The Lord of Berkeley is so pitiful
As Leicester that had charge of him before.
Q. Isab. Then let some other be his guardian.
Y. Mor. Let me alone; here is the privy-seal,—
[*Exit the Bish. of Win.*
Who's there? Call hither Gurney and Matrevis.—
[*To Attendants within.*
To dash the heavy-headed Edmund's drift,
Berkeley shall be discharg'd, the king remov'd,
And none but we shall know where he lieth.
Q. Isab. But, Mortimer, as long as he survives,
What safety rests for us or for my son?
Y. Mor. Speak, shall he presently be despatch'd and die?
Q. Isab. I would he were, so 'twere not by my means!

Enter MATREVIS *and* GURNEY.

Y. Mor. Enough.—Matrevis, write a letter presently

Unto the Lord of Berkeley from ourself,
That he resign the king to thee and Gurney;
And, when 'tis done, we will subscribe our name.

Mat. It shall be done, my lord. [*Writes.*

Y. Mor. Gurney,—

Gur. My lord?

Y. Mor. As thou intend'st to rise by Mortimer,
Who now makes Fortune's wheel turn as he please,
Seek all the means thou canst to make him droop,
And neither give him kind word nor good look.

Gur. I warrant you, my lord.

Y. Mor. And this above the rest: because we hear
That Edmund casts to work his liberty,
Remove him still from place to place by night,
Till at the last he come to Killingworth,
And then from thence to Berkeley back again;
And by the way, to make him fret the more,
Speak curstly to him; and in any case
Let no man comfort him, if he chance to weep,
But amplify his grief with bitter words.

Mat. Fear not, my lord; we'll do as you command.

Y. Mor. So, now away! post thitherwards amain.

Q. Isab. Whither goes this letter? to my lord the king?
Commend me humbly to his majesty,
And tell him that I labour all in vain
To ease his grief and work his liberty;
And bear him this as witness of my love. [*Gives ring.*

Mat. I will, madam. [*Exit with Gurney.*

Y. Mor. Finely dissembled! do so still, sweet queen.
Here comes the young prince with the Earl of Kent.

Q. Isab. Something he whispers in his childish ears.

Y. Mor. If he have such access unto the prince,
Our plots and stratagems will soon be dash'd.

Q. Isab. Use Edmund friendly, as if all were well.

Enter PRINCE EDWARD, *and* KENT *talking with him.*

Y. Mor. How fares my honourable Lord of Kent?

Kent. In health, sweet Mortimer.—How fares your grace?

Q. Isab. Well, if my lord your brother were enlarg'd.

Kent. I hear of late he hath depos'd himself.

Q. Isab. The more my grief.

Y. Mor. And mine.

Kent. Ah, they do dissemble! [*Aside.*

Q. Isab. Sweet son, come hither; I must talk with thee.
Y. Mor. You, being his uncle and the next of blood,
Do look to be protector o'er the prince.
Kent. Not I, my lord: who should protect the son,
But she that gave him life? I mean the queen.
P. Edw. Mother, persuade me not to wear the crown:
Let him be king; I am too young to reign.
Q. Isab. But be content, seeing it his highness' pleasure.
P. Edw. Let me but see him first, and then I will.
Kent. Ay, do, sweet nephew.
Q. Isab. Brother, you know it is impossible.
P. Edw. Why, is he dead?
Q. Isab. No, God forbid!
Kent. I would those words proceeded from your heart!
Y. Mor. Inconstant Edmund, dost thou favour him,
That wast a cause of his imprisonment?
Kent. The more cause have I now to make amends.
Y. Mor. [*aside to* Q. ISAB.] I tell thee, 'tis not meet that one so false
Should come about the person of a prince.—
My lord, he hath betray'd the king his brother,
And therefore trust him not.
P. Edw. But he repents, and sorrows for it now.
Q. Isab. Come, son, and go with this gentle lord and me.
P. Edw. With you I will, but not with Mortimer.
Y. Mor. Why, youngling, 'sdain'st thou so of Mortimer?
Then I will carry thee by force away.
P. Edw. Help, uncle Kent! Mortimer will wrong me.
Q. Isab. Brother Edmund, strive not; we are his friends;
Isabel is nearer than the Earl of Kent.
Kent. Sister, Edward is my charge; redeem him.
Q. Isab. Edward is my son, and I will keep him.
Kent. Mortimer shall know that he hath wronged me.
Hence will I haste to Killingworth Castle,
And rescue aged Edward from his foes,
To be reveng'd on Mortimer and thee. [*Aside.*
[*Exeunt, on one side, Queen Isabella, Prince Edward, and the younger Mortimer; on the other, Kent.*

Enter MATREVIS, GURNEY, *and* Soldiers, *with* KING EDWARD.

Mat. My lord, be not pensive; we are your friends:
Men are ordain'd to live in misery;

Therefore, come; dalliance dangereth our lives.
K. Edw. Friends, whither must unhappy Edward go?
Will hateful Mortimer appoint no rest?
Must I be vexed like the nightly bird,
Whose sight is loathsome to all winged fowls?
When will the fury of his mind assuage?
When will his heart be satisfied with blood?
If mine will serve, unbowel straight this breast,
And give my heart to Isabel and him:
It is the chiefest mark they level at.
Gur. Not so, my liege: the queen hath given this charge,
To keep your grace in safety:
Your passions make your dolours to increase.
K. Edw. This usage makes my misery increase.
But can my air of life continue long,
When all my senses are annoy'd with stench?
Within a dungeon England's king is kept,
Where I am starv'd for want of sustenance;
My daily diet is heart-breaking sobs,
That almost rent the closet of my heart:
Thus lives old Edward not reliev'd by any,
And so must die, though pitied by many.
O, water, gentle friends, to cool my thirst,
And clear my body from foul excrements!
Mat. Here's channel-water, as our charge is given:
Sit down, for we'll be barbers to your grace.
K. Edw. Traitors, away! what, will you murder me,
Or choke your sovereign with puddle-water?
Gur. No, but wash your face, and shave away your beard,
Lest you be known, and so be rescued.
Mat. Why strive you thus? your labour is in vain.
K. Edw. The wren may strive against the lion's strength,
But all in vain: so vainly do I strive
To seek for mercy at a tyrant's hand.
[*They wash him with puddle-water, and shave his beard away.*
Immortal powers, that know the painful cares
That wait upon my poor distressed soul,
O, level all your looks upon these daring men
That wrong their liege and sovereign, England's king!
O Gaveston, it is for thee that I am wrong'd!
For me both thou and both the Spensers died;
And for your sakes a thousand wrongs I'll take.

The Spensers' ghosts, wherever they remain,
Wish well to mine; then, tush, for them I'll die.
Mat. 'Twixt theirs and yours shall be no enmity.
Come, come, away! Now put the torches out:
We'll enter in by darkness to Killingworth.
Gur. How now! who comes there?

Enter KENT.

Mat. Guard the king sure: it is the Earl of Kent.
K. Edw. O gentle brother, help to rescue me!
Mat. Keep them asunder; thrust in the king.
Kent. Soldiers, let me but talk to him one word.
Gur. Lay hands upon the earl for this assault.
Kent. Lay down your weapons, traitors! yield the king!
Mat. Edmund, yield thou thyself, or thou shalt die.
Kent. Base villains, wherefore do you gripe me thus?
Gur. Bind him, and so convey him to the court.
Kent. Where is the court but here? here is the king
And I will visit him: why stay you me?
Mat. The court is where Lord Mortimer remains:
Thither shall your honour go; and so, farewell.
[*Exeunt Matrevis and Gurney with King Edward.*
Kent. O, miserable is that common-weal,
Where lords keep courts, and kings are lock'd in prison!
First Sold. Wherefore stay we? on, sirs, to the court!
Kent. Ay, lead me whither you will, even to my death,
Seeing that my brother cannot be releas'd. [*Exeunt.*

Enter the younger MORTIMER.

Y. Mor. The king must die, or Mortimer goes down;
The commons now begin to pity him:
Yet he that is the cause of Edward's death,
Is sure to pay for it when his son's of age;
And therefore will I do it cunningly.
This letter, written by a friend of ours,
Contains his death, yet bids them save his life;
[*Reads.*

Edwardum occidere nolite timere, bonum est,
Fear not to kill the king, 'tis good he die:
But read it thus, and that's another sense;
Edwardum occidere nolite, timere bonum est,
Kill not the king, 'tis good to fear the worst.
Unpointed as it is, thus shall it go.

That, being dead, if it chance to be found,
Matrevis and the rest may bear the blame,
And we be quit that caus'd it to be done.
Within this room is lock'd the messenger
That shall convey it, and perform the rest;
And, by a secret token that he bears,
Shall he be murder'd when the deed is done.—
Lightborn, come forth!

Enter LIGHTBORN.

Art thou as resolute as thou wast?

Light. What else, my lord? and far more resolute.

Y. Mor. And hast thou cast how to accomplish it?

Light. Ay, ay; and none shall know which way he died.

Y. Mor. But at his looks, Lightborn, thou wilt relent.

Light. Relent! ha, ha! I use much to relent.

Y. Mor. Well, do it bravely, and be secret.

Light. You shall not need to give instructions;
'Tis not the first time I have kill'd a man:
I learn'd in Naples how to poison flowers;
To strangle with a lawn thrust down the throat;
To pierce the wind pipe with a needle's point;
Or, whilst one is asleep, to take a quill,
And blow a little powder in his ears;
Or open his mouth, and pour quick-silver down.
But yet I have a braver way than these.

Y. Mor. What's that?

Light. Nay, you shall pardon me; none shall know my tricks.

Y. Mor. I care not how it is, so it be not spied.
Deliver this to Gurney and Matrevis: [*Gives letter.*
At every ten miles' end thou hast a horse:
Take this [*Gives money*]: away, and never see me more!

Light. No?

Y. Mor. No; unless thou bring me news of Edward's death.

Light. That will I quickly do. Farewell, my lord. [*Exit.*

Y. Mor. The prince I rule, the queen do I command,
And with a lowly congé to the ground
The proudest lords salute me as I pass;
I seal, I cancel, I do what I will.
Fear'd am I more than lov'd;—let me be fear'd,
And, when I frown, make all the court look pale.
I view the prince with Aristarchus' eyes,

Whose looks were as a breeching to a boy.
They thrust upon me the protectorship,
And sue to me for that that I desire;
While at the council-table, grave enough,
And not unlike a bashful puritan,
First I complain of imbecility,
Saying it is *onus quam gravissimum ;*
Till, being interrupted by my friends,
Suscepi that *provinciam,* as they term it;
And, to conclude, I am Protector now.
Now is all sure: the queen and Mortimer
Shall rule the realm, the king; and none rule us.
Mine enemies will I plague, my friends advance;
And what I list command who dare control?
Major sum quàm cui possit fortuna nocere :
And that this be the coronation-day,
It pleaseth me and Isabel the queen. [*Trumpets within.*
The trumpets sound; I must go take my place.

Enter KING EDWARD THE THIRD, QUEEN ISABELLA, *the* ARCHBISHOP OF CANTERBURY, Champion, *and* Nobles.

Archb. of Cant. Long live King Edward, by the grace of God
King of England and Lord of Ireland!
Cham. If any Christian, Heathen, Turk, or Jew,
Dares but affirm that Edward's not true king,
And will avouch his saying with the sword,
I am the Champion that will combat him.
Y. Mor. None comes: sound, trumpets! [*Trumpets.*
K. Edw. Third. Champion, here's to thee. [*Gives purse.*
Q. Isab. Lord Mortimer, now take him to your charge.

Enter Soldiers *with* KENT *prisoner.*

Y. Mor. What traitor have we there with blades and bills?
First Sold. Edmund the Earl of Kent.
K. Edw. Third. What hath he done?
First Sold. 'A would have taken the king away perforce,
As we were bringing him to Killingworth.
Y. Mor. Did you attempt his rescue, Edmund? speak.
Kent. Mortimer, I did: he is our king,
And thou compell'st this prince to wear the crown.
Y. Mor. Strike off his head: he shall have martial law.
Kent. Strike off my head! base traitor, I defy thee!
K. Edw. Third. My lord, he is my uncle, and shall live.

Y. Mor. My lord, he is your enemy, and shall die.
Kent. Stay, villains!
K. Edw. Third. Sweet mother, if I cannot pardon him
Entreat my Lord Protector for his life.
Q. Isab. Son, be content: I dare not speak a word.
K. Edw. Third. Nor I; and yet methinks I should command:
But, seeing I cannot, I'll entreat for him.—
My lord, if you will let my uncle live,
I will requite it when I come to age.
Y. Mor. 'Tis for your highness' good and for the realm's.—
How often shall I bid you bear him hence?
Kent. Art thou king? must I die at thy command?
Y. Mor. At our command.—Once more, away with him!
Kent. Let me but stay and speak; I will not go:
Either my brother or his son is king,
And none of both them thirst for Edmund's blood:
And therefore, soldiers, whither will you hale me?
[*Soldiers hale Kent away, and carry him to be beheaded.*
K. Edw. Third. What safety may I look for at his hands,
If that my uncle shall be murder'd thus?
Q. Isab. Fear not, sweet boy; I'll guard thee from thy foes:
Had Edmund liv'd, he would have sought thy death.
Come, son, we'll ride a-hunting in the park.
K. Edw. Third. And shall my uncle Edmund ride with us?
Q. Isab. He is a traitor; think not on him: come. [*Exeunt.*

Enter MATREVIS *and* GURNEY.

Mat. Gurney, I wonder the king dies not,
Being in a vault up to the knees in water,
To which the channels of the castle run,
From whence a damp continually ariseth,
That were enough to poison any man,
Much more a king, brought up so tenderly.
Gur. And so do I, Matrevis: yesternight
I open'd but the door to throw him meat,
And I was almost stifled with the savour.
Mat. He hath a body able to endure
More than we can inflict: and therefore now
Let us assail his mind another while.
Gur. Send for him out thence, and I will anger him.
Mat. But stay; who's this?

Enter LIGHTBORN.

Light. My Lord Protector greets you. [*Gives letter.*
Gur. What's here? I know not how to conster it.
Mat. Gurney, it was left unpointed for the nonce;
Edwardum occidere nolite timere,
That's his meaning.
Light. Know you this token? I must have the king.
[*Gives token.*
Mat. Ay, stay a while; thou shalt have answer straight.—
This villain's sent to make away the king.
Gur. I thought as much.
Mat. And, when the murder's done,
See how he must be handled for his labour,—
Pereat iste! Let him have the king;
What else?—Here is the keys, this is the lake:
Do as you are commanded by my lord.
Light. I know what I must do. Get you away:
Yet be not far off; I shall need your help:
See that in the next room I have a fire,
And get me a spit, and let it be red-hot.
Mat. Very well.
Gur. Need you anything besides?
Light. What else? a table and a feather-bed.
Gur. That's all?
Light. Ay, ay: so, when I call you, bring it in.
Mat. Fear not you that.
Gur. Here's a light to go into the dungeon.
[*Gives light to Lightborn, and then exit with Matrevis*
Light. So, now
Must I about this gear: ne'er was there any
So finely handled as this king shall be.—
Foh, here's a place indeed with all my heart!
K. Edw. Who's there? what light is that? wherefore comes thou?
Light. To comfort you, and bring you joyful news.
K. Edw. Small comfort finds poor Edward in thy looks:
Villain, I know thou com'st to murder me.
Light. To murder you, my most gracious lord?
Far is it from my heart to do you harm.
The queen sent me to see how you were us'd,
For she relents at this your misery:
And what eye can refrain from shedding tears,

To see a king in this most piteous state?

K. Edw. Weep'st thou already? list a while to me,
And then thy heart, were it as Gurney's is,
Or as Matrevis', hewn from the Caucasus,
Yet will it melt ere I have done my tale.
This dungeon where they keep me is the sink
Wherein the filth of all the castle falls.

Light. O villains!

K. Edw. And there, in mire and puddle, have I stood
This ten days' space; and, lest that I should sleep,
One plays continually upon a drum;
They give me bread and water, being a king;
So that, for want of sleep and sustenance,
My mind's distemper'd, and my body's numb'd,
And whether I have limbs or no I know not.
O, would my blood dropp'd out from every vein,
As doth this water from my tatter'd robes!
Tell Isabel the queen, I look'd not thus,
When for her sake I ran at tilt in France,
And there unhors'd the Duke of Cleremont.

Light. O, speak no more, my lord! this breaks my heart.
Lie on this bed, and rest yourself a while.

K. Edw. These looks of thine can harbour naught but death;
I see my tragedy written in thy brows.
Yet stay a while; forbear thy bloody hand,
And let me see the stroke before it comes,
That even then when I shall lose my life,
My mind may be more steadfast on my God.

Light. What means your highness to mistrust me thus?

K. Edw. What mean'st thou to dissemble with me thus?

Light. These hands were never stain'd with innocent blood,
Nor shall they now be tainted with a king's.

K. Edw. Forgive my thought for having such a thought.
One jewel have I left; receive thou this: [*Giving jewel.*
Still fear I, and I know not what's the cause,
But every joint shakes as I give it thee.
O, if thou harbour'st murder in thy heart,
Let this gift change thy mind, and save thy soul!
Know that I am a king: O, at that name
I feel a hell of grief! where is my crown?
Gone, gone! and do I remain alive?

Light. You're overwatch'd, my lord: lie down and rest.

K. Edw. But that grief keeps me waking, I should sleep;
For not these ten days have these eyes' lids clos'd.
Now, as I speak, they fall; and yet with fear
Open again. O, wherefore sitt'st thou here?
Light. If you mistrust me, I'll be gone, my lord.
K. Edw. No, no; for, if thou mean'st to murder me,
Thou wilt return again; and therefore stay. [*Sleeps.*
Light. He sleeps.
K. Edw. [*waking*] O, let me not die yet! O, stay a while!
Light. How now, my lord!
K. Edw. Something still buzzeth in mine ears,
And tells me, if I sleep, I never wake:
This fear is that which makes me tremble thus;
And therefore tell me, wherefore art thou come?
Light. To rid thee of thy life.—Matrevis, come!

Enter MATREVIS *and* GURNEY.

K. Edw. I am too weak and feeble to resist.—
Assist me, sweet God, and receive my soul!
Light. Run for the table.
K. Edw. O, spare me, or despatch me in a trice!
[*Matrevis brings in a table. King Edward is murdered by holding him down on the bed with the table, and stamping on it.*
Light. So, lay the table down, and stamp on it,
But not too hard, lest that you bruise his body.
Mat. I fear me that this cry will raise the town,
And therefore let us take horse and away.
Light. Tell me, sirs, was it not bravely done?
Gur. Excellent well: take this for thy reward.
[*Stabs Lightborn, who dies.*
Come, let us cast the body in the moat,
And bear the king's to Mortimer our lord:
Away! [*Exeunt with the bodies.*

Enter the younger MORTIMER *and* MATREVIS.

Y. Mor. Is't done, Matrevis, and the murderer dead?
Mat. Ay, my good lord: I would it were undone!
Y. Mor. Matrevis, if thou now grow'st penitent,
I'll be thy ghostly father; therefore choose,
Whether thou wilt be secret in this,
Or else die by the hand of Mortimer.
Mat. Gurney, my lord, is fled, and will, I fear,

Betray us both; therefore let me fly.
Y. Mor. Fly to the savages!
Mat. I humbly thank your honour. [*Exit.*
Y. Mor. As for myself, I stand as Jove's huge tree,
And others are but shrubs compar'd to me:
All tremble at my name, and I fear none:
Let's see who dare impeach me for his death!

Enter QUEEN ISABELLA.

Q. Isab. Ah, Mortimer, the king my son hath news,
His father's dead, and we have murder'd him!
Y. Mor. What if he have? the king is yet a child.
Q. Isab. Ay, but he tears his hair, and wrings his hands,
And vows to be reveng'd upon us both.
Into the council-chamber he is gone,
To crave the aid and succour of his peers.
Ay me, see where he comes, and they with him!
Now, Mortimer, begins our tragedy.

Enter KING EDWARD THE THIRD, Lords, *and* Attendants.

First Lord. Fear not, my lord; know that you are a king.
K. Edw. Third. Villain!—
Y. Mor. Ho, now, my lord!
K. Edw. Third. Think not that I am frighted with thy words:
My father's murder'd through thy treachery;
And thou shalt die, and on his mournful hearse
Thy hateful and accursed head shall lie,
To witness to the world that by thy means
His kingly body was too soon interr'd.
Q. Isab. Weep not, sweet son.
K. Edw. Third. Forbid not me to weep; he was my father;
And had you lov'd him half so well as I,
You could not bear his death thus patiently:
But you, I fear, conspir'd with Mortimer.
First Lord. Why speak you not unto my lord the king?
Y. Mor. Because I think scorn to be accus'd.
Who is the man dare say I murder'd him?
K. Edw. Third. Traitor, in me my loving father speaks,
And plainly saith, 'twas thou that murder'dst him.
Y. Mor. But hath your grace no other proof than this?
K. Edw. Third. Yes, if this be the hand of Mortimer. [*Showing letter.*

Y. Mor. False Gurney hath betray'd me and himself.
[*Aside to Queen Isabella.*
Q. Isab. I fear'd as much: murder can not be hid.
Y. Mor. It is my hand; what gather you by this?
K. Edw. Third. That thither thou didst send a murderer.
Y. Mor. What murderer? bring forth the man I sent.
K. Edw. Third. Ah, Mortimer, thou know'st that he is slain!
And so shalt thou be too.—Why stays he here?
Bring him unto a hurdle, drag him forth;
Hang him, I say, and set his quarters up:
And bring his head back presently to me.
Q. Isab. For my sake, sweet son, pity Mortimer!
Y. Mor. Madam, entreat not: I will rather die
Than sue for life unto a paltry boy.
K. Edw. Third. Hence with the traitor, with the murderer!
Y. Mor. Base Fortune, now I see, that in thy wheel
There is a point, to which when men aspire,
They tumble headlong down: that point I touch'd,
And, seeing there was no place to mount up higher,
Why should I grieve at my declining fall?—
Farewell, fair queen: weep not for Mortimer,
That scorns the world, and, as a traveller,
Goes to discover countries yet unknown.
K. Edw. Third. What, suffer you the traitor to delay?
[*Exit the younger Mortimer with First Lord and some of the Attendants.*
Q. Isab. As thou received thy life from me,
Spill not the blood of gentle Mortimer!
K. Edw. Third. This argues that you spilt my father's blood,
Else would you not entreat for Mortimer.
Q. Isab. I spill his blood! no.
K. Edw. Third. Ay, madam, you; for so the rumour runs.
Q. Isab. That rumour is untrue: for loving thee,
Is this report rais'd on poor Isabel.
K. Edw. Third. I do not think her so unnatural.
Sec. Lord. My lord, I fear me it will prove too true.
K. Edw. Third. Mother, you are suspected for his death,
And therefore we commit you to the Tower,
Till further trial may be made thereof.
If you be guilty, though I be your son,
Think not to find me slack or pitiful.
Q. Isab. Nay, to my death; for too long have I liv'd,
Whenas my son thinks to abridge my days.

K. Edw. Third. Away with her! her words enforce these tears,
And I shall pity her, if she speak again.
Q. Isab. Shall I not mourn for my beloved lord?
And with the rest accompany him to his grave.
Sec. Lord. Thus, madam, 'tis the king's will you shall hence
Q. Isab. He hath forgotten me: stay; I am his mother.
Sec. Lord. That boots not; therefore, gentle madam, go.
Q. Isab. Then come, sweet death, and rid me of this grief!
[*Exit with Second Lord and some of the Attendants.*

Re-enter First Lord, *with the head of the younger* MORTIMER.

First Lord. My lord, here is the head of Mortimer.
K. Edw. Third. Go fetch my father's hearse, where it shall lie;
And bring my funeral robes. [*Exeunt Attendants.*
Accursed head,
Could I have rul'd thee then, as I do now,
Thou hadst not hatch'd this monstrous treachery!—
Here comes the hearse: help me to mourn, my lords.

Re-enter Attendants, *with the hearse and funeral robes.*

Sweet father, here unto thy murder'd ghost
I offer up the wicked traitor's head;
And let these tears, distilling from mine eyes,
Be witness of my grief and innocency. [*Exeunt.*

THE MASSACRE AT PARIS

DRAMATIS PERSONÆ

CHARLES THE NINTH, *King of France.*
DUKE OF ANJOU, *his brother, afterwards* KING HENRY THE THIRD.
KING OF NAVARRE.
PRINCE OF CONDÉ, *his cousin.*
DUKE OF GUISE, CARDINAL OF LORRAINE, DUKE DUMAINE, } *brothers.*
SON TO THE DUKE OF GUISE, *a boy.*
THE LORD HIGH ADMIRAL.
DUKE JOYEUX.
EPERNOUN.
PLESHÉ.
BARTUS.
TWO LORDS OF POLAND.
GONZAGO.
RETES.
MOUNTSORRELL.
MUGEROUN.
THE CUTPURSE.
LOREINE, *a preacher.*
SEROUNE.
RAMUS.
TALÆUS.
FRIAR.
SURGEON.
ENGLISH AGENT.
APOTHECARY.
CAPTAIN OF THE GUARD, PROTESTANTS, SCHOOLMASTERS, SOLDIERS, MURDERERS, ATTENDANTS, *etc.*

CATHERINE, *the Queen-Mother of France.*
MARGARET, *her daughter, wife to the* KING OF NAVARRE.
THE OLD QUEEN OF NAVARRE.
DUCHESS OF GUISE.
WIFE *to* SEROUNE.
MAID *to the* DUCHESS OF GUISE.

Enter CHARLES, *the French king;* CATHERINE, *the Queen-Mother;* *the* KING OF NAVARRE; MARGARET, *Queen of Navarre;* *the* PRINCE OF CONDÉ; *the* LORD HIGH ADMIRAL; *the* OLD QUEEN OF NAVARRE; *with others.*

Char. Prince of Navarre, my honourable brother,
Prince Condé, and my good Lord Admiral,
I wish this union and religious league,
Knit in these hands, thus join'd in nuptial rites,
May not dissolve till death dissolve our lives;
And that the native sparks of princely love,
That kindled first this motion in our hearts,
May still be fuell'd in our progeny.
Nav. The many favours which your grace hath shown,
From time to time, but specially in this,
Shall bind me ever to your highness' will,
In what Queen-Mother or your grace commands.

Cath. Thanks, son Navarre. You see we love you well,
That link you in marriage with our daughter here;
And, as you know, our difference in religion
Might be a means to cross you in your love.—
Char. Well, madam, let that rest.—
And now, my lords, the marriage-rites perform'd,
We think it good to go and consummate
The rest with hearing of a holy mass.—
Sister, I think yourself will bear us company.
Mar. I will, my good lord.
Char. The rest that will not go, my lords, may stay.—
Come, mother,
Let us go to honour this solemnity.
Cath. Which I'll dissolve with blood and cruelty. [*Aside.*
[*Exeunt all except the King of Navarre, Condé, and the Admiral.*
Nav. Prince Condé, and my good Lord Admiral,
Now Guise may storm, but do us little hurt,
Having the king, Queen-mother on our sides,
To stop the malice of his envious heart,
That seeks to murder all the Protestants.
Have you not heard of late how he decreed
(If that the king had given consent thereto)
That all the protestants that are in Paris
Should have been murdered the other night?
Adm. My lord, I marvel that th' aspiring Guise
Dares once adventure, without the king's consent,
To meddle or attempt such dangerous things.
Con. My lord, you need not marvel at the Guise,
For what he doth, the Pope will ratify,
In murder, mischief, or in tyranny.
Nav. But he that sits and rules above the clouds
Doth hear and see the prayers of the just,
And will revenge the blood of innocents,
That Guise hath slain by treason of his heart,
And brought by murder to their timeless ends.
Adm. My lord, but did you mark the Cardinal,
The Guise's brother, and the Duke Dumaine,
How they did storm at these your nuptial rites,
Because the house of Bourbon now comes in,
And joins your lineage to the crown of France?
Nav. And that's the cause that Guise so frowns at us,
And beats his brains to catch us in his trap,

Which he hath pitch'd within his deadly toil.
Come, my lords, let's go to the church, and pray
That God may still defend the right of France,
And make his Gospel flourish in this land. [*Exeunt.*

Enter GUISE.

Guise. If ever Hymen lour'd at marriage-rites,
And had his altars deck'd with dusky lights;
If ever sun stain'd heaven with bloody clouds,
And made it look with terror on the world;
If ever day were turn'd to ugly night,
And night made semblance of the hue of hell;
This day, this hour, this fatal night,
Shall fully show the fury of them all.—
Apothecary!

Enter APOTHECARY.

Apoth. My lord?
Guise. Now shall I prove, and guerdon to the full,
The love thou bear'st unto the house of Guise.
Where are those perfum'd gloves which I sent
To be poison'd? hast thou done them? speak;
Will every savour breed a pang of death?
Apoth. See where they be, my good lord; and he that smells
But to them, dies.
Guise. Then thou remain'st resolute?
Apoth. I am, my lord, in what your grace commands,
Till death.
Guise. Thanks, my good friend: I will requite thy love.
Go, then, present them to the Queen Navarre;
For she is that huge blemish in our eye,
That makes these upstart heresies in France:
Be gone, my friend, present them to her straight.
[*Exit Apothecary.*
Soldier!

Enter a Soldier.

Sold. My lord?
Guise. Now come thou forth, and play thy tragic part.
Stand in some window, opening near the street,
And when thou see'st the Admiral ride by,
Discharge thy musket, and perform his death;
And then I'll guerdon thee with store of crowns.
Sold. I will, my lord. [*Exit.*
Guise. Now, Guise, begin those deep-engender'd thoughts

To burst abroad those never-dying flames
Which cannot be extinguished but by blood.
Oft have I levell'd, and at last have learn'd
That peril is the chiefest way to happiness,
And resolution honour's fairest aim.
What glory is there in a common good,
That hangs for every peasant to achieve?
That like I best, that flies beyond my reach.
Set me to scale the high Pyramides,
And thereon set the diadem of France;
I'll either rend it with my nails to naught,
Or mount the top with my aspiring wings,
Although my downfall be the deepest hell.
For this I wake, when others think I sleep;
For this I wait, that scorn attendance else;
For this, my quenchless thirst, whereon I build,
Hath often pleaded kindred to the king;
For this, this head, this heart, this hand, and sword,
Contrives, imagines, and fully executes,
Matters of import aimed at by many,
Yet understood by none;
For this, hath heaven engender'd me of earth;
For this, this earth sustains my body's weight,
And with this weight I'll counterpoise a crown,
Or with seditions weary all the world;
For this, from Spain the stately Catholics
Send Indian gold to coin me French ecues;
For this, have I a largess from the Pope,
A pension, and a dispensation too;
And by that privilege to work upon,
My policy hath fram'd religion.
Religion! *O Diabole!*
Fie, I am asham'd, however that I seem,
To think a word of such a simple sound,
Of so great matter should be made the ground!
The gentle king, whose pleasure uncontroll'd
Weakeneth his body, and will waste his realm,
If I repair not what he ruinates,—
Him, as a child, I daily win with words,
So that for proof he barely bears the name;
I execute, and he sustains the blame.
The Mother-Queen works wonders for my sake,
And in my love entombs the hope of France,

Rifling the bowels of her treasury,
To supply my wants and necessity.
Paris hath full five hundred colleges,
As monasteries, priories, abbeys, and halls,
Wherein are thirty thousand able men,
Besides a thousand sturdy student Catholics;
And more,—of my knowledge, in one cloister keep
Five hundred fat Franciscan friars and priests:
All this, and more, if more may be compris'd,
To bring the will of our desires to end.
Then, Guise,
Since thou hast all the cards within thy hands,
To shuffle or cut, take this as surest thing,
That, right or wrong, thou deal thyself a king.—
Ay, but, Navarre,—'tis but a nook of France,
Sufficient yet for such a petty king,
That, with a rabblement of his heretics,
Blinds Europe's eyes, and troubleth our estate.
Him will we—[*Pointing to his sword.*] but first let's follow
    those in France
That hinder our possession to the crown.
As Cæsar to his soldiers, so say I,—
Those that hate me will I learn to loathe.
Give me a look, that, when I bend the brows,
Pale death may walk in furrows of my face;
A hand, that with a grasp may gripe the world;
An ear to hear what my detractors say;
A royal seat, a sceptre, and a crown;
That those which do behold them may become
As men that stand and gaze against the sun.
The plot is laid, and things shall come to pass
Where resolution strives for victory. [*Exit.*

Enter the KING OF NAVARRE, QUEEN MARGARET, *the* OLD QUEEN OF NAVARRE, *the* PRINCE OF CONDÉ, *and the* ADMIRAL; *they are met by the* Apothecary *with the gloves, which he gives to the* OLD QUEEN.

Apoth. Madam,
I beseech your grace to accept this simple gift.

Old Q. of Nav. Thanks, my good friend. Hold, take thou this reward. [*Gives a purse.*

Apoth. I humbly thank your majesty. [*Exit.*

Old Q. of Nav. Methinks the gloves have a very strong perfume,
The scent whereof doth make my head to ache.
Nav. Doth not your grace know the man that gave them you?
Old Q. of Nav. Not well; but do remember such a man.
Adm. Your grace was ill-advis'd to take them, then,
Considering of these dangerous times.
Old Q. of Nav. Help, son Navarre! I am poison'd!
Mar. The heavens forbid your highness such mishap!
Nav. The late suspicion of the Duke of Guise
Might well have mov'd your highness to beware
How you did meddle with such dangerous gifts.
Mar. Too late, it is, my lord, if that be true,
To blame her highness; but I hope it be
Only some natural passion makes her sick.
Old Q. of Nav. O, no, sweet Margaret! the fatal poison
Works within my head; my brain-pan breaks;
My heart doth faint; I die! [*Dies.*
Nav. My mother poison'd here before my face!
O gracious God, what times are these!
O, grant, sweet God, my days may end with hers,
That I with her may die and live again!
Mar. Let not this heavy chance, my dearest lord,
(For whose effects my soul is massacred),
Infect thy gracious breast with fresh supply
To aggravate our sudden misery.
Adm. Come, my lords, let us bear her body hence,
And see it honoured with just solemnity.
[*As they are going out, the Soldier dischargeth his musket at the Admiral.*
Con. What, are you hurt, my Lord High Admiral?
Adm. Ay, my good lord, shot through the arm.
Nav. We are betray'd! Come, my lords,
And let us go tell the king of this.
Adm. These are
The cursed Guisians, that do seek our death.
O, fatal was this marriage to us all.
[*Exeunt, bearing out the body of the Old Queen of Navarre.*

Enter KING CHARLES, CATHERINE *the Queen-Mother,* GUISE, ANJOU, *and* DUMAINE.

Cath. My noble son, and princely Duke of Guise,
Now have we got the fatal, straggling deer

Within the compass of a deadly toil,
And, as we late decreed, we may perform.
Char. Madam, it will be noted through the world
An action bloody and tyrannical;
Chiefly, since under safety of our word
They justly challenge their protection:
Besides, my heart relents that noble men,
Only corrupted in religion,
Ladies of honour, knights, and gentlemen,
Should, for their conscience, taste such ruthless ends.
Anj. Though gentle minds should pity others' pains,
Yet will the wisest note their proper griefs,
And rather seek to scourge their enemies
Than be themselves base subjects to the whip.
Guise. Methinks my Lord Anjou hath well advis'd
Your highness to consider of the thing,
And rather choose to seek your country's good
Than pity or relieve these upstart heretics.
Cath. I hope these reasons may serve my princely son
To have some care for fear of enemies.
Char. Well, madam, I refer it to your majesty,
And to my nephew here, the Duke of Guise:
What you determine, I will ratify.
Cath. Thanks to my princely son.—Then tell me, Guise,
What order will you set down for the massacre?
Guise. Thus, madam. They
That shall be actors in this massacre
Shall wear white crosses on their burgonets,
And tie white linen scarfs about their arms;
He that wants these, and is suspect of heresy,
Shall die, be he king or emperor. Then I'll have
A peal of ordnance shot from the tower, at which
They all shall issue out, and set the streets,
And then,
The watchword being given, a bell shall ring,
Which when they hear, they shall begin to kill,
And never cease until that bell shall cease;
Then breathe a while.

Enter the ADMIRAL's Serving-Man.

Char. How now, fellow! what news?
Serv.-M. An it please your grace, the Lord High Admiral,
Riding the streets, was traitorously shot;

And most humbly entreats your majesty
To visit him, sick in his bed,
Char. Messenger, tell him I will see him straight.
[*Exit Serv.-M.*

What shall we do now with the Admiral?
Cath. Your majesty were best go visit him,
And make a show as if all were well.
Char. Content; I will go visit the Admiral.
Guise. And I will go take order for his death.
[*Exeunt Catherine and Guise.*

The ADMIRAL *discovered in bed.*

Char. How fares it with my Lord High Admiral?
Hath he been hurt with villains in the street?
I vow and swear, as I am King of France,
To find and to repay the man with death,
With death delay'd and torments never us'd,
That durst presume, for hope of any gain,
To hurt the noble man his sovereign loves.
Adm. Ah, my good lord, these are the Guisians,
That seek to massacre our guiltless lives!
Char. Assure yourself, my good Lord Admiral,
I deeply sorrow for your treacherous wrong;
And that I am not more secure myself
Than I am careful you should be preserv'd.—
Cousin, take twenty of our strongest guard,
And, under your direction, see they keep
All treacherous violence from our noble friend;
Repaying all attempts with present death
Upon the cursed breakers of our peace.—
And so be patient, good Lord Admiral,
And every hour I will visit you.
Adm. I humbly thank your royal majesty.
[*Exeunt Charles, etc. Scene closes.*

Enter GUISE, ANJOU, DUMAINE, GONZAGO, RETES, MOUNTSORRELL, *and* Soldiers, *to the massacre.*

Guise. Anjou, Dumaine, Gonzago, Retes, swear,
By the argent crosses in your burgonets,
To kill all that you suspect of heresy.
Dum. I swear by this, to be unmerciful.
Anj. I am disguis'd, and none knows who I am,
And therefore mean to murder all I meet.

Gon. And so will I.
Retes. And I.
Guise. Away, then! break into the Admiral's house.
Retes. Ay, let the Admiral be first despatch'd.
Guise. The Admiral,
Chief standard-bearer to the Lutherans,
Shall in the entrance of this massacre
Be murder'd in his bed.
Gonzago, conduct them thither; and then
Beset his house, that not a man may live.
Anj. That charge is mine.—Switzers, keep you the streets;
And at each corner shall the king's guard stand.
Gon. Come, sirs, follow me. [*Exit Gonzago with others.*
Anj. Cousin, the captain of the Admiral's guard,
Plac'd by my brother, will betray his lord.
Now, Guise, shall Catholics flourish once again;
The head being off, the members cannot stand.
Retes. But look, my lord, there's some in the Admiral's house.

[*The Admiral discovered in bed; Gonzago and others in the house.*

Anj. In lucky time: come, let us keep this lane,
And slay his servants that shall issue out.
Gon. Where is the Admiral?
Adm. O, let me pray before I die!
Gon. Then pray unto our Lady; kiss this cross. [*Stabs him.*
Adm. O God, forgive my sins! [*Dies.*
Guise. Gonzago, what, is he dead?
Gon. Ay, my lord.
Guise. Then throw him down.

[*The body of the Admiral is thrown down.*

Anj. Now, cousin, view him well:
It may be 'tis some other, and he escap'd.
Guise. Cousin, 'tis he; I know him by his look:
See where my soldier shot him through the arm;
He miss'd him near, but we have struck him now.—
Ah, base Chatillon and degenerate,
Chief standard-bearer to the Lutherans,
Thus, in despite of thy religion,
The Duke of Guise stamps on thy lifeless bulk!
Anj. Away with him! cut off his head and hands,
And send them for a present to the Pope;
And, when this just revenge is finished,

Unto Mount Faucon will we drag his corse;
And he, that living hated so the Cross,
Shall, being dead, be hang'd thereon in chains.

Guise. Anjou, Gonzago, Retes, if that you three
Will be as resolute as I and Dumaine,
There shall not be a Huguenot breathe in France.

Anj. I swear by this cross, we'll not be partial,
But slay as many as we can come near.

Guise. Mountsorrell, go shoot the ordnance off,
That they, which have already set the street,
May know their watchword; then toll the bell,
And so let's forward to the massacre.

Mount. I will, my lord. [*Exit.*

Guise. And now, my lords, let's closely to our business.

Anj. Anjou will follow thee.

Dum. And so will Dumaine.

[*The ordnance being shot off, the bell tolls.*

Guise. Come, then, let's away. [*Exeunt.*

Enter GUISE, *and the rest, with their swords drawn, chasing the Protestants.*

Guise. Tuez, tuez, tuez!
Let none escape! murder the Huguenots!

Anj. Kill them! kill them! [*Exeunt.*

Enter LOREINE, *running;* GUISE *and the rest pursuing him.*

Guise. Loreine, Loreine! follow Loreine!—Sirrah,
Are you a preacher of these heresies?

Lor. I am a preacher of the word of God;
And thou a traitor to thy soul and him.

Guise. "Dearly beloved brother,"—thus 'tis written.

[*Stabs Loreine, who dies.*

Anj. Stay, my lord, let me begin the psalm.

Guise. Come, drag him away, and throw him in a ditch.

[*Exeunt with the body.*

Enter MOUNTSORRELL, *and knocks at* SEROUNE'S *door.*

Seroune's Wife [*within*]. Who is that which knocks there?

Mount. Mountsorrell, from the Duke of Guise.

Seroune's Wife [*within*]. Husband, come down; here's one would speak with you.
From the Duke of Guise.

Enter SEROUNE *from the house.*

Ser. To speak with me, from such a man as he?
Mount. Ay, ay, for this, Seroune; and thou shalt ha't.
[*Showing his dagger.*
Ser. O, let me pray, before I take my death!
Mount. Despatch, then, quickly.
Ser. O Christ, my Saviour!
Mount. Christ, villain!
Why, darest thou to presume to call on Christ,
Without the intercession of some saint?
Sanctus Jacobus, he's my saint; pray to him.
Ser. O, let me pray unto my God!
Mount. Then take this with you.
[*Stabs Seroune, who dies; and then exit.*

Enter RAMUS, *in his study.*

Ramus. What fearful cries come from the river Seine,
That fright poor Ramus sitting at his book!
I fear the Guisians have pass'd the bridge,
And mean once more to menace me.

Enter TALÆUS.

Tal. Fly, Ramus, fly, if thou wilt save thy life!
Ramus. Tell me, Talæus, wherefore should I fly?
Tal. The Guisians are
Hard at thy door, and mean to murder us:
Hark, hark, they come! I'll leap out at the window.
Ramus. Sweet Talæus, stay.

Enter GONZAGO *and* RETES.

Gon. Who goes there?
Retes. 'Tis Talæus, Ramus' bedfellow.
Gon. What art thou?
Tal. I am, as Ramus is, a Christian.
Retes. O, let him go; he is a Catholic. [*Exit Talæus.*
Gon. Come, Ramus, more gold, or thou shalt have the stab.
Ramus. Alas, I am a scholar! how should I have gold?
All that I have is but my stipend from the king,
Which is no sooner receiv'd but it is spent.

Enter GUISE, ANJOU, DUMAINE, MOUNTSORRELL, *and* Soldiers.

Anj. Who have you there?
Retes. 'Tis Ramus, the king's Professor of Logic.

Guise. Stab him.
Ramus. O, good my lord,
  Wherein hath Ramus been so offensious?
Guise. Marry, sir, in having a smack in all,
  And yet didst never sound anything to the depth.
  Was it not thou that scoff'st the *Organon*,
  And said it was a heap of vanities?
  He that will be a flat dichotomist,
  And seen in nothing but epitomes,
  Is in your judgment thought a learned man;
  And he, forsooth, must go and preach in Germany,
  Excepting against doctors' axioms,
  And *ipse dixi* with this quiddity,
  Argumentum testimonii est inartificiale.
  To contradict which, I say, Ramus shall die:
  How answer you that? your *nego argumentum*
  Cannot serve, sirrah.—Kill him.
Ramus. O, good my lord, let me but speak a word!
Anj. Well, say on.
Ramus. Not for my life do I desire this pause;
  But in my latter hour to purge myself,
  In that I know the things that I have wrote,
  Which, as I hear, one Scheckius takes it ill,
  Because my places, being but three, contain all his.
  I knew the *Organon* to be confus'd,
  And I reduc'd it into better form:
  And this for Aristotle will I say,
  That he that despiseth him can ne'er
  Be good in logic or philosophy;
  And that's because the blockish Sorbonnists
  Attribute as much unto their [own] works
  As to the service of the eternal God.
Guise. Why suffer you that peasant to declaim?
  Stab him, I say, and send him to his friends in hell.
Anj. Ne'er was there collier's son so full of pride.
[*Stabs Ramus, who dies.*
Guise. My Lord of Anjou, there are a hundred Protestants,
  Which we have chas'd into the river Seine,
  That swim about, and so preserve their lives:
  How may we do? I fear me they will live.
Dum. Go place some men upon the bridge,
  With bows and darts, to shoot at them they see,
  And sink them in the river as they swim.

Guise. 'Tis well advis'd, Dumaine; go see it straight be done. [*Exit Dumaine.*
And in the meantime, my lord, could we devise
To get those pedants from the King Navarre,
That are tutors to him and the Prince of Condé—
Anj. For that, let me alone: cousin, stay you here
And when you see me in, then follow hard.

ANJOU *knocketh at the door; and enter the* KING OF NAVARRE *and the* PRINCE OF CONDÉ, *with their two* Schoolmasters.

How now, my lords! how fare you?
Nav. My lord, they say
That all the Protestants are massacred.
Anj. Ay, so they are; but yet, what remedy?
I have done what I could to stay this broil.
Nav. But yet, my lord, the report doth run,
That you were one that made this massacre.
Anj. Who, I? you are deceiv'd; I rose but now.

GUISE, GONZAGO, RETES, MOUNTSORRELL, *and* Soldiers, *come forward.*

Guise. Murder the Huguenots! take those pedants hence!
Nav. Thou traitor, Guise, lay off thy bloody hands!
Con. Come, let us go tell the king.
[*Exit with the King of Navarre.*
Guise. Come, sirs,
I'll whip you to death with my poniard's point.
[*Stabs the Schoolmasters, who die.*
Anj. Away with them both!
[*Exeunt Anjou and Soldiers with the bodies.*
Guise. And now, sirs, for this night let our fury stay.
Yet will we not that the massacre shall end:
Gonzago, post you to Orleans,
Retes to Dieppe, Mountsorrell unto Rouen,
And spare not one that you suspect of heresy.
And now stay
That bell, that to the devil's matins rings.
Now every man put off his burgonet,
And so convey him closely to his bed. [*Exeunt.*

Enter ANJOU, *with two* Lords of Poland.

Anj. My lords of Poland, I must needs confess,
The offer of your Prince Elector's far
Beyond the reach of my deserts;

For Poland is, as I have been inform'd,
A martial people, worthy such a king
As hath sufficient counsel in himself
To lighten doubts, and frustrate subtle foes;
And such a king, whom practice long hath taught
To please himself with manage of the wars,
The greatest wars within our Christian bounds,—
I mean our wars against the Muscovites,
And, on the other side, against the Turk,
Rich princes both, and mighty emperors.
Yet, by my brother Charles, our king of France,
And by his grace's council, it is thought
That, if I undertake to wear the crown
Of Poland, it may prejudice their hope
Of my inheritance to the crown of France;
For, if th' Almighty take my brother hence,
By due descent the regal seat is mine.
With Poland, therefore, must I covenant thus,—
That if, by death of Charles, the diadem
Of France be cast on me, then, with your leaves,
I may retire me to my native home.
If your commission serve to warrant this,
I thankfully shall undertake the charge
Of you and yours, and carefully maintain
The wealth and safety of your kingdom's right.

First Lord. All this, and more, your highness shall command,
For Poland's crown and kingly diadem.

Anj. Then, come, my lords, let's go. [*Exeunt.*

Enter two Men, *with the* ADMIRAL's *body.*

First Man. Now, sirrah, what shall we do with the Admiral?

Sec. Man. Why, let us burn him for an heretic.

First Man. O, no! his body will infect the fire, and the fire the air, and so we shall be poisoned with him.

Sec. Man. What shall we do, then?

First Man. Let's throw him into the river.

Sec. Man. O, 'twill corrupt the water, and the water the fish, and the fish ourselves, when we eat them!

First Man. Then throw him into the ditch.

Sec. Man. No, no. To decide all doubts, be ruled by me: let's hang him here upon this tree.

First Man. Agreed.

[*They hang up the body on a tree, and then exeunt.*

Enter GUISE, CATHERINE *the Queen-Mother, and the* CARDINAL OF LORRAINE, *with* Attendants.

Guise. Now, madam, how like you our lusty Admiral?
Cath. Believe me, Guise, he becomes the place so well
As I could long ere this have wish'd him there.
But come,
Let's walk aside; the air's not very sweet.
Guise. No, by my faith, madam.—
Sirs, take him away, and throw him in some ditch.
[*The Attendants bear off the Admiral's body.*
And now, madam, as I understand,
There are a hundred Huguenots and more,
Which in the woods do hold their synagogue,
And daily meet about this time of day;
And thither will I, to put them to the sword.
Cath. Do so, sweet Guise; let us delay no time;
For, if these stragglers gather head again,
And disperse themselves throughout the realm of France,
It will be hard for us to work their deaths.
Be gone; delay no time, sweet Guise.
Guise. Madam,
I go as whirlwinds rage before a storm. [*Exit.*
Cath. My Lord of Lorraine, have you mark'd of late,
How Charles our son begins for to lament
For the late night's-work which my Lord of Guise
Did make in Paris amongst the Huguenots?
Card. Madam, I have heard him solemnly vow,
With the rebellious King of Navarre,
For to revenge their deaths upon us all.
Cath. Ay, but, my lord, let me alone for that;
For Catherine must have her will in France.
As I do live, so surely shall he die,
And Henry then shall wear the diadem;
And, if he grudge or cross his mother's will,
I'll disinherit him and all the rest;
For I'll rule France, but they shall wear the crown,
And, if they storm, I then may pull them down.
Come, my lord, let us go. [*Exeunt.*

Enter five or six Protestants, *with books, and kneel together. Then enter* GUISE *and others.*

Guise. Down with the Huguenots! murder them!
First Pro. O Monsieur de Guise, hear me but speak!

Guise. No, villain; that tongue of thine,
That hath blasphem'd the holy Church of Rome.
Shall drive no plaints into the Guise's ears,
To make the justice of my heart relent.—
Tuez, tuez, tuez! let none escape.
[*They kill the Protestants.*
So, drag them away. [*Exeunt with the bodies.*

Enter KING CHARLES, *supported by the* KING OF NAVARRE *and* EPERNOUN; CATHERINE *the Queen-Mother, the* CARDINAL OF LORRAINE, PLESHÉ, *and* Attendants.

Char. O, let me stay, and rest me here a while!
A griping pain hath seiz'd upon my heart;
A sudden pang, the messenger of death.
Cath. O, say not so! thou kill'st thy mother's heart.
Char. I must say so; pain forceth me complain.
Nav. Comfort yourself, my lord, and have no doubt
But God will sure restore you to your health.
Char. O, no, my loving brother of Navarre!
I have deserv'd a scourge, I must confess;
Yet is there patience of another sort
Than to misdo the welfare of their king:
God grant my nearest friends may prove no worse!
O, hold me up! my sight begins to fail,
My sinews shrink, my brains turn upside down;
My heart doth break: I faint and die. [*Dies.*
Cath. What, art thou dead, sweet son? speak to thy mother!
O, no, his soul is fled from out his breast,
And he nor hears nor sees us what we do!
My lords, what resteth there now for to be done,
But that we presently despatch ambassadors
To Poland, to call Henry back again,
To wear his brother's crown and dignity?
Epernoun, go see it presently be done,
And bid him come without delay to us.
Eper. Madam, I will. [*Exit.*
Cath. And now, my lords, after these funerals done,
We will, with all the speed we can, provide
For Henry's coronation from Polony.
Come, let us take his body hence.
[*The body of King Charles is borne out; and exeunt all except the King of Navarre and Pleshé.*
Nav. And now, Pleshé, whilst that these broils do last,

My opportunity may serve me fit
To steal from France, and hie me to my home,
For here's no safety in the realm for me:
And now that Henry is recall'd from Poland,
It is my due, by just succession;
And therefore, as speedily as I can perform,
I'll muster up an army secretly,
For fear that Guise, join'd with the king of Spain,
Might seek to cross me in mine enterprise.
But God, that always doth defend the right,
Will show his mercy, and preserve us still.

Pleshé. The virtues of our true religion
Cannot but march, with many graces more,
Whose army shall discomfit all your foes,
And, at the length, in Pampeluna crown
(In spite of Spain, and all the popish power,
That holds it from your highness wrongfully)
Your majesty her rightful lord and sovereign.

Nav. Truth, Pleshé; and God so prosper me in all,
As I intend to labour for the truth,
And true profession of his holy word!
Come, Pleshé, let's away whilst time doth serve.

[*Exeunt.*

Trumpets sounded within, and a cry of "Vive le Roi," two or three times. Enter ANJOU *crowned as King Henry the Third;* CATHERINE *the Queen-Mother, the* CARDINAL OF LORRAINE, GUISE, EPERNOUN, MUGEROUN, *the* Cutpurse, *and others.*

All. Vive le Roi, Vive le Roi! [*A flourish of trumpets.*

Cath. Welcome from Poland, Henry, once again!
Welcome to France, thy father's royal seat!
Here hast thou a country void of fears,
A warlike people to maintain thy right,
A watchful senate for ordaining laws,
A loving mother to preserve thy state,
And all things that a king may wish besides;
All this, and more, hath Henry with his crown.

Card. And long may Henry enjoy all this, and more!

All. Vive le Roi, Vive le Roi! [*A flourish of trumpets.*

Henry. Thanks to you all. The guider of all crowns
Grant that our deeds may well deserve your loves!
And so they shall, if fortune speed my will,

And yield your thoughts to height of my deserts.
What say our minions? think they Henry's heart
Will not both harbour love and majesty?
Put off that fear, they are already join'd:
No person, place, or time, or circumstance,
Shall slack my love's affections from his bent:
As now you are, so shall you still persist,
Removeless from the favours of your king.

Mug. We know that noble minds change not their thoughts
For wearing of a crown, in that your grace
Hath worn the Poland diadem before
You were invested in the crown of France.

Henry. I tell thee, Mugeroun, we will be friends,
And fellows too, whatever storms arise.

Mug. Then may it please your majesty to give me leave
To punish those that do profane this holy feast.

Henry. How mean'st thou that?

[*Mugeroun cuts off the Cutpurse's ear, for cutting the gold buttons off his cloak.*

Cutp. O Lord, mine ear!

Mug. Come, sir, give me my buttons, and here's your ear.

Guise. Sirrah, take him away.

Henry. Hands off, good fellow; I will be his bail
For this offence.—Go, sirrah, work no more
Till this our coronation-day be past.—
And now,
Our solemn rites of coronation done,
What now remains but for a while to feast,
And spend some days in barriers, tourney, tilt,
And like disports, such as do fit the court?
Let's go, my lords; our dinner stays for us.

[*Exeunt all except Catherine the Queen-mother and the Cardinal of Lorraine.*

Cath. My Lord Cardinal of Lorraine, tell me,
How likes your grace my son's pleasantness?
His mind, you see, runs on his minions,
And all his heaven is to delight himself;
And, whilst he sleeps securely thus in ease,
Thy brother Guise and we may now provide
To plant ourselves with such authority
As not a man may live without our leaves.
Then shall the Catholic faith of Rome
Flourish in France, and none deny the same.

Card. Madam, as in secrecy I was told,
My brother Guise hath gather'd a power of men,
Which are, he saith, to kill the Puritans;
But 'tis the house of Bourbon that he means.
Now, madam, must you insinuate with the king,
And tell him that 'tis for his country's good,
And common profit of religion.
Cath. Tush, man, let me alone with him,
To work the way to bring this thing to pass;
And, if he do deny what I do say,
I'll despatch him with his brother presently,
And then shall Monsieur wear the diadem.
Tush, all shall die unless I have my will;
For, while she lives, Catherine will be queen.
Come, my lord, let us go seek the Guise,
And then determine of this enterprise. [*Exeunt.*

Enter the DUCHESS OF GUISE *and her* Maid.

Duch. of G. Go fetch me pen and ink,—
Maid. I will, madam.
Duch. That I may write unto my dearest lord.
[*Exit Maid.*
Sweet Mugeroun, 'tis he that hath my heart,
And Guise usurps it 'cause I am his wife,
Fain would I find some means to speak with him,
But cannot, and therefore am enforc'd to write,
That he may come and meet me in some place,
Where we may one enjoy the other's sight.

Re-enter the Maid, *with pen, ink, and paper.*

So, set it down, and leave me to myself.
[*Exit Maid. The Duchess writes*
O, would to God, this quill that here doth write,
Had late been pluck'd from out fair Cupid's wing,
That it might print these lines within his heart!

Enter GUISE.

Guise. What, all alone, my love? and writing too?
I prithee, say to whom thou writ'st.
Duch. To such
A one, my lord, as, when she reads my lines,
Will laugh, I fear me, at their good array.
Guise. I pray thee, let me see.

Duch. O, no, my lord; a woman only must
Partake the secrets of my heart.
Guise. But, madam, I must see. [*Seizes the paper.*
Are these your secrets that no man must know?
Duch. O, pardon me, my lord!
Guise. Thou trothless and unjust! what lines are these?
Am I grown old, or is thy lust grown young?
Or hath my love been so obscur'd in thee,
That others need to comment on my text?
Is all my love forgot, which held thee dear,
Ay, dearer than the apple of mine eye?
Is Guise's glory but a cloudy mist,
In sight and judgment of thy lustful eye?
Mort Dieu! were not the fruit within thy womb,
Of whose increase I set some longing hope,
This wrathful hand should strike thee to the heart.
Hence, strumpet! hide thy head for shame;
And fly my presence, if thou look to live! [*Exit Duchess.*
O wicked sex, perjured and unjust!
Now do I see that from the very first
Her eyes and looks sow'd seeds of perjury.
But villain, he, to whom these lines should go,
Shall buy her love even with his dearest blood. [*Exit.*

Enter the KING OF NAVARRE, PLESHÉ, BARTUS, *and train, with drums and trumpets.*

Nav. My lords, sith in a quarrel just and right
We undertake to manage these our wars
Against the proud disturbers of the faith,
(I mean the Guise, the Pope, and king of Spain,
Who set themselves to tread us under foot,
And rent our true religion from this land;
But for you know our quarrel is no more
But to defend their strange inventions,
Which they will put us to with sword and fire,)
We must with resolute minds resolve to fight,
In honour of our God, and country's good.
Spain is the council-chamber of the Pope,
Spain is the place where he makes peace and war;
And Guise for Spain hath now incens'd the king
To send his power to meet us in the field.
Bar. Then in this bloody brunt they may behold
The sole endeavour of your princely care,

To plant the true succession of the faith,
In spite of Spain and all his heresies.

Nav. The power of vengeance now encamps itself
Upon the haughty mountains of my breast;
Plays with her gory colours of revenge,
Whom I respect as leaves of boasting green,
That change their colour when the winter comes,
When I shall vaunt as victor in revenge.

Enter a Messenger.

How now, sirrah! what news?

Mes. My lord, as by our scouts we understand,
A mighty army comes from France with speed;
Which are already muster'd in the land,
And mean to meet your highness in the field.

Nav. In God's name, let them come!
This is the Guise that hath incens'd the king
To levy arms, and make these civil broils.
But canst thou tell who is their general?

Mes. Not yet, my lord, for thereon do they stay;
But, as report doth go, the Duke of Joyeux
Hath made great suit unto the king therefore.

Nav. It will not countervail his pains, I hope.
I would the Guise in his stead might have come!
But he doth lurk within his drowsy couch,
And makes his footstool on security:
So he be safe, he cares not what becomes
Of king or country; no, not for them both.
But come, my lords, let us away with speed,
And place ourselves in order for the fight. [*Exeunt.*

Enter KING HENRY, GUISE, EPERNOUN, *and* JOYEUX.

Henry. My sweet Joyeux, I make thee general
Of all my army, now in readiness
To march 'gainst the rebellious King Navarre;
At thy request I am content thou go,
Although my love to thee can hardly suffer't,
Regarding still the danger of thy life.

Joyeux. Thanks to your majesty: and so, I take my leave.—
Farewell to my Lord of Guise, and Epernoun.

Guise. Health and hearty farewell to my Lord Joyeux.
[*Exit Joyeux.*

Henry. So kindly, cousin of Guise, you and your wife

Do both salute our lovely minions.
Remember you the letter, gentle sir,
Which your wife writ
To my dear minion, and her chosen friend?
[*Makes horns at Guise.*

Guise. How now, my lord! faith, this is more than need.
Am I thus to be jested at and scorn'd?
'Tis more than kingly or emperious:
And, sure, if all the proudest kings
In Christendom should bear me such derision,
They should know how I scorn'd them and their mocks.
I love your minions! dote on them yourself;
I know none else but holds them in disgrace;
And here, by all the saints in heaven, I swear,
That villain for whom I bear this deep disgrace,
Even for your words that have incens'd me so,
Shall buy that strumpet's favour with his blood!
Whether he have dishonour'd me or no,
Par la mort de Dieu, il mourra! [*Exit.*

Henry. Believe me, this jest bites sore.

Eper. My lord, 'twere good to make them friends,
For his oaths are seldom spent in vain.

Enter MUGEROUN.

Henry. How now, Mugeroun! met'st thou not the Guise at the door?

Mug. Not I, my lord; what if I had?

Henry. Marry, if thou hadst, thou mightst have had the stab.
For he hath solemnly sworn thy death.

Mug. I may be stabb'd, and live till he be dead:
But wherefore bears he me such deadly hate?

Henry. Because his wife bears thee such kindly love.

Mug. If that be all, the next time that I meet her,
I'll make her shake off love with her heels.
But which way is he gone? I'll go take a walk
On purpose from the court to meet with him. [*Exit.*

Henry. I like not this. Come, Epernoun,
Let us go seek the duke, and make them friends. [*Exeunt.*

Alarums, within, and a cry—" The DUKE JOYEUX *is slain."*
Enter the KING OF NAVARRE, BARTUS, *and train.*

Nav. The duke is slain, and all his power dispers'd,
And we are grac'd with wreaths of victory.

Thus God, we see, doth ever guide the right,
To make his glory great upon the earth.
Bar. The terror of this happy victory,
I hope, will make the king surcease his hate,
And either never manage army more,
Or else employ them in some better cause.
Nav. How many noblemen have lost their lives
In prosecution of these cruel arms,
Is ruth, and almost death, to call to mind.
But God we know will always put them down
That lift themselves against the perfect truth;
Which I'll maintain so long as life doth last,
And with the Queen of England join my force
To beat the papal monarch from our lands,
And keep those relics from our countries' coasts.
Come, my lords; now that this storm is overpast,
Let us away with triumph to our tents. [*Exeunt.*

Enter a Soldier.

Sold. Sir, to you, sir, that dares make the duke a cuckold, and use a counterfeit key to his privy-chamber-door; and although you take out nothing but your own, yet you put in that which displeaseth him, and so forestall his market, and set up your standing where you should not; and whereas he is your landlord, you will take upon you to be his, and till the ground that he himself should occupy, which is his own free land; if it be not too free—there's the question; and though I come not to take possession (as I would I might!) yet I mean to keep you out; which I will, if this gear hold.

Enter MUGEROUN.

What, are ye come so soon? have at ye, sir!
[*Shoots at Mugeroun and kills him.*

Enter GUISE *and* Attendants.

Guise. [*Giving a purse*] Hold thee, tall soldier, take thee this, and fly. [*Exit Soldier.*
Lie there, the king's delight, and Guise's scorn!
Revenge it, Henry, as thou list or dare;
I did it only in despite of thee.
[*Attendants bear off Mugeroun's body.*

Enter KING HENRY *and* EPERNOUN.

Henry. My Lord of Guise, we understand
That you have gathered a power of men:
What your intent is yet we cannot learn,
But we presume it is not for our good.
Guise. Why, I am no traitor to the crown of France;
What I have done, 'tis for the Gospel's sake.
Eper. Nay, for the Pope's sake, and thine own benefit.
What peer in France, but thou, aspiring Guise,
Durst be in arms without the king's consent?
I challenge thee for treason in the cause.
Guise. Ah, base Epernoun! were not his highness here,
Thou shouldst perceive the Duke of Guise is mov'd.
Henry. Be patient, Guise, and threat not Epernoun,
Lest thou perceive the king of France be mov'd.
Guise. Why, I'm a prince of the Valois line,
Therefore an enemy to the Bourbonites;
I am a juror in the holy league,
And therefore hated of the Protestants:
What should I do but stand upon my guard?
And, being able, I'll keep an host in pay.
Eper. Thou able to maintain an host in pay,
That liv'st by foreign exhibition!
The Pope and King of Spain are thy good friends;
Else all France knows how poor a duke thou art.
Henry. Ay, those are they that feed him with their gold,
To countermand our will, and check our friends.
Guise. My lord, to speak more plainly, thus it is.
Being animated by religious zeal,
I mean to muster all the power I can,
To overthrow those factious Puritans:
And know, my lord, the Pope will sell his triple crown,
Ay, and the Catholic Philip, king of Spain,
Ere I shall want, will cause his Indians
To rip the golden bowels of America.
Navarre, that cloaks them underneath his wings,
Shall feel the house of Lorraine is his foe.
Your highness needs not fear mine army's force;
'Tis for your safety, and your enemies' wreck.
Henry. Guise, wear our crown, and be thou king of France,
And, as dictator, make or war or peace,
Whilst I cry *placet*, like a senator!

I cannot brook thy haughty insolence:
Dismiss thy camp, or else by our edict
Be thou proclaim'd a traitor throughout France.

Guise. The choice is hard; I must dissemble.— [*Aside*.
My lord, in token of my true humility,
And simple meaning to your majesty,
I kiss your grace's hand, and take my leave,
Intending to dislodge my camp with speed.

Henry. Then farewell, Guise; the king and thou are friends.
[*Exit Guise*.

Eper. But trust him not, my lord; for, had your highness
Seen with what a pomp he enter'd Paris,
And how the citizens with gifts and shows
Did entertain him,
And promised to be at his command—
Nay, they fear'd not to speak in the streets,
That the Guise durst stand in arms against the king,
For not effecting of his holiness' will.

Henry. Did they of Paris entertain him so?
Then means he present treason to our state.
Well, let me alone.—Who's within there?

Enter an Attendant.

Make a discharge of all my council straight,
And I'll subscribe my name, and seal it straight.
[*Attendant writes*.
My head shall be my council; they are false;
And, Epernoun, I will be rul'd by thee.

Eper. My lord,
I think, for safety of your royal person,
It would be good the Guise were made away,
And so to quite your grace of all suspect.

Henry. First let us set our hand and seal to this,
And then I'll tell thee what I mean to do.— [*Writes*.
So; convey this to the council presently.
[*Exit Attendant*.
And, Epernoun, though I seem mild and calm,
Think not but I am tragical within.
I'll secretly convey me unto Blois;
For, now that Paris takes the Guise's part,
Here is no staying for the king of France,
Unless he mean to be betray'd and die:
But, as I live, so sure the Guise shall die. [*Exeunt*.

Enter the KING OF NAVARRE, *reading a letter, and* BARTUS.

Nav. My lord, I am advertised from France
That the Guise hath taken arms against the king,
And that Paris is revolted from his grace.
Bar. Then hath your grace fit opportunity
To show your love unto the king of France,
Offering him aid against his enemies,
Which cannot but be thankfully receiv'd.
Nav. Bartus, it shall be so: post, then, to France,
And there salute his highness in our name;
Assure him all the aid we can provide
Against the Guisians and their complices.
Bartus, be gone: commend me to his grace,
And tell him, ere it be long, I'll visit him.
Bar. I will, my lord. [*Exit.*
Nav. Pleshé!

Enter PLESHÉ.

Pleshé. My lord!
Nav. Pleshé, go muster up our men with speed,
And let them march away to France amain,
For we must aid the king against the Guise.
Be gone, I say; 'tis time that we were there.
Pleshé. I go, my lord. [*Exit.*
Nav. That wicked Guise, I fear me much will be
The ruin of that famous realm of France;
For his aspiring thoughts aim at the crown:
'A takes his vantage on religion,
To plant the Pope and Popelings in the realm,
And bind it wholly to the see of Rome.
But, if that God do prosper mine attempts,
And send us safely to arrive in France,
We'll beat him back, and drive him to his death.
That basely seeks the ruin of his realm. [*Exit.*

Enter the Captain of the Guard, *and three* Murderers.

Cap. Come on, sirs. What, are you resolutely bent,
Hating the life and honour of the Guise?
What, will you not fear, when you see him come?
First Murd. Fear him, said you? tush, were he here, we would kill him presently.
Sec. Murd. O, that his heart were leaping in my hand!

Third Murd. But when will he come, that we may murder him?
Cap. Well, then, I see you are resolute.
First Murd. Let us alone; I warrant you.
Cap. Then, sirs, take your standings within this chamber;
For anon the Guise will come.
All three Murderers. You will give us our money?
Cap. Ay, ay, fear not: stand close: so; be resolute.
[*Exeunt Murderers.*
Now falls the star whose influence governs France,
Whose light was deadly to the Protestants:
Now must he fall, and perish in his height.

Enter KING HENRY *and* EPERNOUN.

Henry. Now, captain of my guard, are these murderers ready?
Cap. They be, my good lord.
Henry. But are they resolute, and arm'd to kill,
Hating the life and honour of the Guise?
Cap. I warrant ye, my lord. [*Exit.*
Henry. Then come, proud Guise, and here disgorge thy breast,
Surcharg'd with surfeit of ambitious thoughts;
Breathe out that life wherein my death was hid,
And end thy endless treasons with thy death.
[*Knocking within.*
Guise. [*within*] *Holà, varlet, hé!*—Epernoun, where is the king?
Eper. Mounted his royal cabinet.
Guise. [*within*] I prithee, tell him that the Guise is here.
Eper. An please your grace, the Duke of Guise doth crave
Access unto your highness.
Henry. Let him come in.—
Come, Guise, and see thy traitorous guile outreach'd,
And perish in the pit thou mad'st for me.

Enter GUISE.

Guise. Good morrow to your majesty.
Henry. Good morrow to my loving cousin of Guise:
How fares it this morning with your excellence?
Guise. I heard your majesty was scarcely pleas'd,
That in the court I bare so great a train.
Henry. They were to blame that said I was displeas'd;

And you, good cousin, to imagine it.
'Twere hard with me, if I should doubt my kin,
Or be suspicious of my dearest friends.
Cousin, assure you I am resolute,
Whatsoever any whisper in mine ears,
Not to suspect disloyalty in thee:
And so, sweet coz, farewell. [*Exit with Epernoun*

Guise. So;
Now sues the king for favour to the Guise,
And all his minions stoop when I command:
Why, this 'tis to have an army in the field.
Now, by the holy sacrament, I swear,
As ancient Romans o'er their captive lords,
So will I triumph o'er this wanton king;
And he shall follow my proud chariot's wheels.
Now do I but begin to look about,
And all my former time was spent in vain.
Hold, sword,
For in thee is the Duke of Guise's hope.

Re-enter Third Murderer.

Villain, why dost thou look so ghastly? speak.

Third Murd. O, pardon me, my Lord of Guise!

Guise. Pardon thee! why, what hast thou done?

Third Murd. O my lord, I am one of them that is set to murder you!

Guise. To murder me, villain!

Third Murd. Ay, my lord: the rest have ta'en their standings in the next room; therefore, good my lord, go not forth.

Guise. Yet Cæsar shall go forth.
Let mean conceits and baser men fear death:
Tut, they are peasants; I am Duke of Guise;
And princes with their looks engender fear.

First Murd. [*within*] Stand close; he is coming; I know him by his voice.

Guise. As pale as ashes! nay, then, it is time
To look about.

Enter First *and* Second Murderers.

First and Sec. Murderers. Down with him, down with him! [*They stab Guise.*

Guise. O, I have my death's wound! give me leave to speak.

Sec. Murd. Then pray to God, and ask forgiveness of the king.
Guise. Trouble me not; I ne'er offended him,
Nor will I ask forgiveness of the king.
O, that I have not power to stay my life,
Nor immortality to be reveng'd!
To die by peasants, what a grief is this!
Ah, Sixtus, be reveng'd upon the king!
Philip and Parma, I am slain for you!
Pope, excommunicate, Philip, depose
The wicked branch of curs'd Valois his line!
Vive la messe! perish Huguenots!
Thus Cæsar did go forth, and thus he died. [*Dies.*

Enter the Captain of the Guard.

Cap. What, have you done?
Then stay a while, and I'll go call the king.
But see, where he comes.

Enter KING HENRY, EPERNOUN, *and* Attendants.

My lord, see, where the Guise is slain.
Henry. Ah, this sweet sight is physic to my soul!
Go fetch his son for to behold his death.—
[*Exit an Attendant.*
Surcharg'd with guilt of thousand massacres,
Monsieur of Lorraine, sink away to hell!
And, in remembrance of those bloody broils,
To which thou didst allure me, being alive.
And here in presence of you all, I swear,
I ne'er was king of France until this hour.
This is the traitor that hath spent my gold
In making foreign wars and civil broils.
Did he not draw a sort of English priests
From Douay to the seminary at Rheims.
To hatch forth treason 'gainst their natural queen?
Did he not cause the king of Spain's huge fleet
To threaten England, and to menace me?
Did he not injure Monsieur that's deceas'd?
Hath he not made me, in the Pope's defence,
To spend the treasure, that should strength my land,
In civil broils between Navarre and me?
Tush, to be short, he meant to make me monk,
Or else to murder me, and so be king.

Let Christian princes, that shall hear of this,
(As all the world shall know our Guise is dead),
Rest satisfied with this, that here I swear,
Ne'er was there king of France so yok'd as I.

Eper. My lord, here is his son.

Enter GUISE'S Son.

Henry. Boy, look, where your father lies.

G.'s Son. My father slain! who hath done this deed?

Henry. Sirrah, 'twas I that slew him; and will slay
Thee too, an thou prove such a traitor.

G.'s Son. Art thou king, and hast done this bloody deed?
I'll be reveng'd. [*Offers to throw his dagger.*

Henry. Away to prison with him! I'll clip his wings
Or e'er he pass my hands. Away with him.
[*Some of the Attendants bear off Guise's Son.*
But what availeth that this traitor's dead,
When Duke Dumaine, his brother, is alive,
And that young cardinal that is grown so proud?
Go to the governor of Orleans,
And will him, in my name, to kill the duke.
[*To the Captain of the Guard.*
Get you away, and strangle the cardinal.
[*To the Murderers.*
[*Exeunt Captain of the Guard and Murderers.*
These two will make one entire Duke of Guise,
Especially with our old mother's help.

Eper. My lord, see, where she comes, as if she droop'd
To hear these news.

Henry. And let her droop; my heart is light enough.

Enter CATHERINE *the* QUEEN-MOTHER.

Mother, how like you this device of mine?
I slew the Guise, because I would be king.

Cath. King! why, so thou wert before:
Pray God thou be a king now this is done!

Henry. Nay, he was king, and countermanded me:
But now I will be king, and rule myself,
And make the Guisians stoop that are alive.

Cath. I cannot speak for grief.—When thou wast born,
I would that I had murder'd thee, my son!
My son! thou art a changeling, not my son:
I curse thee, and exclaim thee miscreant,

Traitor to God and to the realm of France!

Henry. Cry out, exclaim, howl till thy throat be hoarse!
The Guise is slain, and I rejoice therefore:
And now will I to arms.—Come, Epernoun,
And let her grieve her heart out, if she will.
[*Exit with Epernoun.*

Cath. Away! leave me alone to meditate.
[*Exeunt Attendants.*
Sweet Guise, would he had died, so thou wert here!
To whom shall I bewray my secrets now,
Or who will help to build religion?
The Protestants will glory and insult;
Wicked Navarre will get the crown of France;
The Popedom cannot stand; all goes to wreck;
And all for thee, my Guise! What may I do?
But sorrow seize upon my toiling soul!
For, since the Guise is dead, I will not live. [*Exit.*

Enter two Murderers, *dragging in the* CARDINAL.

Card. Murder me not; I am a cardinal.

First Murd. Wert thou the Pope, thou mightst not 'scape from us.

Card. What, will you file your hands with churchmen's blood?

Sec. Murd. Shed your blood! O Lord, no! for we intend to strangle you.

Card. Then there is no remedy, but I must die?

First Murd. No remedy; therefore prepare yourself.

Card. Yet lives my brother Duke Dumaine, and many more,
To revenge our death upon that cursed king;
Upon whose heart may all the Furies gripe,
And with their paws drench his black soul in hell!

First Murd. Yours, my Lord Cardinal, you should have said.— [*They strangle him.*
So, pluck amain:
He is hard-hearted; therefore pull with violence.
Come, take him away. [*Exeunt with the body.*

Enter DUMAINE, *reading a letter; with others.*

Dum. My noble brother murder'd by the king!
O, what may I do for to revenge thy death?
The king's alone, it cannot satisfy.
Sweet Duke of Guise, our prop to lean upon,
Now thou art dead, here is no stay for us.

I am thy brother, and I'll revenge thy death,
And root Valois his line from forth of France;
And beat proud Bourbon to his native home,
That basely seeks to join with such a king,
Whose murderous thoughts will be his overthrow.
He will'd the governor of Orleans, in his name,
That I with speed should have been put to death;
But that's prevented, for to end his life,
And all those traitors to the Church of Rome
That durst attempt to murder noble Guise.

Enter Friar.

Fri. My lord, I come to bring you news that your brother the Cardinal of Lorraine, by the king's consent, is lately strangled to death.

Dum. My brother [the] Cardinal slain, and I alive?
O words of power to kill a thousand men!—
Come, let us away, and levy men;
'Tis war that must assuage this tyrant's pride.

Fri. My lord, hear me but speak.
I am a friar of the order of the Jacobins,
That for my conscience' sake will kill the king.

Dum. But what doth move thee, above the rest, to do the deed?

Fri. O, my lord, I have been a great sinner in my days! and the deed is meritorious.

Dum. But how wilt thou get opportunity?

Fri. Tush, my lord, let me alone for that.

Dum. Friar, come with me;
We will go talk more of this within. [*Exeunt.*

Drums and Trumpets. Enter KING HENRY, *the* KING OF NAVARRE, EPERNOUN, BARTUS, PLESHÉ, Soldiers, *and* Attendants.

Henry. Brother of Navarre, I sorrow much
That ever I was prov'd your enemy,
And that the sweet and princely mind you bear
Was ever troubled with injurious wars.
I vow, as I am lawful King of France,
To recompense your reconciled love
With all the honours and affections
That ever I vouchsaf'd my dearest friends.

Nav. It is enough if that Navarre may be

Esteemed faithful to the King of France,
Whose service he may still command till death.
Henry. Thanks to my kingly brother of Navarre.
Then here we'll lie before Lutetia walls,
Girting this strumpet city with our siege,
Till, surfeiting with our afflicting arms,
She cast her hateful stomach to the earth.

Enter a Messenger.

Mes. An it please your majesty, here is a friar of the order of the Jacobins, sent from the President of Paris, that craves access unto your grace.
Henry. Let him come in. [*Exit Mess.*

Enter Friar, *with a letter.*

Eper. I like not this friar's look:
'Twere not amiss, my lord, if he were search'd.
Henry. Sweet Epernoun, our friars are holy men,
And will not offer violence to their king,
For all the wealth and treasure of the world.—
Friar, thou dost acknowledge me thy king?
Fri. Ay, my good lord, and will die therein.
Henry. Then come thou near, and tell what news thou bring'st.
Fri. My lord,
The President of Paris greets your grace
And sends his duty by these speedy lines,
Humbly craving your gracious reply. [*Gives letter.*
Henry. I'll read them, friar, and then I'll answer thee.
Fri. *Sancte Jacobe*, now have mercy upon me!
[*Stabs the king with a knife, as he reads the letter; and then the king gets the knife, and kills him.*
Eper. O, my lord, let him live a while!
Henry. No, let the villain die, and feel in hell
Just torments for his treachery.
Nav. What, is your highness hurt?
Henry. Yes, Navarre; but not to death, I hope.
Nav. God shield your grace from such a sudden death!—
Go call a surgeon hither straight.
[*Exit an Attendant.*
Henry. What irreligious pagans' parts be these,
Of such as hold them of the holy church!

Take hence that damned villain from my sight.
[*Attendants carry out the Friar's body.*

Eper. Ah, had your highness let him live,
We might have punish'd him to his deserts!

Henry. Sweet Epernoun, all rebels under heaven
Shall take example by his punishment,
How they bear arms against their sovereign.—
Go call the English agent hither straight:
[*Exit an Attendant.*
I'll send my sister England news of this,
And give her warning of her treacherous foes.

Enter a Surgeon.

Nav. Pleaseth your grace to let the surgeon search your wound?

Henry. The wound, I warrant ye, is deep, my lord.—
Search, surgeon, and resolve me what thou see'st.
[*The Surgeon searches the wound.*

Enter the English Agent.

Agent for England, send thy mistress word
What this detested Jacobin hath done.
Tell her, for all this, that I hope to live;
Which if I do, the papal monarch goes
To wreck, and [th'] antichristian kingdom falls:
These bloody hands shall tear his triple crown,
And fire accursed Rome about his ears;
I'll fire his crazed buildings, and enforce
The papal towers to kiss the lowly earth.—
Navarre, give me thy hand: I here do swear
To ruinate that wicked Church of Rome,
That hatcheth up such bloody practices;
And here protest eternal love to thee,
And to the Queen of England specially,
Whom God hath bless'd for hating papistry.

Nav. These words revive my thoughts, and comfort me,
To see your highness in this virtuous mind,

Henry. Tell me, surgeon, shall I live?

Surg. Alas, my lord, the wound is dangerous,
For you are stricken with a poison'd knife!

Henry. A poison'd knife! what, shall the French king die,
Wounded and poison'd both at once?

Eper. O, that
That damned villain were alive again,
That we might torture him with some new-found death!
Bar. He died a death too good:
The devil of hell torture his wicked soul!
Henry. Ah, curse him not, sith he is dead!—
O, the fatal poison works within my breast!—
Tell me, surgeon, and flatter not—may I live?
Surg. Alas, my lord, your highness cannot live!
Nav. Surgeon, why say'st thou so? the king may live.
Henry. O, no, Navarre! thou must be king of France!
Nav. Long may you live, and still be King of France.
Eper. Or else, die Epernoun!
Henry. Sweet Epernoun, thy king must die.—My lords,
Fight in the quarrel of this valiant prince,
For he's your lawful king, and my next heir;
Valois's line ends in my tragedy.
Now let the house of Bourbon wear the crown;
And may it ne'er end in blood, as mine hath done!—
Weep not, sweet Navarre, but revenge my death.—
Ah, Epernoun, is this thy love to me?
Henry, thy king, wipes off these childish tears,
And bids thee whet thy sword on Sixtus' bones,
That it may keenly slice the Catholics.
He loves me not [the most] that sheds most tears,
But he that makes most lavish of his blood.
Fire Paris, where these treacherous rebels lurk.—
I die, Navarre; come bear me to my sepulchre.
Salute the Queen of England in my name,
And tell her, Henry dies her faithful friend. [*Dies.*
Nav. Come, lords, take up the body of the king,
That we may see it honourably interr'd:
And then I vow so to revenge his death
As Rome, and all those popish prelates there,
Shall curse the time that e'er Navarre was king,
And rul'd in France by Henry's fatal death.
[*They march out, with the body of King Henry lying on four men's shoulders, with a dead march, drawing weapons on the ground.*

THE TRAGEDY OF

DIDO, QUEEN OF CARTHAGE

DRAMATIS PERSONÆ

JUPITER.
GANYMEDE.
HERMES.
CUPID.

JUNO.
VENUS.

ÆNEAS.
ASCANIUS, *his son.*
ACHATES.

ILIONEUS.
CLOANTHUS.
SERGESTUS.
OTHER TROJANS.
IARBAS.
CARTHAGINIAN LORDS.

DIDO.
ANNA, *her sister.*
NURSE.

ACT I

Here the curtains draw: there is discovered JUPITER *dandling* GANYMEDE *upon his knee, and* HERMES *lying asleep.*

Jup. Come, gentle Ganymede, and play with me;
I love thee well, say Juno what she will.
Gan. I am much better for your worthless love,
That will not shield me from her shrewish blows!
To day, whenas I fill'd into your cups,
And held the cloth of pleasance whiles you drank,
She reach'd me such a rap for that I spill'd,
As made the blood run down about mine ears.
Jup. What, dares she strike the darling of my thoughts?
By Saturn's soul, and this earth-threatening hair,
That, shaken thrice, makes nature's buildings quake,
I vow, if she but once frown on thee more,
To hang her, meteor like, 'twixt heaven and earth,
And bind her, hand and foot, with golden cords,
As once I did for harming Hercules!
Gan. Might I but see that pretty sport a-foot,
O, how would I with Helen's brother laugh,

And bring the gods to wonder at the game!
Sweet Jupiter, if e'er I pleas'd thine eye,
Or seemed fair, wall'd-in with eagle's wings,
Grace my immortal beauty with this boon,
And I will spend my time in thy bright arms.
Jup. What is't, sweet wag, I should deny thy youth?
Whose face reflects such pleasure to mine eyes,
As I, exhal'd with thy fire-darting beams,
Have oft driven back the horses of the Night,
Whenas they would have hal'd thee from my sight.
Sit on my knee, and call for thy content,
Control proud Fate, and cut the thread of Time:
Why, are not all the gods at thy command,
And heaven and earth the bounds of thy delight?
Vulcan shall dance to make thee laughing sport,
And my nine daughters sing when thou art sad;
From Juno's bird I'll pluck her spotted pride,
To make thee fans wherewith to cool thy face;
And Venus' swans shall shed their silver down,
To sweeten out the slumbers of thy bed;
Hermes no more shall show the world his wings,
If that thy fancy in his feathers dwell,
But, as this one, I'll tear them all from him.
[*Plucks a feather from Hermes' wings.*
Do thou but say, "their colour pleaseth me."
Hold here, my little love; these linked gems
[*Gives jewels.*
My Juno ware upon her marriage-day,
Put thou about thy neck, my own sweet heart,
And trick thy arms and shoulders with my theft.
Gan. I would have a jewel for mine ear,
And a fine brooch to put in my hat,
And then I'll hug with you an hundred times.
Jup. And shalt have, Ganymede, if thou wilt be my love.

Enter VENUS.

Ven. Ay, this is it: you can sit toying there,
And playing with that female wanton boy,
Whiles my Æneas wanders on the seas,
And rests a prey to every billow's pride.
Juno, false Juno, in her chariot's pomp,
Drawn through the heavens by steeds of Boreas' brood,
Made Hebe to direct her airy wheels

Into the windy country of the clouds;
Where, finding Æolus entrench'd with storms,
And guarded with a thousand grisly ghosts,
She humbly did beseech him for our bane,
And charg'd him drown my son with all his train.
Then gan the winds break ope their brazen doors,
And all Æolia to be up in arms:
Poor Troy must now be sack'd upon the sea,
And Neptune's waves be envious men of war;
Epeus' horse, to Ætna's hill transform'd,
Prepared stands to wreck their wooden walls;
And Æolus, like Agamemnon, sounds
The surges, his fierce soldiers, to the spoil:
See how the night, Ulysses-like, comes forth,
And intercepts the day, as Dolon erst!
Ay, me! the stars suppris'd, like Rhesus' steeds,
Are drawn by darkness forth Astræus' tents.
What shall I do to save thee, my sweet boy?
Whenas the waves do threat our crystal world,
And Proteus, raising hills of floods on high,
Intends, ere long, to sport him in the sky.
False Jupiter, reward'st thou virtue so?
What, is not piety exempt from woe?
Then die, Æneas, in thine innocence,
Since that religion hath no recompense.

Jup. Content thee, Cytherea, in thy care,
Since thy Æneas' wandering fate is firm,
Whose weary limbs shall shortly make repose
In those fair walls I promis'd him of yore.
But, first, in blood must his good fortune bud,
Before he be the lord of Turnus' town,
Or force her smile that hitherto hath frown'd:
Three winters shall he with the Rutiles war,
And, in the end, subdue them with his sword;
And full three summers likewise shall he waste
In managing those fierce barbarian minds;
Which once perform'd, poor Troy, so long suppress'd,
From forth her ashes shall advance her head,
And flourish once again, that erst was dead.
But bright Ascanius, beauty's better work,
Who with the sun divides one radiant shape,
Shall build his throne amidst those starry towers
That earth-born Atlas, groaning, underprops:

No bounds, but heaven, shall bound his empery,
Whose azur'd gates enchased with his name,
Shall make the Morning haste her grey uprise,
To feed her eyes with his engraven fame.
Thus, in stout Hector's race, three hundred years
The Roman sceptre royal shall remain,
Till that a princess-priest conceiv'd by Mars,
Shall yield to dignity a double birth,
Who will eternish Troy in their attempts.

Ven. How may I credit these thy flattering terms,
When both sea and sands beset their ships,
And Phœbus, as in Stygian pools, refrains
To taint his tresses in the Tyrrhene main?

Jup. I will take order for that presently.—
Hermes, awake! and haste to Neptune's realm,
Whereas the wind-god, warring now with fate,
Beseige[s] th' offspring of our kingly loins:
Charge him from me to turn his stormy powers,
And fetter them in Vulcan's sturdy brass,
That durst thus proudly wrong our kinsman's peace.
[*Exit Hermes.*
Venus, farewell; thy son shall be our care.—
Come, Ganymede, we must about this gear.
[*Exeunt Jupiter and Ganymede.*

Ven. Disquiet seas, lay down your swelling looks,
And court Æneas with your calmy cheer,
Whose beauteous burden well might make you proud,
Had not the heavens, conceived with hell-born clouds,
Veil'd his resplendent glory from your view:
For my sake, pity him, Oceanus,
That erstwhile issu'd from thy watery loins,
And had my being from thy bubbling froth.
Triton, I know, hath fill'd his trump with Troy,
And therefore will take pity on his toil,
And call both Thetis and Cymodoce
To succour him in this extremity.

Enter ÆNEAS, ASCANIUS, ACHATES, *and others.*

What, do I see my son now come on shore?
Venus, how art thou compass'd with content,
The while thine eyes attract their sought-for joys!
Great Jupiter, still honour'd may'st thou be
For this so friendly aid in time of need!

Here in this bush disguised will I stand,
Whiles my Æneas spends himself in plaints,
And heaven and earth with his unrest acquaints.

Æn. You sons of care, companions of my course,
Priam's misfortune follows us by sea,
And Helen's rape doth haunt ye at the heels.
How many dangers have we overpass'd!
Both barking Scylla, and the sounding rocks,
The Cyclops' shelves, and grim Ceraunia's seat.
Have you o'ergone, and yet remain alive.
Pluck up your hearts, since Fate still rests our friend,
And changing heavens may those good days return.
Which Pergama did vaunt in all her pride.

Ach. Brave prince of Troy, thou only art our god,
That by thy virtues free'st us from annoy,
And mak'st our hopes survive to coming joys:
Do thou but smile, and cloudy heaven will clear,
Whose night and day descendeth from thy brows.
Though we be now in extreme misery,
And rest the map of weather-beaten woe,
Yet shall the aged sun shed forth his hair,
To make us live unto our former heat,
And every beast the forest doth send forth
Bequeath her young ones to our scanted food.

Asc. Father, I faint; good father, give me meat.

Æn. Alas, sweet boy, thou must be still a while.
Till we have fire to dress the meat we kill'd!—
Gentle Achates, reach the tinder box,
That we may make a fire to warm us with,
And roast our new found victuals on this shore.

Ven. See, what strange arts necessity finds out!
How near, my sweet Æneas, art thou driven! [*Aside.*

Æn. Hold; take this candle, and go light a fire;
You shall have leaves and windfall boughs enow,
Near to these woods, to roast you meat withal.—
Ascanius, go and dry thy drenched limbs,
Whiles I with my Achates rove abroad,
To know what coast the wind hath driven us on,
Or whether men or beasts inhabit it.
[*Exeunt Ascanius and others.*

Ach. The air is pleasant, and the soil most fit
For cities and society's supports;
Yet much I marvel that I cannot find

No steps of men imprinted in the earth.
Ven. Now is the time for me to play my part.— [*Aside.*
Ho, young men! saw you, as you came,
Any of all my sisters wandering here,
Having a quiver girded to her side,
And clothed in a spotted leopard's skin?
Æn. I neither saw nor heard of any such.
But what may I, fair virgin, call your name,
Whose looks set forth no mortal form to view,
Nor speech bewrays aught human in thy birth?
Thou art a goddess that delud'st our eyes,
And shroud'st thy beauty in this borrow'd shape;
But whether thou the Sun's bright sister be,
Or one of chaste Diana's fellow nymphs,
Live happy in the height of all content,
And lighten our extremes with this one boon,
As to instruct us under what good heaven
We breathe as now, and what this world is call'd
On which by tempests' fury we are cast:
Tell us, O, tell us, that are ignorant!
And this right hand shall make thy altars crack
With mountain-heaps of milk-white sacrifice.
Ven. Such honour, stranger, do I not affect:
It is the use for Tyrian maids to wear
Their bow and quiver in this modest sort,
And suit themselves in purple for the nonce,
That they may trip more lightly o'er the lawnds,
And overtake the tusked boar in chase.
But for the land whereof thou dost inquire,
It is the Punic kingdom, rich and strong,
Adjoining on Agenor's stately town,
The kingly seat of Southern Libya,
Whereas Sidonian Dido rules as queen.
But what are you that ask of me these things?
Whence may you come, or whither will you go?
Æn. Of Troy am I, Æneas is my name;
Who, driven by war from forth my native world,
Put sails to sea to seek out Italy;
And my divine descent from sceptred Jove:
With twice twelve Phrygian ships I plough'd the deep,
And made that way my mother Venus led;
But of all them scarce seven do anchor safe,
And they so wrack'd and welter'd by the waves,

As every tide tilts 'twixt their oaken sides;
And all of them, unburden'd of their load,
Are ballassed with billows' watery weight.
But hapless I, God wot, poor and unknown,
Do trace these Libyan deserts, all despis'd,
Exil'd forth Europe and wide Asia both,
And have not any coverture but heaven.

Ven. Fortune hath favour'd thee, whate'er thou be,
In sending thee unto this courteous coast.
A' God's name, on! and haste thee to the court,
Where Dido will receive ye with her smiles:
And for thy ships, which thou supposest lost,
Not one of them hath perish'd in the storm,
But are arrived safe, not far from hence:
And so, I leave thee to thy fortune's lot,
Wishing good luck unto thy wandering steps. [*Exit.*

Æn. Achates, 'tis my mother that is fled;
I know her by the movings of her feet.—
Stay, gentle Venus, fly not from thy son!
Too cruel, why wilt thou forsake me thus,
Or in these shades deceiv'st mine eyes so oft?
Why talk we not together hand in hand,
And tell our griefs in more familiar terms?
But thou art gone, and leav'st me here alone
To dull the air with my discoursive moan. [*Exeunt.*

Enter IARBAS, *followed by* ILIONEUS, CLOANTHUS, SERGESTUS, *and others.*

Ili. Follow, ye Trojans, follow this brave lord,
And plain to him the sum of your distress.

Iar. Why, what are you, or wherefore do you sue?

Ili. Wretches of Troy, envied of all the winds,
That crave such favour at your honour's feet,
As poor distressed misery may plead:
Save, save, O, save our ships from cruel fire,
That do complain the wounds of thousand waves,
And spare our lives, whom every spite pursues!
We come not, we, to wrong your Libyan gods,
Or steal your household Lares from their shrines;
Our hands are not prepar'd to lawless spoil,
Nor armed to offend in any kind;
Such force is far from our unweapon'd thoughts,
Whose fading weal, of victory forsook,

Forbids all hope to harbour near our hearts.
Iar. But tell me, Trojans, Trojans if you be,
Unto what fruitful quarters were ye bound,
Before that Boreas buckled with your sails?
Clo. There is a place, Hesperia term'd by us,
An ancient empire, famoused for arms,
And fertile in fair Ceres' furrow'd wealth,
Which now we call Italia, of his name
That in such peace long time did rule the same.
Thither made we;
When, suddenly, gloomy Orion rose,
And led our ships into the shallow sands,
Whereas the southern wind with brackish breath,
Dispers'd them all amongst the wreckful rocks:
From thence a few of us escap'd to land;
The rest, we fear, are folded in the floods.
Iar. Brave men-at-arms, abandon fruitless fears,
Since Carthage knows to entertain distress.
Serg. Ay, but the barbarous sort do threat our steps,
And will not let us lodge upon the sands;
In multitudes they swarm unto the shore,
And from the first earth interdict our feet.
Iar. Myself will see they shall not trouble ye:
Your men and you shall banquet in our court,
And every Trojan be as welcome here
As Jupiter to silly Baucis' house.
Come in with me; I'll bring you to my queen.
Who shall confirm my words with further deeds.
Serg. Thanks, gentle lord, for such unlook'd-for grace:
Might we but once more see Æneas' face,
Then would we hope to quite such friendly turns,
As shall surpass the wonder of our speech. [*Exeunt.*

ACT II

Enter ÆNEAS, ACHATES, ASCANIUS, *and others.*

Æn. Where am I now? these should be Carthage walls.
Ach. Why stands my sweet Æneas thus amaz'd?
Æn. O my Achates, Theban Niobe,
Who for her sons' death wept out life and breath,
And, dry with grief, was turn'd into a stone,
Had not such passions in her head as I!

Methinks,
That town there should be Troy, yon Ida's hill,
There Xanthus' stream, because here's Priamus;
And when I know it is not, then I die.

Ach. And in this humour is Achates too;
I cannot choose but fall upon my knees,
And kiss his hand. O, where is Hecuba?
Here she was wont to sit; but, saving air,
Is nothing here; and what is this but stone?

Æn. O, yet this stone doth make Æneas weep!
And would my prayers (as Pygmalion's did)
Could give it life, that under his conduct
We might sail back to Troy, and be reveng'd
On these hard-hearted Grecians which rejoice
That nothing now is left of Priamus!
O, Priamus is left, and this is he!
Come, come aboard; pursue the hateful Greeks.

Ach. What means Æneas?

Æn. Achates, though mine eyes say this is stone,
Yet thinks my mind that this is Priamus;
And when my grieved heart sighs and says no,
Then would it leap out to give Priam life.—
O, were I not at all, so thou mightst be!—
Achates, see, King Priam wags his hand!
He is alive; Troy is not overcome!

Ach. Thy mind, Æneas, that would have it so,
Deludes thy eyesight; Priamus is dead.

Æn. Ah, Troy is sack'd, and Priamus is dead!
And why should poor Æneas be alive?

Asc. Sweet father, leave to weep; this is not he,
For, were it Priam, he would smile on me.

Ach. Æneas, see, here come the citizens:
Leave to lament, lest they laugh at our fears.

Enter CLOANTHUS, SERGESTUS, ILIONEUS, *and others.*

Æn. Lords of this town, or whatsoever style
Belongs unto your name, vouchsafe of ruth
To tell us who inhabits this fair town,
What kind of people, and who governs them;
For we are strangers driven on this shore,
And scarcely know within what clime we are.

Ili. I hear Æneas' voice, but see him not,
For none of these can be our general.

Ach. Like Ilioneus, speaks this nobleman,
But Ilioneus goes not in such robes.
Serg. You are Achates, or I [am] deceiv'd.
Ach. Æneas, see, Sergestus, or his ghost!
Ili. He names Æneas; let us kiss his feet.
Clo. It is our captain; see, Ascanius!
Serg. Live long Æneas and Ascanius!
Æn. Achates, speak, for I am overjoy'd.
Ach. O Ilioneus, art thou yet alive?
Ili. Blest be the time I see Achates' face!
Clo. Why turns Æneas from his trusty friends?
Æn. Sergestus, Ilioneus, and the rest,
Your sight amaz'd me. O, what destinies
Have brought my sweet companions in such plight?
O, tell me, for I long to be resolv'd!
Ili. Lovely Æneas, these are Carthage walls;
And here Queen Dido wears th' imperial crown.
Who for Troy's sake hath entertain'd us all,
And clad us in these wealthy robes we wear.
Oft hath she ask'd us under whom we serv'd;
And, when we told her, she would weep for grief,
Thinking the sea had swallow'd up thy ships;
And, now she sees thee, how will she rejoice!
Serg. See, where her servitors pass through the hall
Bearing a banquet: Dido is not far.
Ili. Look, where she comes; Æneas, view her well.
Æn. Well may I view her; but she sees not me.

Enter DIDO, ANNA, IARBAS, *and train.*

Dido. What stranger art thou, that dost eye me thus?
Æn. Sometime I was a Trojan, mighty queen;
But Troy is not:—what shall I say I am?
Ili. Renowmed Dido, 'tis our general,
Warlike Æneas.
Dido. Warlike Æneas, and in these base robes!—
Go fetch the garment which Sichæus ware.—
[*Exit an Attendant who brings in the garment, which Æneas puts on.*
Brave prince, welcome to Carthage and to me,
Both happy that Æneas is our guest.
Sit in this chair, and banquet with a queen:
Æneas is Æneas, were he clad
In weeds as bad as ever Irus ware.

Æn. This is no seat for one that's comfortless:
May it please your grace to let Æneas wait;
For though my birth be great, my fortune's mean,
Too mean to be companion to a queen.
Dido. Thy fortune may be greater than thy birth:
Sit down, Æneas, sit in Dido's place;
And, if this be thy son, as I suppose,
Here let him sit.—Be merry, lovely child.
Æn. This place beseems me not; O pardon me!
Dido. I'll have it so; Æneas, be content.
Asc. Madam, you shall be my mother.
Dido. And so I will, sweet child.—Be merry, man:
Here's to thy better fortune and good stars. [*Drinks*
Æn. In all humility, I thank your grace.
Dido. Remember who thou art; speak like thyself:
Humility belongs to common grooms.
Æn. And who so miserable as Æneas is?
Dido. Lies it in Dido's hands to make thee blest?
Then be assur'd thou art not miserable.
Æn. O Priamus, O Troy, O Hecuba!
Dido. May I entreat thee to discourse at large,
And truly too, how Troy was overcome?
For many tales go of that city's fall,
And scarcely do agree upon one point:
Some say Antenor did betray the town;
Others report 'twas Sinon's perjury;
But all in this, that Troy is overcome,
And Priam dead; yet how, we hear no news.
Æn. A woeful tale bids Dido to unfold,
Whose memory, like pale Death's stony mace,
Beats forth my senses from this troubled soul,
And makes Æneas sink at Dido's feet.
Dido. What, faints Æneas to remember Troy,
In whose defence he fought so valiantly?
Look up, and speak.
Æn. Then speak, Æneas, with Achilles' tongue:
And, Dido, and you Carthaginian peers,
Hear me; but yet with Myrmidons' harsh ears,
Daily inur'd to broils and massacres,
Lest you be mov'd too much with my sad tale.
The Grecian soldiers, tir'd with ten years' war,
Began to cry, "Let us unto our ships,
Troy is invincible, why stay we here?"

With whose outcries Atrides being appall'd,
Summon'd the captains to his princely tent;
Who, looking on the scars we Trojans gave,
Seeing the number of their men decreas'd,
And the remainder weak and out of heart,
Gave up their voices to dislodge the camp,
And so in troops all march'd to Tenedos:
Where when they came, Ulysses on the sand
Assay'd with honey words to turn them back;
And, as he spoke, to further his intent,
The winds did drive huge billows to the shore,
And heaven was darken'd with tempestuous clouds;
Then he alleg'd the gods would have them stay,
And prophesied Troy should be overcome:
And therewithal he call'd false Sinon forth,
A man compact of craft and perjury,
Whose ticing tongue was made of Hermes' pipe,
To force an hundred watchful eyes to sleep;
And him, Epeus having made the horse,
With sacrificing wreaths upon his head,
Ulysses sent to our unhappy town;
Who, grovelling in the mire of Xanthus' banks,
His hands bound at his back, and both his eyes
Turn'd up to heaven, as one resolv'd to die,
Our Phrygian shepherd[s] hal'd within the gates,
And brought unto the court of Priamus;
To whom he us'd action so pitiful,
Looks so remorseful, vows so forcible,
As therewithal the old man overcome,
Kiss'd him, embrac'd him, and unloos'd his bands:
And then—O Dido, pardon me!

Dido. Nay, leave not here; resolve me of the rest.

Æn. O, the enchanting words of that base slave
Made him to think Epeus' pine-tree horse
A sacrifice t' appease Minerva's wrath!
The rather, for that one Laocoon,
Breaking a spear upon his hollow breast,
Was with two winged serpents stung to death.
Whereat aghast, we were commanded straight
With reverence to draw it into Troy:
In which unhappy work was I employ'd;
These hands did help to hale it to the gates,
Through which it could not enter, 'twas so huge,—

O, had it never enter'd, Troy had stood!
But Priamus, impatient of delay,
Enforc'd a wide breach in that rampir'd wall
Which thousand battering-rams could never pierce,
And so came in this fatal instrument:
At whose accursed feet, as overjoy'd,
We banqueted, till, overcome with wine,
Some surfeited, and others soundly slept.
Which Sinon viewing, caus'd the Greekish spies
To haste to Tenedos, and tell the camp:
Then he unlock'd the horse; and suddenly,
From out his entrails, Neoptolemus,
Setting his spear upon the ground, leapt forth,
And, after him, a thousand Grecians more,
In whose stern faces shin'd the quenchless fire
That after burnt the pride of Asia.
By this, the camp was come unto the walls,
And through the breach did march into the streets,
Where, meeting with the rest, " Kill, kill! " they cried.
Frighted with this confused noise, I rose,
And, looking from a turret, might behold
Young infants swimming in their parents' blood,
Headless carcasses piled up in heaps,
Virgins half-dead, dragg'd by their golden hair,
And with main force flung on a ring of pikes,
Old men with swords thrust through their aged sides,
Kneeling for mercy to a Greekish lad,
Who with steel pole-axes dash'd out their brains.
Then buckled I mine armour, drew my sword.
And thinking to go down, came Hector's ghost,
With ashy visage, blueish sulphur eyes,
His arms torn from his shoulders, and his breast
Furrow'd with wounds, and, that which made me weep,
Thongs at his heels, by which Achilles' horse
Drew him in triumph through the Greekish camp,
Burst from the earth, crying " Æneas, fly!
Troy is a-fire, the Grecians have the town! "

Dido. O Hector, who weeps not to hear thy name?

Æn. Yet flung I forth, and, desperate of my life,
Ran in the thickest throngs, and with this sword
Sent many of their savage ghosts to hell.
At last came Pyrrhus, fell and full of ire,
His harness dropping blood, and on his spear

The mangled head of Priam's youngest son;
And, after him, his band of Myrmidons,
With balls of wild-fire in their murdering paws,
Which made the funeral flame that burnt fair Troy:
All which hemm'd me about, crying, "This is he!"

Dido. Ah, how could poor Æneas scape their hands?

Æn. My mother Venus, jealous of my health,
Convey'd me from their crooked nets and bands;
So I escap'd the furious Pyrrhus' wrath:
Who then ran to the palace of the king,
And at Jove's altar finding Priamus,
About whose wither'd neck hung Hecuba,
Folding his hand in hers, and jointly both
Beating their breasts, and falling on the ground,
He, with his falchion's point rais'd up at once,
And with Megæra's eyes, star'd in their face,
Threatening a thousand deaths at every glance:
To whom the aged king thus, trembling, spoke;
"Achilles' son, remember what I was,
Father of fifty sons, but they are slain;
Lord of my fortune, but my fortune's turn'd;
King of this city, but my Troy is fir'd;
And now am neither father, lord, nor king:
Yet who so wretched but desires to live?
O, let me live, great Neoptolemus!"
Not mov'd at all, but smiling at his tears,
This butcher, whilst his hands were yet held up,
Treading upon his breast, struck off his hands.

Dido. O, end, Æneas! I can hear no more.

Æn. At which the frantic queen leap'd on his face,
And in his eyelids hanging by the nails,
A little while prolong'd her husband's life.
At last, the soldiers pull'd her by the heels,
And swung her howling in the empty air,
Which sent an echo to the wounded king:
Whereat he lifted up his bed-rid limbs,
And would have grappled with Achilles' son,
Forgetting both his want of strength and hands;
Which he disdaining, whisk'd his sword about,
And with the wind thereof the king fell down;
Then from the navel to the throat at once
He ripp'd old Priam; at whose latter gasp
Jove's marble statue gan to bend the brow,

As loathing Pyrrhus for this wicked act.
Yet he, undaunted, took his father's flag,
And dipp'd it in the old king's chill-cold blood,
And then in triumph ran into the streets,
Through which he could not pass for slaughter'd men;
So, leaning on his sword, he stood stone still,
Viewing the fire wherewith rich Ilion burnt.
By this, I got my father on my back,
This young boy in mine arms, and by the hand
Led fair Creusa, my beloved wife;
When thou, Achates, with thy sword mad'st way,
And we were round environ'd with the Greeks:
O, there I lost my wife! and, had not we
Fought manfully, I had not told this tale.
Yet manhood would not serve; of force we fled;
And, as we went unto our ships, thou know'st
We saw Cassandra sprawling in the streets,
Whom Ajax ravish'd in Diana's fane,
Her cheeks swollen with sighs, her hair all rent;
Whom I took up to bear unto our ships;
But suddenly the Grecians follow'd us,
And I, alas, was forc'd to let her lie!
Then got we to our ships, and, being aboard,
Polyxena cried out, "Æneas, stay!
The Greeks pursue me; stay, and take me in!"
Mov'd with her voice, I leap'd into the sea,
Thinking to bear her on my back aboard,
For all our ships were launch'd into the deep,
And, so I swom, she, standing on the shore,
Was by the cruel Myrmidons surpris'd
And, after that, by Pyrrhus sacrific'd.

Dido. I die with melting ruth; Æneas, leave.

Anna. O, what became of aged Hecuba?

Iar. How got Æneas to the fleet again?

Dido. But how scap'd Helen, she that caus'd this war?

Æn. Achates, speak; sorrow hath tir'd me quite.

Ach. What happen'd to the queen we cannot show;
We hear they led her captive into Greece:
As for Æneas, he swom quickly back;
And Helena betray'd Deiphobus,
Her lover, after Alexander died,
And so was reconcil'd to Menelaus.

Dido. O, had that ticing strumpet ne'er been born!—

Trojan, thy ruthful tale hath made me sad:
Come, let us think upon some pleasing sport,
To rid me from these melancholy thoughts.

[*Exeunt all except Ascanius, whom Venus, entering with Cupid at another door, takes by the sleeve as he is going off.*

Ven. Fair child, stay thou with Dido's waiting maid:
I'll give thee sugar almonds, sweet conserves,
A silver girdle, and a golden purse,
And this young prince shall be thy playfellow.

Asc. Are you Queen Dido's son?

Cup. Ay; and my mother gave me this fine bow.

Asc. Shall I have such a quiver and a bow?

Ven. Such bow, such quiver, and such golden shafts,
Will Dido give to sweet Ascanius.
For Dido's sake I take thee in my arms,
And stick these spangled feathers in thy hat:
Eat comfits in mine arms, and I will sing. [*Sings.*
Now is he fast asleep; and in this grove,
Amongst green brakes, I'll lay Ascanius,
And strew him with sweet-smelling violets,
Blushing roses, purple hyacinths:
These milk-white doves shall be his centronels,
Who, if that any seek to do him hurt,
Will quickly fly to Cytherea's fist.
Now, Cupid, turn thee to Ascanius' shape,
And go to Dido, who, instead of him,
Will set thee on her lap, and play with thee:
Then touch her white breast with this arrow head,
That she may dote upon Æneas' love,
And by that means repair his broken ships,
Victual his soldiers, give him wealthy gifts,
And he, at last, depart to Italy,
Or else in Carthage make his kingly throne.

Cup. I will, fair mother; and so play my part
As every touch shall wound Queen Dido's heart.
[*Exit.*

Ven. Sleep, my sweet nephew, in these cooling shades,
Free from the murmur of these running streams,
The cry of beasts, the rattling of the winds,
Or whisking of these leaves: all shall be still,
And nothing interrupt thy quiet sleep,
Till I return, and take thee hence again. [*Exit.*

ACT III

Enter CUPID *as* ASCANIUS.

Cup. Now, Cupid, cause the Carthaginian queen
To be enamour'd of thy brother's looks;
Convey this golden arrow in thy sleeve,
Lest she imagine thou art Venus' son;
And when she strokes thee softly on the head,
Then shall I touch her breast and conquer her.

Enter DIDO, ANNA, *and* IARBAS.

Iar. How long, fair Dido, shall I pine for thee?
'Tis not enough that thou dost grant me love,
But that I may enjoy what I desire:
That love is childish which consists in words.
Dido. Iarbas, know, that thou, of all my wooers,—
And yet have I had many mightier kings,—
Hast had the greatest favours I could give.
I fear me, Dido hath been counted light
In being too familiar with Iarbas;
Albeit the gods do know, no wanton thought
Had ever residence in Dido's breast.
Iar. But Dido is the favour I request.
Dido. Fear not, Iarbas; Dido may be thine.
Anna. Look, sister, how Æneas' little son
Plays with your garments and embraceth you.
Cup. No, Dido will not take me in her arms;
I shall not be her son, she loves me not.
Dido. Weep not, sweet boy; thou shalt be Dido's son:
Sit in my lap, and let me hear thee sing. [*Cupid sings.*
No more, my child; now talk another while,
And tell me where learn'dst thou this pretty song.
Cup. My cousin Helen taught it me in Troy.
Dido. How lovely is Ascanius when he smiles!
Cup. Will Dido let me hang about her neck?
Dido. Ay, wag; and give thee leave to kiss her too.
Cup. What will you give me now? I'll have this fan.
Dido. Take it, Ascanius, for thy father's sake.
Iar. Come, Dido, leave Ascanius; let us walk.
Dido. Go thou away; Acsanius shall stay.

Iar. Ungentle queen, is this thy love to me?
Dido. O stay, Iarbas, and I'll go with thee!
Cup. An if my mother go, I'll follow her.
Dido. Why stay'st thou here? thou art no love of mine.
Iar. Iarbas, die, seeing she abandons thee!
Dido. No; live, Iarbas: what hast thou deserv'd,
That I should say thou art no love of mine?
Something thou hast deserv'd.—Away, I say!
Depart from Carthage; come not in my sight.
Iar. Am I not king of rich Gætulia?
Dido. Iarbas, pardon me, and stay a while.
Cup. Mother, look here.
Dido. What tell'st thou me of rich Gætulia?
Am not I queen of Libya? then depart.
Iar. I go to feed the humour of my love,
Yet not from Carthage for a thousand worlds.
Dido. Iarbas!
Iar. Doth Dido call me back?
Dido. No; but I charge thee never look on me.
Iar. Then pull out both mine eyes, or let me die. [*Exit.*
Anna. Wherefore doth Dido bid Iarbas go?
Dido. Because his loathsome sight offends mine eye,
And in my thoughts is shrin'd another love.
O Anna, didst thou know how sweet love were,
Full soon wouldst thou abjure this single life!
Anna. Poor soul, I know too well the sour of love:
O, that Iarbas could but fancy me! [*Aside.*
Dido. Is not Æneas fair and beautiful?
Anna. Yes, and Iarbas foul and favourless.
Dido. Is he not eloquent in all his speech?
Anna. Yes; and Iarbas rude and rustical.
Dido. Name not Iarbas: but, sweet Anna, say,
Is not Æneas worthy Dido's love?
Anna. O sister, were you empress of the world,
Æneas well deserves to be your love!
So lovely is he, that, where'er he goes,
The people swarm to gaze him in the face.
Dido. But tell them, none shall gaze on him but I,
Lest their gross eye-beams taint my lover's cheeks.
Anna, good sister Anna, go for him,
Lest with these sweet thoughts I melt clean away.
Anna. Then, sister, you'll abjure Iarbas' love?
Dido. Yet must I hear that loathsome name again?

Run for Æneas, or I'll fly to him. [*Exit Anna.*

Cup. You shall not hurt my father when he comes.

Dido. No; for thy sake I'll love thy father well.—
O dull-conceited Dido, that till now
Didst never think Æneas beautiful!
But now, for quittance of this oversight,
I'll make me bracelets of his golden hair;
His glistening eyes shall be my looking-glass;
His lips an altar, where I'll offer up
As many kisses as the sea hath sands;
Instead of music I will hear him speak;
His looks shall be my only library;
And thou, Æneas, Dido's treasury,
In whose fair bosom I will lock more wealth
Than twenty thousand Indias can afford.
O, here he comes! Love, love, give Dido leave
To be more modest than her thoughts admit,
Lest I be made a wonder to the world.

Enter ÆNEAS, ACHATES, SERGESTUS, ILIONEUS, *and* CLOANTHUS.

Achates, how doth Carthage please your lord?

Ach. That will Æneas show your majesty.

Dido. Æneas, art thou there?

Æn. I understand, your highness sent for me.

Dido. No; but, now thou art here, tell me, in sooth,
In what might Dido highly pleasure thee.

Æn. So much have I receiv'd at Dido's hands,
As, without blushing, I can ask no more:
Yet, queen of Afric, are my ships unrigg'd,
My sails all rent in sunder with the wind,
My oars broken, and my tackling lost,
Yea, all my navy split with rocks and shelves;
Nor stern nor anchor have our maimed fleet;
Our masts the furious winds struck overboard:
Which piteous wants if Dido will supply,
We will account her author of our lives.

Dido. Æneas, I'll repair thy Trojan ships,
Conditionally that thou wilt stay with me,
And let Achates sail to Italy:
I'll give thee tackling made of rivell'd gold,
Wound on the barks of odoriferous trees;
Oars of massy ivory, full of holes,

Through which the water shall delight to play;
Thy anchors shall be hew'd from crystal rocks,
Which, if thou lose, shall shine above the waves;
The masts, whereon thy swelling sails shall hang,
Hollow pyramides of silver plate;
The sails of folded lawn, where shall be wrought
The wars of Troy,—but not Troy's overthrow;
For ballass, empty Dido's treasury:
Take what ye will, but leave Æneas here.
Achates, thou shalt be so newly clad,
As sea-born nymphs shall swarm about thy ships,
And wanton mermaids court thee with sweet songs,
Flinging in favours of more sovereign worth
Than Thetis hangs about Apollo's neck,
So that Æneas may but stay with me.

Æn. Wherefore would Dido have Æneas stay?

Dido. To war against my bordering enemies.
Æneas, think not Dido is in love;
For, if that any man could conquer me,
I had been wedded ere Æneas came:
See, where the pictures of my suitors hang;
And are not these as fair as fair may be?

Ach. I saw this man at Troy, ere Troy was sack'd.

Serg. I this in Greece, when Paris stole fair Helen.

Ili. This man and I were at Olympia's games.

Serg. I know this face; he is a Persian born:
I travell'd with him to Ætolia.

Cloan. And I in Athens with this gentleman,
Unless I be deceiv'd, disputed once.

Dido. But speak, Æneas; know you none of these?

Æn. No, madam; but it seems that these are kings.

Dido. All these, and others which I never saw,
Have been most urgent suitors for my love;
Some came in person, others sent their legates,
Yet none obtain'd me: I am free from all;
And yet, God knows, entangled unto one.
This was an orator, and thought by words
To compass me; but yet he was deceiv'd:
And this a Spartan courtier, vain and wild:
But his fantastic humours pleas'd not me:
This was Alcion, a musician;
But, play'd he ne'er so sweet, I let him go:
This was the wealthy king of Thessaly;

But I had gold enough, and cast him off:
This, Meleager's son, a warlike prince;
But weapons gree not with my tender years:
The rest are such as all the world well knows:
Yet now I swear, by heaven and him I love,
I was as far from love as they from hate.

Æn. O, happy shall he be whom Dido loves!

Dido. Then never say that thou art miserable,
Because, it may be, thou shalt be my love:
Yet boast not of it, for I love thee not,—
And yet I hate thee not.—O, if I speak,
I shall betray myself! [*Aside*]—Æneas, come:
We two will go a-hunting in the woods;
But not so much for thee,—thou art but one,—
As for Achates and his followers. [*Exeunt.*

Enter JUNO *to* ASCANIUS, *who lies asleep.*

Juno. Here lies my hate, Æneas' cursed brat,
The boy wherein false Destiny delights,
The heir of Fury, the favourite of the Fates,
That ugly imp that shall outwear my wrath,
And wrong my deity with high disgrace.
But I will take another order now,
And raze th' eternal register of Time:
Troy shall no more call him her second hope,
Nor Venus triumph in his tender youth;
For here, in spite of heaven, I'll murder him,
And feed infection with his let-out life.
Say, Paris, now shall Venus have the ball?
Say, vengeance, now shall her Ascanius die?
O, no! God wot, I cannot watch my time,
Nor quit good turns with double fee down told!
Tut, I am simple, without mind to hurt,
And have no gall at all to grieve my foes!
But lustful Jove and his adulterous child
Shall find it written on confusion's front,
That only Juno rules in Rhamnus' town.

Enter VENUS.

Ven. What should this mean? my doves are back return'd,
Who warn me of such danger prest at hand
To harm my sweet Ascanius' lovely life.—
Juno, my mortal foe, what make you here?

Avaunt, old witch! and trouble not my wits.
Juno. Fie, Venus, that such causeless words of wrath
Should e'er defile so fair a mouth as thine!
Are not we both sprung of celestial race,
And banquet, as two sisters, with the gods?
Why is it, then, displeasure should disjoin
Whom kindred and acquaintance co-unites?
Ven. Out, hateful hag! thou wouldst have slain my son,
Had not my doves discover'd thy intent:
But I will tear thy eyes fro forth thy head,
And feast the birds with their blood-shotten balls,
If thou but lay thy fingers on my boy.
Juno. Is this, then, all the thanks that I shall have
For saving him from snakes' and serpents' stings,
That would have kill'd him, sleeping, as he lay?
What, though I was offended with thy son,
And wrought him mickle woe on sea and land,
When, for the hate of Trojan Ganymede,
That was advanced by my Hebe's shame,
And Paris' judgment of the heavenly ball,
I muster'd all the winds unto his wreck,
And urg'd each element to his annoy?
Yet now I do repent me of his ruth,
And wish that I had never wrong'd him so.
Bootless, I saw, it was to war with fate
That hath so many unresisted friends:
Wherefore I chang'd my counsel with the time,
And planted love where envy erst had sprung.
Ven. Sister of Jove, if that thy love be such
As these thy protestations do paint forth,
We two, as friends, one fortune will divide:
Cupid shall lay his arrows in thy lap,
And to a sceptre change his golden shafts;
Fancy and modesty shall live as mates,
And thy fair peacocks by my pigeons perch:
Love my Æneas, and desire is thine;
The day, the night, my swans, my sweets, are thine.
Juno. More than melodious are these words to me,
That overcloy my soul with their content;
Venus, sweet Venus, how may I deserve
Such amorous favours at thy beauteous hand?
But, that thou mayst more easily perceive
How highly I do prize this amity,

Hark to a motion of eternal league,
Which I will make in quittance of thy love.
Thy son, thou know'st, with Dido now remains
And feeds his eyes with favours of her court;
She, likewise, in admiring spends her time,
And cannot talk nor think of aught but him;
Why should not they, then, join in marriage,
And bring forth mighty kings to Carthage town,
Whom casualty of sea hath made such friends?
And, Venus, let there be a match confirm'd
Betwixt these two, whose loves are so alike;
And both our deities, conjoin'd in one,
Shall chain felicity unto their throne.

Ven. Well could I like this reconcilement's means;
But much I fear, my son will ne'er consent,
Whose armed soul, already on the sea,
Darts forth her light to Lavinia's shore.

Juno. Fair queen of love, I will divorce these doubts,
And find the way to weary such fond thoughts.
This day they both a-hunting forth will ride
Into the woods adjoining to these walls;
When, in the midst of all their gamesome sports,
I'll make the clouds dissolve their watery works,
And drench Silvanus' dwellings with their showers;
Then in one cave the queen and he shall meet,
And interchangeably discourse their thoughts,
Whose short conclusion will seal up their hearts
Unto the purpose which we now propound.

Ven. Sister, I see you savour of my wiles;
Be it as you will have [it] for this once.
Meantime Ascanius shall be my charge;
Whom I shall bear to Ida in mine arms,
And couch him in Adonis' purple down. [*Exeunt.*

Enter DIDO, ÆNEAS, ANNA, IARBAS, ACHATES, CUPID *as* ASCANIUS, *and* Followers.

Dido. Æneas, think not but I honour thee,
That thus in person go with thee to hunt:
My princely robes, thou see'st, are laid aside,
Whose glittering pomp Diana's shroud supplies;
All fellows now, dispos'd alike to sport;
The woods are wide, and we have store of game.
Fair Trojan, hold my golden bow a while,

Until I gird my quiver to my side.—
Lords, go before; we two must talk alone.

Iar. Ungentle, can she wrong Iarbas so?
I'll die before a stranger have that grace.
" We two will talk alone "—what words be these? [*Aside.*

Dido. What makes Iarbas here of all the rest?
We could have gone without your company.

Æn. But love and duty led him on perhaps
To press beyond acceptance to your sight.

Iar. Why, man of Troy, do I offend thine eyes?
Or art thou griev'd thy betters press so nigh?

Dido. How now, Gætulian! are you grown so brave,
To challenge us with your comparisons?
Peasant, go seek companions like thyself,
And meddle not with any that I love.—
Æneas, be not mov'd at what he says;
For otherwhile he will be out of joint.

Iar. Women may wrong by privilege of love;
But, should that man of men, Dido except,
Have taunted me in these opprobrious terms,
I would have either drunk his dying blood,
Or else I would have given my life in gage.

Dido. Huntsmen, why pitch you not your toils apace,
And rouse the light-foot deer from forth their lair?

Anna. Sister, see, see Ascanius in his pomp,
Bearing his hunt-spear bravely in his hand!

Dido. Yea, little son, are you so forward now?

Cup. Ay, mother; I shall one day be a man,
And better able unto other arms;
Meantime these wanton weapons serve my war,
Which I will break betwixt a lion's jaws.

Dido. What, dar'st thou look a lion in the face?

Cup. Ay; and outface him too, do what he can.

Anna. How like his father speaketh he in all!

Æn. And mought I live to see him sack rich Thebes,
And load his spear with Grecian princes' heads,
Then would I wish me with Anchises' tomb,
And dead to honour that hath brought me up.

Iar. And might I live to see thee shipp'd away,
And hoist aloft on Neptune's hideous hills,
Then would I wish me in fair Dido's arms,
And dead to scorn that hath pursu'd me so. [*Aside.*

Æn. Stout friend Achates, dost thou know this wood?

Ach. As I remember, here you shot the deer
That sav'd your famish'd soldiers' lives from death,
When first you set your foot upon the shore;
And here we met fair Venus, virgin-like,
Bearing her bow and quiver at her back.
Æn. O, how these irksome labours now delight,
And overjoy my thoughts with their escape!
Who would not undergo all kind of toil,
To be well stor'd with such a winter's tale?
Dido. Æneas, leave these dumps, and let's away,
Some to the mountains, some unto the soil,
You to the valleys,—thou unto the house.
[*Exeunt all except Iarbas.*
Iar. Ay, this it is which wounds me to the death,
To see a Phrygian, far-fet o' the sea,
Preferr'd before a man of majesty.
O love! O hate! O cruel women's hearts,
That imitate the moon in every change,
And, like the planets, ever love to range!
What shall I do, thus wronged with disdain?
Revenge me on Æneas or on her?
On her! fond man, that were to war 'gainst heaven,
And with one shaft provoke ten thousand darts.
This Trojan's end will be thy envy's aim,
Whose blood will reconcile thee to content,
And make love drunken with thy sweet desire.
But Dido, that now holdeth him so dear,
Will die with very tidings of his death:
But time will discontinue her content,
And mould her mind unto new fancy's shapes.
O God of heaven, turn the hand of Fate
Unto that happy day of my delight!
And then—what then? Iarbas shall but love:
So doth he now, though not with equal gain;
That resteth in the rival of thy pain,
Who ne'er will cease to soar till he be slain. [*Exit.*

The storm. Enter ÆNEAS *and* DIDO *in the cave, at several times.*

Dido. Æneas!
Æn. Dido!
Dido. Tell me, dear love, how found you out this cave?
Æn. By chance, sweet queen, as Mars and Venus met.

Dido. Why, that was in a net, where we are loose;
And yet I am not free,—O, would I were!
Æn. Why, what is it that Dido may desire
And not obtain, be it in human power?
Dido. The thing that I will die before I ask,
And yet desire to have before I die.
Æn. It is not aught Æneas may achieve?
Dido. Æneas! no; although his eyes do pierce.
Æn. What, hath Iarbas anger'd her in aught?
And will she be avenged on his life?
Dido. Not anger'd me, except in angering thee.
Æn. Who, then, of all so cruel may he be
That should detain thy eye in his defects?
Dido. The man that I do eye where'er I am;
Whose amorous face, like Pæan, sparkles fire,
Whenas he butts his beams on Flora's bed.
Prometheus hath put on Cupid's shape,
And I must perish in his burning arms:
Æneas, O Æneas, quench these flames!
Æn. What ails my queen? is she faln sick of late?
Dido. Not sick, my love; but sick I must conceal
The torment that it boots me not reveal:
And yet I'll speak,—and yet I'll hold my peace.
Do shame her worst, I will disclose my grief:
Æneas, thou art he—what did I say?
Something it was that now I have forgot.
Æn. What means fair Dido by this doubtful speech?
Dido. Nay, nothing; but Æneas loves me not.
Æn. Æneas' thoughts dare not ascend so high
As Dido's heart, which monarchs might not scale.
Dido. It was because I saw no king like thee,
Whose golden crown might balance my content;
But now that I have found what to affect,
I follow one that loveth fame 'fore me,
And rather had seem fair [in] Sirens' eyes,
Than to the Carthage queen that dies for him.
Æn. If that your majesty can look so low
As my despised worths that shun all praise,
With this my hand I give to you my heart,
And vow, by all the gods of hospitality,
By heaven and earth, and my fair brother's bow,
By Paphos, Capys, and the purple sea
From whence my radiant mother did ascend,

And by this sword that sav'd me from the Greeks,
Never to leave these new-upreared walls,
Whiles Dido lives and rules in Juno's town,—
Never to like or love any but her!

Dido. What more than Delian music do I hear,
That calls my soul from forth his living seat
To move unto the measures of delight?
Kind clouds, that sent forth such a courteous storm
As made disdain to fly to fancy's lap!
Stout love, in mine arms make thy Italy,
Whose crown and kingdom rests at thy command:
Sichæus, not Æneas, be thou call'd;
The king of Carthage, not Anchises' son:
Hold, take these jewels at thy lover's hand,
[*Giving jewels, etc.*
These golden bracelets, and this wedding-ring,
Wherewith my husband woo'd me yet a maid,
And be thou king of Libya by my gift.
[*Exeunt to the cave.*

ACT IV

Enter ACHATES, CUPID *as* ASCANIUS, IARBAS, *and* ANNA.

Ach. Did ever men see such a sudden storm,
Or day so clear so suddenly o'ercast?

Iar. I think some fell enchantress dwelleth here,
That can call them forth whenas she please,
And dive into black tempest's treasury,
Whenas she means to mask the world with clouds.

Anna. In all my life I never knew the like;
It hailed, it snow'd, it lighten'd, all at once.

Ach. I think, it was the devils' revelling night,
There was such hurly-burly in the heavens:
Doubtless Apollo's axle-tree is crack'd,
Or aged Altas' shoulder out of joint,
The motion was so over-violent.

Iar. In all this coil, where have ye left the queen?

Asc. Nay, where's my warlike father, can you tell?

Anna. Behold where both of them come forth the cave.

Iar. Come forth the cave! can heaven endure this sight?
Iarbas, curse that unrevenging Jove,

Whose flinty darts slept in Typhœus' den,
Whiles these adulterers surfeited with sin.
Nature, why mad'st me not some poisonous beast,
That with the sharpness of my edged sting
I might have stak'd them both unto the earth,
Whilst they were sporting in this darksome cave?

Enter, from the cave, ÆNEAS *and* DIDO.

Æn. The air is clear, and southern winds are whist.
Come, Dido, let us hasten to the town,
Since gloomy Æolus doth cease to frown.
Dido. Achates and Ascanius, well met.
Æn. Fair Anna, how escap'd you from the shower?
Anna. As others did, by running to the wood.
Dido. But where were you, Iarbus, all this while?
Iar. Not with Æneas in the ugly cave.
Dido. I see, Æneas sticketh in your mind;
But I will soon put by that stumbling-block,
And quell those hopes that thus employ your cares.
[*Exeunt.*

Enter IARBAS *to sacrifice.*

Iar. Come, servants, come; bring forth the sacrifice,
That I may pacify that gloomy Jove,
Whose empty altars have enlarg'd our ills.—
[*Servants bring in the sacrifice, and then exeunt.*
Eternal Jove, great master of the clouds,
Father of gladness and all frolic thoughts,
That with thy gloomy hand corrects the heaven,
When airy creatures war amongst themselves;
Hear, hear, O, hear Iarbas' plaining prayers,
Whose hideous echoes make the welkin howl,
And all the woods Elissa to resound!
The woman that thou will'd us entertain,
Where, straying in our borders up and down,
She crav'd a hide of ground to build a town,
With whom we did divide both laws and land,
And all the fruits that plenty else sends forth,
Scorning our loves and royal marriage-rites,
Yields up her beauty to a stranger's bed;
Who, having wrought her shame, is straightway fled:
Now, if thou be'st a pitying god of power,
On whom ruth and compassion ever waits,

Redress these wrongs, and warn him to his ships,
That now afflicts me with his flattering eyes.

Enter ANNA.

Anna. How now, Iarbas! at your prayers so hard?
Iar. Ay, Anna: is there aught you would with me?
Anna. Nay, no such weighty busines of import,
But may be slack'd until another time:
Yet, if you would partake with me the cause
Of this devotion that detaineth you,
I would be thankful for such courtesy.
Iar. Anna, against this Trojan do I pray,
Who seeks to rob me of thy sister's love,
And dive into her heart by colour'd looks.
Anna. Alas, poor king, that labours so in vain
For her that so delighteth in thy pain!
Be rul'd by me, and seek some other love,
Whose yielding heart may yield thee more relief.
Iar. Mine eye is fix'd where fancy cannot start:
O, leave me, leave me to my silent thoughts,
That register the numbers of my ruth,
And I will either move the thoughtless flint,
Or drop out both mine eyes in drizzling tears,
Before my sorrow's tide have any stint!
Anna. I will not leave Iarbas, whom I love,
In this delight of dying pensiveness.
Away with Dido! Anna be thy song;
Anna, that doth admire thee more than heaven.
Iar. I may nor will list to such loathsome change,
That intercepts the course of my desire.—
Servants, come fetch these empty vessels here;
For I will fly from these alluring eyes,
That do pursue my peace where'e it goes.
[*Exit.—Servants re-enter, and carry out the vessels, etc.*
Anna. Iarbas, stay, loving Iarbas, stay!
For I have honey to present thee with.
Hard-hearted, wilt not deign to hear me speak?
I'll follow thee with outcries ne'ertheless,
And strew thy walks with my dishevell'd hair. [*Exit.*

Enter ÆNEAS.

Æn. Carthage, my friendly host, adieu!
Since destiny doth call me from the shore:

Hermes this night, descending in a dream,
Hath summon'd me to fruitful Italy;
Jove wills it so; my mother wills it so;
Let my Phœnissa grant, and then I go.
Grant she or no, Æneas must away;
Whose golden fortunes, clogg'd with courtly ease,
Cannot ascend to Fame's immortal house,
Or banquet in bright Honour's burnish'd hall,
Till he hath furrow'd Neptune's glassy fields,
And cut a passage through his topless hills.—
Achates, come forth! Sergestus, Ilioneus,
Cloanthus, haste away! Æneas calls.

Enter ACHATES, CLOANTHUS, SERGESTUS, *and* ILIONEUS.

Ach. What wills our lord, or wherefore did he call?
Æn. The dream, brave mates, that did beset my bed,
When sleep but newly had embrac'd the night,
Commands me leave these unrenowmed realms,
Whereas nobility abhors to stay,
And none but base Æneas will abide.
Aboard, aboard! since Fates do bid aboard,
And slice the sea with sable-coloured ships,
On whom the nimble winds may all day wait,
And follow them, as footmen, through the deep.
Yet Dido casts her eyes, like anchors, out,
To stay my fleet from loosing forth the bay:
"Come back, come back," I hear her cry a-far,
"And let me link my body to thy lips,
That, tied together by the striving tongues,
We may, as one, sail into Italy."
Ach. Banish that ticing dame from forth your mouth,
And follow your fore-seeing stars in all:
This is no life for men-at-arms to live,
Where dalliance doth consume a soldier's strength,
And wanton motions of alluring eyes
Effiminate our minds, inur'd to war.
Ili. Why, let us build a city of our own,
And not stand lingering here for amorous looks.
Will Dido raise old Priam forth his grave,
And build the town again the Greeks did burn?
No, no; she cares not how we sink or swim,
So she may have Æneas in her arms.
Clo. To Italy, sweet friends, to Italy!

We will not stay a minute longer here.

Æn. Trojans, aboard, and I will follow you,
[*Exeunt all except Æneas.*
I fain would go, yet beauty calls me back:
To leave her so, and not once say farewell,
Were to transgress against all laws of love.
But, if I use such ceremonious thanks
As parting friends accustom on the shore,
Her silver arms will coll me round about,
And tears of pearl cry, "Stay, Æneas, stay!"
Each word she says will then contain a crown,
And every speech be ended with a kiss:
I may not dure this female drudgery:
To sea, Æneas! find out Italy! [*Exit.*

Enter DIDO *and* ANNA.

Dido. O Anna, run unto the water side!
They say Æneas' men are going aboard;
It may be, he will steal away with them:
Stay not to answer me: run, Anna, run! [*Exit Anna.*
O foolish Trojans, that would steal from hence,
And not let Dido understand their drift!
I would have given Achates store of gold,
And Ilioneus gum and Libyan spice;
The common soldiers rich embroider'd coats,
And silver whistles to control the winds,
Which Circe sent Sichæus when he liv'd;
Unworthy are they of a queen's reward.
See, where they come: how might I do to chide?

Re-enter ANNA, *with* ÆNEAS, ACHATES, CLOANTHUS, ILIONEUS, SERGESTUS, *and* Carthaginian Lords.

Anna. 'Twas time to run, Æneas had been gone;
The sails were hoising up, and he aboard.

Dido. Is this thy love to me?

Æn. O princely Dido, give me leave to speak!
I went to take my farewell of Achates.

Dido. How haps Achates bid me not farewell?

Acha. Because I fear'd your grace would keep me here.

Dido. To rid thee of that doubt, aboard again:
I charge thee put to sea, and stay not here.

Ach. Then let Æneas go aboard with us.

Dido. Get you aboard; Æneas means to stay.

Æn. The sea is rough, the winds blow to the shore.
Dido. O false Æneas! now the sea is rough;
But, when you were aboard, 'twas calm enough:
Thou and Achates meant to sail away.
Æn. Hath not the Carthage queen mine only son?
Thinks Dido I will go and leave him here?
Dido. Æneas, pardon me; for I forgot
That young Ascanius lay with me this night;
Love made me jealous: but, to make amends,
Wear the imperial crown of Libya,
[*Giving him her crown and sceptre.*
Sway thou the Punic sceptre in my stead,
And punish me, Æneas, for this crime.
Æn. This kiss shall be fair Dido's punishment.
Dido. O, how a crown becomes Æneas' head!
Stay here, Æneas, and command as king.
Æn. How vain am I to wear this diadem,
And bear this golden sceptre in my hand!
A burgonet of steel, and not a crown,
A sword, and not a sceptre, fits Æneas.
Dido. O keep them still, and let me gaze my fill!
Now looks Æneas like immortal Jove:
O where is Ganymede, to hold his cup,
And Mercury, to fly for what he calls?
Ten thousand Cupids hover in the air,
And fan it in Æneas' lovely face!
O that the clouds were here wherein thou fled'st,
That thou and I unseen might sport ourselves!
Heaven, envious of our joys, is waxen pale;
And when we whisper, then the stars fall down,
To be partakers of our honey talk.
Æn. O Dido, patroness of all our lives,
When I leave thee, death be my punishment!
Swell, raging seas! frown, wayward Destinies!
Blow, winds! threaten, ye rocks and sandy shelves!
This is the harbour that Æneas seeks:
Let's see what tempests can annoy me now.
Dido. Not all the world can take thee from mine arms.
Æneas may command as many Moors
As in the sea are little water drops:
And now, to make experience of my love,—
Fair sister Anna, lead my lover forth,
And, seated on my jennet, let him ride,

As Dido's husband, through the Punic streets;
And will my guard, with Mauritanian darts
To wait upon him as their sovereign lord.

Anna. What if the citizens repine thereat?

Dido. Those that dislike what Dido gives in charge,
Command my guard to slay for their offence.
Shall vulgar peasants storm at what I do?
The ground is mine that gives them sustenance,
The air wherein they breathe, the water, fire,
All that they have, their lands, their goods, their lives,
And I, the goddess of all these, command
Æneas ride as Carthaginian king.

Ach. Æneas, for his parentage, deserves
As large a kingdom as is Libya.

Æn. Ay, and, unless the Destinies be false,
I shall be planted in as rich a land.

Dido. Speak of no other land; this land is thine;
Dido is thine, henceforth I'll call thee lord.—
Do as I bid thee, sister; lead the way;
And from a turret I'll behold my love.

Æn. Then here in me shall flourish Priam's race;
And thou and I, Achates, for revenge
For Troy, for Priam, for his fifty sons,
Our kinsmen's lives and thousand guiltless souls,
Will lead an host against the hateful Greeks,
And fire proud Lacedæmon o'er their heads.

[*Exeunt all except Dido and Carthaginian Lords.*

Dido. Speaks not Æneas like a conqueror?
O blessed tempests that did drive him in!
O happy sand that made him run aground!
Henceforth you shall be our Carthage gods.
Ay, but it may be, he will leave my love,
And seek a foreign land call'd Italy:
O that I had a charm to keep the winds
Within the closure of a golden ball;
Or that the Tyrrhene sea were in mine arms,
That he might suffer shipwreck on my breast,
As oft as he attempts to hoist up sail!
I must prevent him; wishing will not serve.—
Go bid my nurse take young Ascanius,
And bear him in the country to her house;
Æneas will not go without his son;
Yet, lest he should, for I am full of fear,

Bring me his oars, his tackling, and his sails.
[*Exit First Lord.*
What if I sink his ships? O, he will frown!
Better he frown than I should die for grief.
I cannot see him frown; it may not be:
Armies of foes resolv'd to win this town,
Or impious traitors vow'd to have my life,
Affright me not; only Æneas' frown
Is that which terrifies poor Dido's heart:
Not bloody spears, appearing in the air,
Presage the downfall of my empery,
Nor blazing comets threaten Dido's death;
It is Æneas' frown that ends my days.
If he forsake me not, I never die;
For in his looks I see eternity,
And he'll make me immortal with a kiss.

Re-enter First Lord, *with* Attendants *carrying tackling, etc.*

First Lord. Your nurse is gone with young Ascanius;
And here's Æneas' tackling, oars, and sails.
Dido. Are these the sails that, in despite of me,
Pack'd with the winds to bear Æneas hence?
I'll hang ye in the chamber where I lie;
Drive, if you can, my house to Italy:
I'll set the casement open, that the winds
May enter in, and once again conspire
Against the life of me, poor Carthage queen:
But, though ye go, he stays in Carthage still;
And let rich Carthage fleet upon the seas,
So I may have Æneas in mine arms.
Is this the wood that grew in Carthage plains,
And would be toiling in the watery billows,
To rob their mistress of her Trojan guest?
O cursed tree, hadst thou but wit or sense,
To measure how I prize Æneas' love,
Thou wouldst have leapt from out the sailors' hands,
And told me that Æneas meant to go!
And yet I blame thee not; thou art but wood.
The water, which our poets term a nymph,
Why did it suffer thee to touch her breast,
And shrunk not back, knowing my love was there?
The water is an element, no nymph.

Why should I blame Æneas for his flight?
O Dido, blame not him, but break his oars!
These were the instruments that launch'd him forth.
There's not so much as this base tackling too,
But dares to heap up sorrow to my heart:
Was it not you that hoised up these sails?
Why burst you not, and they fell in the seas?
For this will Dido tie ye full of knots,
And shear ye all asunder with her hands:
Now serve to chastise shipboys for their faults;
Ye shall no more offend the Carthage queen.
Now, let him hang my favours on his masts,
And see if those will serve instead of sails;
For tackling, let him take the chains of gold
Which I bestow'd upon his followers;
Instead of oars, let him use his hands,
And swim to Italy. I'll keep these sure.—
Come, bear them in. [*Exeunt.*

Enter Nurse, *with* CUPID *as* ASCANIUS.

Nurse. My Lord Ascanius, you must go with me.
Cup. Whither must I go? I'll stay with my mother.
Nurse. No, thou shalt go with me unto my house.
I have an orchard that hath store of plums,
Brown almonds, services, ripe figs, and dates,
Dewberries, apples, yellow oranges;
A garden where are bee-hives full of honey,
Musk-roses, and a thousand sort of flowers;
And in the midst doth run a silver stream,
Where thou shalt see the red-gill'd fishes leap,
White swans, and many lovely water-fowls.
Now speak, Ascanius, will you go or no?
Cup. Come, come, I'll go. How far hence is your house?
Nurse. But hereby, child; we shall get thither straight.
Cup. Nurse, I am weary; will you carry me?
Nurse. Ay, so you'll dwell with me, and call me mother.
Cup. So you'll love me, I care not if I do.
Nurse. That I might live to see this boy a man!
How prettily he laughs! Go, you wag!
You'll be a twigger when you come to age.—
Say Dido what she will, I am not old;
I'll be no more a widow; I am young;
I'll have a husband, I, or else a lover.

Cup. A husband, and no teeth!
Nurse. O, what mean I to have such foolish thoughts?
Foolish is love, a toy.—O sacred love!
If there be any heaven in earth, 'tis love,
Especially in women of your years.—
Blush, blush for shame! why shouldst thou think of love?
A grave, and not a lover, fits thy age.—
A grave! why, I may live a hundred years;
Fourscore is but a girl's age: love is sweet.—
My veins are wither'd, and my sinews dry:
Why do I think of love, now I should die?
Cup. Come, nurse.
Nurse. Well, if he come a-wooing, he shall speed:
O, how unwise was I to say him nay! [*Exeunt.*

ACT V

Enter ÆNEAS, *with a paper in his hand, drawing the platform of the city;* ACHATES, SERGESTUS, CLOANTHUS, *and* ILIONEUS.

Æn. Triumph, my mates! our travels are at end:
Here will Æneas build a statelier Troy
Than that which grim Atrides overthrew.
Carthage shall haunt her petty walls no more;
For I will grace them with a fairer frame,
And clad her in a crystal livery,
Wherein the day may evermore delight;
From golden India Ganges will I fetch,
Whose wealthy streams may wait upon her towers,
And triple-wise entrench her round about;
The sun from Egypt shall rich odours bring,
Wherewith his burning beams (like labouring bees
That load their thighs with Hybla's honey's spoils)
Shall here unburden their exhaled sweets,
And plant our pleasant suburbs with their fumes.
Ach. What length or breadth shall this brave town contain?
Æn. Not past four thousand paces at the most.
Ili. But what shall it be call'd? Troy, as before?
Æn. That have I not determin'd with myself.
Clo. Let it be term'd Ænea, by your name.
Serg. Rather Ascania, by your little son.

Æn. Nay, I will have it called Anchisæon,
Of my old father's name.

Enter HERMES *with* ASCANIUS.

Her. Æneas, stay; Jove's herald bids thee stay.
Æn. Whom do I see? Jove's winged messenger!
Welcome to Carthage' new-erected town.
Her. Why, cousin, stand you building cities here,
And beautifying the empire of this queen,
While Italy is clean out of thy mind?
Too-too forgetful of thine own affairs,
Why wilt thou so betray thy son's good hap?
The king of gods sent me from highest heaven,
To sound this angry message in thine ears:
Vain man, what monarchy expect'st thou here?
Or with what thought sleep'st thou in Libya shore?
If that all glory hath forsaken thee,
And thou despise the praise of such attempts,
Yet think upon Ascanius' prophecy,
And young Iulus' more than thousand years,
Whom I have brought from Ida, where he slept,
And bore young Capid unto Cyprus' isle.
Æn. This was my mother that beguil'd the queen,
And made me take my brother for my son:
No marvel, Dido, though thou be in love,
That daily dandlest Cupid in thy arms.—
Welcome, sweet child: where hast thou been this long?
Asc. Eating sweet comfits with Queen Dido's maid,
Who ever since hath lull'd me in her arms.
Æn. Sergestus, bear him hence unto our ships,
Lest Dido, spying him, keep him for a pledge.
[*Exit Sergestus with Ascanius.*
Her. Spend'st thou thy time about this little boy,
And giv'st not ear unto the charge I bring?
I tell thee, thou must straight to Italy,
Or else abide the wrath of frowning Jove. [*Exit.*
Æn. How should I put into the raging deep,
Who have no sails nor tackling for my ships?
What, would the gods have me, Deucalion-like,
Float up and down where'er the billows drive?
Though she repair'd my fleet and gave me ships,
Yet hath she ta'en away my oars and masts,
And left me neither sail nor stern aboard.

Enter IARBAS.

Iar. How now, Æneas! sad! what mean these dumps?
Æn. Iarbas, I am clean besides myself;
Jove hath heap'd on me such a desperate charge,
Which neither art nor reason may achieve,
Nor I devise by what means to contrive.
Iar. As how, I pray? may I entreat you tell?
Æn. With speed he bids me sail to Italy,
Whenas I want both rigging for my fleet.
And also furniture for these my men.
Iar. If that be all, then cheer thy drooping looks,
For I will furnish thee with such supplies.
Let some of those thy followers go with me,
And they shall have what thing soe'er thou need'st.
Æn. Thanks, good Iarbas, for thy friendly aid:
Achates and the rest shall wait on thee,
Whilst I rest thankful for this courtesy.
[*Exeunt all except Æneas.*
Now will I haste unto Lavinian shore,
And raise a new foundation to old Troy.
Witness the gods, and witness heaven and earth,
How loath I am to leave these Libyan bounds,
But that eternal Jupiter commands!

Enter DIDO.

Dido. I fear I saw Æneas' little son
Led by Achates to the Trojan fleet.
If it be so, his father means to fly:—
But here he is; now, Dido, try thy wit.— [*Aside.*
Æneas, wherefore go thy men aboard?
Why are thy ships new-rigg'd? or to what end,
Launch'd from the haven, lie they in the road?
Pardon me, though I ask; love makes me ask.
Æn. O, pardon me, if I resolve thee why!
Æneas will not feign with his dear love.
I must from hence: this day, swift Mercury,
When I was laying a platform for these walls,
Sent from his father Jove, appear'd to me,
And in his name rebuk'd me bitterly
For lingering here, neglecting Italy.
Dido. But yet Æneas will not leave his love.
Æn. I am commanded by immortal Jove

To leave this town and pass to Italy;
And therefore must of force.
Dido. These words proceed not from Æneas' heart.
Æn. Not from my heart, for I can hardly go;
And yet I may not stay. Dido, farewell.
Dido. Farewell! is this the 'mends for Dido's love?
Do Trojans use to quit their lovers thus?
Fare well may Dido, so Æneas stay;
I die, if my Æneas say farewell;
Æn. Then let me go, and never say farewell:
Dido. 'Let me go; farewell; I must from hence.'
These words are poison to poor Dido's soul:
O, speak like my Æneas, like my love!
Why look'st thou toward the sea? the time hath been
When Dido's beauty chain'd thine eyes to her.
Am I less fair than when thou saw'st me first?
O, then, Æneas, 'tis for grief of thee!
Say thou wilt stay in Carthage with thy queen,
And Dido's beauty will return again.
Æneas, say, how canst thou take thy leave?
Wilt thou kiss Dido? O, thy lips have sworn
To stay with Dido! canst thou take her hand?
Thy hand and mine have plighted mutual faith;
Therefore, unkind Æneas, must thou say,
"Then let me go, and never say farewell"?
Æn. O queen of Carthage, wert thou ugly-black,
Æneas could not choose but hold thee dear!
Yet must he not gainsay the gods' behest.
Dido. The gods! what gods be those that seek my death?
Wherein have I offended Jupiter,
That he should take Æneas from mine arms?
O, no! the gods weigh not what lovers do:
It is Æneas calls Æneas hence;
And woful Dido, by these blubber'd cheeks,
By this right hand, and by our spousal rites,
Desires Æneas to remain with her;
Si bene quid de te merui, fuit aut tibi quidquam
Dulce meum, miserere domus labentis, et istam,
Oro, si quis adhuc precibus locus, exue mentem.
Æn. Desine meque tuis incendere teque querelis;
Italiam non sponte sequor.
Dido. Hast thou forgot how many neighbour kings
Were up in arms, for making thee my love?

How Carthage did rebel, Iarbas storm,
And all the world calls me a second Helen,
For being entangled by a stranger's looks?
So thou wouldst prove as true as Paris did,
Would, as fair Troy was, Carthage might be sack'd,
And I be call'd a second Helena!
Had I a son by thee, the grief were less,
That I might see Æneas in his face:
Now if thou go'st, what canst thou leave behind,
But rather will augment than ease my woe?

Æn. In vain, my love, thou spend'st thy fainting breath:
If words might move me, I were overcome.

Dido. And wilt thou not be mov'd with Dido's words?
Thy mother was no goddess, perjur'd man,
Nor Dardanus the author of thy stock;
But thou art sprung from Scythian Caucasus,
And tigers of Hyrcania gave thee suck.—
Ah, foolish Dido, to forbear this long!—
Wast thou not wreck'd upon this Libyan shore,
And cam'st to Dido like a fisher swain?
Repair'd not I thy ships, made thee a king,
And all thy needy followers noblemen?
O serpent, that came creeping from the shore,
And I for pity harbour'd in my bosom,
Wilt thou now slay me with thy venom'd sting,
And hiss at Dido for preserving thee?
Go, go, and spare not; seek out Italy:
I hope that that which love forbids me do,
The rocks and sea-gulfs will perform at large,
And thou shalt perish in the billows' ways,
To whom poor Dido doth bequeath revenge:
Ay, traitor! and the waves shall cast thee up,
Where thou and false Achates first set foot;
Which if it chance, I'll give ye burial,
And weep upon your lifeless carcasses,
Though thou nor he will pity me a whit.
Why star'st thou in my face? If thou wilt stay,
Leap in mine arms; mine arms are open wide;
If not, turn from me, and I'll turn from thee;
For though thou hast the heart to say farewell,
I have not power to stay thee. [*Exit Æneas.*
Is he gone?
Ay, but he'll come again; he cannot go;

He loves me too-too well to serve me so:
Yet he that in my sight would not relent,
Will, being absent, be obdurate still.
By this, is he got to the water-side;
And, see, the sailors take him by the hand;
But he shrinks back; and now, remembering me,
Returns amain: welcome, welcome, my love!
But where's Æneas? ah, he's gone, he's gone!

Enter ANNA.

Anna. What means my sister, thus to rave and cry?
Dido. O Anna, my Æneas is aboard,
And, leaving me, will sail to Italy!
Once didst thou go, and he came back again:
Now bring him back, and thou shalt be a queen,
And I will live a private life with him.
Anna. Wicked Æneas!
Dido. Call him not wicked, sister: speak him fair,
And look upon him with a mermaid's eye;
Tell him, I never vow'd at Aulis' gulf
The desolation of his native Troy.
Nor sent a thousand ships unto the walls,
Nor ever violated faith to him;
Request him gently, Anna, to return:
I crave but this,—he stay a tide or two,
That I may learn to bear it patiently;
If he depart thus suddenly, I die.
Run, Anna, run; stay not to answer me.
Anna. I go, fair sister: heavens grant good success! [*Exit.*

Enter Nurse.

Nurse. O Dido, your little son Ascanius
Is gone! he lay with me last night,
And in the morning he was stoln from me:
I think, some fairies have beguiled me.
Dido. O cursed hag and false dissembling wretch,
That slay'st me with thy harsh and hellish tale!
Thou for some petty gift hast let him go,
And I am thus deluded of my boy.—
Away with her to prison presently,

Enter Attendants.

Trait'ress too keend and cursed sorceress!
Nurse. I know not what you mean by treason, I;
I am as true as any one of yours.
Dido. Away with her! suffer her not to speak.
[*Exit Nurse with Attendants.*
My sister comes: I like not her sad looks.

Re-enter ANNA.

Anna. Before I came, Æneas was aboard,
And, spying me, hois'd up the sails amain;
But I cried out, "Æneas, false Æneas, stay!"
Then gan he wag his hand, which, yet held up,
Made me suppose he would have heard me speak;
Then gan they drive into the ocean:
Which when I view'd, I cried, "Æneas, stay!
Dido, fair Dido wills Æneas stay!"
Yet he, whose heart['s] of adamant or flint,
My tears nor plaints could mollify a whit.
Then carelessly I rent my hair for grief:
Which seen to all, though he beheld me not,
They gan to move him to redress my ruth,
And stay a while to hear what I could say;
But he, clapp'd under hatches, sail'd away.
Dido. O Anna, Anna, I will follow him!
Anna. How can you go, when he hath all your fleet?
Dido. I'll frame me wings of wax, like Icarus,
And, o'er his ships, will soar unto the sun,
That they may melt, and I fall in his arms;
Or else I'll make a prayer unto the waves,
That I may swim to him, like Triton's niece.
O Anna, fetch Arion's harp,
That I may tice a dolphin to the shore,
And ride upon his back unto my love!
Look, sister, look! lovely Æneas' ships!
See, see, the billows heave 'em up to heaven,
And now down fall the keels into the deep!
O sister, sister, take away the rocks!
They'll break his ships. O Proteus, Neptune, Jove,
Save, save Æneas, Dido's liefest love!
Now is he come on shore, safe without hurt:
But, see, Achates wills him put to sea,
And all the sailors merry-make for joy;

But he, remembering me, shrinks back again:
See, where he comes! welcome, welcome, my love!

Anna. Ah, sister, leave these idle fantasies!
Sweet sister, cease; remember who you are.

Dido. Dido I am, unless I be deceiv'd:
And must I rave thus for a runagate?
Must I make ships for him to sail away?
Nothing can bear me to him but a ship,
And he hath all my fleet.—What shall I do,
But die in fury of this oversight?
Ay, I must be the murderer of myself:
No, but I am not; yet I will be straight.— [*Aside.*
Anna, be glad; now have I found a mean
To rid me from these thoughts of lunacy:
Not far from hence
There is a woman famoused for arts,
Daughter unto the nymphs Hesperides,
Who will'd me sacrifice his ticing relics:
Go, Anna, bid my servants bring me fire. [*Exit Anna.*

Enter IARBAS.

Iar. How long will Dido mourn a stranger's flight
That hath dishonour'd her and Carthage both?
How long shall I with grief consume my days,
And reap no guerdon for my truest love?

Enter Attendants *with wood and torches.*

Dido. Iarbas, talk not of Æneas; let him go:
Lay to thy hands, and help me make a fire,
That shall consume all that this stranger left;
For I intend a private sacrifice,
To cure my mind, that melts for unkind love.

Iar. But, afterwards, will Dido grant me love?

Dido. Ay, ay, Iarbas; after this is done,
None in the world shall have my love but thou.
[*They make a fire.*
So, leave me now; let none approach this place.
[*Exeunt Iarbas and Attendants.*
Now, Dido, with these relics burn thyself,
And make Æneas famous through the world
For perjury and slaughter of a queen.
Here lie[s] the sword that in the darksome cave
He drew, and swore by, to be true to me;

Thou shalt burn first; thy crime is worse than his.
Here lie[s] the garment which I cloth'd him in
When first he came on shore: perish thou too.
These letters, lines, and perjur'd papers, all
Shall burn to cinders in this precious flame.
And now, ye gods, that guide the starry frame,
And order all things at your high dispose,
Grant, though the traitors land in Italy,
They may be still tormented with unrest;
And from mine ashes let a conqueror rise,
That may revenge this treason to a queen
By ploughing up his countries with the sword!
Betwixt this land and that be never league;
Litora litoribus contraria, fluctibus undas
Imprecor, arma armis; pugnent ipsique nepotes!
Live, false Æneas! truest Dido dies;
Sic, sic juvat ire sub umbras.

[*Throws herself into the flames.*

Re-enter ANNA.

Anna. O, help, Iarbas! Dido in these flames
Hath burnt herself! ay me, unhappy me!

Re-enter IARBAS, *running.*

Iar. Cursed Iarbas, die to expiate
The grief that tires upon thine inward soul!—
Dido, I come to thee.—Ay me, Æneas!

[*Stabs himself, and dies.*

Anna. What can my tears or cries prevail me now?
Dido is dead!
Iarbas slain, Iarbas my dear love!
O sweet Iarbas, Anna's sole delight!
What fatal Destiny envies me thus,
To see my sweet Iarbas slay himself?
But Anna now shall honour thee in death,
And mix her blood with thine; this shall I do,
That gods and men may pity this my death,
And rue our ends, senseless of life or breath:
Now, sweet Iarbas, stay! I come to thee.

[*Stabs herself, and dies.*

HERO AND LEANDER

TO THE RIGHT WORSHIPFUL SIR THOMAS WALSINGHAM, KNIGHT.

Sir, we think not ourselves discharged of the duty we owe to our friend when we have brought the breathless body to the earth; for, albeit the eye there taketh his ever-farewell of that beloved object, yet the impression of the man that hath been dear unto us, living an after-life in our memory, there putteth us in mind of farther obsequies due unto the deceased; and namely of the performance of whatsoever we may judge shall make to his living credit and to the effecting of his determinations prevented by the stroke of death. By these meditations (as by an intellectual will) I suppose myself executor to the unhappily deceased author of this poem; upon whom knowing that in his lifetime you bestowed many kind favours, entertaining the parts of reckoning and worth which you found in him with good countenance and liberal affection, I cannot but see so far into the will of him dead, that whatsoever issue of his brain should chance to come abroad, that the first breath it should take might be the gentle air of your liking; for, since his self had been accustomed thereunto, it would prove more agreeable and thriving to his right children than any other foster countenance whatsoever. At this time seeing that this unfinished tragedy happens under my hands to be imprinted, of a double duty, the one to yourself, the other to the deceased, I present the same to your most favourable allowance, offering my utmost self now and ever to be ready at your worship's disposing.

EDWARD BLUNT.

THE FIRST SESTIAD[1]

The Argument of the First Sestiad.

Hero's description and her love's;
The fane of Venus where he moves
His worthy love-suit, and attains;
Whose bliss the wrath of Fates restrains
For Cupid's grace to Mercury:
Which tale the author doth imply.

On Hellespont, guilty of true love's blood,
In view and opposite two cities stood,
Sea-borderers, disjoin'd by Neptune's might;
The one Abydos, the other Sestos hight.
At Sestos Hero dwelt; Hero the fair,
Whom young Apollo courted for her hair,
And offer'd as a dower his burning throne,
Where she should sit, for men to gaze upon.
The outside of her garments were of lawn,
The lining purple silk, with gilt stars drawn;
Her wide sleeves green, and border'd with a grove,
Where Venus in her naked glory strove
To please the careless and disdainful eyes
Of proud Adonis, that before her lies;
Her kirtle blue, whereon was many a stain,
Made with the blood of wretched lovers slain.
Upon her head she ware a myrtle wreath,
From whence her veil reach'd to the ground beneath:
Her veil was artificial flowers and leaves,
Whose workmanship both man and beast deceives:
Many would praise the sweet smell as she past,
When 'twas the odour which her breath forth cast;
And there for honey bees have sought in vain,
And, beat from thence, have lighted there again.
About her neck hung chains of pebble-stone,
Which, lighten'd by her neck, like diamonds shone.
She ware no gloves; for neither sun nor wind
Would burn or parch her hands, but to her mind,
Or warm or cool them, for they took delight
To play upon those hands, they were so white,
Buskins of shells, all silver'd, used she,

[1] The first two Sestiads were written by Marlowe; the last four by Chapman, who supplied also the Arguments for the six Sestiads.

And branch'd with blushing coral to the knee;
Where sparrows perch'd, of hollow pearl and gold,
Such as the world would wonder to behold:
Those with sweet water oft her handmaid fills,
Which, as she went, would cherup through the bills.
Some say, for her the fairest Cupid pin'd,
And, looking in her face, was strooken blind.
But this is true; so like was one the other,
As he imagin'd Hero was his mother;
And oftentimes into her bosom flew,
About her naked neck his bare arms threw,
And laid his childish head upon her breast,
And, with still panting rock'd, there took his rest.
So lovely-fair was Hero, Venus' nun,
As Nature wept, thinking she was undone,
Because she took more from her than she left,
And of such wondrous beauty her bereft:
Therefore, in sign her treasure suffer'd wrack,
Since Hero's time hath half the world been black.
  Amorous Leander, beautiful and young,
(Whose tragedy divine Musæus sung,)
Dwelt at Abydos; since him dwelt there none
For whom succeeding times make greater moan.
His dangling tresses, that were never shorn,
Had they been cut, and unto Colchos borne,
Would have allur'd the venturous youth of Greece
To hazard more than for the golden fleece.
Fair Cynthia wish'd his arms might be her sphere;
Grief makes her pale, because she moves not there.
His body was as straight as Circe's wand;
Jove might have sipt out nectar from his hand.
Even as delicious meat is to the tast,
So was his neck in touching, and surpast
The white of Pelops' shoulder: I could tell ye,
How smooth his breast was, and how white his belly;
And whose immortal fingers did imprint
That heavenly path with many a curious dint
That runs along his back; but my rude pen
Can hardly blazon forth the loves of men,
Much less of powerful gods: let it suffice
That my slack Muse sings of Leander's eyes;
Those orient cheeks and lips, exceeding his
That leapt into the water for a kiss

Of his own shadow, and, despising many,
Died ere he could enjoy the love of any.
Had wild Hippolytus Leander seen,
Enamour'd of his beauty had he been:
His presence made the rudest peasant melt,
That in the vast uplandish country dwelt;
The barbarous Thracian soldier, mov'd with nought,
Was mov'd with him, and for his favour sought.
Some swore he was a maid in man's attire,
For in his looks were all that men desire,—
A pleasant-smiling cheek, a speaking eye,
A brow for love to banquet royally;
And such as knew he was a man, would say,
" Leander, thou art made for amorous play:
Why art thou not in love, and lov'd of all?
Though thou be fair, yet be not thine own thrall."
The men of wealthy Sestos every year,
For his sake whom their goddess held so dear,
Rose-cheek'd Adonis, kept a solemn feast:
Thither resorted many a wandering guest
To meet their loves: such as had none at all,
Came lovers home from this great festival;
For every street, like to a firmament,
Glister'd with breathing stars, who, where they went,
Frighted the melancholy earth, which deem'd
Eternal heaven to burn, for so it seem'd,
As if another Phaëton had got
The guidance of the sun's rich chariot.
But, far above the loveliest, Hero shin'd,
And stole away th' enchanted gazers' mind;
For like sea nymphs' inveigling harmony,
So was her beauty to the standers by;
Nor that night-wandering, pale, and watery star
(When yawning dragons draw her thirling car
From Latmus' mount up to the gloomy sky,
Where, crown'd with blazing light and majesty,
She proudly sits) more over-rules the flood
Than she the hearts of those that near her stood.
Even as when gaudy nymphs pursue the chase,
Wretched Ixion's shaggy-footed race,
Incens'd with savage heat, gallop amain
From steep pine-bearing mountains to the plain,
So ran the people forth to gaze upon her,

And all that view'd her were enamour'd on her:
And as in fury of a dreadful fight,
Their fellows being slain or put to flight,
Poor soldiers stand with fear of death dead-strooken,
So at her presence all surpris'd and tooken
Await the sentence of her scornful eyes;
He whom she favours lives; the other dies:
There might you see one sigh; another rage;
And some, their violent passions to assuage,
Compile sharp satires; but, alas, too late!
For faithful love will never turn to hate;
And many, seeing great princes were denied,
Pin'd as they went, and thinking on her died.
On this feast-day,—O cursed day and hour!—
Went Hero thorough Sestos, from her tower
To Venus' temple, where unhappily,
As after chanc'd, they did each other spy.
So fair a church as this had Venus none:
The walls were of discolour'd jasper-stone,
Wherein was Proteus carved, and o'er-head
A lively vine of green sea-agate spread,
Where by one hand light-headed Bacchus hung,
And with the other wine from grapes out-wrung.
Of crystal shining fair the pavement was;
The town of Sestos call'd it Venus' glass:
There might you see the gods, in sundry shapes,
Committing heady riots, incest, rapes;
For know, that underneath this radiant flour
Was Danäe's statue in a brazen tower;
Jove slily stealing from his sister's bed,
To dally with Idalian Ganymed,
And for his love Europa bellowing loud,
And tumbling with the Rainbow in a cloud;
Blood-quaffing Mars heaving the iron net
Which limping Vulcan and his Cyclops set;
Love kindling fire, to burn such towns as Troy;
Silvanus weeping for the lovely boy
That now is turn'd into a cypress-tree,
Under whose shade the wood-gods love to be.
And in the midst a silver altar stood:
There Hero, sacrificing turtles' blood,
Vail'd to the ground, veiling her eyelids close;
And modestly they open'd as she rose:

Thence flew Love's arrow with the golden head;
And thus Leander was enamoured.
Stone-still he stood, and evermore he gaz'd,
Till with the fire, that from his countenance blaz'd,
Relenting Hero's gentle heart was strook:
Such force and virtue hath an amorous look.
  It lies not in our power to love or hate,
For will in us is over-rul'd by fate.
When two are stript long ere the course begin,
We wish that one should lose, the other win;
And one especially do we affect
Of two gold ingots, like in each respect:
The reason no man knows; let it suffice,
What we behold is censur'd by our eyes.
Where both deliberate, the love is slight:
Who ever lov'd, that lov'd not at first sight?
  He kneel'd; but unto her devoutly pray'd:
Chaste Hero to herself thus softly said,
"Were I the saint he worships, I would hear him;"
And, as she spake those words, came somewhat near
    him.
He started up; she blush'd as one asham'd;
Wherewith Leander much more was inflam'd.
He touch'd her hand; in touching it she trembled:
Love deeply grounded, hardly is dissembled.
These lovers parled by the touch of hands:
True love is mute, and oft amazed stands.
Thus while dumb signs their yielding hearts entangled,
The air with sparks of living fire was spangled;
And Night, deep-drench'd in misty Acheron,
Heav'd up her head, and half the world upon
Breath'd darkness forth (dark night is Cupid's day):
And now begins Leander to display
Love's holy fire, with words, with sighs, and tears;
Which, like sweet music, enter'd Hero's ears;
And yet at every word she turn'd aside,
And always cut him off, as he replied.
At last, like to a bold sharp sophister,
With cheerful hope thus he accosted her.
"Fair creature, let me speak without offence:
I would my rude words had the influence
To lead thy thoughts as thy fair looks do mine!
Then shouldst thou be his prisoner, who is thine.

Be not unkind and fair; mis-shapen stuff
Are of behaviour boisterous and rough.
O, shun me not, but hear me ere you go!
God knows, I cannot force love as you do:
My words shall be as spotless as my youth,
Full of simplicity and naked truth.
This sacrifice, whose sweet perfume descending
From Venus' altar, to your footsteps bending,
Doth testify that you exceed her far,
To whom you offer, and whose nun you are.
Why should you worship her? her you surpass
As much as sparkling diamonds flaring glass.
A diamond set in lead his worth retains;
A heavenly nymph, belov'd of human swains,
Receives no blemish, but oftimes more grace;
Which makes me hope, although I am but base,
Base in respect of thee divine and pure,
Dutiful service may thy love procure;
And I in duty will excel all other,
As thou in beauty dost exceed Love's mother.
Nor heaven nor thou were made to gaze upon:
As heaven preserves all things, so save thou one.
A stately builded ship, well rigg'd and tall,
The ocean maketh more majestical:
Why vow'st thou, then, to live in Sestos here,
Who on Love's seas more glorious wouldst appear?
Like untun'd golden strings all women are,
Which long time lie untouch'd, will harshly jar.
Vessels of brass, oft handled, brightly shine:
What difference betwixt the richest mine
And basest mould, but use? for both, not us'd,
Are of like worth. Then treasure is abus'd,
When misers keep it: being put to loan,
In time it will return us two for one.
Rich robes themselves and others do adorn;
Neither themselves nor others, if not worn.
Who builds a palace, and rams up the gate,
Shall see it ruinous and desolate:
Ah, simple Hero, learn thyself to cherish!
Lone women, like to empty houses, perish.
Less sins the poor rich man, that starves himself
In heaping up a mass of drossy pelf,
Than such as you: his golden earth remains,

Which, after his decease, some other gains;
But this fair gem, sweet in the loss alone,
When you fleet hence, can be bequeath'd to none;
Or, if it could, down from th' enamell'd sky
All heaven would come to claim this legacy,
And with intestine broils the world destroy,
And quite confound Nature's sweet harmony.
Well therefore by the gods decreed it is,
We human creatures should enjoy that bliss.
One is no number; maids are nothing, then,
Without the sweet society of men.
Wilt thou live single still? one shalt thou be,
Though never-singling Hymen couple thee.
Wild savages, that drink of running springs,
Think water far excels all earthly things;
But they, that daily taste neat wine, despise it:
Virginity, albeit some highly prize it,
Compar'd with marriage, had you tried them both,
Differs as much as wine and water doth.
Base bullion for the stamp's sake we allow:
Even so for men's impression do we you;
By which alone, our reverend fathers say,
Women receive perfection every way.
This idol, which you term virginity,
Is neither essence subject to the eye,
No, nor to any one exterior sense,
Nor hath it any place of residence,
Nor is't of earth or mould celestial,
Or capable of any form at all.
Of that which hath no being, do not boast:
Things that are not at all, are never lost.
Men foolishly do call it virtuous:
What virtue is it, that is born with us?
Much less can honour be ascrib'd thereto:
Honour is purchas'd by the deeds we do;
Believe me, Hero, honour is not won,
Until some honourable deed be done.
Seek you, for chastity, immortal fame,
And know that some have wrong'd Diana's name?
Whose name is it, if she be false or not,
So she be fair, but some vile tongues will blot?
But you are fair, ay me! so wondrous fair,
So young, so gentle, and so debonair,

As Greece will think, if thus you live alone,
Some one or other keeps you as his own.
Then, Hero, hate me not, nor from me fly,
To follow swiftly blasting infamy.
Perhaps thy sacred priesthood makes thee loath:
Tell me, to whom mad'st thou that heedless oath?"
"To Venus," answer'd she; and, as she spake,
Forth from those two tralucent cisterns brake
A stream of liquid pearl, which down her face
Made milk-white paths, whereon the gods might trace
To Jove's high court. He thus replied: "The rites
In which love's beauteous empress most delights,
Are banquets, Doric music, midnight revel,
Plays, masks, and all that stern age counteth evil.
Thee as a holy idiot doth she scorn;
For thou, in vowing chastity, hast sworn
To rob her name and honour, and thereby
Committ'st a sin far worse than perjury,
Even sacrilege against her deity,
Through regular and formal purity.
To expiate which sin, kiss and shake hands:
Such sacrifice as this Venus demands."
  Thereat she smil'd, and did deny him so,
As put thereby, yet might he hope for mo;
Which makes him quickly reinforce his speech,
And her in humble manner thus beseech:
"Though neither gods nor men may thee deserve,
Yet for her sake, whom you have vow'd to serve,
Abandon fruitless cold virginity.
The gentle queen of love's sole enemy.
Then shall you most resemble Venus' nun,
When Venus' sweet rites are perform'd and done.
Flint-breasted Pallas joys in single life;
But Pallas and your mistress are at strife.
Love, Hero, then, and be not tyrannous;
But heal the heart that thou hast wounded thus;
Nor stain thy youthful years with avarice:
Fair fools delight to be accounted nice.
The richest corn dies, if it be not reapt;
Beauty alone is lost, too warily kept."
These arguments he us'd, and many more;
Wherewith she yielded, that was won before.
Hero's looks yielded, but her words made war:

Women are won when they begin to jar.
Thus, having swallow'd Cupid's golden hook,
The more she striv'd, the deeper was she strook:
Yet, evilly feigning anger, strove she still,
And would be thought to grant against her will.
So having paus'd a while, at last she said,
"Who taught thee rhetoric to deceive a maid?
Ay me! such words as these should I abhor,
And yet I like them for the orator."
With that, Leander stoop'd to have embrac'd her,
But from his spreading arms away she cast her,
And thus bespake him: "Gentle youth, forbear
To touch the sacred garments which I wear.
Upon a rock, and underneath a hill,
Far from the town, (where all is whist and still,
Save that the sea, playing on yellow sand,
Sends forth a rattling murmur to the land,
Whose sound allures the golden Morpheus
In silence of the night to visit us,)
My turret stands; and there, God knows, I play
With Venus' swans and sparrows all the day.
A dwarfish beldam bears me company,
That hops about the chamber where I lie,
And spends the night, that might be better spent,
In vain discourse and apish merriment:—
Come thither." As she spake this, her tongue tripp'd,
For unawares "Come thither" from her slipp'd;
And suddenly her former colour chang'd,
And here and there her eyes through anger rang'd;
And, like a planet moving several ways
At one self instant, she, poor soul, assays,
Loving, not to love at all, and every part
Strove to resist the motions of her heart:
And hands so pure, so innocent, nay, such
As might have made Heaven stoop to have a touch,
Did she uphold to Venus, and again
Vow'd spotless chastity; but all in vain;
Cupid beats down her prayers with his wings;
Her vows above the empty air he flings:
All deep enrag'd, his sinewy bow he bent,
And shot a shaft that burning from him went;
Wherewith she strooken, look'd so dolefully,
As made Love sigh to see his tyranny;

And, as she wept, her tears to pearl he turn'd,
And wound them on his arm, and for her mourn'd.
Then towards the palace of the Destinies,
Laden with languishment and grief, he flies,
And to those stern nymphs humbly made request,
Both might enjoy each other, and be blest.
But with a ghastly dreadful countenance,
Threatening a thousand deaths at every glance,
They answer'd Love, nor would vouchsafe so much
As one poor word, their hate to him was such:
Hearken a while, and I will tell you why.
  Heaven's winged herald, Jove-born Mercury,
The self-same day that he asleep had laid
Enchanted Argus, spied a country maid,
Whose careless hair, instead of pearl t'adorn it,
Glister'd with dew, as one that seem'd to scorn it;
Her breath as fragrant as the morning rose;
Her mind pure, and her tongue untaught to glose:
Yet proud she was (for lofty Pride that dwells
In towered courts, is oft in shepherds' cells),
And too-too well the fair vermilion knew
And silver tincture of her cheeks, that drew
The love of every swain. On her this god
Enamour'd was, and with his snaky rod
Did charm her nimble feet, and made her stay,
The while upon a hillock down he lay,
And sweetly on his pipe began to play,
And with smooth speech her fancy to assay,
Till in his twining arms he lock'd her fast,
And then he woo'd with kisses; and at last,
As shepherds do, her on the ground he laid,
And, tumbling in the grass, he often stray'd
Beyond the bounds of shame, in being bold
To eye those parts which no eye should behold;
And, like an insolent commanding lover,
Boasting his parentage, would needs discover
The way to new Elysium. But she,
Whose only dower was her chastity,
Having striven in vain, was now about to cry,
And crave the help of shepherds that were nigh.
Herewith he stay'd his fury, and began
To give her leave to rise: away she ran;
After went Mercury, who us'd such cunning,

As she, to hear his tale, left off her running;
(Maids are not won by brutish force and might,
But speeches full of pleasure, and delight;)
And, knowing Hermes courted her, was glad
That she such loveliness and beauty had
As could provoke his liking; yet was mute,
And neither would deny nor grant his suit.
Still vow'd he love: she, wanting no excuse
To feed him with delays, as women use,
Or thirsting after immortality,
(All women are ambitious naturally,)
Impos'd upon her lover such a task,
As he ought not perform, nor yet she ask;
A draught of flowing nectar she requested,
Wherewith the king of gods and men is feasted.
He, ready to accomplish what she will'd,
Stole some from Hebe (Hebe Jove's cup fill'd),
And gave it to his simple rustic love:
Which being known,—as what is hid from Jove?—
He inly storm'd, and wax'd more furious
Than for the fire filch'd by Prometheus;
And thrusts him down from heaven. He, wandering here,
In mournful terms, with sad and heavy cheer,
Complain'd to Cupid: Cupid, for his sake,
To be reveng'd on Jove did undertake;
And those on whom heaven, earth, and hell relies,
I mean the adamantine Destinies,
He wounds with love, and forc'd them equally
To dote upon deceitful Mercury.
They offer'd him the deadly fatal knife
That shears the slender threads of human life;
At his fair feather'd feet the engines laid,
Which th' earth from ugly Chaos' den upweigh'd.
These he regarded not; but did entreat
That Jove, usurper of his father's seat,
Might presently he banish'd into hell,
And aged Saturn in Olympus dwell.
They granted what he crav'd; and once again
Saturn and Ops began their golden reign:
Murder, rape, war, lust, and treachery,
Were with Jove clos'd in Stygian empery.
But long this blessed time continu'd not:

As soon as he his wished purpose got,
He, reckless of his promise, did despise
The love of th' everlasting Destinies.
They, seeing it, both Love and him abhorr'd,
And Jupiter unto his place restor'd:
And, but that learning, in despite of Fate,
Will mount aloft, and enter heaven-gate,
And to the seat of Jove itself advance,
Hermes had slept in hell with Ignorance.
Yet, as a punishment, they added this,
That he and Poverty should always kiss;
And to this day is every scholar poor:
Gross gold from them runs headlong to the boor.
Likewise the angry Sisters, thus deluded,
To venge themselves on Hermes, have concluded
That Midas' brood shall sit in Honour's chair,
To which the Muses' sons are only heir;
And fruitful wits, that inaspiring are,
Shall discontent run into regions far;
And few great lords in virtuous deeds shall joy
But be surpris'd with every garish toy,
And still enrich the lofty servile clown,
Who with encroaching guile keeps learning down.
Then muse not Cupid's suit no better sped,
Seeing in their loves the Fates were injured.

THE SECOND SESTIAD

The Argument of the Second Sestiad

Hero of love takes deeper sense,
And doth her love more recompense:
Their first night's meeting, where sweet kisses
Are th' only crowns of both their blisses.
He swims t' Abydos, and returns:
Cold Neptune with his beauty burns;
Whose suit he shuns, and doth aspire
Hero's fair tower and his desire.

By this, sad Hero, with love unacquainted,
Viewing Leander's face, fell down and fainted.
He kiss'd her, and breath'd life into her lips;
Wherewith, as one displeas'd, away she trips;
Yet, as she went, full often look'd behind,

And many poor excuses did she find
To linger by the way, and once she stay'd,
And would have turn'd again, but was afraid,
In offering parley, to be counted light:
So on she goes, and, in her idle flight,
Her painted fan of curled plumes let fall,
Thinking to train Leander therewithal.
He, being a novice, knew not what she meant,
But stay'd, and after her a letter sent;
Which joyful Hero answer'd in such sort,
As he had hope to scale the beauteous fort
Wherein the liberal Graces lock'd their wealth;
And therefore to her tower he got by stealth.
Wide-open stood the door; he need not climb;
And she herself, before the pointed time,
Had spread the board, with roses strew'd the room,
And oft look'd out, and mus'd he did not come.
At last he came: O, who can tell the greeting
These greedy lovers had at their first meeting?
He ask'd; she gave; and nothing was denied;
Both to each other quickly were affied:
Look how their hands, so were their hearts united,
And what he did she willingly requited.
(Sweet are the kisses, the embracements sweet,
When like desires and affections meet;
For from the earth to heaven is Cupid rais'd,
Where fancy is in equal balance pais'd.)
Yet she this rashness suddenly repented,
And turn'd aside, and to herself lamented,
As if her name and honour had been wrong'd,
By being possess'd of him for whom she long'd;
Ay, and she wish'd, albeit not from her heart,
That he would leave her turret and depart.
The mirthful god of amorous pleasure smil'd
To see how he this captive nymph beguil'd;
For hitherto he did but fan the fire,
And kept it down, that it might mount the higher.
Now wax'd she jealous lest his love abated,
Fearing her own thoughts made her to be hated.
Therefore unto him hastily she goes,
And, like light Salmacis, her body throws
Upon his bosom, where with yielding eyes
She offers up herself a sacrifice.

To slake his anger, if he were displeas'd:
O, what god would not therewith be appeas'd?
Like Æsop's cock, this jewel he enjoy'd,
And as a brother with his sister toy'd,
Supposing nothing else was to be done,
Now he her favour and goodwill had won.
But know you not that creatures wanting sense,
By nature have a mutual appetence,
And, wanting organs to advance a step,
Mov'd by love's force, unto each other lep?
Much more in subjects having intellect
Some hidden influence breeds like effect.
Albeit Leander, rude in love and raw,
Long dallying with Hero, nothing saw
That might delight him more, yet he suspected
Some amorous rites or other were neglected.
Therefore unto his body hers he clung:
She, fearing on the rushes to be flung,
Striv'd with redoubled strength; the more she striv'd,
The more a gentle pleasing heat reviv'd,
Which taught him all that elder lovers know;
And now the same gan so to scorch and glow,
As in plain terms, yet cunningly, he crav'd it:
Love always makes those eloquent that have it.
She, with a kind of granting, put him by it,
And ever, as he thought himself most nigh it,
Like to the tree of Tantalus, she fled,
And, seeming lavish, sav'd her maidenhead.
Ne'er king more sought to keep his diadem,
Than Hero this inestimable gem:
Above our life we love a steadfast friend;
Yet when a token of great worth we send,
We often kiss it, often look thereon,
And stay the messenger that would be gone;
No marvel, then, though Hero would not yield
So soon to part from that she dearly held:
Jewels being lost are found again; this never;
'Tis lost but once, and once lost, lost for ever.
  Now had the Morn espied her lover's steeds;
Whereat she starts, puts on her purple weeds,
And, red for anger that he stay'd so long,
All headlong throws herself the clouds among.
And now Leander, fearing to be miss'd,

Embrac'd her suddenly, took leave, and kiss'd:
Long was he taking leave, and loathe to go,
And kiss'd again, as lovers use to do.
Sad Hero wrung him by the hand, and wept,
Saying, " Let your vows and promises be kept ":
Then standing at the door, she turn'd about,
As loathe to see Leander going out.
And now the sun, that through th' horizon peeps,
As pitying these lovers, downward creeps;
So that in silence of the cloudy night,
Though it was morning, did he take his flight.
But what the secret trusty night conceal'd,
Leander's amorous habit soon reveal'd:
With Cupid's myrtle was his bonnet crown'd,
About his arms the purple riband wound,
Wherewith she wreath'd her largely-spreading hair;
Nor could the youth abstain, but he must wear
The sacred ring wherewith she was endow'd,
When first religious chastity she vow'd;
Which made his love through Sestos to be known,
And thence unto Abydos sooner blown
Than he could sail; for incorporeal Fame,
Whose weight consists in nothing but her name,
Is swifter than the wind, whose tardy plumes
Are reeking water and dull earthly fumes.
  Home when he came, he seem'd not to be there,
But, like exiled air thrust from his sphere,
Set in a foreign place; and straight from thence,
Alcides-like, by mighty violence,
He would have chas'd away the swelling main,
That him from her unjustly did detain.
Like as the sun in a diameter
Fires and inflames objects removed far,
And heateth kindly, shining laterally;
So beauty sweetly quickens when 'tis nigh,
But being separated and remov'd,
Burns where it cherish'd, murders where it lov'd.
Therefore even as an index to a book,
So to his mind was young Leander's look.
O, none but gods have power their love to hide!
Affection by the countenance is descried;
The light of hidden fire itself discovers,
And love that is conceal'd betrays poor lovers.

His secret flame apparently was seen:
Leander's father knew where he had been,
And for the same mildly rebuk'd his son,
Thinking to quench the sparkles new-begun.
But love resisted once, grows passionate,
And nothing more than counsel lovers hate;
For as a hot proud horse highly disdains
To have his head controll'd, but breaks the reins,
Spits forth the ringled bit, and with his hoves
Checks the submissive ground; so he that loves,
The more he is restrain'd, the worse he fares:
What is it now but mad Leander dares?
"O Hero, Hero!" thus he cried full oft;
And then he got him to a rock aloft,
Where having spied her tower, long star'd he on't,
And pray'd the narrow toiling Hellespont
To part in twain, that he might come and go;
But still the rising billows answer'd, "No."
With that, he stripp'd him to the ivory skin,
And, crying, "Love, I come," leap'd lively in:
Whereat the sapphire-visag'd god grew proud,
And made his capering Triton sound aloud,
Imagining that Ganymede, displeas'd,
Had left the heavens; therefore on him he seiz'd.
Leander striv'd; the waves about him wound,
And pull'd him to the bottom, where the ground
Was strew'd with pearl, and in low coral groves
Sweet-singing mermaids sported with their loves
On heaps of heavy gold, and took great pleasure
To spurn in careless sort the shipwreck treasure;
For here the stately azure palace stood,
Where kingly Neptune and his train abode.
The lusty god embrac'd him, call'd him "love,"
And swore he never should return to Jove:
But when he knew it was not Ganymed,
For under water he was almost dead,
He heav'd him up, and, looking on his face,
Beat down the bold waves with his triple mace,
Which mounted up, intending to have kiss'd him.
And fell in drops like tears because they miss'd him.
Leander, being up, began to swim,
And, looking back, saw Neptune follow him:
Whereat aghast, the poor soul gan to cry,

"O, let me visit Hero ere I die!"
The god put Helle's bracelet on his arm,
And swore the sea should never do him harm.
He clapp'd his plump cheeks, with his tresses play'd,
And, smiling wantonly, his love bewray'd;
He watch'd his arms, and, as they open'd wide
At every stroke, betwixt them would he slide,
And steal a kiss, and then run out and dance,
And, as he turn'd, cast many a lustful glance,
And throw him gaudy toys to please his eye,
And dive into the water, and there pry
Upon his breast, his thighs, and every limb,
And up again, and close beside him swim,
And talk of love. Leander made reply,
"You are deceiv'd; I am no woman, I."
Thereat smil'd Neptune, and then told a tale,
How that a shepherd, sitting in a vale,
Play'd with a boy so fair and kind,
As for his love both earth and heaven pin'd;
That of the cooling river durst not drink,
Lest water-nymphs should pull him from the brink;
And when he sported in the fragrant lawns,
Goat-footed Satyrs and up-staring Fauns
Would steal him thence. Ere half this tale was done,
"Ay me," Leander cried, "th' enamour'd sun,
That now should shine on Thetis' glassy bower,
Descends upon my radiant Hero's tower:
O, that these tardy arms of mine were wings!"
And, as he spake, upon the waves he springs.
Neptune was angry that he gave no ear,
And in his heart revenging malice bare:
He flung at him his mace; but, as it went,
He call'd it in, for love made him repent:
The mace, returning back, his own hand hit,
As meaning to be veng'd for darting it.
When this fresh-bleeding wound Leander view'd,
His colour went and came, as if he ru'd
The grief which Neptune felt: in gentle breasts
Relenting thoughts, remorse, and pity rests;
And who have hard hearts and obdurate minds,
But vicious, hare-brain'd, and illiterate hinds?
The god, seeing him with pity to be mov'd,
Thereon concluded that he was belov'd;

(Love is too full of faith, too credulous,
With folly and false hope deluding us;)
Wherefore, Leander's fancy to surprise,
To the rich ocean for gifts he flies;
'Tis wisdom to give much; a gilt prevails
When deep-persuading oratory fails.
By this, Leander, being near the land,
Cast down his weary feet, and felt the sand.
Breathless albeit he were, he rested not
Till to the solitary tower he got;
And knock'd, and call'd: at which celestial noise
The longing heart of Hero much more joys
Than nymphs and shepherds when the timbrel rings,
Or crooked dolphin when the sailor sings.
She stay'd not for her robes, but straight arose,
And, drunk with gladness, to the door she goes;
Where seeing a naked man, she screech'd for fear,
(Such sights as this to tender maids are rare,)
And ran into the dark herself to hide
(Rich jewels in the dark are soonest spied).
Unto her was he led, or rather drawn
By those white limbs which sparkled through the lawn.
The nearer that he came, the more she fled,
And, seeking refuge, slipt into her bed;
Whereon Leander sitting, thus began,
Through numbing cold all feeble, faint, and wan.
" If not for love, yet, love, for pity-sake,
Me in thy bed and maiden bosom take;
At least vouchsafe these arms some little room,
Who, hoping to embrace thee, cheerly swum:
This head was beat with many a churlish billow,
And therefore let it rest upon thy pillow."
Herewith affrighted, Hero shrunk away,
And in her lukewarm place Leander lay;
Whose lively heat, like fire from heaven fet,
Would animate gross clay, and higher set
The drooping thoughts of base-declining souls,
Than dreary-Mars-carousing nectar bowls.
His hands he cast upon her like a snare:
She, overcome with shame and sallow fear,
Like chaste Diana when Actæon spied her,
Being suddenly betray'd, div'd down to hide her;
And, as her silver body downward went,

With both her hands she made the bed a tent,
And in her own mind thought herself secure,
O'ercast with dim and darksome coverture.
And now she lets him whisper in her ear,
Flatter, entreat, promise, protest, and swear:
Yet ever, as he greedily assay'd
To touch those dainties, she the harpy play'd,
And every limb did, as a soldier stout,
Defend the fort, and keep the foeman out;
For though the rising ivory mount he scal'd,
Which is with azure circling lines empal'd.
Much like a globe (a globe may I term this,
By which Love sails to regions full of bliss,)
Yet there with Sisyphus he toil'd in vain,
Till gentle parley did the truce obtain.
Even as a bird, which in our hands we wring,
Forth plungeth, and oft flutters with her wing,
She trembling strove: this strife of hers, like that
Which made the world, another world begat
Of unknown joy. Treason was in her thought,
And cunningly to yield herself she sought.
Seeming not won, yet won she was at length:
In such wars women use but half their strength.
Leander now, like Theban Hercules,
Enter'd the orchard of th' Hesperides;
Whose fruit none rightly can describe, but he
That pulls or shakes it from the golden tree.
Wherein Leander, on her quivering breast,
Breathless spoke something, and sigh'd out the rest;
Which so prevail'd, as he, with small ado,
Enclos'd her in his arms, and kiss'd her too:
And every kiss to her was as a charm,
And to Leander as a fresh alarm:
So that the truce was broke, and she, alas,
Poor silly maiden, at his mercy was.
Love is not full of pity, as men say,
But deaf and cruel where he means to prey

And now she wish'd this night were never done,
And sigh'd to think upon th' approaching sun;
For much it griev'd her that the bright day-light
Should know the pleasure of this blessed night,
And them, like Mars and Erycine, display
Both in each other's arms chain'd as they lay.

Again, she knew not how to frame her look,
Or speak to him, who in a moment took
That which so long, so charily she kept;
And fain by stealth away she would have crept,
And to some corner secretly have gone,
Leaving Leander in the bed alone.
But as her naked feet were whipping out,
He on the sudden cling'd her so about,
That, mermaid-like, unto the floor she slid;
One half appear'd, the other half was hid.
Thus near the bed she blushing stood upright,
And from her countenance behold ye might
A kind of twilight break, which through the hair,
As from an orient cloud, glimps'd here and there;
And round about the chamber this false morn
Brought forth the day before the day was born.
So Hero's ruddy cheek Hero betray'd,
And her all naked to his sight display'd:
Whence his admiring eyes more pleasure took
Than Dis, on heaps of gold fixing his look.
By this, Apollo's golden harp began
To sound forth music to the ocean;
Which watchful Hesperus no sooner heard,
But he the bright Day-bearing car prepar'd,
And ran before, as harbinger of light,
And with his flaring beams mock'd ugly Night,
Till she, o'ercome with anguish, shame, and rage,
Dang'd down to hell her loathsome carriage.[1]

[1] Here Marlowe's work ends. The rest of the poem is by Chapman.

THE THIRD SESTIAD

The Argument of the Third Sestiad.

Leander to the envious light
Resigns his night-sports with the night,
And swims the Hellespont again.
Thesme, the deity sovereign
Of customs and religious rites,
Appears, reproving his delights,
Since nuptial honours he neglected;
Which straight he vows shall be effected.
Fair Hero, left devirginate,
Weighs, and with fury wails her state:
But with her love and woman's wit
She argues and approveth it.

New light gives new directions, fortunes new
To fashion our endeavours that ensue.
More harsh, at least more hard, more grave and high
Our subject runs, and our stern Muse must fly.
Love's edge is taken off, and that light flame,
Those thoughts, joys, longings, that before became
High unexperienc'd blood, and maids' sharp plights,
Must now grow staid, and censure the delights,
That, being enjoy'd, ask judgment; now we praise,
As having parted: evenings crown the days.
And now, ye wanton Loves, and young Desires,
Pied Vanity, the mint of strange attires,
Ye lisping Flatteries, and obsequious Glances,
Relentful Musics, and attractive Dances,
And you detested Charms constraining love!
Shun love's stoln sports by that these lovers prove.
By this, the sovereign of heaven's golden fires,
And young Leander, lord of his desires,
Together from their lover's arms arose:
Leander into Hellespontus throws
His Hero-handled body, whose delight
Made him disdain each other epithite.
And so amidst th' enamour'd waves he swims,
The god of gold of purpose gilt his limbs,
That, this word *gilt* including double sense,
The double guilt of his incontinence
Might be express'd, that had no stay t' employ
The treasure which the love-god let him joy
In his dear Hero, with such sacred thrift

As had beseem'd so sanctified a gift;
But, like a greedy vulgar prodigal,
Would on the stock dispend, and rudely fall,
Before his time, to that unblessed blessing
Which, for lust's plague, doth perish with possessing:
Joy graven in sense, like snow in water, wasts;
Without preserve of virtue, nothing lasts.
What man is he, that with a wealthy eye
Enjoys a beauty richer than the sky,
Through whose white skin, softer than soundest sleep,
With damask eyes the ruby blood doth peep,
And runs in branches through her azure veins,
Whose mixture and first fire his love attains;
Whose both hands limit both love's deities,
And sweeten human thoughts like paradise;
Whose disposition silken and is kind,
Directed with an earth-exempted mind;—
Who thinks not heaven with such a love is given?
And who, like earth, would spend that dower of heaven,
With rank desire to joy it all at first?
What simply kills our hunger, quencheth thirst,
Clothes but our nakedness, and makes us live,
Praise doth not any of her favours give:
But what doth plentifully minister
Beauteous apparel and delicious cheer,
So order'd that it still excites desire,
And still gives pleasure freeness to aspire,
The palm of Bounty ever moist preserving;
To Love's sweet life this is the courtly carving.
Thus Time and all-states-ordering Ceremony
Had banish'd all offence: Time's golden thigh
Upholds the flowery body of the earth
In sacred harmony, and every birth
Of men and actions makes legitimate,
Being us'd aright; *the use of time is fate.*
Yet did the gentle flood transfer once more
This prize of love home to his father's shore,
Where he unlades himself of that false wealth
That makes few rich,—treasures compos'd by stealth;
And to his sister, kind Hermione,
(Who on the shore kneel'd, praying to the sea
For his return,) he all love's goods did show,
In Hero seis'd for him, in him for Hero.

His most kind sister all his secrets knew,
And to her, singing, like a shower, he flew,
Sprinkling the earth, that to their tombs took in
Streams dead for love, to leave his ivory skin,
Which yet a snowy foam did leave above,
As soul to the dead water that did love;
And from thence did the first white roses spring
(For love is sweet and fair in every thing),
And all the sweeten'd shore, as he did go,
Was crown'd with odorous roses, white as snow.
Love-blest Leander was with love so fill'd,
That love to all that touch'd him he instill'd;
And as the colours of all things we see,
To our sight's powers communicated be,
So to all objects that in compass came
Of any sense he had, his senses' flame
Flow'd from his parts with force so virtual,
It fir'd with sense things were insensual.
Now, with warm baths and odours comforted,
When he lay down, he kindly kiss'd his bed,
As consecrating it to Hero's right,
And vow'd thereafter, that whatever sight
Put him in mind of Hero or her bliss,
Should be her altar to prefer a kiss.
Then laid he forth his late-enriched arms,
In whose white circle Love writ all his charms,
And made his characters sweet Hero's limbs,
When on his breast's warm sea she sideling swims;
And as those arms, held up in circle, met,
He said, " See, sister, Hero's carquenet!
Which she had rather wear about her neck,
Than all the jewels that do Juno deck."
But, as he shook with passionate desire
To put in flame his other secret fire,
A music so divine did pierce his ear,
As never yet his ravish'd sense did hear;
When suddenly a light of twenty hues
Brake through the roof, and, like the rainbow, views
Amaz'd Leander: in whose beams came down
The goddess Ceremony, with a crown
Of all the stars; and Heaven with her descended:
Her flaming hair to her bright feet extended,
By which hung all the bench of deities;

And in a chain, compact of ears and eyes,
She led Religion: all her body was
Clear and transparent as the purest glass,
For she was all presented to the sense:
Devotion, Order, State, and Reverence,
Her shadows were; Society, Memory;
All which her sight made live, her absence die.
A rich disparent pentacle she wears,
Drawn full of circles and strange characters.
Her face was changeable to every eye;
One way look'd ill, another graciously;
Which while men view'd, they cheerful were and holy,
But looking off, vicious and melancholy.
The snaky paths to each observed law
Did Policy in her broad bosom draw.
One hand a mathematic crystal sways,
Which, gathering in one line a thousand rays
From her bright eyes, Confusion burns to death,
And all estates of men distinguisheth:
By it Morality and Comeliness
Themselves in all their sightly figures dress.
Her other hand a laurel rod applies.
To beat back Barbarism and Avarice,
That follow'd, eating earth and excrement
And human limbs; and would make proud ascent
To seats of gods, were Ceremony slain.
The Hours and Graces bore her glorious train;
And all the sweets of our society
Were spher'd and treasur'd in her bounteous eye.
Thus she appear'd, and sharply did reprove
Leander's bluntness in his violent love;
Told him how poor was substance without rites,
Like bills unsign'd; desires without delights;
Like meats unseason'd; like rank corn that grows
On cottages, that none or reaps or sows;
Not being with civil forms confirm'd and bounded,
For human dignities and comforts founded;
But loose and secret all their glories hide;
Fear fills the chamber, Darkness decks the bride.
She vanish'd, leaving pierc'd Leander's heart
With sense of his unceremonious part,
In which, with plain neglect of nuptial rites,
He close and flatly fell to his delights:

And instantly he vow'd to celebrate
All rites pertaining to his married state.
So up he gets, and to his father goes,
To whose glad ears he doth his vows disclose.
The nuptials are resolv'd with utmost power;
And he at night would swim to Hero's tower,
From whence he meant to Sestos' forked bay
To bring her covertly, where ships must stay,
Sent by his father, throughly rigg'd and mann'd,
To waft her safely to Abydos' strand.
There leave we him; and with fresh wing pursue
Astonish'd Hero, whose most wished view
I thus long have forborne, because I left her
So out of countenance, and her spirits bereft her:
To look of one abashed is impudence,
When of slight faults he hath too deep a sense.
Her blushing het her chamber: she look'd out,
And all the air she purpled round about;
And after it a foul black day befell,
Which ever since a red morn doth foretell,
And still renews our woes for Hero's woe;
And foul it prov'd, because it figur'd so
The next night's horror; which prepare to hear;
I fail, if it profane your daintiest ear.
  Then, ho, most strangely-intellectual fire,
That, proper to my soul, hast power t'inspire
Her burning faculties, and with the wings
Of thy unsphered flame visit'st the springs
Of spirits immortal! Now (as swift as Time
Doth follow Motion) find th' eternal clime
Of his free soul, whose living subject stood
Up to the chin in the Pierian flood,
And drunk to me half this Musæan story,
Inscribing it to deathless memory:
Confer with it, and make my pledge as deep,
That neither's draught be consecrate to sleep;
Tell it how much his late desires I tender
(If yet it know not), and to light surrender
My soul's dark offspring, willing it should die
To loves, to passions, and society.
  Sweet Hero, left upon her bed alone,
Her maidenhead, her vows, Leander gone,
And nothing with her but a violent crew

Of new-come thoughts, that yet she never knew.
Even to herself a stranger, was much like
Th' Iberian city that War's hand did strike
By English force in princely Essex' guide,
When Peace assur'd her towers had fortified,
And golden-finger'd India had bestow'd
Such wealth on her, that strength and empire flow'd
Into her turrets, and her virgin waist
The wealthy girdle of the sea embrac'd;
Till our Leander, that made Mars his Cupid,
For soft love suits with iron thunders chid;
Swum to her towers, dissolv'd her virgin zone;
Led in his power, and made Confusion
Run through her streets amaz'd, that she suppos'd
She had not been in her own walls enclos'd,
But rapt by wonder to some foreign state,
Seeing all her issue so disconsolate,
And all her peaceful mansions possess'd
With war's just spoil, and many a foreign guest
From every corner driving an enjoyer,
Supplying it with power of a destroyer.
So far'd fair Hero in th' expugned fort
Of her chaste bosom; and of every sort
Strange thoughts possess'd her, ransacking her breast
For that that was not there, her wonted rest.
She was a mother straight, and bore with pain
Thoughts that spake straight, and wish'd their mother slain;
She hates their lives, and they their own and hers:
Such strife still grows where sin the race prefers:
Love is a golden bubble, full of dreams,
That waking breaks, and fills us with extremes.
She mus'd how she could look upon her sire,
And not show that without, that was intire;
For as a glass is an inanimate eye,
And outward forms embraceth inwardly,
So is the eye an animate glass, that shows
In-forms without us; and as Phœbus throws
His beams abroad, though he in clouds be clos'd,
Still glancing by them till he find oppos'd
A loose and rorid vapour that is fit
T' event his searching beams, and useth it
To form a tender twenty-colour'd eye,

Cast in a circle round about the sky;
So when our fiery soul, our body's star,
(That ever is in motion circular,)
Conceives a form, in seeking to display it
Through all our cloudy parts, it doth convey it
Forth at the eye, as the most pregnant place,
And that reflects it round about the face.
And this event uncourtly Hero thought,
Her inward guilt would in her looks have wrought;
For yet the world's stale cunning she resisted,
To bear foul thoughts, yet forge what looks she listed,
And held it for a very silly sleight,
To make a perfect metal counterfeit.
Glad to disclaim herself, proud of an art
That makes the face a pandar to the heart.
Those be the painted moons, whose lights profane
Beauty's true heaven, at full still in their wane;
Those be the lapwing faces that still cry,
" Here 'tis! " when that they vow is nothing nigh:
Base fools! when every moorish fool can teach
That which men think the height of human reach.
But custom, that the apoplexy is
Of bed-rid nature and lives led amiss,
And takes away all feeling of offence,
Yet braz'd not Hero's brow with impudence;
And this she thought most hard to bring to pass,
To seem in countenance other than she was,
As if she had two souls, one for the face,
One for the heart, and that they shifted place
As either list to utter or conceal
What they conceiv'd, or as one soul did deal
With both affairs at once, keeps and ejects
Both at an instant contrary effects;
Retention and ejection in her powers
Being acts alike; for this one vice of ours,
That forms the thought, and sways the countenance,
Rules both our motion and our utterance.
These and more grave conceits toil'd Hero's spirits;
For, though the light of her discoursive wits
Perhaps might find some little hole to pass
Through all these worldly cinctures, yet, alas!
There was a heavenly flame encompass'd her,—
Her goddess, in whose fane she did prefer

Her virgin vows, from whose impulsive sight
She knew the black shield of the darkest night
Could not defend her, nor wit's subtlest art:
This was the point pierc'd Hero to the heart;
Who, heavy to the death, with a deep sigh,
And hand that languish'd, took a robe was nigh,
Exceeding large, and of black cypres made,
In which she sate, hid from the day in shade,
Even over head and face, down to her feet;
Her left hand made it at her bosom meet,
Her right hand lean'd on her heart-bowing knee,
Wrapp'd in unshapeful folds, 'twas death to see;
Her knee stay'd that, and that her falling face;
Each limb help'd other to put on disgrace:
No form was seen, where form held all her sight;
But, like an embryon that saw never light,
Or like a scorched statue made a coal
With three-wing'd lightning, or a wretched soul
Muffled with endless darkness, she did sit:
The night had never such a heavy spirit.
Yet might a penetrating eye well see
How fast her clear tears melted on her knee
Through her black veil, and turn'd as black as it,
Mourning to be her tears. Then wrought her wit
With her broke vow, her goddess' wrath, her fame,—
All tools that enginous despair could frame:
Which made her strew the floor with her torn hair,
And spread her mantle piece-meal in the air.
Like Jove's son's club, strong passion struck her down
And with a piteous snriek enforc'd her swoun:
Her shriek made with another shriek ascend
The frighted matron that on her did tend;
And as with her own cry her sense was slain,
So with the other it was call'd again.
She rose, and to her bed made forced way,
And laid her down even where Leander lay;
And all this while the red sea of her blood
Ebb'd with Leander: but now turn'd the flood,
And all her fleet of spirits came swelling in,
With child of sail, and did hot fight begin
With those severe conceits she too much mark'd:
And here Leander's beauties were embark'd.
He came in swimming, painted all with joys,

Such as might sweeten hell: his thought destroys
All her destroying thoughts; she thought she felt
His heart in hers with her contentions melt,
And chide her soul that it could so much err,
To check the true joys he deserv'd in her.
Her fresh heat-blood cast figures in her eyes,
And she suppos'd she saw in Neptune's skies
How her star wander'd, wash'd in smarting brine,
For her love's sake, that with immortal wine
Should be embath'd, and swim in more heart's-ease
Than there was water in the Sestian seas.
Then said her Cupid-prompted spirit: "Shall I
Sing moans to such delightsome harmony?
Shall slick-tongu'd Fame, patch'd up with voices rude,
The drunken bastard of the multitude,
(Begot when father Judgment is away,
And, gossip-like, says because others say,
Takes news as if it were too hot to eat,
And spits it slavering forth for dog-fees meat,)
Make me, for forging a fantastic vow,
Presume to bear what makes grave matrons bow?
Good vows are never broken with good deeds,
For then good deeds were bad: vows are but seeds,
And good deeds fruits; even those good deeds that grow
From other stocks than from th' observed vow.
That is a good deed that prevents a bad;
Had I not yielded, slain myself I had.
Hero Leander is, Leander Hero;
Such virtue love hath to make one of two.
If, then, Leander did my maidenhead git,
Leander being myself, I still retain it:
We break chaste vows when we live loosely ever,
But bound as we are, we live loosely never:
Two constant lovers being join'd in one,
Yielding to one another, yield to none.
We know not how to vow till love unblind us,
And vows made ignorantly never bind us.
Too true it is, that, when 'tis gone, men hate
The joys as vain they took in love's estate:
But that's since they have lost the heavenly light
Should show them way to judge of all things right.
When life is gone, death must implant his terror:

As death is foe to life, so love to error.
Before we love, how range we through this sphere,
Searching the sundry fancies hunted here!
Now with desire of wealth transported quite
Beyond our free humanity's delight;
Now with ambition climbing falling towers,
Whose hope to scale, our fear to fall devours;
Now rapt with pastimes, pomp, all joys impure:
In things without us no delight is sure.
But love, with all joys crown'd, within doth sit:
O goddess, pity love, and pardon it!"
Thus spake she weeping: but her goddess' ear
Burn'd with too stern a heat, and would not hear.
Ay me! hath heaven's strait fingers no more graces
For such as Hero than for homeliest faces?
Yet she hop'd well, and in her sweet conceit
Weighing her arguments, she thought them weight,
And that the logic of Leander's beauty,
And them together, would bring proofs of duty;
And if her soul, that was a skilful glance
Of heaven's great essence, found such imperance
In her love's beauties, she had confidence
Jove lov'd him too, and pardon'd her offence:
Beauty in heaven and earth this grace doth win,
It supples rigour, and it lessens sin.
Thus, her sharp wit, her love, her secrecy,
Trooping together, made her wonder why
She should not leave her bed, and to the temple;
Her health said she must live; her sex, dissemble.
She view'd Leander's place, and wish'd he were
Turn'd to his place, so his place were Leander.
" Ay me," said she, " that love's sweet life and sense
Should do it harm! my love had not gone hence,
Had he been like his place: O blessed place,
Image of constancy! Thus my love's grace
Parts nowhere, but it leaves something behind
Worth observation: he renowns his kind:
His motion is, like heaven's, orbicular,
For where he once is, he is ever there.
This place was mine; Leander, now 'tis thine,
Thou being myself, then it is double mine,
Mine, and Leander's mine, Leander's mine.
O, see what wealth it yields me, nay, yields him!

For I am in it, he for me doth swim.
Rich, fruitful love, that, doubling self, estates
Elixir-like contracts, though separates!
Dear place, I kiss thee, and do welcome thee,
As from Leander ever sent to me."

THE FOURTH SESTIAD

The Argument of the Fourth Sestiad.

Hero, in sacred habit deckt,
Doth private sacrifice effect.
Her scarf's description, wrought by Fate;
Ostents that threaten her estate;
The strange, yet physical, events,
Leander's counterfeit presents.
In thunder Cyprides descends,
Presaging both the lovers' ends:
Ecte, the goddess of remorse,
With vocal and articulate force
Inspires Leucote, Venus' swan,
T' excuse the beauteous Sestian.
Venus, to wreak her rites' abuses,
Creates the monster Eronusis,
Inflaming Hero's sacrifice
With lightning darted from her eyes;
And thereof springs the painted beast
That ever since taints every breast.

Now from Leander's place she rose, and found
Her hair and rent robe scatter'd on the ground;
Which taking up, she every piece did lay
Upon an altar, where in youth of day
She us'd t' exhibit private sacrifice:
Those would she offer to the deities
Of her fair goddess and her powerful son,
As relics of her late-felt passion;
And in that holy sort she vow'd to end them,
In hope her violent fancies, that did rend them,
Would as quite fade in her love's holy fire,
As they should in the flames she meant t' inspire.
Then she put on all her religious weeds,
That deck'd her in her secret sacred deeds;
A crown of icicles, that sun nor fire
Could ever melt, and figur'd chaste desire;
A golden star shin'd in her naked breast,
In honour of the queen-light of the east.

In her right hand she held a silver wand,
On whose bright top Peristera did stand,
Who was a nymph, but now transform'd a dove,
And in her life was dear in Venus' love;
And for her sake she ever since that time
Choos'd doves to draw her coach through heaven's blue
clime.
Her plenteous hair in curled billows swims
On her bright shoulder: her harmonious limbs
Sustain'd no more but a most subtile veil,
That hung on them, as it durst not assail
Their different concord; for the weakest air
Could raise it swelling from her beauties fair;
Nor did it cover, but adumbrate only
Her most heart-piercing parts, that a blest eye
Might see, as it did shadow, fearfully,
All that all-love-deserving paradise:
It was as blue as the most freezing skies;
Near the sea's hue, for thence her goddess came:
On it a scarf she wore of wondrous frame;
In midst whereof she wrought a virgin's face,
From whose each cheek a fiery blush did chase
Two crimson flames, that did two ways extend,
Spreading the ample scarf to either end;
Which figur'd the division of her mind,
Whiles yet she rested bashfully inclined,
And stood not resolute to wed Leander;
This serv'd her white neck for a purple sphere,
And cast itself at full breadth down her back:
There, since the first breath that begun the wrack
Of her free quiet from Leander's lips,
She wrought a sea, in one flame, full of ships;
But that one ship where all her wealth did pass,
Like simple merchants' goods, Leander was;
For in that sea she naked figur'd him;
Her diving needle taught him how to swim,
And to each thread did such resemblance give,
For joy to be so like him it did live:
Things senseless live by art, and rational die
By rude contempt of art and industry.
Scarce could she work, but, in her strength of thought,
She fear'd she prick'd Leander as she wrought,
And oft would shriek so, that her guardian, frighted,

Would staring haste, as with some mischief cited:
They double life that dead things' grief sustain;
They kill that feel not their friends' living pain.
Sometimes she fear'd he sought her infamy;
And then, as she was working of his eye.
She thought to prick it out to quench her ill;
But, as she prick'd, it grew more perfect still:
Trifling attempts no serious acts advance;
The fire of love is blown by dalliance.
In working his fair neck she did so grace it,
She still was working her own arms t' embrace it.
That, and his shoulders, and his hands were seen
Above the stream; and with a pure sea-green
She did so quaintly shadow every limb,
All might be seen beneath the waves to swim.
In this conceited scarf she wrought beside
A moon in change, and shooting stars did glide
In number after her with bloody beams;
Which figur'd her affects in their extremes,
Pursuing nature in her Cynthian body,
And did her thoughts running on change imply;
For maids take more delight, when they prepare,
And think of wives' states, than when wives they are.
Beneath all these she wrought a fisherman,
Drawing his nets from forth the ocean;
Who drew so hard, ye might discover well
The toughen'd sinews in his neck did swell:
His inward strains drave out his blood-shot eyes
And springs of sweat did in his forehead rise;
Yet was of naught but of a serpent sped,
That in his bosom flew and stung him dead:
And this by Fate into her mind was sent,
Not wrought by mere instinct of her intent.
At the scarf's other end her hand did frame,
Near the fork'd point of the divided flame,
A country virgin keeping of a vine,
Who did of hollow bulrushes combine
Snares for the stubble-loving grasshopper,
And by her lay her scrip that nourish'd her.
Within a myrtle shade she sate and sung;
And tufts of waving reeds about her sprung
Where lurk'd two foxes, that, while she applied
Her trifling snares, their thieveries did divide,

One to the vine, another to her scrip,
That she did negligently overslip;
By which her fruitful vine and wholesome fare
She suffer'd spoil'd, to make a childish snare.
These ominous fancies did her soul express,
And every finger made a prophetess,
To show what death was hid in love's disguise,
And make her judgment conquer Destinies.
O, what sweet forms fair ladies' souls do shroud,
Were they made seen and forced through their blood;
If through their beauties, like rich work through lawn,
They would set forth their minds with virtues drawn,
In letting graces from their fingers fly,
To still their eyas thoughts with industry:
That their plied wits in number'd silks might sing
Passion's huge conquest, and their needles leading
Affection prisoner through their own-built cities,
Pinion'd with stories and Arachnean ditties.
  Proceed we now with Hero's sacrifice:
She odours burn'd, and from their smoke did rise
Unsavoury fumes, that air with plagues inspir'd;
And then the consecrated sticks she fir'd,
On whose pale flame an angry spirit flew,
And beat it down still as it upward grew;
The virgin tapers that on th' altar stood,
When she inflam'd them, burn'd as red as blood:
All sad ostents of that too near success,
That made such moving beauties motionless.
Then Hero wept; but her affrighted eyes
She quickly wrested from the sacrifice,
Shut them, and inwards for Leander look'd.
Search'd her soft bosom, and from thence she pluck'd
His lovely picture: which when she had view'd,
Her beauties were with all love's joys renew'd;
The odours sweeten'd, and the fires burn'd clear,
Leander's form left no ill object there:
Such was his beauty, that the force of light,
Whose knowledge teacheth wonders infinite,
The strength of number and proportion,
Nature had plac'd in it to make it known,
Art was her daughter, and what human wits
For study lost, entomb'd in drossy spirits.
After this accident, (which for her glory

Hero could not but make a history,)
Th' inhabitants of Sestos and Abydos
Did every year, with feasts propitious,
To fair Leander's picture sacrifice:
And they were persons of especial price
That were allow'd it, as an ornament
T' enrich their houses, for the continent
Of the strange virtues all approv'd it held;
For even the very look of it repell'd
All blastings, witchcrafts, and the strifes of nature
In those diseases that no herbs could cure:
The wolfy sting of avarice it would pull,
And make the rankest miser bountiful;
It kill'd the fear of thunder and of death;
The discords that conceit engendereth
'Twixt man and wife, it for the time would cease;
The flames of love it quench'd, and would increase;
Held in a prince's hand, it would put out
The dreadful'st comet; it would ease all doubt
Of threatened mischiefs; it would bring asleep
Such as were mad; it would enforce to weep
Most barbarous eyes; and many more effects
This picture wrought, and sprung Leandrian sects;
Of which was Hero first; for he whose form,
Held in her hand, clear'd such a fatal storm,
From hell she thought his person would defend her,
Which night and Hellespont would quickly send her.
With this confirm'd, she vow'd to banish quite
All thought of any check to her delight;
And, in contempt of silly bashfulness,
She would the faith of her desires profess,
Where her religion should be policy,
To follow love with zeal her piety;
Her chamber her cathedral-church should be,
And her Leander her chief deity;
For in her love these did the gods forego;
And though her knowledge did not teach her so,
Yet did it teach her this, that what her heart
Did greatest hold in her self-greatest part,
That she did make her god; and 'twas less naught
To leave gods in profession and in thought,
Than in her love and life; for therein lies
Most of her duties and their dignities;

And, rail the brain-bald world at what it will,
That's the grand atheism that reigns in it still.
Yet singularity she would use no more,
For she was singular too much before;
But she would please the world with fair pretext;
Love would not leave her conscience perplext:
Great men that will have less do for them still,
Must bear them out, though th' acts be ne'er so ill;
Meanness must pander be to Excellence;
Pleasure atones Falsehood and Conscience:
Dissembling was the worst, thought Hero then,
And that was best, now she must live with men.
O virtuous love, that taught her to do best
When she did worst, and when she thought it least!
Thus would she still proceed in works divine,
And in her sacred state of priesthood shine,
Handling the holy rites with hands as bold,
As if therein she did Jove's thunder hold,
And need not fear those menaces of error,
Which she at others threw with greatest terror.
O lovely Hero, nothing is thy sin,
Weigh'd with those foul faults other priests are in!
That having neither faiths, nor works, nor beauties,
T' engender any 'scuse for slubber'd duties,
With as much countenance fill their holy chairs,
And sweat denouncements 'gainst profane affairs,
As if their lives were cut out by their places,
And they the only fathers of the Graces.
  Now, as with settled mind she did repair
Her thoughts to sacrifice her ravish'd hair
And her torn robe, which on the altar lay,
And only for religion's fire did stay,
She heard a thunder by the Cyclops beaten,
In such a volley as the world did threaten,
Given Venus as she parted th' airy sphere,
Descending now to chide with Hero here:
When suddenly the goddess' waggoners,
The swans and turtles that, in coupled pheres,
Through all worlds' bosoms draw her influence,
Lighted in Hero's window, and from thence
To her fair shoulders flew the gentle doves,—
Graceful Ædone that sweet pleasure loves,
And ruff-foot Chreste with the tufted crown;

Both which did kiss her, though their goddess frown.
The swans did in the solid flood, her glass,
Preen their fair plumes; of which the fairest was
Jove-lov'd Leucote, that pure brightness is;
The other bounty-loving Dapsilis,
All were in heaven, now they with Hero were:
But Venus' looks brought wrath, and urged fear.
Her robe was scarlet; black her head's attire;
And through her naked breast shin'd streams of fire,
As when the rarified air is driven
In flashing streams, and opes the darken'd heaven.
In her white hand a wreath of yew she bore;
And, breaking th' icy wreath sweet Hero wore,
She forc'd about her brows her wreath of yew,
And said, "Now, minion, to thy fate be true,
Though not to me; endure what this portends:
Begin where lightness will, in shame it ends.
Love makes thee cunning; thou art current now,
By being counterfeit: thy broken vow
Deceit with her pied garters must rejoin,
And with her stamp thou countenances must coin;
Coyness, and pure deceits, for purities,
And still a maid wilt seem in cozen'd eyes,
And have an antic face to laugh within,
While thy smooth looks make men digest thy sin,
But since thy lips (lest thought forsworn) forswore,
Be never virgin's vow worth trusting more!"
  When Beauty's dearest did her goddess hear
Breathe such rebukes 'gainst that she could not clear,
Dumb sorrow spake aloud in tears and blood,
That from her grief-burst veins, in piteous flood,
From the sweet conduits of her favour fell.
The gentle turtles did with moans make swell
Their shining gorges; the white black-ey'd swans
Did sing as woful epicedians,
As they would straightways die: when Pity's queen,
The goddess Ecte, that had ever been
Hid in a watery cloud near Hero's cries,
Since the first instant of her broken eyes,
Gave bright Leucote voice, and made her speak,
To ease her anguish, whose swoln breast did break
With anger at her goddess, that did touch
Hero so near for that she us'd so much;

And, thrusting her white neck at Venus, said:
"Why may not amorous Hero seem a maid,
Though she be none, as well as you suppress
In modest cheeks your inward wantonness?
How often have we drawn you from above,
T' exchange with mortals rites for rites in love!
Why in your priest, then, call you that offence,
That shines in you, and is your influence?"
With this, the Furies stopp'd Leucote's lips,
Enjoin'd by Venus; who with rosy whips
Beat the kind bird. Fierce lightning from her eyes
Did set on fire fair Hero's sacrifice,
Which was her torn robe and enforced hair;
And the bright flame became a maid most fair
For her aspect: her tresses were of wire,
Knit like a net, where hearts, set all on fire,
Struggled in pants, and could not get releast;
Her arms were all with golden pincers drest,
And twenty-fashion'd knots, pulleys, and brakes,
And all her body girdled with painted snakes;
Her down-parts in a scorpion's tail combin'd,
Freckled with twenty colours; pied wings shin'd
Out of her shoulders; cloth had never dye,
Nor sweeter colours never viewed eye,
In scorching Turkey, Cares, Tartary,
Than shin'd about this spirit notorious;
Nor was Arachne's web so glorious.
Of lightning, and of shreds she was begot;
More hold in base dissemblers is there not.
Her name was Eronusis. Venus flew
From Hero's sight, and at her chariot drew
This wondrous creature to so steep a height,
That all the world she might command with sleight
Of her gay wings; and then she bade her haste,—
Since Hero had dissembled, and disgrac'd
Her rites so much,—and every breast infect
With her deceits: she made her architect
Of all dissimulation, and since then
Never was any trust in maids nor men.
O, it spited
Fair Venus' heart to see her most delighted,
And one she choos'd, for temper of her mind,
To be the only ruler of her kind,

So soon to let her virgin race be ended!
Not simply for the fault a whit offended,
But that in strife for chasteness with the Moon,
Spiteful Diana bade her show but one
That was her servant vow'd, and liv'd a maid;
And, now she thought to answer that upbraid,
Hero had lost her answer: who knows not
Venus would seem as far from any spot
Of light demeanour, as the very skin
'Twixt Cynthia's brows? sin is asham'd of sin.
Up Venus flew, and scarce durst up for fear
Of Phœbe's laughter, when she pass'd her sphere:
And so most ugly-clouded was the light,
That day was hid in day; night came ere night;
And Venus could not through the thick air pierce,
Till the day's king, god of undaunted verse,
Because she was so plentiful a theme
To such as wore his laurel anademe,
Like to a fiery bullet made descent,
And from her passage those fat vapours rent,
That, being not throughly rarefied to rain,
Melted like pitch, as blue as any vein;
And scalding tempests made the earth to shrink
Under their fervour, and the world did think
In every drop a torturing spirit flew,
It pierc'd so deeply, and it burn'd so blue.
  Betwixt all this and Hero, Hero held
Leander's picture, as a Persian shield;
And she was free from fear of worst success:
The more ill threats us, we suspect the less:
As we grow hapless, violence subtle grows,
Dumb, deaf, and blind, and comes when no man knows.

THE FIFTH SESTIAD

The Argument of the Fifth Sestiad.

Day doubles her accustomed date,
As loath the Night, incens'd by Fate,
Should wreck our lovers. Hero's plight;
Longs for Leander and the night:
Which ere her thirsty wish recovers,
She sends for two betrothed lovers,
And marries them, that, with their crew,
Their sports, and ceremonies due,
She covertly might celebrate,
With secret joy, her own estate.
She makes a feast, at which appears
The wild nymph Teras, that still bears
An ivory lute, tells ominous tales,
And sings at solemn festivals.

Now was bright Hero weary of the day,
Thought an Olympiad in Leander's stay.
Sol and the soft-foot Hours hung on his arms,
And would not let him swim, foreseeing his harms:
That day Aurora double grace obtain'd
Of her love Phœbus; she his horses rein'd,
Sat on his golden knee, and, as she list,
She pull'd him back; and, as she pull'd, she kiss'd,
To have him turn to bed: he lov'd her more,
To see the love Leander Hero bore:
Examples profit much; ten times in one,
In persons full of note, good deeds are done.
Day was so long, men walking fell asleep;
The heavy humours that their eyes did steep
Made them fear mischiefs. The hard streets were beds
For covetous churls and for ambitious heads,
That, spite of Nature, would their business ply:
All thought they had the falling epilepsy,
Men grovell'd so upon the smother'd ground;
And pity did the heart of Heaven confound.
The Gods, the Graces, and the Muses came
Down to the Destinies, to stay the frame
Of the true lovers' deaths, and all worlds' tears:
But Death before had stopp'd their cruel ears.
All the celestials parted mourning then,
Pierc'd with our human miseries more than men:

Ah, nothing doth the world with mischief fill,
But want of feeling one another's ill!
  With their descent the day grew something fair,
And cast a brighter robe upon the air.
Hero, to shorten time with merriment,
For young Alcmane and bright Mya sent,
Two lovers that had long crav'd marriage-dues
At Hero's hands: but she did still refuse;
For lovely Mya was her consort vow'd
In her maid's state, and therefore not allow'd
To amorous nuptials: yet fair Hero now
Intended to dispense with her cold vow,
Since hers was broken, and to marry her:
The rites would pleasing matter minister
To her conceits, and shorten tedious day.
They came; sweet Music usher'd th' odorous way,
And wanton Air in twenty sweet forms danc'd
After her fingers; Beauty and Love advanc'd
Their ensigns in the downless rosy faces
Of youths and maids, led after by the Graces.
For all these Hero made a friendly feast,
Welcom'd them kindly, did much love protest,
Winning their hearts with all the means she might,
That, when her fault should chance t' abide the light,
Their loves might cover or extenuate it,
And high in her worst fate make pity sit.
  She married them; and in the banquet came,
Borne by the virgins. Hero striv'd to frame
Her thoughts to mirth: ay me! but hard it is
To imitate a false and forced bliss;
Ill may a sad mind forge a merry face,
Nor hath constrained laughter any grace.
Then laid she wine on cares to make them sink:
Who fears the threats of Fortune, let him drink.
  To these quick nuptials enter'd suddenly
Admired Teras with the ebon thigh;
A nymph that haunted the green Sestian groves,
And would consort soft virgins in their loves,
At gaysome triumphs and on solemn days,
Singing prophetic elegies and lays,
And fingering of a silver lute she tied
With black and purple scarfs by her left side.
Apollo gave it, and her skill withal,

And she was term'd his dwarf, she was so small:
Yet great in virtue, for his beams enclos'd
His virtues in her; never was propos'd
Riddle to her, or augury, strange or new,
But she resolv'd it; never slight tale flew
From her charm'd lips without important sense,
Shown in some grave succeeding consequence.
  This little sylvan, with her songs and tales,
Gave such estate to feasts and nuptials,
That though ofttimes she forewent tragedies,
Yet for her strangeness still she pleas'd their eyes;
And for her smallness they admir'd her so,
They thought her perfect born, and could not grow.
  All eyes were on her. Hero did command
An altar deck'd with sacred state should stand
At the feast's upper end, close by the bride,
On which the pretty nymph might sit espied.
Then all were silent; every one so hears,
As all their senses climb'd into their ears:
And first this amorous tale, that fitted well
Fair Hero and the nuptials, she did tell.

The Tale of Teras.

  Hymen, that now is god of nuptial rites,
And crowns with honour Love and his delights,
Of Athens was a youth, so sweet of face,
That many thought him of the female race;
Such quickening brightness did his clear eyes dart,
Warm went their beams to his beholder's heart,
In such pure leagues his beauties were combin'd,
That there your nuptial contracts first were sign'd;
For as proportion, white and crimson, meet
In beauty's mixture, all right clear and sweet,
The eye responsible, the golden hair,
And none is held, without the other, fair;
All spring together, all together fade;
Such intermix'd affections should invade
Two perfect lovers; which being yet unseen,
Their virtues and their comforts copied been
In beauty's concord, subject to the eye;
And that, in Hymen, pleas'd so matchlessly,
That lovers were esteem'd in their full grace,

Like form and colour mix'd in Hymen's face;
And such sweet concord was thought worthy then
Of torches, music, feasts, and greatest men:
So Hymen look'd, that even the chastest mind
He mov'd to join in joys of sacred kind;
For only now his chin's first down consorted
His head's rich fleece, in golden curls contorted;
And as he was so lov'd, he lov'd so too:
So should best beauties, bound by nuptials, do.
  Bright Eucharis, who was by all men said
The noblest, fairest, and the richest maid
Of all th' Athenian damsels, Hymen lov'd
With such transmission, that his heart remov'd
From his white breast to hers: but her estate,
In passing his, was so interminate
For wealth and honour, that his love durst feed
On naught but sight and hearing, nor could breed
Hope of requital, the grand prize of love;
Nor could he hear or see, but he must prove
How his rare beauty's music would agree
With maids in consort; therefore robbed he
His chin of those same few first fruits it bore,
And, clad in such attire as virgins wore,
He kept them company; and might right well,
For he did all but Eucharis excel
In all the fair of beauty: yet he wanted
Virtue to make his own desires implanted
In his dear Eucharis; for women never
Love beauty in their sex, but envy ever.
His judgment yet, that durst not suit address,
Nor, past due means, presume of due success,
Reason gat Fortune in the end to speed
To his best prayers: but strange it seem'd, indeed,
That Fortune should a chaste affection bless:
Preferment seldom graceth bashfulness.
Nor grac'd it Hymen yet; but many a dart,
And many an amorous thought, enthrall'd his heart,
Ere he obtain'd her; and he sick became,
Forc'd to abstain her sight; and then the flame
Rag'd in his bosom. O, what grief did fill him!
Sight made him sick, and want of sight did kill him.
The virgins wonder'd where Diætia stay'd,
For so did Hymen term himself, a maid.

At length with sickly looks he greeted them:
'Tis strange to see 'gainst what an extreme stream
A lover strives; poor Hymen look'd so ill,
That as in merit he increased still
By suffering much, so he in grace decreas'd:
Women are most won, when men merit least:
If Merit look not well, Love bids stand by;
Love's special lesson is to please the eye.
And Hymen soon recovering all he lost,
Deceiving still these maids, but himself most,
His love and he with many virgin dames,
Noble by birth, noble by beauty's flames,
Leaving the town with songs and hallow'd lights,
To do great Ceres Eleusina rites
Of zealous sacrifice, were made a prey
To barbarous rovers, that in ambush lay,
And with rude hands enforc'd their shining spoil,
Far from the darken'd city, tir'd with toil:
And when the yellow issue of the sky
Came trooping forth, jealous of cruelty
To their bright fellows of this under-heaven,
Into a double night they saw them driven,—
A horrid cave, the thieves' black mansion;
Where weary of the journey they had gone,
Their last night's watch, and drunk with their sweet gains,
Dull Morpheus enter'd, laden with silken chains,
Stronger than iron, and bound the swelling veins
And tired senses of these lawless swains.
But when the virgin lights thus dimly burn'd,
O, what a hell was heaven in! how they mourn'd,
And wrung their hands, and wound their gentle forms
Into the shapes of sorrow! golden storms
Fell from their eyes; as when the sun appears,
And yet it rains, so show'd their eyes their tears:
And, as when funeral dames watch a dead corse,
Weeping about it, telling with remorse
What pains he felt, how long in pain he lay,
How little food he eat, what he would say,
And then mix mournful tales of others' deaths,
Smothering themselves in clouds of their own breaths;
At length, one cheering other, call for wine;
The golden bowl drinks tears out of their eyne,

As they drink wine from it; and round it goes,
Each helping other to relieve their woes;
So cast these virgins' beauties mutual rays,
One lights another, face the face displays;
Lips by reflection kiss'd, and hands hands shook,
Even by the whiteness each of other took.
 But Hymen now us'd friendly Morpheus' aid,
Slew every thief, and rescu'd every maid:
And now did his enamour'd passion take
Heart from his hearty deed, whose worth did make
His hope of bounteous Eucharis more strong;
And now came Love with Proteus, who had long
Juggled the little god with prayers and gifts,
Ran through all shapes, and varied all his shifts,
To win Love's stay with him, and make him love him;
And when he saw no strength of sleight could move him
To make him love or stay, he nimbly turn'd
Into Love's self, he so extremely burn'd.
And thus came Love, with Proteus and his power,
T' encounter Eucharis: first, like the flower
That Juno's milk did spring, the silver lily,
He fell on Hymen's hand, who straight did spy
The bounteous godhead, and with wondrous joy
Offer'd it Eucharis. She, wondrous coy,
Drew back her hand: the subtle flower did woo it,
And, drawing it near, mix'd so you could not know it:
As two clear tapers mix in one their light,
So did the lily and the hand their white.
She view'd it; and her view the form bestows
Amongst her spirits: for, as colour flows
From superficies of each thing we see,
Even so with colours forms emitted be;
And where Love's form is, Love is; Love is form:
He enter'd at the eye; his sacred storm
Rose from the hand, Love's sweetest instrument:
It stirr'd her blood's sea so, that high it went,
And beat in bashful waves 'gainst the white shore
Of her divided cheeks; it rag'd the more,
Because the tide went 'gainst the haughty wind
Of her estate and birth: and, as we find,
In fainting ebbs, the flowery Zephyr hurls
The green-hair'd Hellespont, broke in silver curls,
'Gainst Hero's tower; but in his blast's retreat,

The waves obeying him, they after beat,
Leaving the chalky shore a great way pale,
Then moist it freshly with another gale;
So ebb'd and flow'd the blood in Eucharis' face,
Coyness and Love striv'd which had greatest grace;
Virginity did fight on Coyness' side,
Fear of her parents' frowns, and female pride
Loathing the lower place, more than it loves
The high contents desert and virtue moves.
With Love fought Hymen's beauty and his valure,
Which scarce could so much favour yet allure
To come to strike, but fameless idle stood:
Action is fiery valour's sovereign good.
But Love, once enter'd, wish'd no greater aid
Than he could find within; thought thought betray'd;
The brib'd, but incorrupted, garrison
Sung "Io Hymen"; there those songs begun,
And Love was grown so rich with such a gain,
And wanton with the ease of his free reign,
That he would turn into her roughest frowns
To turn them out; and thus he Hymen crowns
King of his thoughts, man's greatest empery:
This was his first brave step to deity.
  Home to the mourning city they repair,
With news as wholesome as the morning air,
To the sad parents of each saved maid:
But Hymen and his Eucharis had laid
This plat, to make the flame of their delight
Round as the moon at full, and full as bright.
  Because the parents of chaste Eucharis
Exceeding Hymen's so, might cross their bliss;
And as the world rewards deserts, that law
Cannot assist with force; so when they saw
Their daughter safe, take vantage of their own,
Praise Hymen's valour much, nothing bestown;
Hymen must leave the virgins in a grove
Far off from Athens, and go first to prove,
If to restore them all with fame and life,
He should enjoy his dearest as his wife.
This told to all the maids, the most agree:
The riper sort, knowing what 'tis to be
The first mouth of a news so far deriv'd,
And that to hear and bear news brave folks liv'd,

As being a carriage special hard to bear
Occurrents, these occurrents being so dear,
They did with grace protest, they were content
T' accost their friends with all their compliment,
For Hymen's good; but to incur their harm,
There he must pardon them. This wit went warm
To Adolesche's brain, a nymph born high,
Made all of voice and fire, that upwards fly:
Her heart and all her forces' nether train
Climb'd to her tongue, and thither fell her brain,
Since it could go no higher; and it must go;
All powers she had, even her tongue, did so:
In spirit and quickness she much joy did take,
And lov'd her tongue, only for quickness' sake;
And she would haste and tell. The rest all stay:
Hymen goes one, the nymph another way;
And what became of her I'll tell at last:
Yet take her visage now;—moist-lipp'd, long-fac'd,
Thin like an iron wedge, so sharp and tart,
As 'twere of purpose made to cleave Love's heart:
Well were this lovely beauty rid of her.
And Hymen did at Athens now prefer
His welcome suit, which he with joy aspir'd:
A hundred princely youths with him retir'd
To fetch the nymphs; chariots and music went
And home they came: heaven with applauses rent.
The nuptials straight proceed, whiles all the town,
Fresh in their joys, might do them most renown.
First, gold-lock'd Hymen did to church repair,
Like a quick offering burn'd in flames of hair;
And after, with a virgin firmament
The godhead-proving bride attended went
Before them all: she look'd in her command,
As if form-giving Cypria's silver hand
Gripp'd all their beauties, and crushed out one flame;
She blush'd to see how beauty overcame
The thoughts of all men. Next, before her went
Five lovely children, deck'd with ornament
Of her sweet colours, bearing torches by;
For light was held a happy augury
Of generation, whose efficient right
Is nothing else but to produce to light.
The odd disparent number they did choose,

To show the union married loves should use,
Since in two equal parts it will not sever,
But the midst holds one to rejoin it ever,
As common to both parts: men therefore deem
That equal number gods do not esteem,
Being authors of sweet peace and unity,
But pleasing to th' infernal empery,
Under whose ensigns Wars and Discords fight,
Since an even number you may disunite
In two parts equal, naught in middle left
To reunite each part from other reft;
And five they hold in most especial prize,
Since 'tis the first odd number that doth rise
From the two foremost numbers' unity,
That odd and even are; which are two and three;
For one no number is; but thence doth flow
The powerful race of number. Next did go
A noble matron, that did spinning bear
A huswife's rock and spindle, and did wear
A wether's skin, with all the snowy fleece,
To intimate that even the daintiest piece
And noblest-born dame should industrious be:
That which does good disgraceth no degree.
  And now to Juno's temple they are come,
Where her grave priest stood in the marriage-room:
On his right arm did hang a scarlet veil,
And from his shoulders to the ground did trail,
On either side, ribands of white and blue:
With the red veil he hid the bashful hue
Of the chaste bride, to show the modest shame,
In coupling with a man, should grace a dame.
Then took he the disparent silks, and tied
The lovers by the waists, and side by side,
In token that hereafter they must bind
In one self-sacred knot each other's mind.
Before them on an altar he presented
Both fire and water, which was first invented,
Since to ingenerate every human creature
And every other birth produc'd by Nature,
Moisture and heat must mix; so man and wife
For human race must join in nuptial life.
Then one of Juno's birds, the painted jay,
He sacrific'd, and took the gall away;

All which he did behind the altar throw,
In sign no bitterness of hate should grow
'Twixt married loves, nor any least disdain.
Nothing they spake, for 'twas esteem'd too plain
For the most silken mildness of a maid,
To let a public audience hear it said
She boldly took the man; and so respected
Was bashfulness in Athens, it erected
To chaste Agneia, which is Shamefastness,
A sacred temple, holding her a goddess.
And now to feasts, masks, and triumphant shows,
The shining troops return'd, even till earth-throes
Brought forth with joy the thickest part of night,
When the sweet nuptial song, that us'd to cite
All to their rest, was by Phemonöe sung,
First Delphian prophetess, whose graces sprung
Out of the Muses' well: she sung before
The bride into her chamber; at which door
A matron and a torch-bearer did stand:
A painted box of comfits in her hand
The matron held, and so did other some
That compass'd round the honour'd nuptial room.
The custom was that every maid did wear,
During her maidenhead, a silken sphere
About her waist, above her inmost weed,
Knit with Minerva's knot, and that was freed
By the fair bridegroom on the marriage-night,
With many ceremonies of delight:
And yet eternis'd Hymen's tender bride,
To suffer it dissolv'd so sweetly cried.
The maids that heard, so lov'd and did adore her,
They wish'd with all their hearts to suffer for her.
So had the matrons, that with comfits stood
About the chamber, such affectionate blood,
And so true feeling of her harmless pains,
That every one a shower of comfits rains;
For which the bride-youths scrambling on the ground,
In noise of that sweet hail her cries were drown'd.
And thus blest Hymen joy'd his gracious bride,
And for his joy was after deified.
The saffron mirror by which Phœbus' love,
Green Tellus, decks her, now he held above
The cloudy mountains: and the noble maid,

Sharp-visag'd Adolesche, that was stray'd
Out of her way, in hasting with her news,
Not till this hour th' Athenian turrets views;
And now brought home by guides, she heard by all,
That her long kept occurrents would be stale,
And how fair Hymen's honours did excel
For those rare news which she came short to tell.
To hear her dear tongue robb'd of such a joy,
Made the well-spoken nymph take such a toy,
That down she sunk: when lightning from above
Shrunk her lean body, and, for mere free love,
Turn'd her into the pied-plum'd Psittacus,
That now the Parrot is surnam'd by us,
Who still with counterfeit confusion prates
Naught but news common to the common'st mates.—
This told, strange Teras touch'd her lute, and sung
This ditty, that the torchy evening sprung.

Epithalamion Teratos.

Come, come, dear Night! Love's mart of kisses,
  Sweet close of his ambitious line,
The fruitful summer of his blisses!
  Love's glory doth in darkness shine.
O, come, soft rest of cares! come, Night!
  Come, naked Virtue's only tire,
The reaped harvest of the light,
  Bound up in sheaves of sacred fire!
    Love calls to war;
      Sighs his alarms,
    Lips his swords are,
      The field his arms.

Come, Night, and lay thy velvet hand
  On glorious Day's outfacing face;
And all thy crowned flames command,
  For torches to our nuptial grace!
    Love calls to war;
      Sighs his alarms,
    Lips his swords are,
      The field his arms.

No need have we of factious Day,
  To cast, in envy of thy peace,

Her balls of discord in thy way:
  Here Beauty's day doth never cease;
Day is abstracted here,
And varied in a triple sphere.
Hero, Alcmane, Mya, so outshine thee,
Ere thou come here, let Thetis thrice refine thee.
    Love calls to war;
      Sighs his alarms,
    Lips his swords are,
      The field his arms.

    The evening star I see:
      Rise, youths! the evening star
      Helps Love to summon war;
    Both now embracing be.
Rise, youths! Love's rite claims more than banquets; rise!
Now the bright marigolds, that deck the skies,
Phœbus' celestial flowers, that, contrary
To his flowers here, ope when he shuts his eye,
And shut when he doth open, crown your sports:
Now Love in Night, and Night in Love exhorts
Courtship and dances: all your parts employ,
And suit Night's rich expansure with your joy.
Love paints his longings in sweet virgins' eyes:
Rise, youths! Love's rite claims more than banquets; rise!
  Rise, virgins! let fair nuptial loves enfold
Your fruitless breasts: the maidenheads ye hold
Are not your own alone, but parted are;
Part in disposing them your parents share,
And that a third part is; so must ye save
Your loves a third, and you your thirds must have.
Love paints his longings in sweet virgins' eyes:
Rise, youths! Love's rites claim more than banquets; rise!

  Herewith the amorous spirit, that was so kind
To Teras' hair, and comb'd it down with wind,
Still as it, comet-like, brake from her brain,
Would needs have Teras gone, and did refrain
To blow it down: which, staring up, dismay'd
The timorous feast; and she no longer stay'd;

But, bowing to the bridegroom and the bride,
Did, like a shooting exhalation, glide
Out of their sights: the turning of her back
Made them all shriek, it look'd so ghastly black.
O hapless Hero! that most hapless cloud
Thy soon-succeeding tragedy foreshow'd.
Thus all the nuptial crew to joys depart;
But much-wrung Hero stood Hell's blackest dart:
Whose wound because I grieve so to display,
I use digressions thus t'increase the day.

THE SIXTH SESTIAD

The Argument of the Sixth Sestiad.

Leucote flies to all the Winds,
And from the Fates their outrage binds,
That Hero and her love may meet.
Leander, with Love's complete fleet
Mann'd in himself, puts forth to seas;
When straight the ruthless Destinies,
With Até, stir the winds to war
Upon the Hellespont: their jar
Drowns poor Leander. Hero's eyes,
Wet witnesses of his surprise,
Her torch blown out, grief casts her down
Upon her love, and both doth drown:
In whose just ruth the god of seas
Transforms them to th' Acanthides.

No longer could the Day nor Destinies
Delay the Night, who now did frowning rise
Into her throne; and at her humorous breasts
Visions and Dreams lay sucking: all men's rests
Fell like the mists of death upon their eyes,
Day's too-long darts so kill'd their faculties.
The Winds yet, like the flowers, to cease began;
For bright Leucote, Venus' whitest swan,
That held sweet Hero dear, spread her fair wings,
Like to a field of snow, and message brings
From Venus to the Fates, t'entreat them lay
Their charge upon the Winds their rage to stay,
That the stern battle of the seas might cease,
And guard Leander to his love in peace.
The Fates consent;—ay me, dissembling Fates!

They show'd their favours to conceal their hates,
And draw Leander on, lest seas too high
Should stay his too obsequious destiny:
Who like a fleering slavish parasite,
In warping profit or a traitorous sleight,
Hoops round his rotten body with devotes,
And pricks his descant face full of false notes;
Praising with open throat, and oaths as foul
As his false heart, the beauty of an owl;
Kissing his skipping hand with charmed skips,
That cannot leave, but leaps upon his lips
Like a cock-sparrow, or a shameless quean
Sharp at a red-lipp'd youth, and naught doth mean
Of all his antic shows, but doth repair
More tender fawns, and takes a scatter'd hair
From his tame subject's shoulder; whips and calls
For everything he lacks; creeps 'gainst the walls
With backward humbless, to give needless way:
Thus his false fate did with Leander play.
  First to black Eurus flies the white Leucote.
(Born 'mongst the negroes in the Levant sea,
On whose curl'd head[s] the glowing sun doth rise,)
And shows the sovereign will of Destinies,
To have him cease his blasts; and down he lies.
Next, to the fenny Notus course she holds,
And found him leaning, with his arms in folds,
Upon a rock, his white hair full of showers;
And him she chargeth by the fatal powers,
To hold in his wet cheeks his cloudy voice.
To Zephyr then that doth in flowers rejoice:
To snake-foot Boreas next she did remove,
And found him tossing of his ravish'd love,
To heat his frosty bosom hid in snow;
Who with Leucote's sight did cease to blow.
Thus all were still to Hero's heart's desire;
Who with all speed did consecrate a fire
Of flaming gums and comfortable spice,
To light her torch, which in such curious price
She held, being object to Leander's sight,
That naught but fires perfum'd must give it light.
She lov'd it so, she griev'd to see it burn,
Since it would waste, and soon to ashes turn:
Yet, if it burn'd not, 'twere not worth her eyes;

What made it nothing, gave it all the prize.
Sweet torch, true glass of our society!
What man does good, but he consumes thereby?
But thou wert lov'd for good, held high, given show;
Poor virtue loath'd for good, obscur'd, held low:
Do good, be pin'd,—be deedless good, disgrac'd;
Unless we feed on men, we let them fast.
Yet Hero with these thoughts her torch did spend:
When bees make wax, Nature doth not intend
It shall be made a torch; but we, that know
The proper virtue of it, make it so,
And, when 'tis made, we light it: nor did Nature
Propose one life to maids; but each such creature
Makes by her soul the best of her free state,
Which without love is rude, disconsolate,
And wants love's fire to make it mild and bright,
Till when, maids are but torches wanting light.
Thus 'gainst our grief, not cause of grief, we fight:
The right of naught is glean'd, but the delight.
Up went she: but to tell how she descended,
Would God she were not dead, or my verse ended!
She was the rule of wishes, sum, and end,
For all the parts that did on love depend:
Yet cast the torch his brightness further forth;
But what shines nearest best, holds truest worth.
Leander did not through such tempests swim
To kiss the torch, although it lighted him:
But all his powers in her desires awaked,
Her love and virtues cloth'd him richly naked.
Men kiss but fire that only shows pursue;
Her torch and Hero, figure show and virtue.
  Now at oppos'd Abydos naught was heard
But bleating flocks, and many a bellowing herd,
Slain for the nuptials; cracks of falling woods;
Blows of broad axes; pourings out of floods.
The guilty Hellespont was mix'd and stain'd
With bloody torrents, that the shambles rain'd;
Not arguments of feast, but shows that bled,
Foretelling that red night that followed.
More blood was spilt, more honours were addrest,
Than could have graced any happy feast;
Rich banquets, triumphs, every pomp employs
His sumptuous hand; no miser's nuptial joys.

Air felt continual thunder with the noise
Made in the general marriage-violence;
And no man knew the cause of this expense,
But the two hapless lords, Leander's sire,
And poor Leander, poorest where the fire
Of credulous love made him most rich surmis'd:
As short was he of that himself he priz'd,
As is an empty gallant full of form,
That thinks each look an act, each drop a storm,
That falls from his brave breathings; most brought up
In our metropolis, and hath his cup
Brought after him to feasts; and much palm bears
For his rare judgment in th' attire he wears;
Hath seen the hot Low-Countries, not their heat,
Observes their rampires and their buildings yet;
And, for your sweet discourse with mouths, is heard
Giving instructions with his very beard;
Hath gone with an ambassador, and been
A great man's mate in travelling, even to Rhene;
And then puts all his worth in such a face
As he saw brave men make, and strives for grace
To get his news forth: as when you descry
A ship, with all her sail contends to fly
Out of the narrow Thames with winds unapt,
Now crosseth here, then there, then this way rapt,
And then hath one point reach'd, then alters all,
And to another crooked reach doth fall
Of half a bird-bolt's shoot, keeping more coil
Than if she danc'd upon the ocean's toil;
So serious is his trifling company,
In all his swelling ship of vacantry.
And so short of himself in his high thought
Was our Leander in his fortunes brought,
And in his fort of love that he thought won;
But otherwise he scorns comparison.
O sweet Leander, thy large worth I hide
In a short grave! ill-favour'd storms must chide
Thy sacred favour; I in floods of ink
Must drown thy graces, which white papers drink,
Even as thy beauties did the foul black seas;
I must describe the hell of thy decease,
That heaven did merit: yet I needs must see
Our painted fools and cockhorse peasantry

Still, still usurp, with long lives, loves, and lust,
The seats of Virtue, cutting short as dust
Her dear-bought issue: ill to worse converts,
And tramples in the blood of all deserts.
Night close and silent now goes fast before
The captains and the soldiers to the shore,
On whom attended the appointed fleet
At Sestos' bay, that should Leander meet,
Who feign'd he in another ship would pass:
Which must not be, for no one mean there was
To get his love home, but the course he took.
Forth did his beauty for his beauty look,
And saw her through her torch, as you behold
Sometimes within the sun a face of gold,
Form'd in strong thoughts, by that tradition's force
That says a god sits there and guides his course.
His sister was with him; to whom he show'd
His guide by sea, and said, " Oft have you view'd
In one heaven many stars, but never yet
In one star many heavens till now were met.
See, lovely sister! see, now Hero shines,
No heaven but her appears; each star repines,
And all are clad in clouds, as if they mourn'd
To be by influence of earth out-burn'd.
Yet doth she shine, and teacheth Virtue's train
Still to be constant in hell's blackest reign,
Though even the gods themselves do so entreat them
As they did hate, and earth as she would eat them."
Off went his silken robe, and in he leapt,
Whom the kind waves so licorously cleapt,
Thickening for haste, one in another, so,
To kiss his skin, that he might almost go
To Hero's tower, had that kind minute lasted.
But now the cruel Fates with Até hasted
To all the Winds, and made them battle fight
Upon the Hellespont, for either's right
Pretended to the windy monarchy;
And forth they brake, the seas mix'd with the sky,
And toss'd distress'd Leander, being in hell,
As high as heaven: bliss not in height doth dwell.
The Destinies sate dancing on the waves,
To see the glorious Winds with mutual braves
Consume each other: O, true glass, to see

How ruinous ambitious statists be
To their own glories! Poor Leander cried
For help to sea-born Venus; she denied;
To Boreas, that, for his Atthæa's sake,
He would some pity on his Hero take,
And for his own love's sake, on his desires;
But Glory never blows cold Pity's fires.
Then call'd he Neptune, who, through all the noise,
Knew with affright his wreck'd Leander's voice,
And up he rose; for haste his forehead hit
'Gainst heaven's hard crystal; his proud waves he smit
With his fork'd sceptre, that could not obey;
Much greater powers than Neptune's gave them sway.
They lov'd Leander so, in groans they brake
When they came near him; and such space did take
'Twixt one another, loath to issue on,
That in their shallow furrows earth was shown,
And the poor lover took a little breath:
But the curst Fates sate spinning of his death
On every wave, and with the servile Winds
Tumbled them on him. And now Hero finds,
By that she felt, her dear Leander's state:
She wept, and pray'd for him to every Fate;
And every Wind that whipp'd her with her hair
About the face, she kiss'd and spake it fair,
Kneel'd to it, gave it drink out of her eyes
To quench his thirst: but still their cruelties
Even her poor torch envi'd, and rudely beat
The bating flame from that dear food it eat;
Dear, for it nourish'd her Leander's life;
Which with her robe she rescu'd from their strife:
But silk too soft was, such hard hearts to break,
And she, dear soul, even as her silk, faint, weak,
Could not preserve it; out, O, out it went!
Leander still call'd Neptune, that now rent
His brackish curls, and tore his wrinkled face,
Where tears in billows did each other chase;
And, burst with ruth, he hurl'd his marble mace
At the stern Fates; it wounded Lachesis
That drew Leander's thread, and could not miss
The thread itself, as it her hand did hit,
But smote it full, and quite did sunder it.
The more kind Neptune rag'd, the more he raz'd

His love's life fort, and kill'd as he embrac'd:
Anger doth still his own mishap increase;
If any comfort live, it is in peace.
O thievish Fates, to let blood, flesh, and sense,
Build two fair temples for their excellence,
To rob it with a poison'd influence!
Though souls' gifts starve, the bodies are held dear
In ugliest things; sense-sport preserves a bear:
But here naught serves our turns: O heaven and earth,
How most most wretched is our human birth!
And now did all the tyrannous crew depart,
Knowing there was a storm in Hero's heart,
Greater than they could make, and scorn'd their smart.
She bow'd herself so low out of her tower,
That wonder 'twas she fell not ere her hour,
With searching the lamenting waves for him:
Like a poor snail, her gentle supple limb
Hung on her turret's top, so most downright,
As she would dive beneath the darkness quite,
To find her jewel;—jewel!—her Leander,
A name of all earth's jewels pleas'd not her
Like his dear name: "Leander, still my choice,
Come naught but my Leander! O my voice,
Turn to Leander! henceforth be all sounds,
Accents, and phrases, that show all grief's wounds,
Analys'd in Leander! O black change!
Trumpets, do you, with thunder of your clange,
Drive out this change's horror! My voice faints:
Where all joy was, now shriek out all complaints!"
Thus cried she; for her mixed soul could tell
Her love was dead: and when the Morning fell
Prostrate upon the weeping earth for woe,
Blushes, that bled out of her cheeks, did show
Leander brought by Neptune, bruis'd and torn
With cities' ruins he to rocks had worn,
To filthy usuring rocks, that would have blood,
Though they could get of him no other good.
She saw him, and the sight was much much more
Than might have serv'd to kill her: should her store
Of giant sorrows speak?—Burst,—die,—bleed,
And leave poor plaints to us that shall succeed.
She fell on her love's bosom, hugg'd it fast,
And with Leander's name she breath'd her last.

Neptune for pity in his arms did take them,
Flung them into the air, and did awake them
Like two sweet birds, surnam'd th' Acanthides,
Which we call Thistle-warps, that near no seas
Dare ever come, but still in couples fly,
And feed on thistle-tops, to testify
The hardness of their first life in their last;
The first, in thorns of love, that sorrows past:
And so most beautiful their colours show
As none (so little) like them; her sad brow
A sable velvet feather covers quite,
Even like the forehead-cloth that, in the night,
Or when they sorrow, ladies use to wear:
Their wings, blue, red, and yellow, mix'd appear;
Colours that, as we construe colours, paint
Their states to life;—the yellow shows their saint,
The dainty Venus, left them; blue, their truth;
The red and black, ensigns of death and ruth.
And this true honour from their love-death sprung,—
They were the first that ever poet sung.

THE PASSIONATE SHEPHERD TO HIS LOVE

COME live with me, and be my love;
And we will all the pleasures prove
That hills and valleys, dales and fields,
Woods or steepy mountain yields.

And we will sit upon the rocks,
Seeing the shepherds feed their flocks
By shallow rivers, to whose falls
Melodious birds sing madrigals.

And I will make thee beds of roses,
And a thousand fragrant posies;
A cap of flowers, and a kirtle
Embroider'd all with leaves of myrtle;

A gown made of the finest wool
Which from our pretty lambs we pull;
Fair-lined slippers for the cold,
With buckles of the purest gold;

A belt of straw and ivy-buds,
With coral clasps and amber studs:
An if these pleasures may thee move,
Come live with me, and be my love.

The shepherd-swains shall dance and sing
For thy delight each May morning:
If these delights thy mind may move,
Then live with me, and be my love.

OVID'S AMORES

BOOK I. Elegy iii. *To His Mistress*

I ask but right: let her that caught me late
Either love, or cause that I may never hate.
I ask too much, would she but let me love her!
Love knows with such-like prayers I daily move her.
Accept him that will serve thee all his youth,
Accept him that will love with spotless truth.
If lofty titles cannot make me thine,
That am descended but of knightly line,
(Soon may you plough the little land I have,
I gladly grant my parents given to save),
Apollo, *Bacchus*, and the Muses may,
And Cupid who hath mark'd me for thy prey;
My spotless life, which but to Gods gives place,
Naked simplicity, and modest grace.
I love but one, and her I love change never;
If men have faith, I'll live with thee for ever.
The years that fatal destiny shall give
I'll live with thee, and die ere thou shall grieve,
Be thou the happy subject of my books,
That I may write things worthy thy fair looks.
By verses horned *Io* got her name,
And she to whom in shape of swan *Jove* came,
And she that on a feign'd bull swam to land,
Griping his false horns with her virgin hand.
So likewise we will through the world be rung,
And with my name shall thine be always sung,

Elegy v. *Corinna in Bed*

In summer's heat and mid-time of the day
To rest my limbs upon a bed I lay;
One window shut, the other open stood,
Which gave such light as twinkles in a wood,
Like twilight glimpse at setting of the sun,
Or night being past, and yet not day begun.

Such light to shamefast maidens must be shown,
Where they may sport, and seem to be unknown.
Then came *Corinna* in a long loose gown,
Her white neck hid with tresses hanging down,
Resembling fair *Semiramis* going to bed,
Or *Lais* of a thousand wooers sped.
I snatch'd her gown; being thin, the harm was small,
Yet striv'd she to be cover'd therewithal.
And striving thus as one that would be cast
Betray'd herself, and yielded at the last.
Stark naked as she stood before mine eye,
Not one wen on her body could I spy.
What arms and shoulders did I touch and see,
How apt her breasts were to be press'd by me!
How smooth a belly under her waist saw I!
How large a leg, and what a lusty thigh!
To leave the rest, all lik'd me passing well,
I cling'd her naked body, down she fell;
Judge you the rest; being tir'd she bade me kiss;
Jove send me more such afternoons as this.

ELEGY XI. *Instructions for carrying a Letter to Corinna*

In skilful gathering ruffled hairs in order,
Nape, free-born, whose cunning hath no border,
Thy service for night's scapes is known commodious,
And to give signs dull wit to thee is odious.
Corinna clips 'em oft by thy persuasion,
Never to harm me made thy faith evasion.
Receive these lines, them to my mistress carry,
Be sedulous, let no stay cause thee tarry.
Nor flint, nor iron, are in thy soft breast,
But pure simplicity in thee doth rest.
And 'tis suppos'd Love's bow hath wounded thee:
Defend the ensigns of thy war in me.
If what I do she asks, say "hope for night,"
The rest my hand doth in my letters write.
Time passeth while I speak; give her my writ,
But see that forthwith she peruseth it.
I charge thee mark her eyes and front in reading;
By speechless looks we guess at things succeeding.
Straight being read, will her to write much back,
I hate fair paper should writ matter lack.

Let her make verses, and some blotted letter,
On the last edge to stay mine eyes the better.
What need she tire her hand to hold the quill?
Let this word, " come," alone the tables fill.
Then with triumphant laurel will I grace them
And in the midst of *Venus*' temple place them,
Subscribing that to her I consecrate
My faithful tables being vile maple late.

Elegy xiii. *To the Dawn, not to Hasten*

Now o'er the sea from her old love comes she
That draws the day from heaven's cold axletree.
Aurora, whither slid'st thou? down again,
And birds for *Memnon* yearly shall be slain.
Now in her tender arms I sweetly bide;
If ever, now well lies she by my side.
The air is cold, and sleep is sweetest now,
And birds send forth shrill notes from every bough:
Whither runn'st thou, that men, and women, love not?
Hold in thy rosy horses that they move not.
Ere thou rise, stars teach seamen where to sail,
But when thou com'st they of their courses fail.
Poor travailers, though tir'd, rise at thy sight,
And soldiers make them ready to the fight.
The painful hind by thee to field is sent,
Slow oxen early in the yoke are pent.
Thou cozen'st boys of sleep, and dost betray them
To pedants that with cruel lashes pay them.
Thou mak'st the surety to the lawyer run,
That with one word hath nigh himself undone.
The lawyer and the client hate thy view,
Both whom thou raisest up to toil anew.
By thy means women of their rest are barr'd,
Thou set'st their labouring hands to spin and card.
All could I bear; but that the wench should rise
Who can endure save him with whom none lies?
How oft wish'd I, night would not give thee place,
Nor morning stars shun thy uprising face.
How oft that either wind would break thy coach,
Or steeds might fall forc'd with thick clouds' approach.
Whither go'st thou, hateful Nymph? *Memnon* the elf

Receiv'd his coal-black colour from thyself.
Say that thy love with *Cephalus* were not known,
Then thinkest thou thy loose life is not shown?
Would *Tithon* might but talk of thee awhile,
Not one in heaven should be more base and vile.
Thou leav'st his bed, because he's faint through age,
And early mount'st thy hateful carriage.
But held'st thou in thine arms some *Cephalus*,
Then would'st thou cry, " stay, night, and run not thus."
Dost punish me, because years make him wane?
I did not bid thee wed an aged swain.
The Moon sleeps with *Endymion* every day;
Thou art as fair as she, then kiss and play.
Jove, that thou should'st not haste but wait his leisure,
Made two nights one to finish up his pleasure.
I chid no more; she blush'd and therefore heard me,
Yet linger'd not the day, but morning scar'd me.

Elegy xv. *To those who envy Poets their Eternity of Fame*

Envy, why carp'st thou my time is spent so ill,
And term'st my works fruits of an idle quill?
Or that unlike the line from whence I come
War's dusty honours are refus'd being young?
Nor that I study not the brawling laws,
Nor set my voice to sale in every cause?
Thy scope is mortal, mine eternal, fame,
That all the world may ever chant my name.
Homer shall live while *Tenedos* stands and *Ide*,
Or into sea swift *Simois* doth slide.
Ascræus lives while grapes with new wine swell,
Or men with crooked sickles corn down fell.
The world shall of *Callimachus* ever speak;
His art excell'd, although his wit was weak.
For ever lasts high *Sophocles'* proud vein,
With sun and moon *Aratus* shall remain.
While bondmen cheat, fathers are hard, bawds whorish,
And strumpets flatter, shall *Menander* flourish.
Rude *Ennius*, and *Plautus* full of wit,
Are both in fame's eternal legend writ.
What age of *Varro*'s name shall not be told,
And *Jason*'s *Argo* and the fleece of gold?

Lofty *Lucretius* shall live that hour
That nature shall dissolve this earthly bower.
Æneas' war and *Tityrus* shall be read
While *Rome* of all the conquer'd world is head.
Till *Cupid*'s bow and fiery shafts be broken,
Thy verses, sweet *Tibullus*, shall be spoken.
And *Gallus* shall be known from east to west,
So shall *Licoris* whom he loved best.
Therefore when flint and iron wear away,
Verse is immortal, and shall ne'er decay.
To verse let kings give place, and kingly shows,
And banks o'er which gold-bearing *Tagus* flows.
Let base-conceited wits admire vile things,
Fair *Phœbus* lead me to the Muses' springs.
About my head be quivering myrtle wound,
And in sad lovers' heads let me be found.
The living, not the dead, can envy bite,
For after death all men receive their right.
Then though death rakes my bones in funeral fire,
I'll live, and as he pulls me down mount higher.

BOOK II. Elegy ix. *To Cupid*

O *Cupid*, that dost never cease my smart,
O boy, that liest so slothful in my heart,
Why me that always was thy soldier found
Dost harm, and in thy tents why dost me wound?
Why burns thy brand, why strikes thy bow thy friends?
More glory by thy vanquish'd foes ascends.
Did not Pelides whom his spear did grieve,
Being requir'd, with speedy help relieve?
Hunters leave taken beasts, pursue the chase,
And then things found do ever further pace.
We people wholly giv'n thee feel thine arms,
Thy dull hand stays thy striving enemies' harms.
Dost joy to have thy hooked arrows shaked
In naked bones? love hath my bones left naked.
So many men and maidens without love,
Hence with great laud thou mayst a triumph move.
Rome, if her strength the huge world had not fill'd,
With strawy cabins now her courts should build.
The weary soldier hath the conquer'd fields,
His sword laid by, safe though rude places yields.

The dock inharbours ships drawn from the floods,
Horse freed from service range abroad the woods,
And time it was for me to live in quiet,
That have so oft serv'd pretty wenches' diet.
Yet should I curse a God, if he but said,
" Live without love, so sweet ill is a maid."
For when my loathing it of heat deprives me,
I know not whither my mind's whirlwind drives me.
Even as a headstrong courser bears away
His rider vainly striving him to stay,
Or as a sudden gale thrusts into sea
The haven-touching bark now near the lee,
So wavering *Cupid* brings me back amain,
And purple love resumes his darts again.
Strike, boy, I offer thee my naked breast,
Here thou hast strength, here thy right hand doth rest.
Here of themselves thy shafts come, as if shot,
Better than I their quiver knows them not.
Hapless is he that all the night lies quiet,
And slumb'ring thinks himself much blessed by it.
Fool, what is sleep but image of cold death?
Long shalt thou rest when Fates expire thy breath.
But me let crafty damsels' words deceive;
Great joys by hope I inly shall conceive.
Now let her flatter me, now chide me hard,
Let me enjoy her oft, oft be debarr'd.
Cupid, by thee *Mars* in great doubt doth trample,
And thy step-father fights by thy example.
Light art thou, and more windy than thy wings,
Joys with uncertain faith thou tak'st and brings.
Yet, Love, if thou with thy fair mother hear,
Within my breast no desert empire bear;
Subdue the wand'ring wenches to thy reign,
So of both people shalt thou homage gain.

ELEGY XVI. *To His Mistress, to come to His Country Dwelling*

Sulmo, Peligne's third part, me contains,
A small but wholesome soil with wat'ry veins.
Although the sun to rive the earth incline,
And the Icarian froward Dog-star shine,
Pelignian fields with liquid rivers flow,

And on the soft grounds fertile green grass grow;
With corn the earth abounds, with vines much more,
And some few pastures Pallas' olives bore.
And by the rising herbs, where clear springs slide,
A grassy turf the moisten'd earth doth hide.
But absent is my fire—lies I'll tell none—
My heat is here, what moves my heat is gone.
Pollux and *Castor* might I stand betwixt,
In heaven without thee would I not be fix'd.
Upon the cold earth pensive let them lay
That mean to travel some long irksome way.
Or else will maidens, young men's mates, to go
If they determine to persever so.
Then on the rough *Alps* should I tread aloft,
My hard way with my mistress would seem soft.
With her I durst the Libyan Syrtes break through,
And raging seas in boist'rous south winds plough.
No barking dogs that *Scylla*'s entrails bear,
Nor thy gulfs, crooked *Malea*, would I fear,
No flowing waves with drowned ships forth pour'd
By cloy'd *Charybdis*, and again devour'd.
But if stern *Neptune*'s windy power prevail,
And water's force force helping gods to fail,
With thy white arms upon my shoulders seize,
So sweet a burden I will bear with ease.
The youth oft swimming to his *Hero* kind
Had then swum over, but the way was blind.
But without thee, although vine-planted ground
Contains me, though the streams in fields surround,
Though hinds in brooks the running waters bring,
And cool gales shake the tall trees' leavy spring,
Healthful Peligne I esteem nought worth,
Nor do I like the country of my birth.
Scythia, *Cilicia*, *Britain* are as good,
And rocks dy'd crimson with *Prometheus*' blood.
Elms love the vines, the vines with elms abide,
Why doth my mistress from me oft divide?
Thou swar'st division should not 'twixt us rise,
By me, and by my stars, thy radiant eyes.
Maid's words, more vain and light than falling leaves,
Which, as it seems, hence wind and sea bereaves.
If any godly care of me thou hast,
Add deeds unto thy promises at last.
And with swift nags drawing thy little coach

(Their reins let loose) right soon my house approach.
But when she comes, you swelling mounts, sink down,
And falling valleys be the smooth ways' crown.

BOOK III. Elegy II. *To his Mistress watching a Chariot Race*

I sit not here the noble horse to see,
Yet whom thou favour'st pray may conqueror be.
To sit and talk with thee I hither came,
That thou mayst know with love thou mak'st me flame.
Thou view'st the course, I thee: let either heed
What please them, and their eyes let either feed.
What horse-driver thou favour'st most is best,
Because on him thy care doth hap to rest.
Such chance let me have: I would bravely run
On swift steeds mounted till the race were done.
Now would I slack the reins, now lash their hide,
With wheels bent inward now the ring-turn ride.
In running if I see thee, I shall stay,
And from my hands the reins will slip away.
Ah, *Pelops* from his coach was almost fell'd,
Hippodameia's looks while he beheld.
Yet he attain'd by her support to have her;
Let us all conquer by our mistress' favour.
In vain why fly'st back? force conjoins us now:
The place's laws this benefit allow.
But spare my wench, thou at her right hand seated;
By thy side's touching ill she is entreated.
And sit thou rounder, that behind us see;
For shame press not her back with thy hard knee.
But on the ground thy clothes too loosely lie,
Gather them up, or lift them lo will I.
Envious garments so good legs to hide,
The more thou look'st, the more the gown envied.
Swift *Atalanta*'s flying legs like these
Wish in his hands grasp'd did *Hippomenes*.
Coat-tuck'd *Diana*'s legs are painted like them,
When strong wild beasts she stronger hunts to strike them.
Ere these were seen, I burn'd: what will these do?
Flames into flame, floods thou pour'st seas into.
By these I judge delight me may the rest,
Which lie hid under her thin veil suppress'd.

Yet in the meantime wilt small winds bestow,
That from thy fan, mov'd by my hand, may blow?
Or is my heat of mind, not of the sky?
Is't women's love my captive breast doth fry?
While thus I speak, black dust her white robes ray:
Foul dust, from her fair body go away.
Now comes the pomp; themselves let all men cheer:
The shout is nigh; the golden pomp comes here.
First victory is brought with large-spread wing,
Goddess, come here, make my love conquering.
Applaud you *Neptune*, that dare trust his wave,
The sea I use not: me my earth must have.
Soldier, applaud thy *Mars*: no wars we move,
Peace pleaseth me, and in mid peace is love.
With augurs *Phœbus*, *Phœbe* with hunters stands,
To thee, *Minerva*, turn the craftsmen's hands.
Ceres and *Bacchus* countrymen adore,
Champions please *Pollux*, *Castor* loves horsemen more.
Thee, gentle *Venus*, and the boy that flies,
We praise: great goddess, aid my enterprise:
Let my new mistress grant to be belov'd.
She beck'd, and prosperous signs gave as she mov'd.
What *Venus* promis'd, promise thou, we pray;
Greater than her by her leave th'art, I'll say.
The Gods, and their rich pomp, witness with me,
For evermore thou shalt my mistress be.
Thy legs hang down; thou mayst, if that be best,
Awhile thy tiptoes on the footstool rest.
Now greatest spectacles the prætor sends,
Four-chariot horses from the lists even ends.
I see whom thou affectest, he shall subdue;
The horses seem as thy desire they knew.
Alas, he runs too far about the ring;
What dost? thy wagon in less compass bring.
What dost, unhappy? her good wishes fade,
Let with strong hand the rein to bend be made.
One slow we favour, Romans him revoke:
And each gives signs by casting up his cloak.
They call him back; lest their gowns toss thy hair,
To hide thee in my bosom straight repair.
But now again the barriers open lie,
And forth the gay troupes on swift horses fly.
At last now conquer, and outrun the rest:
My mistress' wish confirm with my request.

My mistress hath her wish, my wish remain:
He holds the palm: my palm is yet to gain.
She smil'd, and with quick eye behight some grace:
Pay it not here, but in another place.

Elegy viii. *Lament for Tibullus*

If *Thetis* and the Morn their sons did wail,
And envious fates great goddesses assail,
Sad Elegia thy woeful hairs unbind;
Ah, now a name too true thou hast, I find.
Tibullus, thy works' poet, and thy fame,
Burns his dead body in the funeral flame.
Lo, Cupid brings his quiver spoiled quite,
His broken bow, his fire-brand without light.
How piteously with drooping wings he stands,
And knocks his bare breast with self-angry hands.
The locks spread on his neck receive his tears,
And shaking sobs his mouth for speeches bears.
So at *Æneas'* burial, men report,
Fair-fac'd Iülus, he went forth thy court.
And *Venus* grieves, Tibullus' life being spent,
As when the wild boar *Adon*'s groin had rent.
The Gods' care we are called, and men of piety,
And some there be that think we have a deity.
Outrageous death profanes all holy things,
And on all creatures obscure darkness brings.
To Thracian *Orpheus* what did parents good?
Or songs amazing wild beasts of the wood?
Where *Linus* by his father *Phœbus* laid
To sing with his unequall'd harp is said.
See *Homer*, from whose fountain ever fill'd
Pierian dew to poets is distill'd.
Him the last day in black Averne hath drown'd,
Verses alone are with continuance crown'd.
The work of poets lasts *Troy*'s labour's fame,
And that slow web night's falsehood did unframe.
So *Nemesis*, so *Delia* famous are,
The one his first love, th' other his new care.
What profit to us hath our pure life bred?
What to have lain alone in empty bed?
When bad fates take good men, I am forbod
By secret thoughts to think there is a god.

Live godly, thou shalt die; honour thou heaven,
Yet shall thy life be forcibly bereaven.
Trust in good verse, *Tibullus* feels death's pains,
Scarce rests of all what a small urn contains.
Thee, sacred poet, could sad flames destroy?
Nor feared they thy body to annoy?
The holy gods' gilt temples they might fire,
That durst to so great wickedness aspire.
Eryx' bright empress turn'd her looks aside,
And some that she refrain'd tears have denied.
Yet better is't than if *Corcyra's* isle
Had thee unknown interr'd in ground most vile.
Thy dying eyes here did thy mother close,
Nor did thy ashes her last off'rings lose.
Part of her sorrow here thy sister bearing
Comes forth her unkempt locks asunder tearing.
Nemesis and thy first wench join their kisses
With thine, nor this last fire their presence misses.
Delia departing, " happier lov'd," she saith,
" Was I: thou liv'dst, while thou esteem'dst my faith."
Nemesis answers, " what's my loss to thee?
His fainting hand in death engrasped me."
If ought remains of us but name, and spirit,
Tibullus doth *Elysium*'s joy inherit.
Their youthful brows with ivy girt to meet him,
With *Calvus* learn'd *Catullus* comes and greet him,
And thou, if falsely charg'd to wrong thy friend,
Gallus, that car'st not blood and life to spend.
With these thy soul walks, souls if death release,
The godly sweet *Tibullus* doth increase.
Thy bones I pray may in the urn safe rest,
And may th'earth's weight thy ashes nought molest.

LUCAN: PHARSALIA, Book I

Wars worse than civil on Thessalian plains,
And outrage strangling law and people strong,
We sing, whose conquering swords their own breasts lanc'd.
Armies allied, the kingdom's league uprooted,
Th' affrighted world's force bent on public spoil,
Trumpets and drums, 'like deadly, threatning other,
Eagles alike display'd, darts answering darts.
Romans, what madness, what huge lust of war
Hath made Barbarians drunk with Latin blood?
Now Babylon (proud through our spoil) should stoop,
While slaughtered Crassus' ghost walks unreveng'd,
Will ye wage war, for which you shall not triumph?
Ah me, O what a world of land and sea
Might they have won whom civil broils have slain!
As far as Titan springs where night dims heaven,
Ay, to the Torrid Zone where midday burns,
And where stiff winter, whom no spring resolves,
Fetters the Euxine sea with chaines of ice:
Scythia and wild Armenia had been yok'd,
And they of Nilus' mouth (if there live any).
Rome, if thou take delight in impious war,
First conquer all the earth, then turn thy force
Against thy self: as yet thou wants not foes,
That now the walls of houses half rear'd totter,
That rampiers fallen down, huge heaps of stone
Lie in our towns, that houses are abandon'd,
And few live that behold their ancient seats;
Italy many years hath lain untill'd,
And chok'd with thorns, that greedy earth wants hinds.
Fierce Pyrrhus, neither thou nor Hannibal
Art cause, no foreign foe could so afflict us,
These plagues arise from wreak of civil power.
But if for Nero (then unborn) the fates
Would find no other means, (and gods not slightly
Purchase immortal thrones; nor Jove joy'd heaven
Until the cruel Giants' war was done.)
We plain not heavens, but gladly bear these evils
For Nero's sake: Pharsalia groan with slaughter,
And Carthage souls be glutted with our bloods;

At Munda let the dreadful battles join;
Add, Cæsar, to these ills Perusian famine;
The Mutin toils; the fleet at Leuca sunk;
And cruel field near burning Etna fought:
Yet Rome is much bound to these civil arms,
Which made thee Emperor, thee (seeing thou being old
Must shine a star) shall heaven (whom thou lovest)
Receive with shouts; where thou wilt reign as King,
Or mount the sun's plume-bearing chariot,
And with bright restless fire compass the earth,
Undaunted though her former guide be chang'd.
Nature, and every power shall give thee place,
What God it please thee be, or where to sway:
But neither choose the north t'erect thy seat,
Nor yet the adverse reeking southern pole,
Whence thou shouldst view thy Rome with squinting beams.
If any one part of vast heaven thou swayest,
The burdened axes with thy force will bend;
The midst is best; that place is pure, and bright,
There, Cæsar, may'st thou shine and no cloud dim thee;
Then men from war shall bide in league, and ease,
Peace through the world from Janus' fane shall fly,
And bolt the brazen gates with bars of iron:
Thou, Cæsar, at this instant art my God,
Thee if I invocate, I shall not need
To crave Apollo's aid, or Bacchus' help;
Thy power inspires the Muse that sings this war.
The causes first I purpose to unfold
Of these garboils, whence springs a long discourse,
And what made madding people shake off peace.
The fates are envious, high seats quickly perish,
Under great burdens falls are ever grievous;
Rome was so great it could not bear itself:
So when this world's compounded union breaks,
Time ends and to old Chaos all things turn;
Confused stars shall meet, celestial fire
Fleet on the floods, the earth shoulder the sea,
Affording it no shore, and Phœbe's wain
Chase Phœbus and enrag'd affect his place,
And strive to shine by day, and full of strife
Dissolve the engines of the broken world.
All great things crush themselves, such end the gods
Allot the height of honour, men so strong
By land, and sea, no foreign force could ruin:

O Rome, thy self art cause of all these evils,
Thy self thus shivered out to three men's shares:
Dire league of partners in a kingdom last not.
O faintly join'd friends with ambition blind,
Why join you force to share the world betwixt you?
While th' earth the sea, and air the earth sustains;
While Titan strives against the world's swift course;
Or Cynthia, night's Queen, waits upon the day;
Shall never faith be found in fellow kings.
Dominion cannot suffer partnership;
This needs no foreign proof, nor far-fetch'd story:
Rome's infant walls were steep'd in brothers' blood;
Nor then was land, or sea, to breed such hate,
A town with one poor church set them at odds.
Cæsar's and Pompey's jarring love soon ended,
'Twas peace against their wills; betwixt them both
Stepp'd Crassus in: even as the slender Isthmus,
Betwixt the Ægean and the Ionian sea,
Keeps each from other, but being worn away
They both burst out, and each encounter other:
So when as Crassus' wretched death, who stay'd them,
Had fill'd Assyrian Carrhæ's walls with blood,
His loss made way for Roman outrages.
Parthians, y'afflict us more than ye suppose,
Being conquer'd, we are plagu'd with civil war.
Swords share our Empire, fortune that made Rome
Govern the earth, the sea, the world itself,
Would not admit two Lords: for Julia
Snatch'd hence by cruel fates with ominous howls,
Bare down to hell her son, the pledge of peace,
And all bands of that death-presaging alliance:
Julia, had heaven given thee longer life,
Thou hadst restrain'd thy headstrong husband's rage,
Yea, and thy father too, and swords thrown down,
Made all shake hands as once the Sabines did;
Thy death broke amity and train'd to war
These Captains emulous of each other's glory.
Thou feard'st (great Pompey) that late deeds would dim
Old triumphs, and that Cæsar's conquering France
Would dash the wreath thou wear'st for Pirates' wrack.
Thee war's use stirr'd, and thoughts that always scorn'd
A second place; Pompey could bide no equal,
Nor Cæsar no superior; which of both
Had justest cause unlawful 'tis to judge:

Each side had great partakers; Cæsar's cause
The gods abetted; Cato lik'd the other.
Both differed much, Pompey was struck in years,
And by long rest forgot to manage arms,
And, being popular, sought by liberal gifts
To gain the light unstable commons' love,
And joy'd to hear his Theatre's applause;
He liv'd secure, boasting his former deeds,
And thought his name sufficient to uphold him,
Like to a tall oak in a fruitful field,
Bearing old spoils and conquerors' monuments,
Who though his root be weak, and his own weight
Keep him within the ground, his arms all bare,
His body (not his boughs) send forth a shade;
Though every blast it nod, and seem to fall,
When all the woods about stand bolt upright,
Yet he alone is held in reverence.
Cæsar's renown for war was less, he restless,
Shaming to strive but where he did subdue,
When ire or hope provok'd, heady and bold,
At all times charging home, and making havoc;
Urging his fortune, trusting in the gods,
Destroying what withstood his proud desires,
And glad when blood and ruin made him way:
So thunder which the wind tears from the clouds,
With crack of riven air and hideous sound
Filling the world, leaps out and throws forth fire,
Affrights poor fearful men, and blasts their eyes
With overthwarting flames, and raging shoots
Alongst the air and nought resisting it
Falls, and returns, and shivers where it lights.
Such humours stirr'd them up; but this war's seed
Was even the same that wracks all great dominion.
When fortune made us lords of all, wealth flow'd,
And then we grew licentious and rude,
The soldiers' prey and rapine brought in riot,
Men took delight in jewels, houses, plate,
And scorn'd old sparing diet, and ware robes
Too light for women; Poverty (who hatch'd
Rome's greatest wits) was loath'd, and all the world
Ransack'd for gold, which breeds the world decay;
And then large limits had their butting lands,
The ground which Curius and Camillus till'd,
Was stretch'd unto the fields of hinds unknown;

Again, this people could not brook calm peace,
Them freedom without war might not suffice,
Quarrels were rife, greedy desire still poor
Did vile deeds, then 'twas worth the price of blood
And deem'd renown to spoil their native town,
Force master'd right, the strongest govern'd all.
Hence came it that th'edicts were over-rul'd,
That laws were broke, Tribunes with Consuls strove,
Sale made of offices, and people's voices
Bought by themselves and sold, and every year
Frauds and corruption in the field of Mars;
Hence interest and devouring usury sprang,
Faith's breach, and hence came war to most men welcome.
Now Cæsar overpass'd the snowy Alps.
His mind was troubled, and he aim'd at war,
And coming to the ford of Rubicon,
At night in dreadful vision fearful Rome
Mourning appear'd, whose hoary hairs were torn,
And on her turret-bearing head dispers'd,
And arms all naked, who with broken sighs,
And staring, thus bespoke: "What mean'st thou Cæsar?
Whither goes my standard? Romans if ye be,
And bear true hearts, stay here." This spectacle
Struck Cæsar's heart with fear, his hair stood up,
And faintness numb'd his steps there on the brink:
He thus cried out: "Thou thunderer that guard'st
Rome's mighty walls built on Tarpeian rock,
Ye gods of Phrygia and Iülus' line,
Quirinus' rites and Latian Jove advanc'd
On Alba hill, O Vestal flames, O Rome,
My thoughts' sole goddess, aid mine enterprise.
I hate thee not, to thee my conquests stoop,
Cæsar is thine, so please it thee, thy soldier;
He, he afflicts Rome that made me Rome's foe."
This said, he laying aside all lets of war
Approach'd the swelling stream with drum and ensign,
Like to a lion of scorch'd desert Afric,
Who, seeing hunters, pauseth till fell wrath
And kingly rage increase, then having whisk'd
His tail athwart his back, and crest heav'd up,
With jaws wide open ghastly roaring out
(Albeit the Moor's light javelin or his spear
Sticks in his side) yet runs upon the hunter
In summer time the purple Rubicon,

Which issues from a small spring, is but shallow,
And creeps along the vales dividing just
The bounds of Italy from Cisalpine France;
But now the winter's wrath and wat'ry moon,
Being three days old, enforc'd the flood to swell,
And frozen Alps thaw'd with resolving winds.
The thunder-hoov'd horse in a crooked line,
To scape the violence of the stream first waded,
Which being broke the foot had easy passage.
As soon as Cæsar got unto the bank
And bounds of Italy; " here, here " (saith he)
" An end of peace; here end polluted laws;
Hence leagues, and covenants; Fortune, thee I follow,
War and the destinies shall try my cause."
This said, the restless general through the dark
(Swifter than bullets thrown from Spanish slings,
Or darts which Parthians backward shoot) march'd on
And then (when Lucifer did shine alone,
And some dim stars) he Ariminium enter'd:
Day rose and view'd these tumults of the war;
Whether the gods, or blustring south were cause
I know not, but the cloudy air did frown;
The soldiers, having won the market place,
There spread the colours, with confused noise
Of trumpets' clang, shrill cornets, whistling fifes;
The people started; young men left their beds,
And snatch'd arms near their household gods hung up
Such as peace yields; worm-eaten leathern targets,
Through which the wood peer'd, headless darts, old swords
With ugly teeth of black rust foully scarr'd:
But seeing white Eagles, and Rome's flags well known,
And lofty Cæsar in the thickest throng,
They shook for fear, and cold benumb'd their limbs,
And muttering much, thus to themselves complain'd:
" O walls unfortunate too near to France,
Predestinate to ruin; all lands else
Have stable peace, here war's rage first begins,
We bide the first brunt; safer might we dwell
Under the frosty Bear, or parching East,
Wagons or tents, than in this frontier town.
We first sustain'd the uproars of the Gauls,
And furious Cimbrians and of Carthage' Moors,
As oft as Rome was sack'd, here 'gan the spoil."
Thus sighing whisper'd they, and none durst speak

And show their fear, or grief: but as the fields
When birds are silent thorough winter's rage,
Or sea far from the land, so all were whist.
Now light had quite dissolv'd the misty night,
And Cæsar's mind unsettled musing stood;
But gods and fortune prick'd him to this war,
Infringing all excuse of modest shame,
And labouring to approve his quarrel good.
The angry Senate urging Gracchus' deeds,
From doubtful Rome wrongly expell'd the tribunes,
That cross'd them; both which now approach'd the camp,
And with them Curio, sometime tribune too,
One that was fee'd for Cæsar, and whose tongue
Could tune the people to the Nobles' mind.
" Cæsar " (said he) " while eloquence prevail'd,
And I might plead, and draw the commons' minds
To favour thee against the Senate's will,
Five years I lengthen'd thy command in France:
But law being put to silence by the wars,
We from our houses driven, most willingly
Suffer'd exile: let thy sword bring us home.
Now while their part is weak, and fears, march hence.
Where men are ready, lingering ever hurts:
In ten years won'st thou France; Rome may be won
With far less toil, and yet the honours more;
Few battles fought with prosperous success
May bring her down, and with her all the world.
Nor shalt thou triumph when thou com'st to Rome,
Nor capital be adorn'd with sacred bays:
Envy denies all, with thy blood must thou
Aby thy conquest past: the son decrees
To expel the father; share the world thou canst not;
Enjoy it all thou mayst." Thus Curio spake,
And therewith Cæsar, prone enough to war,
Was so incens'd as are Eleius' steeds
With clamours: who though lock'd and chain'd in stalls,
Souse down the walls, and make a passage forth.
Straight summon'd he his several companies
Unto the standard: his grave look appeas'd
The wrestling tumult, and right hand made silence:
And thus he spake: " You that with me have borne
A thousand brunts, and try'd me full ten years,
See how they quit our bloodshed in the North,
Our friends' death, and our wounds, our wintering

Under the Alps; Rome rageth now in arms
As if the Carthage Hannibal were near;
Cornets of horse are muster'd for the field;
Woods turn'd to ships; both land and sea against us.
Had foreign wars ill thriv'd, or wrathful France
Pursu'd us hither, how were we bestead
When, coming conqueror, Rome afflicts me thus?
Let come their leaders whom long peace hath quail'd,
Raw soldiers lately press'd, and troops of gowns;
Brabbling Marcellus; Cato whom fools reverence;
Must Pompey's followers with strangers' aid
(Whom from his youth he brib'd) needs make him king?
And shall he triumph long before his time,
And having once got head still shall he reign?
What should I talk of men's corn reap'd by force,
And by him kept of purpose for a dearth?
Who sees not war sit by the quivering judge;
And sentence given in rings of naked swords,
And laws assail'd, and arm'd men in the Senate?
'Twas his troop hemm'd in Milo being accus'd;
And now lest age might wane his state, he casts
For civil war, wherein through use he's known
To exceed his master, that arch-traitor Sulla.
A brood of barbarous tigers, having lapp'd
The blood of many a herd, whilst with their dams
They kennell'd in Hyrcania, evermore
Will rage and pray: so, Pompey, thou having lick'd
Warm gore from Sulla's sword art yet athirst,
Jaws flesh'd with blood continue murderous.
Speak, when shall this thy long usurp'd power end?
What end of mischief? Sulla teaching thee,
At last learn, wretch, to leave thy monarchy.
What, now Sicilian pirates are suppress'd,
And jaded king of Pontus poison'd slain,
Must Pompey as his last foe plume on me,
Because at his command I wound not up
My conquering eagles? Say I merit nought,
Yet for long service done, reward these men,
And so they triumph, be't with whom ye will.
Whither now shall these old bloodless souls repair?
What seats for their deserts? what store of ground
For servitors to till? what colonies
To rest their bones? Say Pompey, are these worse
Than pirates of Sicilia? They had houses.

Speed, spread these flags that ten years' space have conquer'd,
Let's use our tried force, they that now thwart right
In wars will yield to wrong: the gods are with us.
Neither spoil nor kingdom seek we by these arms,
But Rome at thraldom's feet to rid from tyrants."
This spoke none answer'd, but a murmuring buzz
Th' unstable people made: their household gods
And love to Rome (though slaughter steel'd their hearts
And minds were prone) restrain'd them; but war's love
And Cæsar's awe dash'd all: then Laelius
The chief Centurion, crown'd with oaken leaves
For saving of a Roman Citizen,
Stepp'd forth, and cried: " Chief leader of Rome's force,
So be I may be bold to speak a truth,
We grieve at this thy patience and delay.
What doubtst thou us? Even now when youthful blood
Pricks forth our lively bodies, and strong arms
Can mainly throw the dart, wilt thou endure
These purple grooms? that Senate's tyranny?
Is conquest got by civil war so heinous?
Well, lead us then to Syrtes' desert shore;
Or Scythia; or hot Libya's thirsty sands.
This hand, that all behind us might be quail'd,
Hath with thee past the swelling ocean,
And swept the foaming breast of Arctic's Rhine.
Love over-rules my will, I must obey thee,
Cæsar, he whom I hear thy trumpets charge
I hold no Roman; by these ten blest ensigns
And all thy several triumphs, shouldst thou bid me
Entomb my sword within my brother's bowels;
Or father's throat; or woman's groaning womb;
This hand (albeit unwilling) should perform it;
Or rob the gods; or sacred temples fire:
These troops should soon pull down the church of Jove.
If to encamp on Tuscan Tiber's streams,
I'll boldly quarter out the fields of Rome;
What walls thou wilt be levell'd with the ground,
These hands shall thrust the ram, and make them fly,
Albeit the city thou wouldst have so ras'd
Be Rome itself." Here every band applauded,
And with their hands held up, all jointly cried
They'll follow where he please: the shouts rent heaven,
As when against pine-bearing Ossa's rocks
Beats Thracian Boreas; or when trees bow down,

And rustling swing up as the wind fets breath.
When Cæsar saw his army prone to war,
And fates so bent, lest sloth and long delay
Might cross him, he withdrew his troops from France,
And in all quarters musters men for Rome.
They by Lemannus' nook forsook their tents;
They whom the Lingones foil'd with painted spears,
Under the rocks by crooked Vogesus;
And many came from shallow Isara,
Who, running long, falls in a greater flood,
And ere he sees the sea loseth his name;
The yellow Ruthens left their garrisons;
Mild Atax glad it bears not Roman boats,
And frontier Varus that the camp is far,
Sent aid; so did Alcides' port, whose seas
Eat hollow rocks, and where the north-west wind
Nor Zephyr rules not, but the north alone
Turmoils the coast, and enterance forbids;
And others came from that uncertain shore,
Which is nor sea, nor land, but oft times both,
And changeth as the ocean ebbs and flows:
Whether the sea roll'd always from that point,
Whence the wind blows still forced to and fro;
Or that the wand'ring main follow the moon;
Or flaming Titan (feeding on the deep)
Pulls them aloft, and makes the surge kiss heaven;
Philosophers, look you, for unto me
Thou cause, whate'er thou be whom God assigns
This great effect, art hid. They came that dwell
By Neme's fields, and banks of Satirus,
Where Tarbel's winding shores embrace the sea,
The Santons that rejoice in Cæsar's love,
Those of Bituriges and light Axon pikes;
And they of Rhene and Leuca, cunning darters,
And Sequani that well could manage steeds;
The Belgians apt to govern British cars;
Th' Averni, too, which boldly feign themselves
The Romans' brethren, sprung of Ilian race;
The stubborn Nervians stain'd with Cotta's blood;
And Vangions who like those of Sarmata,
Wear open slops: and fierce Batavians,
Whom trumpets' clang incites, and those that dwell
By Cynga's stream, and where swift Rhodanus
Drives Araris to sea; they near the hills,

Under whose hoary rocks Gebenna hangs;
And Trevier, thou being glad that wars are past thee;
And you late shorn Ligurians, who were wont
In large spread hair to exceed the rest of France;
And where to Hesus, and fell Mercury
They offer human flesh, and where Jove seems
Bloody like Dian, whom the Scythians serve;
And you French Bardi, whose immortal pens
Renown the valiant souls slain in your wars,
Sit safe at home and chant sweet poesie.
And Druides, you now in peace renew
Your barbarous customs, and sinister rites;
In unfell'd woods, and sacred groves you dwell,
And only gods and heavenly powers you know,
Or only know you nothing. For you hold
That souls pass not to silent Erebus
Or Pluto's bloodless kingdom, but elsewhere
Resume a body: so (if truth you sing)
Death brings long life. Doubtless these northern men
Whom death the greatest of all fears affrights not,
Are blest by such sweet error, this makes them
Run on the sword's point and desire to die,
And shame to spare life which being lost is wonne.
You likewise that repuls'd the Caicke foe,
March towards Rome; and you fierce men of Rhene
Leaving your country open to the spoil.
These being come, their huge power made him bold
To manage greater deeds; the bordering towns
He garrison'd; and Italy he fill'd with soldiers.
Vain fame increas'd true fear, and did invade
The people's minds, and laid before their eyes
Slaughter to come, and swiftly bringing news
Of present war, made many lies and tales.
One swears his troops of daring horsemen fought
Upon Mevania's plain, where bulls are graz'd;
Other that Cæsar's barbarous bands were spread
Along Nar flood that into Tiber falls,
And that his own ten ensigns, and the rest,
March'd not entirely, and yet hid the ground,
And that he's much chang'd, looking wild and big,
And far more barbarous than the French (his vassals),
And that he lags behind with them of purpose
Borne 'twixt the Alps and Rhene, which he hath brought
From out their northern parts, and that Rome,

He looking on, by these men should be sack'd.
Thus in his fright did each man strengthen fame,
And without ground, fear'd what themselves had feign'd:
Nor were the commons only strook to heart
With this vain terror, but the court, the Senate,
The fathers' selves leap'd from their seats; and flying
Left hateful war decreed to both the consuls.
Then with their fear and danger all distract,
Their sway of flight carries the heady rout
That in chain'd troops break forth at every port;
You would have thought their houses had been fir'd
Or dropping-ripe, ready to fall with ruin,
So rush'd the inconsiderate multitude
Thorough the city hurried headlong on,
As if the only hope (that did remain
To their afflictions) were t'abandon Rome.
Look how when stormy Auster from the breach
Of Libyan Syrtes rolls a monstrous wave,
Which makes the mainsail fall with hideous sound;
The pilot from the helm leaps in the sea;
And mariners, albeit the keel be sound,
Shipwreck themselves; even so the city left,
All rise in arms; nor could the bed-rid parents
Keep back their sons, or women's tears their husbands;
They stay'd not either to pray or sacrifice,
Their household gods restrain them not, none lingered
As loth to leave Rome whom they held so dear:
Th' irrevocable people fly in troops.
O gods that easy grant men great estates,
But hardly grace to keep them! Rome that flows
With citizens and captives, and would hold
The world (were it together) is by cowards
Left as a prey now Cæsar doth approach:
When Romans are besieg'd by foreign foes,
With slender trench they escape night stratagems,
And sudden rampire rais'd of turf snatch'd up
Would make them sleep securely in their tents.
Thou Rome at name of war runn'st from thyself,
And wilt not trust thy city walls one night:
Well might these fear, when Pompey fear'd and fled.
Now evermore lest some on hope might ease
The commons' jangling minds, apparent signs arose,
Strange sights appear'd, the angry threat'ning gods
Fill'd both the earth and seas with prodigies;

Great store of strange and unknown stars were seen
Wandering about the North, and rings of fire
Fly in the air, and dreadful bearded stars,
And comets that presage the fall of kingdoms.
The flattering sky glitter'd in often flames,
And sundry fiery meteors blaz'd in heaven:
Now spearlike, long; now like a spreading torch
Lightning in silence stole forth without clouds,
And from the northern climate snatching fire
Blasted the Capitol: the lesser stars
Which wont to run their course through empty night
At noon day muster'd; Phoebe, having fill'd
Her meeting horns to match her brother's light,
Strook with th' earth's sudden shadow waxed pale;
Titan himself, thron'd in the midst of heaven,
His burning chariot plung'd in sable clouds,
And whelm'd the world in darkness, making men
Despair of day, as did Thyestes' town
(Mycenæ) Phœbus flying through the East:
Fierce Mulciber unbarred Etna's gate,
Which flamed not on high; but headlong pitch'd
Her burning head on bending Hespery.
Coal-black Charybdis whirl'd a sea of blood;
Fierce mastiffs howl'd; the vestal fires went out,
The flame in Alba consecrate to Jove
Parted in twain, and with a double point
Rose like the Theban brothers' funeral fire;
The earth went off her hinges; and the Alps
Shook the old snow from off their trembling laps.
The ocean swell'd as high as Spanish Calpe,
Or Atlas' head; their saints and household gods
Sweat tears to show the travails of their city.
Crowns fell from holy statues, ominous birds
Defil'd the day, and wild beasts were seen,
Leaving the woods, lodge in the streets of Rome.
Cattle were seen that mutter'd human speech:
Prodigious births, with more and ugly joints
Than nature gives, whose sight appals the mother,
And dismal prophecies were spread abroad:
And they whom fierce Bellona's fury moves
To wound their arms, sing vengeance, Sibyl's priests,
Curling their bloody locks, howl dreadful things,
Souls quiet and appeas'd sigh'd from their graves,
Clashing of arms was heard in untrod woods,

Shrill voices shriek'd, and ghosts encounter men.
Those that inhabited the suburb fields
Fled; foul Erinnys stalk'd about the walls,
Shaking her snaky hair and crooked pine
With flaming top, much like that hellish fiend
Which made the stern Lycurgus wound his thigh,
Or fierce Agave mad; or like Megæra
That scar'd Alcides, when by Juno's task
He had before look'd Pluto in the face.
Trumpets were heard to sound; and with what noise
An armed battle joins, such and more strange
Black night brought forth in secret: Sulla's ghost
Was seen to walk, singing sad oracles,
And Marius' head above cold Tau'ron peering
(His grave broke open) did affright the boors.
To these ostents (as their old custom was)
They call th' Etrurian Augurs, amongst whom
The gravest, Aruns, dwelt in forsaken Luna,
Well skill'd in Pyromancy; one that knew
The hearts of beasts, and flight of wand'ring fowls.
First he commands such monsters Nature hatch'd
Against her kind (the barren mules loath'd issue)
To be cut forth and cast in dismal fires:
Then, that the trembling citizens should walk
About the city; then the sacred priests
That with divine lustration purg'd the walls,
And went the round, in, and without the town.
Next, an inferior troop in tuck'd-up vestures,
After the Gabine manner: then the nuns
And their veil'd matron, who alone might view
Minerva's statue; then, they that keep, and read
Sybilla's secret works, and wash'd their saint
In Almo's flood: next learned Augurs follow,
Apollo's soothsayers, and Jove's feasting priests;
The skipping Salii with shields like wedges;
And Flamens last, with network woollen veils.
While these thus in and out had circled Rome,
Look, what the lightning blasted Aruns takes
And it inters with murmurs dolorous,
And calls the place Bidentall: on the altar
He lays a ne'er-yok'd bull, and pours down wine,
Then crams salt levin on his crooked knife;
The beast long struggled, as being like to prove
An awkward sacrifice, but by the horns

The quick priest pull'd him on his knees and slew him:
No vein sprung out, but from the yawning gash,
Instead of red blood, wallowed venomous gore.
These direful signs made Aruns stand amaz'd,
And searching farther for the gods' displeasure,
The very colour scar'd him; a dead blackness
Ran through the blood, that turn'd it all to jelly,
And stain'd the bowels with dark loathsome spots;
The liver swell'd with filth, and every vein
Did threaten horror from the host of Cæsar;
A small thin skin contain'd the vital parts,
The heart stirr'd not, and from the gaping liver
Squeez'd matter through the caul; the entrails 'pear'd,
And which (ay me!) ever pretendeth ill,
At that bunch where the liver is, appear'd
A knob of flesh, whereof one half did look
Dead, and discolour'd; th' other lean and thin.
By these he seeing what mischiefs must ensue,
Cried out, "O gods! I tremble to unfold
What you intend: great Jove is now displeas'd,
And in the breast of this slain bull are crept
Th' infernal powers. My fear transcends my words,
Yet more will happen than I can unfold.
Turn all to good, be augury vain, and Tages
Th' art's master false." Thus in ambiguous terms,
Involving all, did Aruns darkly sing.
But Figulus more seen in heavenly mysteries,
Whose like Egyptian Memphis never had
For skill in stars, and tuneful planeting,
In this sort spake: "The world's swift course is lawless
And casual; all the stars at random rage:
Or if Fate rule them, Rome, thy citizens
Are near some plague: what mischief shall ensue?
Shall towns be swallowed? shall the thicken'd air
Become intemperate? shall the earth be barren?
Shall water be congeal'd and turn'd to ice?
O Gods, what death prepare ye? with what plague
Mean ye to rage? The death of many men
Meets in one period. If cold noisome Saturn
Were now exalted, and with blue beams shin'd,
Then Ganymede would renew Deucalion's flood,
And in the fleeting sea the earth be drench'd.
O Phœbus, shouldst thou with thy rays now singe
The fell Nemean beast, th' earth would be fired,

And heaven tormented with thy chafing heat,
But thy fires hurt not; Mars, 'tis thou enflam'st
The threat'ning Scorpion with the burning tail
And fir'st his claws. Why art thou thus enrag'd?
King Jupiter hath low declin'd himself;
Venus is faint; swift Hermes retrograde;
Mars only rules the heaven: why do the planets
Alter their course and vainly dim their virtue?
Sword-girt Orion's side glisters too bright.
War's rage draws near; and to the sword's strong hand
Let all laws yield, sin bear the name of virtue,
Many a year these furious broils let last,
Why should we wish the gods should ever end them?
War only gives us peace, O Rome, continue
The course of mischief, and stretch out the date
Of slaughter; only civil broils make peace."
These sad presages were enough to scare
The quivering Romans; but worse things affright them.
As Mænas full of wine on Pindus raves,
So runs a matron through th' amazed streets,
Disclosing Phœbus' fury in this sort:
" Pæan, whither am I hal'd? where shall I fall?
Thus borne aloft I see Pangæus' hill,
With hoary top, and under Hæmus' mount
Philippi plains; Phœbus, what rage is this?
Why grapples Rome, and makes war, having no foes?
Whither turn I now? thou lead'st me toward th' east,
Where Nile augmenteth the Pelusian sea:
This headless trunke that lies on Nilus sand
I know: now throughout the air I fly,
To doubtful Syrtes and dry Afric, where
A fury leads the Emathian bands; from thence
To the pine-bearing hills, hence to the mounts
Pirene, and so back to Rome again.
See, impious war defiles the Senate-house,
New factions rise; now through the world again
I go; O Phœbus, show me Neptune's shore,
And other regions, I have seen Philippi."
This said, being tir'd with fury she sunk down.